Howdunit

Edited by
John Boertlein

D1052877

WRITER'S DIGEST BOOKS
Cincinnati, Ohio
www.writersdigest.com

Howdunit: How Crimes Are Committed and Solved. Copyright © 2001 by Writer's Digest Books. Manufactured in the United States of America. All rights reserved. No part of this book may be reproduced in any form or by any electronic or mechanical means including information storage and retrieval systems without permission in writing from the publisher, except by a reviewer, who may quote brief passages in a review. Published by Writer's Digest Books, an imprint of F&W Publications, Inc., 1507 Dana Avenue, Cincinnati, Ohio 45207. (800) 289-0963. First edition.

Visit our Web site at www.writersdigest.com for information on more resources for writers.

To receive a free weekly e-mail newsletter delivering tips and updates about writing and about Writer's Digest products, send an e-mail with "Subscribe Newsletter" in the body of the message to newsletter-request@writersdigest.com, or register directly at our Web site at www.writersdigest.com.

05   04   03   02   01   5   4   3   2   1

Library of Congress Cataloging-in-Publication Data

Howdunit : how crimes are committed and solved / edited by John Boertlein.
   p.   cm.
  Includes index.
  ISBN 1-58297-015-7 (alk. paper)
   1. Criminology. 2. Crime. 3. Criminal investigation. I. Boertlein, John.

HV6025 .H786   2001
364—dc21   00-043907
                                         CIP

Editors: Jack Heffron and Meg Leder
Interior design: Angela Wilcox
Cover design: Stephanie Redman
Cover photography: "Gunman killed by off-duty cop" Weegee/ICP/Liason Agency
Production coordinator: Mark Griffin

Dedication

For Stewart and Kyla—
thanks for your patience—I'm back!!

Acknowledgments

Special thanks to Jack Heffron for making it all possible. Also, thanks to Barry Vogel, my expert advisor on criminalistics, Debbie Scott for technical support, Kurt Byrd, Dave Ausdenmoore, Dennis Dressler, and everybody else who kindly shared their expertise for "getting this thing out."

About the Editor

John Boertlein is a twenty-year law enforcement veteran. As a police officer with the city of Cincinnati, he served in the capacity of patrol officer, investigator, undercover officer, police academy instructor, field sergeant, recruiting/background investigation supervisor and evidence management commander. He is a graduate of the University of Cincinnati and the College of Mount Saint Joseph on the Ohio.

John resides in Cincinnati with his children Stewart and Kyla.

Table of Contents

How and why a variety of serial-murderer types hunt and kill their human prey—
from the delusional type to the sexually obedient killer. Includes a case study of
Jeffrey Dahmer.

Bizarre Murders

by Mauro V. Corvasce and Joseph R. Paglino
from *Murder One: A Writer's Guide to Homicide*
Voodoo murders, ritual murders and acts of cannibalism.

Controversies Involving Death

by Keith D. Wilson, M.D.
from *Cause of Death: A Writer's Guide to Death, Murder and Forensic Medicine*
A brief look at moral, ethical and political issues associated with death, including
the controversies surrounding voodoo, euthanasia, living wills and more.

How the Body Is Handled

by Keith D. Wilson, M.D.
from *Cause of Death: A Writer's Guide to Death, Murder and Forensic Medicine*
Who handles the body, how they do it and why they do it that way.

The Autopsy

by Keith D. Wilson, M.D.
from *Cause of Death: A Writer's Guide to Death, Murder and Forensic Medicine*
The complete autopsy process as cause of death is established, medical evidence
is gathered and proper photographs are taken.

Larceny, Burglary, Robbery and Assault

by Russell Bintliff
from *Police Procedural: A Writer's Guide to the Police and How They Work*
The crimes and proper investigative techniques that keep police busy.

PART V VICE-RELATED CRIMES

Types of drug use, the most widespread contemporary drugs, and street-level and international drug enforcement.

PART VI BIG BROTHER

Surveillance: Part I
by John Boertlein
The ins and outs of surveillance methods and skills.

Surveillance: Part II
by Greg Fallis
from *Just the Facts, Ma'am: A Writer's Guide to Investigators
and Investigation Techniques*
Overt versus covert surveillance and the techniques necessary to escape detection.

Tailing
by Greg Fallis
from *Just the Facts, Ma'am: A Writer's Guide to Investigators
and Investigation Techniques*
The advantages and disadvantages of tailing on foot and by vehicle, complete with emergency instructions for when you get burned.

Information Sources
by Greg Fallis
from *Just the Facts, Ma'am: A Writer's Guide to Investigators
and Investigation Techniques*
Cultivating contacts and traditional, archival and short-term sources.

PART I

SYSTEMS

Chapter One

Street Cops

by John Boertlein

Cops always prove to be interesting characters for all kinds of writing. Maybe it's because they're made up of the best and worst society has to offer. Maybe it's because, at least on the street, they're granted an immense degree of power. Maybe it's the mystique that cops "know something" the average guy can only scratch the surface of. One thing's for sure—men and women who earn a living by traveling the thin blue line provide plenty of opportunity for the writer's craft.

As in any job, distinct personalities determine how and why cops act the way they do. But everybody in law enforcement experiences the same things at one time or another. From the writer's point of view, you need to be aware of the regimen your subject goes through and the way she was trained to react to situations. Reactions differ, but law enforcement procedures and instructions are, by and large, the same. You get to determine your character's personality and habits. Now we'll discuss some of the factors that will shape your subject's behavior.

Roll Call and Inspection

When cops start a workday (morning, afternoon or night shifts), they ordinarily attend an inspection when they have to display their fitness for duty, verify that they have proper and functional equipment and prove their attendance. Daily inspections I've been a part of follow the same routine. A supervisor, usually a sergeant, gives an order to "fall in," assembling attending officers into a straight line standing shoulder to shoulder. When the formation is complete, inspection goes something like the following.

The supervisor gives the order, "At close intervals," wherein officers straighten the line. At "dress right, dress," officers look to their immediate right and place their right hand on their right hip with the elbow angle near the officer to their immediate right. At this point, the line's straight and everybody's relatively the same distance apart. An order is given to "secure arms, prepare for inspection," and the officers comply by placing the baton under their weaker arm. (If you're right-handed, your left arm is your weaker arm and vice versa.) The supervisor now goes person to person down the line conducting the inspection.

Police command officers commonly believe that a cop's appearance seriously affects the way people react to him and may even influence the cop's own behavior. In short, sloppy appearance equals a lack of respect. Keeping this in mind, the supervisor should be looking for clean, pressed uniforms. Grooming and hygiene are also legitimate concerns. At the same time, flashlights, batons or "nightsticks" and leather goods are examined.

This is also the time to evaluate an officer's fitness for duty. I've witnessed several instances when an officer has not been fit for duty. I know of one routine inspection when the aroma of scotch whiskey lingered over the ranks. The sergeant in charge noticed the inebriate only after she giggled and belched loudly, giving herself away. Another time, a well-meaning young officer went to inspection, trying to work through his flu. He threw up on his, the sergeant's and several co-worker's shoes. After that incident, he decided he'd be better off at home. Another officer showed up with the name of a co-worker (whom he apparently didn't care for) inscribed on his bullets.

After the individual officer's inspection, each officer's firearm is inspected. The supervisor issues the command, "Raise pistols." Upon hearing this command, each officer:

1. Removes the magazine from his holstered pistol.
2. Holds the magazine in his weak hand in such a way that the inspecting supervisor can observe that it is loaded.
3. Draws the pistol from its holster. He then raises the pistol to the inspecting supervisor's eye level with the muzzle straight up so the supervisor can see a bullet in the chamber.

Sometimes these exercises aren't as rigid as they seem, or maybe they are tests for the supervisor. When the Cincinnati Bengals went to the Super Bowl, one particular officer who was a Bengals' fan managed to make it through the daily inspection with a four-foot orange-and-black-striped tail pinned to the back of his uniform's trousers. In another instance, "raise pistols" inspired a cop to produce what appeared to be a marital aid in the form of a portion of the male anatomy fixed to the end of a gun barrel. (That one *did not* go unnoticed by the sergeant.)

After weapons inspection, officers holster their pistols. An order to "replace magazines" causes the officers to return the magazine to the butt of their pistols, which are now loaded and ready.

Finally, officers are directed to "order arms," wherein the baton is placed with the handle in their stronger hand and the long end positioned toward the floor. "Port arms" calls for the officers to raise the baton shaft using their stronger hand, tap their stronger side's shoulder, and rest the baton with the handle in their stronger hand and the shaft in their weaker hand at chest level. A supervisor calls the roll from this position. When an officer's name is called, the officer replies, "Here sir/ma'am," and returns to the "order arms" position.

The exercise ends with an order to "fall out," and the officers find seats for roll call announcements. During roll call, officers receive information about recent crimes, wanted persons, current events and upcoming projects. It's also an opportunity to socialize a little before "hitting the streets." A supervisor conducts roll call as one might conduct a large business meeting. Roll-call scenarios offer the writer a good opportunity to introduce subjects in a semiformal situation where personalities are on open display. Roll calls often range from comedy club-caliber entertainment to heated personality clashes.

Writing about a roll-call setting offers plenty of opportunities for a writer to set the tone for a cop-related story. When I was a field officer, I attended a night shift roll call during a controversial time when the local media was accusing the city of requiring cops to write certain numbers of traffic citations. The administration's official position was, "There is no quota." In fact, there wasn't a quota, even though some felt the pressure to produce.

At that time, frigid weather didn't inspire anybody to do too much ticket writing anyway. However, when the shift fell out for roll call, an old-time sergeant had "words of encouragement" for the group.

"Last night, the people on this relief wrote a total of *two* tickets," he scolded. "I've talked it over with the lieutenant, and we may see about getting somebody fired for neglect of duty." Everybody knew it took a lot more than one night with no "bumps" to get you the ax; consequently, most of us paid little attention. But one senior officer felt the need to push the issue. "Sarge," he asked with a smile, "are you telling us we *do* have a quota?" The sergeant went into a long dissertation about duty and ticket writing, finally concluding with another threat of unemployment while implying the questioning party might be the first one out the door.

The next day, *every roll call everywhere* had something to talk about when a couple of television stations played the recording of our roll call as part of a feature story on police ticket-writing quotas.

The main focus of roll call is the exchange of information including the dissemination of wanted bulletins, descriptions and notifications about recent crimes and other information supposedly useful for the officer's day. Sometimes the information can have more nontraditional value, for example, take the case of an officer who always paid extra attention to the state's "Weekend Fatality Count." The stats were offered every Monday as an incentive for officers to pay attention to traffic safety in their neighborhoods. The count included the "number of crashes involving fatalities," "number of fatalities" and the ever-popular "number pending." The cop wrote these in her notebook without fail while everyone else paid little attention. I had to ask her why.

"Pick three, pick three. It's easy as can be!" she answered.

"What?"

"Pick three, pick three. It's easy as can be!" It finally dawned on me. She was using the weekend fatality count to pick her state lottery numbers. To date, she hasn't hit the jackpot.

Police Uniforms and Related Equipment

An accurate portrayal of cops needs to include some understanding of how and why their dress codes exist and what kind of equipment they're trained with and permitted to use. The following policy statement from the Cincinnati Police Division could apply to any law enforcement organization:

- Sworn personnel will only wear uniforms and equipment issued or approved of by the division.
- Sworn personnel will maintain in good repair and have available a full police uniform and related equipment.
- Uniformed personnel assigned to patrol duties will carry the PR-24 at all times. (The PR-24 is a modified baton with specific capabilities.)
- Division personnel, whether on- or off-duty, will wear their badge or division-issued identification (ID) card while in a police facility.
- Division employees, on-duty, will be properly groomed and dressed, including authorized firearm, badge and ID card. Division employees will wear either the uniform of the day (for their respective unit) or acceptable business attire of conservative color and design.

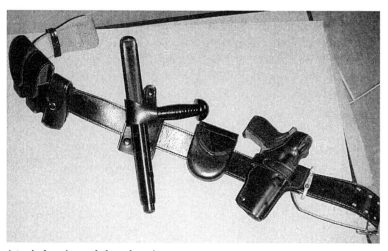

A typical cop's gun belt and equipment.

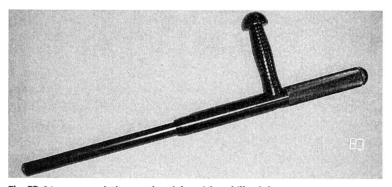

The PR-24, a new variation on the night stick or billy club.

Color and style of uniform parts are generally determined by the chief officer of a particular agency. Equipment selection and issuance, although determined by the command staff, are usually standardized for a number of reasons including liability of the issuing authority. So, if you use it, you'd better be trained to use it, and the people who trained you to use it must be capable of proving that it works. In other words, the government body, head of the agency and supervisors and trainers are responsible for the actions of the people they employ.

Therefore, to be factually correct, your police character will probably never be authorized to use a fragmentation hand grenade or any other high explosive in the performance of her duty. For example, the following list precisely states what equipment is allowed for general use in one law enforcement agency:

- PR-24 and related ring holster
- Issued chemical irritant canister and case

Although it's called "mace," it's actually Tear Gas in a can or a chemical irritant.

- Flashlight that meets one of the following specifications:
  - Division-issued plastic that uses three D-cell batteries.
  - Personally-owned plastic that uses two or three C- or D-cell batteries.
  - Personally-owned rechargeable flashlight, with plastic housing or minilight style, meeting the specifications listed above.
  - Officers may carry a supplemental metal or plastic minilight that uses two AA-cell batteries or is rechargeable.
  - Any other style or size of flashlight must have the written authorization of the police chief. The police chief will authorize other styles for special duty assignment only, not for routine patrol use.
- Firearms—authorized:
  - Smith & Wesson semiautomatic pistol, models 3953, 5906, 5946, 6906 and 6946.
  - Other official firearms designated by the police chief.

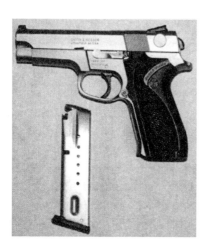

An official police-issue Smith & Wesson 9mm semiautomatic.

These rules and restrictions can go on and on. To be factually correct in your writing, you need to realize that these rules apply to most cops most of the time. Obviously, there will be somebody who operates outside of the rules. I remember an officer who, "because nobody was gonna catch him short," went on patrol with his duty weapon, a shoulder holster with a backup gun just in case they got his duty gun, a sheath knife in his sock just in case they found his backup gun and a switchblade in his pocket just in case they found his sheath knife. Whether your character is operating inside or outside the rules, there are specified regulations.

The need for procedures rises out of concern for safety. Procedure offers guidelines that acknowledge training and precaution in various situations. For example, in this scenario, a field training officer (FTO) and his first-day-on-the-job "rookie" partner are going over an important equipment check at the beginning of their tour of duty:

FTO: "Did you check the shotgun?" (This is a good display of proper procedure. The FTO reinforces the concern for having properly functioning equipment and conveys this feeling to the trainee.)

Rookie: "Yes." (Acknowledges the question by answering in the affirmative.)

FTO (taking shotgun in hand): "Is it unloaded?" (This is an appropriate question. It shows concern for safety.)

Rookie: "Yes."

FTO: "All of the shells are out? You're sure?" (Safety first!)

Rookie: "Yes."

FTO: "Okay, then let's reload." (The FTO follows proper procedure by pointing the shotgun skyward and pulling the trigger to release the mechanism. The shotgun discharges with a loud explosion, causing great concern and alarm to others in the vicinity. The FTO and rookie are showered with branches blown from limbs of a nearby tree.)

FTO: "You said you checked it!"

Rookie: "I did!"

FTO: "You said the damn thing was empty!"

Rookie: "I thought it was."

The FTO and rookie now retire to their supervisor's office where the FTO receives his reprimand for failing to follow safe shotgun-loading procedure by not conducting a visual inspection of his shotgun prior to proceeding with the loading techniques. One can only speculate as to what the FTO put on the rookie's daily performance review. As a writer, you need to be aware that all kinds of policies, procedures and laws exist in the cop's world and many stories could revolve around your character's interpretation, application or disregard of the rules.

Working the Street

We've made it through inspection and roll call and we're on the street. Staying healthy should be the first thing on any cop's mind. What's next? Two things can happen: We can come upon something on our own, or we can be dispatched via radio and/or computer terminal.

Discovering crime on routine patrol is fairly self-explanatory. You can develop any scenario imaginable and probably be within the bound-aries of believability. I've come across all kinds of situations, and they've all taken on different twists and conclusions. For example, one afternoon, while working uniform patrol in an inner-city neighborhood, I came across two young men involved in a drug transaction. The dealer held a brown paper bag in one hand and showed a little plastic baggie of marijuana to his customer with the other. This was not an unusual occur-rence for the area, so I wasn't surprised at what happened next. Some-body whistled, alerting the dopers that I was there. The dealer literally dropped everything and ran off in one direction; the buyer shuffled off in another. I'd witnessed a felony, but what's a poor street cop to do? Go after the suspect? But what do I charge him with when I go back to the scene where there is now no evidence? Or do I go after the drugs and wave goodbye to the pusher forever?

This particular day proved to be an unlucky one for the high-timers. As the dealer ran down the sidewalk, I followed him in my cruiser while watching the buyer in my rearview mirror. Figuring that I wanted the dealer to be too worn-out to run anymore if I spotted him again, I let him sprint around the corner into an alley before backing up to grab the weed. I hadn't had time to make a radio broadcast, but a fellow officer witnessed the chase from an adjacent street and, after circling the block, found the dealer still hoofing it down the street. The other officer figured I wasn't chasing the guy for fun and made the arrest. I got the drugs and the customer, and our case was complete.

Nothing is too bizarre for your character to happen upon, from stopping for a young man who confesses to just committing murder during a burglary, to answering a cockfight complaint from an annoyed neighbor who happens to see a cop driving by.

The other, more common way of responding to crime (or any call for service) is through dispatch using a radio system or, the newer accompaniment, a mobile data terminal (MDT) computer-based system.

The MDT provides written information in a quick, efficient manner while radio communication serves to actively coordinate street police efforts. The system I'm familiar with provides a simple method of identifying an officer by rank and specific location of assignment through a radio dispatch number. For example, there are five districts in my agency. Generally, there are three distinct shifts (with variations) in each district. Each shift is commanded by a lieutenant and sergeants. The cops on each shift are assigned to designated locations (beats) within a district.

Without being too complicated, let's see how we might organize our subjects in a manner frequently used to keep track of beat cops. Using a three-digit system, we'll identify each unit by rank and beat. Remember, beats are established, mapped areas of assignment. The first number in our sequence identifies the district (precinct, division, etc.) of assignment, the second digit identifies the rank and the third identifies the beat assignment. A "0" as the third identifier designates the senior supervisor, who is responsible for an entire district. Here are some examples: "120" designates District One, lieutenant; "322" designates the second sergeant assigned in District Three; "201" is the unit assigned to District Two, beat one; and "406" is District Four, beat six.

You can be as elaborate or simple as your needs call for. For example, an identifier could be added designating the unit's assigned shift: "1204" equals District One, second shift, beat four. However you choose to assign your subjects, there can be a factual basis for it. You may even be able to find out exactly where "Car 54" is or check on "One-Adam-Twelve's" status.

Answering Calls

Now that our characters are assigned with proper identifiers, let's send them on common and often dangerous runs—robbery and burglary. A good illustration of such a run occurred in the early 1980s when I was a rookie. Around 4:00 A.M. on a cold winter morning, a radio broadcast announced that a burglar alarm had gone off in a large machine shop located in a secluded section of a residential neighborhood. A unit arrived on the scene almost immediately, making a radio broadcast that they had discovered a broken window. Backup arrived and everyone took up positions around the building. Our lieutenant, a senior supervisor in the division, showed up and headed right for the broken window. "C'mon guys," he ordered. "Looks like we got one in there." Three of us (the rookies) followed him through the opening and scattered around the dark, crowded shop, searching the equipment and office areas with flashlights. I found a pile of items stacked by a door that was still locked from the inside. The items included an *empty* pistol case.

The lieutenant declared the building secure when we didn't find anyone inside. He asked who would stay to meet the owner and make the report, which fell to me and my fellow rookie partner. As quickly as they had arrived, the senior officers vanished into the night, leaving us to "do the paper."

The owner arrived and turned on the lights in the entire building. We went into the shop area to see if anything was disturbed. Looking past us toward an old car chassis, the businessman matter-of-factly muttered, "Well, there he is."

"What? Who? Where?" we asked in confused unison, looking around. Only then did I notice the burglar trying to hide himself under the chassis.

Case solved, right? Justice served in an efficient manner? Hardly. Luckily, we had a successful conclusion to a situation that, by our own actions, had become potentially disastrous. So let's look at what we should have done as professional police officers. There certainly isn't any particular formula to answer every situation, but if your characters follow certain standards, the odds are in their favor. Back to the "classic" burglary situation.

Answering a Burglar Alarm

A radio broadcast comes out that the burglar alarm went off in a machine shop in a fairly isolated section of a residential neighborhood:

- A "uniform" police car with two officers happens to be a couple of blocks away. (A "uniform" police car is one that's clearly marked with lights, siren and some type of logo.) They arrive on the scene and proceed to check the building's perimeter. Noticing that a window is broken out, they notify dispatch, request backup and position themselves outside the building with the best advantage to see all the routes of departure.
- As other units arrive, they, too, take positions to safely observe the building's perimeter.
- If a supervisor arrives, she assumes command. If a canine search team is available, they're summoned. If an owner or someone familiar with the scene is available, he is asked to respond.
- The canine team gets as much information as possible about the premises before entering. Once inside, the dog and handler perform a thorough, structured search.
- If a canine team isn't available, a group of officers is organized and a search of the building is conducted in an organized manner.

I know, I know. It's painfully boring, but following simple procedures is the safest, most successful method of doing a good job. If your character wants to charge forward as our fearless lieutenant did, it may make for a more exciting story line—but only as long as I'm not the real-life victim of somebody else's Little Big Horn.

Canine Units

Since we just mentioned canines (police dogs) as part of the logical solution to the burglary scenario, let's look at canine operations and how they apply to your writing about street cops.

You should first realize that police dogs are not infallible. Their effectiveness depends largely on the intelligent application of their capabilities. In other words, the dog is only as smart as its handler. Or stupid-lazy-dog-officer equals stupid-lazy-dog.

Here are some points from police procedure that will help you when writing about police dogs:

- Police dogs react instinctively to situations. Anyone making a sudden or threatening move toward the dog or handler risks the chance of the dog attacking them.
- Police dogs can pick up scents for a reasonable time after the departure of a suspect, provided that the scene has not been contaminated by the presence of other persons. No one should enter a search area before the canine team arrives.
- Canine teams are trained to assist in the following:
  - Tracking—Canines can follow a human scent with surprising accuracy, sometimes leading their handlers for blocks on the trail of a suspect.
  - Article searches—A canine's keen sense of smell works well in finding lost or hidden items that possess a human's scent.
  - Area searches—Police dogs are fantastic at finding hidden or lost persons, such as our man hiding inside the machine shop.
  - Crowd control—Be careful here. Crowd control using a vicious, snarling, 120-pound animal is based on the principle that people lose their sense of anonymity in a crowd if they feel they'll be the person singled out to be ripped to pieces. Use of dogs for crowd control is ordinarily tightly restricted by administrative policy.
  - Psychological deterrent in high-crime areas—This is based on the same principle as above, only this time the idea of getting bit keeps one on the straight and narrow.
  - Narcotics detection—Once again, a canine's great nose is fantastic for detecting substances like:
    - Cocaine or crack
    - Heroin
    - Hashish
    - Marijuana
    - Opium
    - Methamphetamine

Answering a Robbery Alarm

Answering a robbery alarm is similar to the burglary call. The key is securing the perimeter and using your best resources to deal with the situation. Let's look at a scenario arguably handled the "right" way.

About 9:00 P.M. on an evening near Thanksgiving, a robbery alarm came from a mom-and-pop corner delicatessen in a busy residential neighborhood. An old-clothes detective had arrived on the scene, taken cover behind a telephone pole and reported seeing nothing inside. Other units had arrived, mine included, and taken cover positions around the building. I crouched behind the engine block of a parked car across from the store's front door. About five minutes passed when a figure appeared behind the glass entrance into the market. It was a person wearing a black trench coat and ski mask and holding a sawed-off shotgun. The robber apparently didn't feel comfortable trying to leave through the front, so he walked back into the store. I made a radio broadcast that at least one subject, armed with a sawed-off shotgun, was in the store. We waited awhile longer. Communications broadcasted that the store clerk was on the phone reporting that she had just been robbed. She stated she was alone in a back room and the suspect had fled into the basement from which there was no exit. From a different vantage point, another officer verified the information. We safely entered the store, taking positions to cover the stairway to the basement. The clerk was removed, and we now knew we had only one armed suspect in the basement.

A supervisor arrived and she decided to send in a canine. When the bad guy heard the barking and growling, he gave up and came out without any trouble.

Obviously, as we saw in the first scenario, cops are liable to do things their own way instead of the right way. In your writing, your characters can do the same, but for accuracy's sake, be aware that cops should have learned the "correct" way of responding to calls:

- Have a plan.
- Use time wisely. Don't rush into any situation.
- Before reacting, get as much information as possible.
- Observe, observe, observe. Use every element of the situation to your advantage.
- Follow proven procedure when possible.
- Never grant others the element of surprise through your actions.
- Before the day begins, be sure you and your equipment can get the job done.

Handling Situations

Now that we've covered the fundamentals of "Street Cop 101," let's do an exercise I put recruits through at the academy. We'll review an actual incident (with names changed) to identify common mistakes made in the field and show that when an officer ignores the fundamentals of procedure or uses poor judgment, the results can be terrible. For your purposes, you may want to put your character into the situation and see where he ends up.

The following is based on an actual situation that occurred a few years ago in an area near Cincinnati. I summarize it here, not to be critical of anyone, but to identify those moments when an officer realizes he's made a mistake and will soon pay for it.

Officer Held Hostage

Rookie officer David Scott didn't know what awaited him when he responded early Saturday morning to a burglar alarm that went off in the temporary police station in Glenview. After he and fellow officer Eric Grayson arrived on the scene, Scott entered through the front door. He was greeted by a gun to his head. The gun, a 9mm semiautomatic, was held by Michael Conley, who had broken through a rear window and hid behind a file cabinet. Conley ordered Scott to drop his gun and radio.

Scott was held hostage inside the station for twenty minutes. Grayson managed to step back outside the station when his partner was captured, and he called on his radio for help. He used his radio to convince Conley to release Scott in exchange for the marked police car. Conley agreed and a chase ensued. City and county police cruisers pursued Conley until he struck a pole and ran from the car into a nearby woods.

An officer from the canine unit tracked Conley into the woods and arrested him after the dog had disarmed him. By the time Conley was arrested, sixty-five officers were involved in the incident.

An Officer's Nightmare

The rookie officer suffered a number of bad moments during this situation. First, he probably approached the alarm in a relaxed way. After all, who'd burglarize the police station? An officer must always be ready for the unexpected.

He should have checked the perimeter first, so that he would know the situation and avoid being caught off guard. By doing this, he would have seen that the rear window was broken and known that someone was inside—someone desperate and confused enough to break into a police station. With this knowledge, he probably would have called for help instead of walking in the front door.

These simple mistakes led to:
- The officer being held hostage
- The patrol car being taken
- A high-speed chase involving city and county officers
- A search involving the canine unit

The rookie officer was embarrassed. He could have been killed, and he could have gotten his partner and other officers killed or injured. As you write about police work, remember that mistakes are made. Officers are only human and capable of errors, and these errors can cause all kinds of problems.

Critical Issue on the Street

The street cop's day is, if anything, unpredictable. We've looked at the structured aspects of inspection and roll call and tried to get a feel for the training or mindset the street cop should use during a tour of duty. As writers, we can use the structure of a police officer's training to determine how and why our characters act the way they do. But in the myriad of issues facing street cops, there's one that can send otherwise well-meaning officers to the penitentiary, cost careers or totally disrupt lives. The most sacred of powers we as a society grant cops is the legal use of force, even deadly force, in the performance of their duties. Because of the implications involved, we'll conclude this chapter by quoting one agency's policy on the use of force. The document, with minor variations, is probably applicable coast to coast. Should your street cop character step outside the bounds of official procedure here, she becomes fair game for a world of trouble.

Policy on the Use of Force

When officers have the right to make an arrest, they may use whatever force is reasonably necessary to apprehend the offender or effect the arrest, and no more. They must avoid using unnecessary violence. Their privilege to use force is not limited to that amount of force necessary to protect themselves, but extends to that amount reasonably necessary to enable them to perform their duty.

If the offender resists, the officer may use such force as required under the circumstances to overcome the resistance, even to the extent of taking a life, if that is necessary. They may not use deadly force merely to prevent escape in misdemeanor cases. The use of force to prevent the escape of felony suspects is constitutionally unreasonable except where the escape presents an immediate risk of death or serious physical harm to the officer or another. Where the suspect poses no immediate threat of death or serious physical harm to others, the harm resulting from failing to apprehend the suspect does not justify the use of deadly force to do so. If officers use unnecessary and excessive force or act wantonly and maliciously, they may be guilty of assault, even of culpable homicide, if they kill the person they are trying to arrest.

The courts could consider a choke hold or other similar type of hold as deadly force. Choke holds should only be used with this in mind. The use of any type of choke hold to prevent the swallowing of evidence is prohibited.

When possible, personnel will use a chemical irritant as the primary response to aggressive citizen behavior.

Conclusion

A street cop's job differs from others for one reason: It's the only occupation requiring practitioners to take things against another's will—evidence, property, liberty, even life. That's why the rules are important, and that's why when writing, you should consider this awesome responsibility and the street cop's success or failure in meeting it.

Chapter Two

The American Criminal Justice System

by Alan March

T here are three fundamental parts to the American criminal justice system: the police, the courts and corrections. The police take the report of a crime and investigate it. Police bring before the courts information they develop in an effort to determine the guilt or innocence of the person accused. Should the defendant be convicted, corrections carries out the sentence of the court, using probation, prison and/or parole.

Our criminal justice system is designed to protect the rights of every American. Another way of looking at our criminal justice system is that it is interested in fair play. For example, if a cop discovers kiddy porn in a man's closet, but didn't have "probable cause" to look inside that closet, the stuff can't be used to prosecute the bad guy. The evidence of the crime, the kiddy porn, is excluded from testimony because the cops didn't play fair. The whole thing is designed to protect the rights of the accused and, by extension, the rights of everyone in America.

The basic design of the criminal justice system is the same from state to state. However, each state has its own subtle ways of protecting the rights of the accused. The concepts addressed in this chapter are used across the country.

The Police

The primary functions of the police are to enforce the law, prevent crime, investigate crimes and maintain order. Crime prevention doesn't seem very exciting to most cops; they'd rather be out catching bad guys or determining who-done-what-to-whom. That's the exciting part, and that's the part most of us like to read (and write!) about. Most cops like getting involved in the action. That's what attracts them to the job. However, crime prevention is a lofty goal. Its aim is to keep people from being victimized in the first place. Of course, if cops were completely successful in crime prevention, there would be no "true-crime" books. And there would be no need for the other parts of the criminal justice system.

Law enforcement—catching bad guys—is the bread and butter of crime novelists and true-crime writers. It can be as simple as observing a car sliding through a stop sign and issuing a citation for the infraction. Or it can be as serious as a SWAT team assaulting a barricaded sniper in a tower. Every incident along that spectrum has its interaction between the infractor and the cop. The cop has to determine if a law was broken, what law it was, who did it and what the appropriate action is.

One of the actions a cop takes is arrest—the seizure of a person's body. The Fourth Amendment to the Constitution addresses such seizures:

> The right of the people to be secure in their persons, houses, papers, and effects, against unreasonable search and seizures, shall not be violated, and no warrants shall issue, but upon probable cause, supported by oath or affirmation, and particularly describing the place to be searched, and the persons or things to be seized.

A cop must have probable cause to make an arrest. Probable cause is more than a simple belief the suspect committed the crime. The belief must be reasonable. (The concept of reasonableness permeates our system.) The cop can't just snatch a guy because he believes he's committed a crime. Probable cause is a reasonable belief that the person under arrest committed the crime. The belief must be more than a hunch or mere suspicion. The belief is based upon any combination of the officer's own observations; witness, victim and/or suspect statements; and evidence at the crime scene. Supreme Court Justice Douglas wrote in 1968, "The term 'probable cause' rings a bell of certainty that is not sounded by such phrases such as 'reasonable suspicion.' " However, the cop doesn't have to be convinced beyond a shadow of a doubt; that level of belief is the responsibility of the court.

An arrested suspect has rights. We all do, but they become important when a person has handcuffs ratcheted around his wrists. An officer can't search a person without probable cause. If a person is under arrest, the arrest itself becomes probable cause to search. This is called "search contemporaneous to the arrest." Before an arrest, however, a cop may only pat down or frisk a subject. The frisk is not a search for evidence or contraband. It is a nonintrusive, cursory examination for weapons.

The case of *Terry v. Ohio* tells us that an officer can stop and frisk a person whom the officer has reasonable suspicion (remember, that's a degree less than probable cause) to believe that person has committed or is likely to commit a crime and that person may be armed.

The frisk is allowed only if the officer can articulate later in court that he was in fear for his safety. The testimony may go something like this: "I observed the subject standing at the corner of Fourteenth and Vine, a location I know has a high incidence of drug traffic. I watched the subject engage in frequent, brief interactions with the occupants of vehicles that had stopped in traffic. I suspected the subject was engaged in drug trafficking." (This is the suspicion of criminal activity.) "Knowing that drug traffickers frequently carry weapons to protect their merchandise and money, I patted down the subject's outer garments. My frisk revealed what felt like a pistol in the subject's front waistband."

At that point, the officer is allowed to retrieve the item he believes is a weapon, for his own safety. If carrying that hidden gun is a crime, then the officer has probable cause to arrest, which then allows a full search. That full search may uncover drugs or other contraband, which may lead to more charges.

If an officer searches without probable cause and finds evidence of a crime, that evidence is likely to be thrown out of court or excluded from testimony. (Recall the example cited at the beginning of the chapter.) This is called the exclusionary rule. The exclusionary rule comes from *Weeks v. United States*. Basically, if a cop violates a person's constitutional rights against unreasonable search and seizure, the evidence he thus uncovers cannot be used. Everything that results from that unconstitutional search is tainted and excluded from the case. The evidence or information that is derived from an unconstitutional search is sometimes referred to as the "fruit of the poisonous tree." If you use it to support your case, the case will be doomed.

If an officer is going to question a suspect while the suspect is in police custody, the cop must first advise the suspect of his rights. Most of us know these as Miranda Rights, from the precedent-setting case,

Miranda v. Arizona: "You have the right to remain silent. If you give up that right, anything you say can be used against you in a court of law."

Miranda says a person being questioned, while in police custody, must be made aware of his Fifth Amendment right not to testify against his own interests. The Fifth Amendment says, in part:

> No person shall . . . be compelled in any criminal case to be a witness against himself. . . .

However, if the cop is not going to ask the suspect any questions, he is not required to read him his rights. A corollary is that a cop does not have to apprise a person of his right against self-incrimination simply when asking him questions on the street. The person must be in police custody for *Miranda* to kick in. *Miranda* also reminds a suspect that he has a right to legal representation: "If you desire an attorney and cannot afford one, the court will provide one for you."

The actual wording of Miranda warnings changes a bit from state to state and agency to agency, depending upon the case law of that state and the experiences of that particular agency.

After arresting the bad guy, the cop takes him to jail. The suspect is processed: He is searched thoroughly by the jailers, and his property is taken, inventoried and noted on a receipt. The suspect is photographed and fingerprinted for identification, and he undergoes a health screening to determine any special health needs. The health screening is important; once a person is taken into custody, that person's welfare is the responsibility of the officer or jailer who has custody.

The arrested person may be able to post a bond to get "bailed out of jail." For most minor crimes, the bond amount is usually predetermined by the courts. A person might even be released simply by signing a piece of paper promising to appear in court, if that person qualifies. (Some of the criteria that qualifies a person for such a release include owning a home in the area, being regularly employed in the area and having no previous history of failing to appear in court.)

The Courts

When a person is arrested, he has the right to have his case heard by a court. There are many levels of courts in the United States, which come under either state or federal jurisdiction. Different courts hear different cases, depending upon the seriousness of the charge.

Essentially, there are two classes of crimes: misdemeanors and felonies. Misdemeanors are less serious crimes for which the penalty is one year or less in jail. Of course, penalties also include fines. Examples of misdemeanors are petty theft, an assault in which no serious injury occurred or a minor case of vandalism. A felony is a more serious crime for which the penalty can be more than a year in prison. Examples of felonies include rape, robbery, burglary and, of course, murder.

Misdemeanors and felonies can be further broken down into classes or degrees. Most states have first-, second-, third- and fourth-degree misdemeanors. Some may use the terms class-A misdemeanor, class-B misdemeanor and so on. A first-degree or class-A misdemeanor is the most serious, warranting the greatest penalty. For example, in Ohio, throwing a rock through a window is a third-degree misdemeanor. The maximum punishment is sixty days in jail, a $250 fine or both. Punching somebody in the nose is a first-degree misdemeanor and will get you 180 days in jail, a $1,000 fine or both.

IS IT JAIL OR ISN'T IT?

Notice that misdemeanor lockup time is done in *jail*, while felony time is done in *prison*. Jail is the local lockup; either the city or county controls it. It is the place less-serious criminals are incarcerated. Prisons are operated by state or federal government.

The term "penitentiary" has lost favor over the years, perhaps because so few of the residents there are truly penitent! However, the more modern term, "correctional facility" may be no more appropriate considering how few of their residents truly correct their behavior.

Felonies come in classes or degrees, too. The more serious the harm, the greater the penalty. Stealing one thousand dollars worth of building supplies will get you a year in prison. Slashing a person with a knife will get you three to ten years and a $20,000 fine. The ultimate penalty is capital punishment. It is meted out for premeditated murder, or murder coupled with other serious crimes, such as rape, robbery or arson. Some states consider these capital crimes a third, and of course, highest degree of crime.

Lower-level state courts, such as justices of the peace, mayor's courts or municipal courts, hear only misdemeanors. Felonies can be tried in county courts, sometimes referred to as common pleas courts. District, circuit and appeals courts hear the most serious crimes in the state's jurisdiction.

They also may hear appeals from lower courts. Ultimately, appeals in state courts can be heard at the state supreme court.

Federal courts include U.S. district courts, which hear most federal cases. Virtually all federal cases are felonies. The U.S. court of appeals hears appeals of cases coming from U.S. district courts. If the prosecution or defense seeks higher appeal, they ask the U.S. Supreme Court to hear the case. The U.S. Supreme Court must decide whether or not it will hear the case. If it chooses not to, the lower court ruling stands. However, if the Supreme Court believes constitutional issues are at the core of the case, then it grants *certiorari*, which means it will hear the case.

Present in the courtroom are a judge, defense attorney and prosecuting attorney, sometimes referred to as a district attorney. The trial judge acts as a referee in an argument. He keeps things moving along, allowing each party to have his say. The prosecutor takes the evidence from the police and presents it to the court in an effort to convince the court the bad guy did it. The defense attorney has to bring doubt upon the prosecutor's case. It is an adversarial system. The judge also makes sure the rights of the accused are protected. Listening to the evidence and arguments of the attorneys, trial judges decide what evidence and testimony will be allowed, based upon case law and court rules. (Technically, testimony *is* evidence. It's just spoken, as opposed to hard evidence, such as a fingerprint.)

There is an old saw in police circles regarding decision making in the use of deadly force. It weighs the practicality of surviving an armed encounter against social values and political considerations. It goes, "It is better to be tried by twelve than carried by six."

Cases are tried before a judge, panel of judges or jury. Most state courts above mayor's court and justices of the peace allow the defendant to choose between having a judge or jury decide guilt or innocence. A bench trial is one in which the judge decides guilt or innocence, as well as runs the trial. Juries can have as few as six people or as many as twelve, depending upon the laws of the state in which the trial is taking place. Mostly, felony trials have twelve jurors.

To attain a conviction in criminal court, the prosecution must prove "beyond a reasonable doubt" that the defendant committed the crime. This means the reasonable, average, prudent person would be convinced by the prosecutor's case that the defendant is guilty.

BURDEN OF PROOF

In civil lawsuits, the burden of proof is simply a preponderance of the evidence. Essentially, the plaintiff, the person who brought the case before the court, must have 51 percent proof the defendant committed the crime. This is much less proof than what is necessary in criminal courts. This is why O.J. Simpson, though acquitted of murder in criminal court, was found by a civil court to have caused the death of his ex-wife. The court simply needed less convincing.

Corrections

If a person is convicted of a crime, the court will pass sentence. Most statutes have penalties as part of their structure. In Ohio, a first-degree misdemeanor can be punished with jail time of up to 180 days and as much as a $1,000 fine. The judge has the discretion to establish the sentence up to those limits. Things that help the judge weigh the decision are the defendant's previous record, his ability to pay the fine (poor people go to jail, wealthy people pay fines) and the seriousness of the harm from the crime.

It's pretty much the same for felonies, too. Felony statutes may have penalty ranges, such as three to five years for a robbery. The judge can determine how much time the convicted person must serve. Some crimes have specific penalties that must be handed out. Many states now have laws that require a mandatory minimum term in prison if a firearm is used in the commission of the offense. That time is in addition to the time spent for the crime itself. So an armed robbery in which a knife is used may get the defendant less time in prison than an armed robbery in which a revolver is used.

Another penalty is probation. Probation places the defendant under the supervision of the court for a set period of time. The defendant must regularly check in with a probation officer during his probation period. The terms of probation can include paying the fine on an installment plan; repaying the victim for his losses; performing community service, such as cutting weeds along a highway; or even requiring a person to get a job.

Probation can include a suspended sentence of incarceration, for example, a person convicted of assault may be sentenced to 180 days in jail. The judge might hold off incarcerating the defendant and place him on probation. The judge could give the defendant a year to repay the victim for his lost earnings and medical bills. During that time, the defendant is on probation. If the defendant fails to complete those payments in one year, he may have to spend the 180 days in jail for probation violation. Also, if the defendant is arrested for another crime while on probation, his probation officer may sign a probation violation warrant, upon which the defendant could be arrested. When appearing before the court on the second charge, the defendant may also be convicted of probation violation and serve the suspended sentence, in addition to anything the new charge would bring.

If a person goes to prison, he may be released before the entire sentence is served. The person would be placed on parole. Parole is similar to probation in that if the defendant violates the terms of his parole, he could be returned to prison for the remainder of his sentence.

The American criminal justice system is always changing. Court rulings, new technologies and changing values drive its evolution. The fundamental concept of our system, though, will never change: There are rules the good guys have to play by. The rights of all Americans are precious and must be protected by the rules and actions of each part of the system.

PART II

CRIME

Chapter Three

An Overview of Murder

by Mauro V. Corvasce and Joseph R. Paglino

from *Murder One: A Writer's Guide to Homicide*

The Legal Terms

The following terms are taken from the New Jersey State Law Code of Criminal Justice. The definitions may vary slightly from state to state, so be sure you check the state code of criminal justice in whichever state your fiction is set. These definitions, however, are fairly standard, and it is unlikely your own state will vary too much from them.

Criminal Homicide: A person is guilty of criminal homicide "if he purposely, knowingly, recklessly . . . causes the death of another human being. Criminal homicide is murder, manslaughter, or death by auto."

Death by Auto or Vessel: "[occurs when death] is caused by driving a vehicle or vessel recklessly."

Manslaughter: "[occurs when the] actor recklessly causes death under circumstances manifesting extreme indifference to human life."

Murder: "[occurs when the] actor purposely [or knowingly] causes death or serious bodily injury resulting in death."

Self-Defense: "[is] the use of force upon or toward another . . . when the actor reasonably believes that such force is immediately necessary for the purpose of protecting himself against the use of unlawful force by such other person on the present occasion."

Homicide Investigations

All homicide investigations follow a basic procedure, which we have outlined below. Before we get into it, however, you need to keep a couple of facts in mind. First, most homicides that get solved are done so within the first forty-eight hours. After that period of time, the trail generally runs cold. This is true for several obvious reasons:

1. Eyewitnesses who have not stepped forward probably will not appear. And their memories of the event, of course, become less clear.
2. New clues at the scene of the crime probably will not surface after the initial investigation and analysis have been completed.
3. If the murderer has left a trail of clues or if the police know where the killer is hiding, an arrest has been made or is imminent.

Secondly, because the first forty-eight-hour period is so important, detectives work around the clock to gather evidence and follow up leads. Throughout the investigation, the homicide squad from the county prosecutor's office lends full assistance.

Finally, in most homicides, the victim knew the killer. For this reason, investigators focus their attention on the victim's immediate circle of family, friends and co-workers. Clues and motives are analyzed with this circle of people in mind. Stranger and familiar stranger murders are very difficult to solve because the killer is not part of this circle. Investigators have no shortlist of likely suspects to keep in mind while analyzing the facts of the crime.

Step 1. Secure the Scene
The responsibility of the first officer at the scene of a crime is to preserve its integrity until the patrol supervisor can arrive. The officer should not move any objects or bodies and should keep bystanders from intruding on the scene. The supervisor—a sergeant or lieutenant—must ensure that the crime scene is preserved. Responsibilities of patrol officers include these tasks:
- Surrounding the area with police tape
- Controlling crowds
- Preventing overzealous members of the media or family members of the victim from destroying or removing crucial evidence

Step 2. Find Eyewitnesses
Although eyewitness testimony is not always considered 100 percent accurate, finding such witnesses is the patrol officers' foremost duty once the crime scene is preserved and the patrol supervisors arrive on the scene. The officers, however, do not interview these eyewitnesses themselves. They record the names and addresses of any people in the area and ask them to wait to speak with the homicide detectives when they arrive.

Step 3. Photograph the Crime Scene

When the detectives arrive, their first job is to photograph the crime scene. Their work is monitored by their own supervisors (who are detective sergeants or detective lieutenants). Several photos must be taken of the crime scene:

- Shot from the four corners of the scene
- Long-distance shots
- Medium-distance shots
- Close-up shots of the body and any evidence
- Shots of any relevant details, selected by the detectives

Step 4. Search for Latent Prints

Fingerprinting at a crime scene is referred to by police officers as searching for latent prints. Police officers and detectives who are qualified should dust for prints. The following are among the most likely targets for fingerprinting:

- Weapons
- Points of entry or exit, such as doors and windows
- Flat, hard surfaces such as tabletops

There are several different types of fingerprint powders used by the detectives, because a fingerprint might only show up when a certain type of powder is used. The most common types:

- Black, for use on light objects
- White, for use on black items
- Silver, for mirrors

As you surely know, no two persons' fingerprints are exactly alike. Also note that fingerprints do not come out clearly on porous material. To search for latent prints, the detectives use an ostrich feather fingerprint duster to apply the appropriate color powder to the area. They then, in a rapid, circular motion, twist the duster to spread the powder over the area. When a potential fingerprint is revealed by the powder, a special strip of tape is used to actually "lift" the fingerprint from the object. This tape is then examined by fingerprint experts and compared to prints stored on local, state and federal crime computers.

If you want to know more about fingerprinting, consult the Howdunit titled *Scene of the Crime*, by Anne Wingate. She covers the topic in greater detail than we can offer here.

Step 5. Gather Evidence

Detectives can be looking for details as subtle as footprints or items as small as clothing fibers, hair strands, blood samples or paint chips. Such "trace evidence" is manipulated through tweezers and other instruments appropriate for dealing with objects of such minute size or substance. It is then transferred to a slide and sent to a forensics lab for examination.

Officers wear gloves when handling larger items, such as weapons, and deposit these items in plastic or paper bags. Whenever evidence is gathered, the name of the detective who found and returned it to the police station is carefully recorded. The name of the police officer who received it at the evidence locker at the local or county police station is also noted. This is called the chain of evidence and is used to ensure the reliability of evidence at trial.

Step 6. Remove the Body

By this stage in the investigation process, the county coroner has arrived. The coroner must make examinations of several key issues:
- The temperature
- The humidity
- The weather in the area

The coroner uses these notations in order to later establish the time of death to a greater degree of accuracy. The body is taken to the county morgue, where an autopsy is performed, revealing (usually) the cause of death.

To learn more about this process—and the next steps in determining cause of death—please consult the Howdunit titled *Cause of Death*, by Dr. Keith Wilson.

Under Arrest

A point before beginning: The following procedure for arresting a suspect does not apply only to murder cases. The same procedure is followed no matter what crime the suspect is alleged to have committed. If you have your detective follow this procedure in booking a murder suspect, you can be assured of its accuracy.

In order to arrest a suspect, the police must have "probable cause"; that is, there must be some substantive evidence linking the suspect to the alleged crime. Either immediately before or immediately after an arrest, the police in some jurisdictions must receive an arrest warrant from a judge, which will determine the initial amount of bail. This figure can later be changed at the formal bail hearing, which is usually within twenty-four hours.

Following an arrest, a variety of forms must be filled out to protect the suspect's constitutional rights, physical safety and personal property.

- **Arrest Report.** This is one of the main forms to be completed. It contains details of the arrest, the bail amount, the suspect's name and information (address, date of birth, Social Security number, employer, address of employer, height, weight, eye color, scars, tattoos, color hair, etc.), and any other relevant facts pertaining to the case.
- **Fingerprint Form.** This is another one of the major forms needed. Upon arrest, each suspect is fingerprinted three times: once for local police records, once for state police records, once for the FBI.
- **Vehicle/Property Report.** Whenever the police impound a car or seize personal property during an arrest or as the result of a warranted search, they are required to fill out one of these forms to ensure the property can be returned if the suspect is found not guilty.
- **Evidence Report Form.** Any evidence seized by the police during an arrest or a warranted search must also be cataloged on these forms, which are sent to the prosecutor. This helps with the efficient development of a case against the suspect.
- **Suicide Evaluation Form.** During any interviews police officers have with the suspect, they observe her behavior. Based on what they notice, the police complete this form to estimate the probability of the suspect's attempting suicide. If that is determined to be a distinct possibility, the police are required to post extra watch on the holding cell.

Writing Accurately About Murder

Before launching into weapons of murder and the specific types of murder, let us remind you that every murder has its own unique qualities. Though we have been investigating murders for many years, we always find something new or surprising. The following information will help you present your fictional murders in accurate ways, but be aware that there are exceptions to every rule.

Now, to close this chapter, let us offer you a few more facts about murder in America. The source of these statistics is a special report compiled by John M. Dawson for the Bureau of Justice Statistics, U.S. Department of Justice.

- More than half of all murder victims in large cities are young black males—who are killed by other young black males. The vast majority of the murderers, and even a large percentage of their victims, have had previous trouble with the law.

- While 48 percent of the general population is between the ages of fifteen and forty-five, 75 percent of the murder victims and 91 percent of defendants are in that age range.
- Seventy-five percent of murder victims and 90 percent of defendants are males.
- In large urban counties, circumstances involving illegal drugs account for 18 percent of the defendants and 16 percent of the victims.
- In large urban counties, handguns are used in 50 percent of the murders; knives are used in 21 percent of the murders.
- While 52 percent of the general population is female, only one in ten murder defendants and just over two in ten murder victims is female.
- A third of the female victims, but only one in ten male victims, are killed by their spouses or romantic partners.
- Six of every ten arrests for murder result in a murder conviction.
- More than 99 percent of defendants in capital offense cases—those with a murder charge that could result in a death penalty—are convicted of some charge.

Chapter Four

Mass Murders

by Mauro V. Corvasce and Joseph R. Paglino

from *Murder One: A Writer's Guide to Homicide*

Mass murders occur when several victims are killed within hours or even moments of each other. In many of these cases, an armed person walks into a restaurant, shopping mall, government office or other such public place and begins randomly shooting innocent bystanders. In April of 1990, for example, a man who had been released only one day from a psychiatric institution went into a mall in Atlanta, Georgia, and began shooting everyone in his way.

In recent years, there has been a growing number of cases where a parent or sibling kills an entire family. Additionally, there have been many cases in which people have gone into schools and playgrounds, armed with semi- or fully automatic weapons and shot everyone, including the children.

While there has not been a tremendous amount of research on these crimes, mass murderers do share certain characteristic traits and habits. The killers are usually white males. From our experience, this type of murderer tends to have a low-paying, semi-skilled job, usually involving shift work or other routine-type tasks.

Profile

In most cases, there is a particular victim whom has been selected to be murdered, such as an ex-wife, a former boss, a friend. But the killer, when he begins the actual process of the murder, such as entering the building where the victim is located, opens fire on whomever is in the area.

Sometimes, however, a person feels overwhelmed and frustrated by a perceived injustice in his life and simply shoots victims who, although not directly related to the killer, represent what he is mentally fighting against. For example, if a man is fired from a job a week after being arrested for an utterly unrelated matter, he may feel the police caused him to be fired. In the killer's mind, the arresting police officer came between him and success, so now anyone in a uniform, most particularly a police officer, is his target.

Characteristics

Although their motivations vary from case to case, mass murderers do share some characteristics that may become reasons for the mass murders. Generally, these traits are severe depression, delusional psychosis, violent changes of temperament, alcoholism and the use of pornography.

One telltale sign of depression is mood swings. The person suffering from depression may be extremely happy and energetic one minute and angry or sobbing the next. These rapid changes may occur within a day, an hour or a few minutes and are usually set off by something to which the reaction seems extreme. For example, the person may be joking around and accidentally spill some water on the floor, at which point he becomes extremely angry, curses vehemently and smashes the glass against the wall.

Lack of interest in what's going on around them is another indication of people's depression. They become bored with their jobs, their friends, their significant others and sometimes life itself. They don't want to leave their homes or their bedrooms, they wear the same clothes day after day and they often neglect personal hygiene. Mass murder may be a way of alleviating this boredom. Similar to their general lack of interest, depressed persons may exhibit a lack of appetite that lasts for weeks. They may eat only their favorite foods or sweets, but even those may become unappetizing to them after a few days.

The mass murderer may also exhibit psychotic behavior, having delusions and losing touch with reality. This may be caused by an organic brain disorder, such as a chemical imbalance or a brain tumor, that impairs his ability for rational thought. Or he could simply be psychopathic, with no sense of his moral or societal obligations. The psychopathic killer is a delusional killer who does not believe what he is doing is wrong.

Mass murderers tend to have violent changes of temperament. For example, a mild, meek person may suddenly become lividly irate and aggressive once certain trigger mechanisms are set off. This often happens because the person has feelings of inadequacy or feels he is being duped by society once again. Michael Douglas's character in the movie *Falling Down* typifies this type of personality.

Also, mass murderers often have problems with alcohol abuse. Although it cannot be implied that alcohol causes people to become mass murderers, there is a high rate of alcoholism among these killers. And alcohol does aggravate the symptoms of depression.

There is also a high incidence of pornography being involved in mass murders. Although pornography may not play a major role in the crime itself, it is one of the higher ranking similarities between mass murderers and serial murderers. Police raids of these killers' homes have often revealed many pornographic videotapes and magazines. Again, as with alcoholism, this does not mean an interest in pornography makes one a mass murderer, but it is nonetheless a common characteristic of these killers.

Motive: Stress

There are some mass murders that appear to be premeditated, as in the case of a Mr. Charles Whitman, who shot at unsuspecting victims from the famous bell tower at the University of Texas in Austin. Whitman carried boxes full of supplies, including food and ammunition, to the top of the bell tower in preparation for his attack on the innocents. Whitman's crime seems to have been motivated by stress, which is why people under great amounts of stress now joke about "going up to the top of the bell tower."

At the opposite end of the spectrum, some cases of multiple murders involve killers whose fury was ignited by a trivial remark, a minor insult or a small provocation. Whether brought on by extreme prolonged stress or an offhand remark, however, multiple-victim murderers do so in an effort to regain some degree of control and pleasure in their lives. To the observer, this motivation may not appear rational, but to the killer, it makes perfect sense, given his psychological dysfunction.

Motive: Hatred of Society

Mass murderers often develop a hatred of society, leading to strong feelings of rejection and failure and the anxiety of not being able to survive on their own. These feelings create frustrations for this murderer that inevitably overwhelm him and motivate him to strike back. For many killers, the best way to lash out against a cold, dark society is to destroy its children. Killing children in a school yard provides the mass murderer with not only a much needed sense of power and control but also a way of taking vengeance where it hurts the community the most. Many of these crimes occur in communities with many schools, shopping malls, office buildings and other such crowded forums.

Methods

The mass murderer often believes that killing innocent people will correct all the wrongs in his life. Since this usually occurs to the killer in a sudden epiphany, he does not usually plan the crime months in advance. Once he does decide to commit the crime, however, he often gathers together more than enough equipment to do the job. In other words, the mass murderer quite frequently has boxes and boxes of ammunition and several semiautomatic or automatic weapons to use to kill suddenly and swiftly. (In one famous case, the killer had enough ammunition to reload his semiautomatic weapons at least 150 times.)

Unlike a serial murderer, who will have enough only to kill the victim and perhaps one or two people at a scene, the mass murderer is prepared to take out as many people as is required to regain his place in the world. He realizes subconsciously that this most likely is his last moment of glory, and he wants to go out with a "bang." A mass murderer almost never runs out of ammunition or is foiled by a jammed weapon.

This is not to say, however, that all mass murderers are this prepared. There are certainly cases on record in which the killers used only one or two guns and gave up or killed themselves after shooting six or seven people.

Investigation and Capture

Unlike serial killers, the mass murderer seems to give very little thought to his possible capture or death. In fact, many are killed by the police during the attack, while many others kill themselves once they have completed the massacres. In some cases, the offenders surrender to the police and offer no resistance. It is almost as if they are finally at peace knowing they have committed the murders and, they hope, righted all the wrongs in their lives.

In cases where families are murdered, the killer usually leaves many, many pieces of evidence that will lead to his arrest. Perhaps because he has killed his loved ones, the familial mass murderer may on some level want to be caught.

Chapter Five

Serial Murders

by Mauro V. Corvasce and Joseph R. Paglino

from *Murder One: A Writer's Guide to Homicide*

Serial murder is the crime of the 1990s, but is it really new? The term is certainly of recent vintage, having been coined around 1980 to differentiate between mass murders and the more methodical killings of those who spin out their crimes over time. In a report from the National Institute of Justice published in 1988, serial murder was defined in the following way:

> A series of three or more murders, committed as separate events, usually, but not always, by one offender acting alone. The crimes may occur over a period of time ranging from hours to years. Quite often the motivation is psychological, and the offender's behavior and the physical evidence observed at the crime scene will reflect sadistic, sexual overtones.

The phrase "committed as separate events" means that a certain amount of time must pass between the murders. No specific time period has ever been stated, but if only a few hours separate the murders, the killer probably will not be considered a serial killer.

Though serial murder is a worldwide phenomenon, North America claims 76 percent of the world's serial murders. The United States must claim an ignominious 74 percent. Europe runs a distant second with 19 percent. Europe's leaders are England (36 percent), Germany (29 percent) and France (11 percent). The formerly Communist Eastern European nations contribute a mere 1.8 percent of the total, with ten cases recorded since 1917, a fact explained by both cultural differences and the tendency of state-owned media to "lose" bad news.

Although most people believe serial murderers are some new phenomenon, you can actually trace their roots back to the early fifteenth century in France. There was a nobleman by the name of Gilles de Rais who was known for his violent attacks of innocent children whom he would rape, torture and eventually kill. Historians believe that he committed these crimes on at least eight hundred children.

Serial murders extended to nineteenth-century England with one of the most famous serial killers of all time, Jack the Ripper. Jack the Ripper, as you recall, went around the streets of London killing prostitutes. His name became a household word as many newspapers printed Jack the Ripper's story as it evolved.

Throughout the early and middle twentieth century, an occasional killer attracted media attention, such as Charlie Starkweather in the late 1950s, but it wasn't until the 1970s that such killers began to surface with alarming frequency. Our society as a whole entered an era of increased violence that's continued the past twenty-five years. And our awareness of this violence, and of serial killers, increased because television brought these stories into our homes every night. Newspapers and magazines, competing with television for our attention, gave greater coverage to stories of violence and murder, increasing our awareness even more. This intensive coverage had an ironic side effect: It turned most serial murderers into cult heroes. They were given nicknames, such as the Freeway Strangler, the Boston Strangler, the Son of Sam, the Zodiac Killer and the Hillside Strangler.

This romanticized view of serial killers has led to their frequent use in mystery and crime fiction. So in this chapter, we will examine some of the common types of serial murders, looking closely at their motivations and how they perform their tasks in real life.

Serial Murders vs. Mass Murders

The terms "mass murderer" and "serial killer" are often used interchangeably in the media. Although they do share a few common traits, the truth is that serial killers and mass murderers are very different. The mass murderer is one who kills a large group of people at one time usually using one device, such as a bomb, or an arsonist who ignites a nightclub filled with people. A serial killer usually commits one murder (sometimes more) at a time over a period of time, which could be days, weeks, months or even years. And the serial killer is one who honestly believes what he is doing is normal and acceptable. To our knowledge, no serial killers kill, then stop; the murders continue throughout the course of a serial killer's lifetime. The only time the slayings actually stop is when the killer is apprehended and placed in jail, where he doesn't have access to his victims.

In the case of the famous Zodiac Killer from California, the murders appeared to have stopped, but a suspect was never apprehended. It could be that the suspect was incarcerated for only one murder and was never linked to the others or perhaps was imprisoned for other crimes. In 1997, a man was arrested in New York City for killing his sister. Some investigators believe this man is the Zodiac Killer, but he has never been charged with any of the Zodiac murders. Yet another possibility is that the Zodiac Killer may have become incapacitated because of an accident or illness or may have died without the story ever being told to law enforcement authorities. While we don't usually associate these kinds of life circumstances with murderers, these things happen to them just as they happen to everyone.

As you can see, there are few similarities, so calling a mass murderer a serial killer (or vice versa) in your work is a glaring error for which many of your readers will take you to task.

Serial Killers

Since so many myths and legends exist about serial killers, let's identify some known facts:

- 85 percent of American serial killers are male; 8 percent are female. Sex remains undetermined in another 7 percent of the cases in which the killers are still at large.
- 82 percent of American serial killers are white; 15 percent are black; 2.5 percent are Hispanic. Native Americans and Asians figure in one case each, with the Asian killer serving as an accomplice to a white male.
- Most serial killers range in age from twenty-two to fifty.
- Surprisingly few serial killers are legally insane. All are cunning, indicated by the fact that more than 18 percent of the cases of serial murder in this century remain unsolved.
- 87 percent of American serial killers are loners; 10 percent hunt in pairs or packs; 59 percent are from all-male groups (ranging from two-man teams to gangs of a dozen or more), while 23 percent are male-female couples and 18 percent include mixed groups of varying sizes.

Geographically Stable vs. Transient Serial Killers

Some serial killers kill in one geographical location and are therefore known as *geographically stable serial killers*. This type doesn't hunt and roam beyond his immediate surroundings; instead, the killer tries to lure victims into his home or car. Famous serial killers Jeffrey Dahmer and John Wayne Gacy fall into this category, as would Atlanta killer Wayne Williams, who patrolled the streets looking for his victims. It has been reported that trace evidence (such as fibers) from Williams's home was found on clothes the victims wore prior to their murders. This suggests the victims had been in Williams's home before Williams committed the murders.

This type of serial killer usually seeks victims that share some similarity, such as age or hair color or social standing. The killer, for example, may seek only young, blond-haired boys or middle-aged, dark-haired women as his victims. Criminal psychologists believe this similarity usually connects to some childhood experience. The victims, for example, may look like the killer's mother or like a special childhood friend.

This type of serial killer is the easiest type to catch because of these two patterns: The victims all live or work in an area near the killer's home, and the victims share some trait or similarity. These patterns allow the police to narrow the focus of the search and locate the killer. Thus, the friends, co-workers and relatives are crucial persons to be interviewed by police as they hold the key to the victim's actions.

Geographically stable serial killers can also be loners, living at home with their mothers and sisters, or come from a dysfunctional family. They may seek their victims during the evening hours. These types of serial killers mainly kill prostitutes. Now, most prostitutes have no family contact. They are often drug abusers and are on the lowest end of the social ladder. Since prostitutes are usually runaways, no one really knows their whereabouts—or that they're missing, so their deaths are unlikely to be reported in a timely manner. Clues will probably be destroyed, leaving the likelihood of catching this type of serial killer next to none.

These victims are usually found in remote locations by hunters, years after they've been killed. We can refer back to the killings in the Green River area of Washington State where a number of prostitutes from the Seattle area were found in various conditions of decomposition, mostly skeletal remains. But the problem with investigating serial killers is that they kill and then transport the victims to other locations, so one is hard pressed to find any type of clues or evidence from a remote dumping area.

The other type of serial killer is the *geographically transient serial killer*. This type moves from location to location, usually to keep his identity unknown. He stays in one location until he feels the police are getting close to him. Most serial killers of this type kill or seek a victim just a short time after moving to a new location. Famous serial killer Ted Bundy, for example, began killing less than two weeks after he moved from Louisville, Kentucky, to Tallahassee, Florida. Most law enforcement officials believe Bundy was responsible for an additional thirty-six unsolved murder cases. But some people believe Bundy actually killed more than three hundred young women throughout the United States.

This could be true. Because murderers of this type are frequently on the move, they're more difficult to catch than those who stay close to home. They therefore remain free to continue killing. One serial killer of this type was the most prolific one on record: Henry Lee Lucas. When he was finally caught, he admitted to killing more than 365 people.

When this serial killer is apprehended, he may or may not cooperate with the police. It has been our finding that these killers cooperate with the police when there's a deal to be made or if they are of low social standing and education.

Psychological Profiles

Serial killers come from all walks of life. They can be rich or poor, old or young, a loner or a socialite. John Wayne Gacy was a well-known politician and a professional businessman whose claim to fame was how nice he was to children. He even dressed up as a clown and went to hospitals and other locations to entertain children. He was liked by many, and it was quite a surprise when the police found in the crawl space underneath his house the bodies of thirty-three young men.

As with any type of human behavior, serial murder can have many motivations. The same motivations that inspire this behavior in some people could inspire other people to different, even constructive, behavior. But motivation is a cornerstone of the FBI's psychological profile. We will describe the major types of serial murderers, examining the motives that seem to dominate each type. It is important to note, however, that many serial killers have more than one profile, so we can't commit ourselves to writing just one profile for each serial killer in all cases. In actuality, the more victims a serial killer murders, the more narrowly we are able to define exactly what type of killer he is. This is because the type of victim often reveals the type of killer. The FBI creates a psychological profile and constantly hones it with each and every murder the serial killer commits.

Delusional Serial Murderers

Many serial murderers are not considered to be psychologically impaired. They are in touch with the real world but have absolutely no feelings for other people. The opposite of that would be the delusional killer who murders because he has seen or heard people or voices that demand he kill a certain type of person or persons. The new breed of police officers would consider these killers psychotic or psychologically impaired; the old school of police officers would simply call them nuts. There is little doubt about the mental state of these serial killers. In psychiatric terms, they would qualify as psychotic.

But are they really as psychotic as they appear? The rationale behind this question: A smart defense attorney would certainly make the case that their delusions make them good candidates to plead insanity.

Motives

David Berkowitz, the "Son of Sam" murderer, is a perfect example of this type of murderer. When interviewed by the police, he said he heard his neighbor's dog speak to him and tell him to kill. Other delusional serial murderers hear a disembodied voice or see a vision, perhaps of a demon, Satan or maybe even God. Harvey Carignan, who was convicted of murdering six women, claimed that God told him to kill. Carignan also had a distaste for women because he thought they were bad, and he declared he was God's savior put on this earth to do away with all the evil in the world.

Another serial killer was a young boy who decapitated an elderly woman and then stabbed her more than two hundred times. Within the next several weeks, he killed several other elderly women by stabbing them in the upper body. Three other elderly women escaped him, though all suffered stabbings. When caught by the police, he informed them that he was possessed by a red demon that stated he must kill in this manner and that the only pleasure he could possibly receive was killing the way he did. In these last two instances, both killers heard voices in their heads, and they both killed because of their delusions. One set of murders was predicated by God, the other by demons—completely opposite ends of the spectrum.

Methods

The delusional serial killer's crime scene is in total disarray. There are probably signs of forced entry, and the scene shows signs of a struggle, such as the victim attempting to flee. The victim is brutally assaulted with either a knife or a club or even both. The victim's body is not carved up, but is stabbed, shot or bludgeoned, not once but numerous times.

When the delusional serial killer goes out looking for his victim, he has an idea he wants to kill but doesn't have a particular person targeted. Experts say there is just something in the killer's mind that clicks before he goes out looking for a victim. When this happens, the victim may be the first person the killer sees or the first person with whom he feels comfortable. Then he attempts to either enter someone's house or apprehend someone from a sidewalk, usually by force, and takes the victim to a secluded area to beat or stab to death.

To aid in abducting the victim, the murderer may use some type of restraining device, such as duct tape or handcuffs, or she may use Mace or pepper spray to overcome the victim. These details are thought out prior to the actual abduction or break-in, which usually occurs during early morning hours. We will go into more detail toward the end of the chapter about just how this type of killer operates.

Goal-Oriented Serial Killers

The goal-oriented serial killer wants to achieve some result from his murders. He may want to eliminate from the world people he perceives as worthless. He typically frequents local hangouts or nightclubs, especially places where women congregate. These women, if provocatively dressed, may unwittingly become victims. Killing provocatively dressed prostitutes is one of the most common themes in serial murders by men, as these killers are obsessed with ridding the world of sexual misconduct.

The serial murderer of this type, when confronted by the police, may actually be proud of the fact that he has made the world a better place by eliminating the lower echelons of society, such as prostitutes, streetwalkers or promiscuous women (promiscuous men in the case of homosexual murders). He believes he should be branded a hero, not a murderer, by the police.

Motives

The goal-oriented serial killer has an obsessive-compulsive mind-set and may have deep-rooted psychosexual problems, but he is not delusional. This type of killer does not hear voices or see visions directing him to kill certain types of people; he simply has in his mind the desire to rid the world of a certain group of people who, as classified in his mind, are undesirable and unworthy to live and work with other people.

Methods

The crime scenes of the goal-oriented serial killer vary from case to case. No two are exactly alike. But through the years, investigators have detected a few patterns. This type of murderer usually does his killings at remote locations, and the victims' bodies are not discovered until years later. And rarely does he murder in one location and then dump the body somewhere else later.

Domineering Serial Killers

This killer actually enjoys seeing his victim suffer. He likes to inspire fear. He gets more enjoyment from the victim's fear, from feeling a sense of control and power over another human being, than he does from the actual killing. Ted Bundy is a good example of this type of killer. This murderer does not suffer from delusions, visions or voices. He is totally aware of what he is doing and may be very well versed in the laws and penal codes of his area. He chooses, however, to completely ignore the law. He is aware of reality and of the consequences of his action but makes a conscious choice to take a life.

Motives

By having complete control of a victim's life, the domineering serial killer experiences extreme pleasure in making the victim totally helpless and having her do whatever he wishes. After all, this is something that has been done to the killer over the years. He can only experience the other side of this while killing another person.

With the domineering serial killer who first rapes his victims, it is not the sexual gratification the killer enjoys, but actually his use of power and control to dominate the victims, who are quite helpless in his clutches.

Let's break this down even further. He may rape his victim or perform some kind of sexual perversion on his victim but not for sexual gratification; he is doing this to strike fear, and it's the fear that becomes his sexual gratification. This is known to law enforcement authorities because the few victims that have survived attacks by serial killers of this nature have told the police that their attackers did not appear to be sexually aroused until the victims became almost "slavelike" persons under the killers' control, forced to follow their every command.

Methods
A domineering serial killer uses what is known in the law enforcement community as signatures—unique ways a person commits a crime, such as removing the victim's head and placing it in a location where the police will immediately see it upon entering. This is done to taunt and torment the police, increasing the killer's sense of power and control.

Sexually Obedient Serial Killers
The sexually obedient serial killer is one who was probably born out of wedlock or whose parents were divorced when he was very young. He is emotionally immature and was probably physically and/or sexually abused as a young child. A lot of these serial killers also abuse narcotics and/or alcohol. He may start out killing small animals, such as cats and dogs, increasing his violent behavior to afflict humans as his sexual fantasies become truer to life.

Motives
This type, unlike the goal-oriented serial killer, kills for the sexual pleasure he derives from his killings.

Methods
The sexually obedient serial killer sexually abuses his victims, whether male or female. In doing this, he uses some type of binding and mutilates the breasts or genital areas of his victims. In one case we remember, the killer actually carved out the woman's breasts. One killer just cut out the woman's nipples, and another actually carved out or cut off the genitalia of his victims. The sexually obedient serial killer's crimes are very violent and savage, and upon searching his home, one is likely to find all types of domineering and sadism and masochism (S & M) equipment and pornographic material.

Thrill-Seeking Serial Killers
Police respond to a crime scene. They find a woman's breasts removed. Additional mutilation of the body is noted.

Another scene in another city. A homeless man is found in an alley. His genitalia have been removed and placed near the scene. His body is mutilated. Are these types of murderers goal oriented? Are they sexual in nature? Apparently not. They are the work of the thrill-seeking serial killer.

Most thrill-seeking murderers are highly intelligent, and the ones who are not possess excellent street smarts. These killers usually move around quite a bit, making it difficult for police to apprehend them.

Motives
Interviews with serial killers of this type reveal that they commit murder for the sheer thrill of doing it. They describe the feeling of plunging a knife into a body as the most exciting experience they have had in their lives. The cutting off of the genitalia or removal of breasts seems to be fixated sexually; however, it should be noted that the thrill-seeking serial murderers are solely excited by the actual rush incurred by inflicting harm. They kill because they enjoy it and because the thrill is an end in itself.

Methods
This type of killer usually likes to kill with his bare hands or with knives or other implements that make contact with the body. Thrill-seeking serial killers almost never utilize firearms because there is no thrill: The thrill is associated with the fact that there is physical contact between the victim and the killer.

Although thrill-seeking serial murders include sexual deviance, necrophilia, dismemberment and other types of bizarre methods of murder, remember that the murderers are motivated by the sheer thrill alone and not by any type of real sexual gratification. Although sexual evidence may be found at a scene, as mentioned earlier, this should not confuse the experienced police detective in tracking down this type of murderer.

Case Study: Jeffrey Dahmer
One of the most infamous serial murderers of all times is Jeffrey Lionel Dahmer. On July 22, 1991, two Milwaukee police officers observed a man running down an avenue in the city's poorly developed district. They noticed he was in handcuffs as he was running down the block, waving in an attempt to make them stop. He informed the police that his name was Tracy Edwards and he was running from the apartment of Jeffrey L. Dahmer, a person who, for the last five hours, had terrorized and threatened to kill Edwards and eat his heart out. He told the police

that he escaped and that he was desperately in need of help.

He accompanied the police officers to Dahmer's apartment, and while there, the police were amazed at what they found. Inside the apartment, they found human remains, including skulls in the freezer and parts of bodies thrown about, and photographs of dead men who had either been mutilated or completely dismembered.

Dahmer, a shy, retiring man, had been arrested by the Milwaukee Police Department on several occasions prior to this for disorderly conduct, for molesting children and for assault. He suddenly became the focus of international notoriety as the gruesome nature of his crimes came to the attention of local law enforcement. A psychological profile of Jeffrey Dahmer revealed he was an insecure alcohol abuser who spent many of his years growing up in a rural area and was deeply affected by his parents' bad marriage. His mother, Joyce, was considered mentally unstable by many neighbors and friends, and after the divorce, she moved to Fresno, California, where she works for a government agency.

In school, Dahmer did not fit the norms and was described by many dates as a likely candidate for killing himself. While his classmates had always seen him as the type to commit suicide, they never considered him violent or dangerous. He joined the military in 1978 and was stationed as a medic in West Germany from 1979 until his discharge in 1981. There, he was recalled to have had incredible drinking binges, drinking until he passed out. On the weekends, he was known to drink all day, pass out, wake up and start drinking again. He had his music playing and seemed to be in a world only known to him. Some weekends, he was reported missing from the base, and when news of the Milwaukee murders came to light, an investigation was conducted by the German police authorities to see if Dahmer was involved in any of several unsolved homicides there.

Dahmer worked for many employers, usually in low positions. He worked for the Ambrosia Chocolate Company as a night worker, but his work habits were constantly under suspicion as he was found sleeping in the lunchroom and was always late. He was also found guilty in 1987 of immoral conduct after urinating publicly in front of several children, but he was put on only one year probation. Years later, an Illinois man informed the authorities that Dahmer had injected him with drugs and stolen his money and jewelry, but that case was eventually dropped due to lack of evidence.

In 1988, he lured a thirteen-year-old boy into his apartment by offering him fifty dollars to pose for a photograph. Dahmer then drugged the child's coffee and molested him before the boy was able to escape. As fate would have it, the boy was the brother of a future victim of Jeffrey Dahmer. Dahmer was arrested and charged with sexual assault and enticement of a child for immoral purposes, and it was judged, in the opinion of the court, that the possibility that Dahmer could be treated and become a stable person in the community was extremely unlikely. Although the prosecutor pushed for a five- or six-year prison term, it was the viewpoint of the judge presiding over the case that Dahmer would benefit more from psychological treatment if he remained outside the prison because the prison did not offer special programs for sex offenders. Dahmer then served a one-year sentence in a correction facility on a work release program that allowed him to continue work at the Ambrosia Chocolate Company.

A profile of Dahmer revealed that he typically found his victims in gay bars, shopping malls or areas of a city frequented by homosexuals. He often lured young men to his apartment on the pretext of watching videos or paying them to pose for photographs. On each occasion after getting these victims to enter his residence, he then attempted to drug, strangle and dismember them. It is also believed by police that, on at least one occasion, he had sex with a dead body. When neighbors in the building complained of the stench coming from his apartment, Dahmer told the neighbors it was simply rotting meat in the refrigerator. He was even known to buy many boxes of Pine Sol, according to the neighbors, as if he were going to try and get rid of the stench, but he always told them it didn't help.

In February of 1992, Jeffrey L. Dahmer was sentenced to fifteen life terms in prison for his crimes. He himself was murdered in prison by a fellow inmate on November 28, 1994.

This serial murder case affected people all over the country. It seemed to bring to light the growing trend of serial murders in all major cities. It is also a classic example of how the quiet, unassuming person is suddenly revealed as a psychopathic murderer.

Chapter Six

Bizarre Murders

by Mauro V. Corvasce and Joseph R. Paglino
from *Murder One: A Writer's Guide to Homicide*

E very once in a while, a homicide comes along that is so strange it does not fit any other pattern we've investigated before. These murders, which for the purpose of this chapter we will identify as bizarre murders, are committed by people from all walks of life and socioeconomic situations.

These bizarre murders do not fit the pattern of other murders for several reasons. It may be that the manner in which the victim was killed does not involve methods or weapons, or it may also be that normal weapons were used but to a different degree or to a certain extreme. Usually these bizarre murders involve rituals, voodoo or extreme degradation of the human body during the murder.

Ritual Murders

The term "ritual murder" implies the taking of a human life for religious purposes in accordance with a religious or magic rite. The term was used to describe a type of murder that became a serious problem in Basutoland, South Africa, in 1947 and 1948. At that time, the British government appointed G. Jones, a lecturer in anthropology at the University of Cambridge, to inquire into the nature and causes of these ritual murders. His investigation revealed that the people of Basutoland were killing other people within their families and exchanging the flesh and blood with their own to keep themselves young or were carving out poisons thought to be detriments to the human body, thus making the body pure.

These types of ritualistic murders usually follow a regular pattern. They are always premeditated and are committed by a group of people for a specific purpose, for example, removing the bad part of the victim's body while he is still alive to improve the body.

In one case we investigated, strips of flesh were removed from the victim and eaten by other members of the family for the betterment of the unit. The family in this investigation was not strictly the blood family but a group of people, including the family of the victim, that had bonded together for the purpose of ritualistic murders. These murders were not committed out of any anger or hate toward the victims; they simply felt that eating the flesh of the victims—who were much younger and in better strength—would enable them to live longer. They believed that the body died and decomposed from the lack of fresh and pure flesh. When any one of them had erred or sinned in any way, they felt their flesh was no longer satisfactory for other members of the family and they had to move on to outside people. Eventually, strangers were being killed for their strips of flesh, which were actually peeled off the victims while they were alive, using scalpels and straight razors. These killings almost always occurred on sandy beaches with small fires for burning incense, which seemed to exhilarate the murderers as they were performing their rituals.

Voodoo Murders

In another bizarre murder, called voodoo murder, the killers are sorcerers who use black magic and other such practices to murder a person who has been the cause of an offense. Voodoo death has been reported from the island of Haiti, Africa, Australia and other countries. It has been suggested that poisons have been used to murder the victims, who have no idea they are being killed. While this may be true in some cases, we've investigated many cases of death occurring as a direct result of voodoo rituals in which the victims were murdered and often dismembered and the killers wanted the victims to know what was being done against them and to fear it.

Case Study: Voodoo Killing

An officer on a routine early-morning patrol of a seashore community stumbled upon a group of people engaging in a voodoo murder under an elevated wooden boardwalk. The officer heard chanting and groaning under the boardwalk and thought it was just the customary late-night couples engaging in a little bit of sexual pleasure. Upon trying to ascertain exactly what was down there, he stumbled on a person who was dressed in full witch doctor regalia and pointing a human bone at another individual.

A large group of people humming and chanting indiscernible phrases and music encircled the two. According to the officer, the person at whom the bone was being pointed stood with his hands lifted as though to ward off a blow from a lethal instrument. His cheeks were extremely white, his eyes were glassy and wide with fear and his face was horribly contorted and twisted. The victim shrieked and began to tremble, his muscles twitching involuntarily as if he were having some type of attack. He shortly fell backward to the ground and, after a small period of time, appeared to be swimming. Then he began twitching on the ground as if he was in agonizing mortal pain, covering his face with his hands and moaning uncontrollably.

At this point, the officer saw what would be his final observation before he, too, became violently ill. Then the person immediately jumped to his feet and began vomiting into a large metal bucket. As the police officer watched in disbelief, all the members of the group dipped their hands into this bucket and actually drank and chewed the vomit from the person that was being placed under this "spell."

While this officer was clutching his own stomach and attempting not to vomit, he observed the final suffering of the victim. The person pointing the bone—apparently the witch doctor—walked over to this groaning individual, doused him with a liquid and immediately set a match to him. The victim screamed in agony, running around under the boardwalk completely immersed in flames. There was nothing the police officer could do but attempt to arrest the witch doctor, since he had been the one to set fire to the victim. The officer moved in and identified himself by screaming that he was the police and telling everyone not to move. The members of the circle then attacked him and began biting him all over different parts of his body. After this prolonged attack, his assailants left the scene, leaving the officer in a pile of burned ash, bones and flesh.

This officer endured mental trauma so severe that he had to be removed from the police department on a medical disability. According to his closest friends, he frequently awakens in the middle of the night screaming and, on many occasions, has attempted suicide. It is believed that the trauma of watching the voodoo murder made him this way, and frequent psychological evaluations confirm that he is suffering from extreme and prolonged trauma. Unfortunately, the murder victim was never identified and neither were any of the participants in the killing.

Links Between Cannibalism, Voodoo Murders and Ritualistic Murders

Cannibalism, voodoo murder and ritualistic murder seem inherently linked. The flesh and blood of the dead are commonly eaten and drunk to inspire bravery, wisdom or other remarkable qualities the victim once had. These qualities are believed to be located in particular parts of the body.

In the mountain tribes of southeastern Africa, there are sects in which youths are formed into guilds or lodges, and one of the rights of initiation is intended to infuse courage, intelligence and other qualities into these novices. Whenever an enemy who has behaved with conspicuous bravery is killed, his liver (considered the seat of valor), his ears (the supposed seat of intelligence), the skin of his forehead (the seat of perseverance), his testicles (the seat of strength) and his arms and legs (the seat of various other virtues) are cut from his body and baked to cinders. The ashes are carefully kept in a bull's horn and during ceremonies are mixed with other ingredients into a kind of paste that is then administered by the tribal priest to the youth. This paste symbolizes all the virtues of the victim, which are believed to be imparted to the eaters.

Modern-Day Bizarre Murders
Cannibalism
There are various motives of cannibalism in modern-day bizarre murders. We all know about Jeffrey Dahmer and his propensity for eating human flesh. He achieved a kind of sexual gratification by doing so, which is not uncommon in bizarre murders where cannibalism is present.

Case Study: Albert Fish
In 1928, a New York couple permitted a casual friend to take their ten-year-old daughter to a children's party. The young girl was never seen again, and all efforts to trace her abductor failed. In 1934, the mother received an unsigned letter in the mail addressed to her. In this letter, the person wrote her that he had been told by a friend of his, who was a deckhand on a steamer in China, about the famine that had occurred there in 1894. He wrote that, according to his friend, the suffering was so great among the poor that children under twelve years old were sold to butchers to be cut up for food in order to keep others from starving. According to this letter writer, his friend had told him that, while in China, a boy or girl under fourteen was not safe on the street. And he wrote that you could go in any shop and ask for steak, chops or stew meat, at which point, parts of a naked body of a boy or girl would be brought out and whatever you wanted was cut from it. A boy or girl's behind, which was considered in China at that time to be the sweetest part of the body, was sold as veal cutlets and commanded the highest price.

In this letter, the bizarre murderer stated that his friend had also told him that once he had arrived in New York, he stole two boys, one seven and one eleven. He took them to his home, stripped them naked, tied them in a closet and burned everything they had on. According to this letter writer, his friend spanked them several times a day and at night, torturing them to make their meat good and tender. Finally, he killed the eleven-year-old boy because he had the fattest behind with, of course, the most meat on it. His friend then said that he cooked the boy's body and ate everything except the head, bone and guts, which he had roasted in the oven. All of his behind was broiled, fried and stewed. The littler boy was next, and he went the same way.

The bizarre murderer finally informed the New York mother about the murder of her daughter. The killer had gone to visit the woman and her family and brought her some fresh fruit. During the time he was there, the victim's mother gave him lunch while the little girl sat on his lap and gave him a kiss. He stated in his letter that he made up his mind at that exact point in time to eat her and would do so on the pretext of taking her to the party. Once he got the mother's permission, he took the girl to an empty home in Westchester that he had already picked out. He wrote that when he got there, he asked the girl to remain outside. While she picked flowers, he went upstairs and took off all of his clothes so he would not get her blood on them. When he was all ready, he went to the window and called her in. He then hid in the closet until the girl was in the room. When he came out, she saw he was naked and began to cry and tried to run downstairs. The bizarre murderer wrote that he then grabbed her and she said she would tell her mother. Then he stripped her naked and she kicked and bit him. Finally, he wrote, he choked her to death and cut her into small pieces so he could take the meat to his room, which was in a boardinghouse, and cook it and eat it. He went on to tell the victim's mother that the girl's sweet and tender little behind was roasted in his oven. It took him nine days, he stated, to eat her entire body. He said he did not have intercourse with her although he could have; she died a virgin, which was the sweetest meat he could possibly eat.

Although the letter was unsigned, the police succeeded in finding the writer, Albert Fish, who was a sixty-five-year-old housepainter and the father of six children. He confessed that he had strangled the girl and dismembered her body. He went on to tell the police that he took parts of her body home with him, cooked them in various ways with carrots, onion and strips of bacon and ate them over a period of nine days. During all this time, he was in a state of sexual excitement. He ate the flesh during the day and thought about it during the night. He spoke in a matter-of-fact way, almost like a homemaker describing her favorite methods of cooking. His previous criminal record included arrests for grand larceny, bad checks and sending obscene letters through the mail. He had been admitted to several mental hospitals, only to be released within a short time on each occasion. However, it was clear he was suffering from a paranoid psychosis.

Upon being analyzed by psychologists, Fish told them that for years he had been sticking needles into his body in his genital area between the rectum and the scrotum. They were needles of assorted sizes, some of them big and some small. He also told police he had done this to other people, too—especially to children. At first, he said, he only stuck these needles into himself a short distance and then pulled them out again. Others he had stuck in so far he wasn't able to get them out and they stayed there. Upon being arrested, he informed the detectives that the needles were in there right now, and when asked how many, he said he didn't know. A series of X-rays and pelvic and abdominal region examinations revealed twenty-nine needles inside his body, twenty-seven of which were in his pelvic region. In some instances, the eyes of the needles were clear. Some of them were eroded to such an extent they must have been there at least seven years. Some were so deeply embedded they were in rather dangerous places, including some just above and beside the transverse and descending colon, several fragments around the rectum and others in the bladder region. These X-rays are unique in the history of medical science.

Fish's explanation for murder was that he had visions of Christ and his angels and saw Christ mumbling words Fish couldn't understand. Sometimes, he was sure the voices he heard came from visions and angels. Other times, he didn't know where the voices came from, but he heard them saying words like *stripes*, *rewardeth* and *delighteth*. He connected these words with the Bible and elaborated upon their meanings to fit his own sadistic wishes. He interpreted *stripes* to mean that he should lash his victims, for example.

In his statement, Fish said he felt driven to torment and kill children. He wanted to offer the children as sacrifices to purge himself of his sins and abnormalities in the eyes of God. Sometimes, he said, he would gag them, tie them up and beat them—although he preferred not to gag them because he liked to hear their cries. Fish also said he was ordered by God to castrate little boys.

The estimate of the number of children Fish murdered varies from five to eighteen. At the trial for the murder of the victim he mentioned in the letter, his plea of insanity was rejected and he was sentenced to death by electrocution.

The most ironic twist in this whole case was that when Fish's little victim noticed he had left the package containing his knife, saw and cleaver on the train on which they'd been traveling, she hurried back and brought it to him. With these tools, she was later dismembered by Fish.

Delusional Killers

Another bizarre murder we have personally investigated involved a young woman addicted to crack cocaine who enjoyed having sex with numerous men in the neighborhood where she rented an apartment. Neighbors frequently complained about the constant parade of men going in and out of the apartment at all times of the day and night. On one occasion, the woman, while having sexual intercourse with a casual friend, had delusions and psychotic fantasies that the man's penis was actually a snake that was going in and out of her. She immediately pulled away and started screaming but would not divulge her fears to the man, who subsequently fell asleep.

The woman, however, remained awake and delusional, deciding she must kill the snake. She remembered seeing on television that a large bolt cutter was frequently used to snip off the head of a snake, thereby rendering it immobile and unable to bite a victim. So she stumbled into her garage where several tools had been left by handymen, with whom she had also engaged in sexual intercourse over the course of years. Armed with a bolt cutter, she proceeded to the sleeping victim and snipped off his penis with one blow. The man, upon awakening in agony, screamed, but he had lost so much blood he could not escape. The woman kept at the genital area with the bolt cutter and eventually succeeded in snipping off his testicles, as well as tearing up both sides of his thighs.

Had it not been for our noticing the bolt cutter, we would have thought he had been shot with a shotgun in the genital area because of the many gorges and open, gaping wounds. Upon interviewing the neighbors, we discovered neighbors a full three blocks away who had heard the bloodcurdling screams.

The Ultimate Revenge

Another case we investigated involved a man who was extremely upset with his spouse, whom he believed was having an affair. He decided to exact the ultimate revenge upon his wife, who was a chef in a local restaurant. He subdued her one evening with an ammonia-soaked rag, then placed her in a double wall oven and proceeded to bake her. The neighbors called the police when they smelled an extremely sour odor that was emanating from the victim's home. The police and the local authorities in the county found the murderer sitting in a chair, laughing hysterically. He obviously was suffering from some type of delusional psychosis, but was absolutely ecstatic he had exacted this revenge upon his wife in the manner he had.

It was later discovered that the wife's suspicious trips were not to her boyfriend's home, as the husband had thought, but to a second part-time job. She had told her friends she was secretly working the second job in order to save up money for a new set of golf clubs her husband wanted for his birthday. And it was the husband's delusions of her infidelity that led him to kill her!

Summary

As you can see, bizarre murders are so extremely contrary to human nature they just do not fit the mold of any other pattern of murder. That Jeffrey Dahmer killed many people and cut up their bodies isn't outside our realm of belief. But the fact that Dahmer dissected these corpses and ate them is beyond our wildest dreams.

Just how bizarre "bizarre murders" will be twenty, thirty or forty years from now depends on the state of society in general. Murders that occurred in the 1950s and 1960s were shocking at the time, but now, thanks to increasingly violent movies and television shows, we've become somewhat inured to all but the most deviant of crimes. Similarly, what seems bizarre today will not likely be bizarre twenty years from now.

Bizarre murderers can come from all walks of life. This type of killer may be rich or poor, an imbecile or a genius. And the manner of the murder will be as bizarre as the murderer's rationale for committing it.

Chapter Seven

Controversies Involving Death

by Keith D. Wilson, M.D.

from *Cause of Death: A Writer's Guide to Death, Murder and Forensic Medicine*

Emotionally Induced Death and Voodoo

It is possible for a person to become scared and weak with fear, almost to the point of death. This is not the same kind of fear one has when standing in front of an audience with trembling voice and knocking knees; that is an adrenaline rush. Rather, it is a cold, dark fear that can actually paralyze a person.

After experiencing sudden fear, psychological stress or tremendous pain, the person breaks into a cold sweat, turns pale, loses blood pressure, then may drop to the floor unconscious.

The scenario described is due to the vaso-vagal reaction and is evoked by great emotional stress associated with fear or pain. It is a transient vascular and neurogenic reaction (mediated by the nervous system); marked by pallor (paleness); nausea; cold, clammy sweating; bradycardia (slow heart rate) and a rapid fall in blood pressure that may lead to unconsciousness.

The large blood vessels inside the abdomen dilate and the blood volume is shunted to the major organs. Peripheral vessels to the arms and legs constrict to compensate, and the patient becomes cold, shakes and is covered with sweat. This vaso-vagal reaction accounts for "sudden death" in the practice of voodoo and witchcraft when curses are placed on the victim. It is actually their own body's response to fear that causes the death they dreaded.

The Journal of the American Medical Association (JAMA) reported on the connection between stress and life-threatening arrhythmias (abnormal, irregular rhythm) of the heart. Some individuals are at high risk of sudden death following stress. There is a clear connection between emotional stress and cardiac vulnerability; this explains why an individual may drop dead from "shock" when told of some family tragedy. There is a similar connection between emotional stress and "voodoo death," where fear and terror are the contributors.

One morning, a Biami tribesman in Papua, New Guinea, who had been in excellent health, believed that some evil sorcery had been cast on him and, thoroughly convinced that it was time to die, he lay down on a rough-hewn mat to wait. By the end of the day he was dead.

The following article appeared in the *Miami Herald*:

Healthy Asian Men Die Unexpectedly; Reason Is Unclear

It seems right out of a Freddie Krueger horror movie, complete with ghastly nightmares, murderous demons and scores of bodies.

All of the victims are Asian men, typically in their 30's. They have strong physiques and no known ailments. One night they head off to bed and fall asleep. Then in the early morning darkness, something awful happens.

The sleeping men utter agonizing groans and begin to writhe and gasp. It often looks as if they've convulsed with a terrible dream. Within minutes, they are dead. The phenomenon is known as the "nightmare death."

The article goes on to state that over the past decade, scores of such cases have been reported in the United States. Hundreds of similar deaths have also been noted in other parts of the world.

As of yet, no one can say for sure what is killing them.

Some have chalked the deaths up to voodoo curses, while others have blamed vindictive, supernatural forces. Blaming female spirits for the killings, the men have begun wearing dresses and red nail polish to fool the spirits into thinking they're women.

But the deaths continue. Autopsies have no sign of anything that could have killed them.

Voodoo practitioners use both spells and poisons to control, cure or kill their victims. Some of the poisons and "medicines" used include toads, bones, plants, lizards and sea worms. But in a closed system of beliefs as strong as voodoo, the mind may in fact be the strongest drug of all. Death comes from a lethal dose of fear!

The Near-Death Experience

There is another gray area concerning death that has given rise to religious, philosophical and scientific debate. That is the near-death experience (NDE)—also called the "Lazarus Syndrome," referring to the biblical Lazarus rising from the dead. Near-death experience is a phrase first termed by Raymond A. Moody in 1975, but NDEs have been reported throughout history by the Greeks, Romans and Egyptians; there are several accounts of it in the Bible as well.

A man is dying and as he reaches the point of greatest physical distress he hears himself pronounced dead by his doctor. There is an utterly black, dark void and he feels himself moving rapidly through a long, dark tunnel. He finds himself outside of his own physical body. He experiences a bright light, a feeling of warmth, peace and quiet, and he sees relatives and friends who have already died, a warm, loving experience of a kind he has never known before.

The bliss that people experience when death approaches has been described by a growing number of people who have "died" (which is to say that their heartbeat and breathing stopped) and have then been revived. The prevailing emotion they describe is euphoria; their flirtation with death so blissful that they often ask, "Why did you bring me back, Doctor?"

Some physicians have suggested that it is nothing more than the effect of hypoxia (decreased oxygen supply) on the temporal lobe of the brain, while others believe that it is a glance forward into that unknown realm of death.

Carl Sagan, in his book *Broca's Brain*, believes that the NDE is latent memories from birth:

> The only alternative, so far as I can see, is that every human being, without exception, has already shared an experience like that of those travelers who return from the land of death; the sensation of flight; the emergence from darkness into light; an experience in which, at least perceived, bathed in radiance and glory. There is only one common experience that matches this description. It is called birth.

There are experiences common to those who have been near death. Raymond A. Moody detailed the near-death experience in his book *The Light Beyond*, and it includes the following:

Experience	Percent
Out of body	26
Accurate visual perception	23
Audible voices and sounds	17
Feeling of peace	32
Light phenomena	14
Life review	32
Being in another world	32
Encountering other beings	23
Tunnel experience	9
Precognition	6

What do these experiences mean? Do they foretell what death itself is like? Or are the experiences merely a part of the dying process, just a quirk of the human brain that mercifully creates "good feelings" as it becomes anoxic and dies?

Melvin Morse, M.D., in his book *Closer to the Light*, describes the near-death experience in dozens of young children that he interviewed in the hospital. The accounts of their NDE's are identical. Over one hundred children, ages three to nine, who had suffered near-fatal trauma or clinical death during surgery were interviewed, and all reported the same experiences as did adults. Since the children were too young to be influenced by religious teaching or to have formed preconceived ideas of death, the meaning of the near-death experience becomes that much more intriguing.

Choosing a Quiet Death

The list of ways that people die is endless, but most people tend to ignore the reality and presume that they will die in their sleep. Unfortunately, people don't get to choose how they will die (except with suicide).

Many people believe that society has mismanaged dying; most people would like to die a quiet, dignified death, a reasonable wish that is almost never fulfilled. Most people still die in hospitals, where respirators, dialysis machines, nasogastric tubes, endless chemotherapy and cardiopulmonary resuscitation change death into a mechanized spectacle.

While we hope for the best concerning our own death, many people have a fear of the worst, a fear that has given rise to the concept of a living will. This is a document designed to give people more control over their dying and to prevent them from being kept in a vegetative state by mechanical devices.

The real issue is that we can't really come to grips with our own death, that moment when we no longer exist. The old and sick may know how they'll die, but even they aren't usually ready to come to terms with death.

> Do not go gentle into that good night,
> Old age should burn and rave at close of day;
> Rage, rage against the dying of the light.
>> Dylan Thomas, "Do Not Go Gentle Into That Good Night"

There are many conflicting attitudes toward death and dying. Complex issues come into play, such as terminally ill individuals who struggle to survive at any cost versus those who search for a quick and easy death. Both groups often find themselves in conflict with family members, clergy, religious beliefs and the law.

The court may try to prevent someone from being taken off life-support, or a lawyer may lobby for euthanasia; clergy may encourage the dying not to give in to suicide since only God can give or take life; family members may not want to give up a loved one or may seek means to help them end their life of pain.

Emotional and Ethical Problems Related to Death
Cryonics
"It's not that I want to come back. It's that I don't want to die." That's how a woman, who is a member of the Immortalist Society, described her interest in cryonics.

Through the ages, people have tried to come up with new ideas to prevent or postpone the inevitable—*death*. One of the more intriguing and unusual methods is freezing your body in a vat of liquid nitrogen at -270° F in the hopes of being thawed out to live again sometime in the future.

Cryonics is the freezing of a person's body at the time of legal death with the intent to be thawed and revived in the future when a cure for the disease or ailment is found. People who believe in cryonics hope that a nap in deep freeze will save them from death. One officer from the Cryonics Institute said, "We're not a bunch of fanatics waiting to plunge into nitrogen. No one is ever sure if it's totally reversible."

A man in California failed to persuade a Superior Court judge to let him freeze his head before he is pronounced legally dead from a brain tumor. "There's a public relations problem involved in heads only, so we avoid it," one of the members of the Cryonics Institute explained.

People magazine reported a story about the death of actor Dick Clair who was determined not to let the grim reaper have the last laugh. Clair's mortal remains are preserved in super-cold storage. If everything goes according to plan, Clair "has not entered The Big Sleep, but merely a Long Nap." He believed he might someday be thawed, cured, revived and returned to the world of the living.

Moments after Clair died, his body was packed in crushed ice, and his blood drained and replaced with a cryo-agent. Liquid nitrogen was then sprayed into a giant Thermos bottle, chilling the body to a final temperature of -320° Fahrenheit.

But those who knew him say death scored its real victory over him while he was still very much alive. He always worried about the future, about living forever. Now he lies frozen in a giant Thermos bottle—not exactly a victor over the grim reaper after all.

This concept—freezing one's body for centuries, only to be thawed out sometime in the future—and those who would choose to do this, is great material for the writer to explore.

Hospice

Many people choose to die in the familiar surroundings of their own homes with friends and family at their bedside, instead of in the sterile, busy and unfamiliar environment of the hospital. Hospice is an organization that was developed to assist those caring for terminally ill family members at home. After the terminally ill person is brought home to die, a nurse from Hospice will make a preliminary visit to answer questions, tell the family what to expect and give them suggestions and guidelines to help them and the dying. Hospice is "on call" at all times to give comfort or to answer questions and give instructions when necessary.

Hospice is a fantastic program that reaches out to millions of people and households each year. Hospice restores control and dignity to both the dying and their family at a time when everything seems impersonal and regulated.

The Right-to-Die and Euthanasia

At the opposite end of the spectrum from those who fight for immortality are those who seek an easy way to end life's struggle.

To them, merely staying alive is not the best choice when faced with constant pain or physical-mental disabilities, and suicide or assisted death seems like the only way out of a hopeless situation. Recent cases such as those involving Nancy Cruzan, Karen Ann Quinlan, Roswell Gilbert and Janet Adkins have forced the right-to-die question into the open.

The "right to die" seems like a ridiculous term since death is so inevitable. But as humans we simply cannot accept death easily and fight to keep others alive at all cost, regardless of *their* desires. Yet suicide is against the law and considered a sin by most religions. We struggle to understand and conquer death, but we cannot.

Dr. Jack Kevorkian, a retired pathologist from Michigan, began working on a suicide machine after meeting a quadriplegic who had to go to court to get permission to have his own ventilator turned off. Dr. Kevorkian, a longtime advocate of euthanasia, wanted the medical and legal establishment to consider the rights of others to choose to die peacefully, when and how they wish. "My ultimate aim is to make euthanasia a positive experience."

Dr. Kevorkian's suicide machine releases sodium pentathol through an intravenous tube; sixty seconds later, when the person is utterly unconscious, a timer triggers a second switch to release potassium chloride into the system, which, when it reaches the heart, immediately stops it. It promises a swift, painless death.

While some argue that it is *too* user-friendly, that it makes suicide too easy, too accessible, too imaginable, Kevorkian argues that the real issue is that it forces people to face their own mortality and stirs up questions they don't want to face. While the Dutch have a euthanasia program in which terminally ill patients can get a lethal injection from their doctors, some medical ethicists argue that the medical profession should not be involved in assisting suicide.

Kevorkian believes that it is cruel and barbaric to keep people alive who must live with horrible intractable pain and feels that doctors have not learned to deal with the agony of the dying. When a woman with an incurable disease came to him because she didn't want to suffer, he hooked her up to his suicide machine. She pushed the button and released potassium chloride into her veins. Just before she died, she looked up at Kevorkian with grateful eyes and said, "Thank you, thank you, thank you."

Kevorkian months later assisted two more women with their suicides. Some consider him a hero who helped those suffering end their misery with dignity. But his critics call him a villain; dubbing him a "serial mercy killer." At the very least, Dr. Kevorkian is forcing society to look at a complex problem, to face questions that need answers.

Dr. Timothy Quill helped a terminally ill woman die because she was facing a painful, agonizing death. He said, "I have been a longtime advocate of a patient's right to die with as much control and dignity as possible."

It was clear to Dr. Quill that the woman knew what she was doing and that she was sad and frightened to be leaving, but that she would be even more terrified to stay and suffer. He suggested that she contact the Hemlock Society, an organization that advocates the right of the terminally ill to commit suicide.

"To think that people do not suffer in the process of dying is an illusion," Dr. Quill said.

When her disease progressed to a stage that she could no longer bear, he provided her with a prescription for barbiturates, along with instructions on what dosage would be fatal. "She taught me about life, death and honesty and about taking charge and facing tragedy squarely when it strikes."

He added sadly, "I wonder whether she struggled in that last hour and whether the Hemlock Society's way of death by suicide is the most benign. I wonder why she, who gave so much to so many of us, had to be alone for the last hour of her life."

Nancy Cruzan was another landmark right-to-die case. Cruzan, age thirty-three, had been in a persistent vegetative state since a 1983 car accident. A judge granted her parents permission to disconnect her feeding tube.

But the day her feeding tube was to be disconnected, nineteen right-to-life protesters were arrested trying to reach her hospital room to prevent it. "She's going to be dead soon, if someone doesn't intervene," said one of the protesters. "Citizens have to stop standing by silently and letting people die."

Many less dramatic day-to-day decisions are made by physicians and family members to allow patients near death to die, cases that never make the headlines.

Derek Humphry founded the National Hemlock Society after he helped his wife of twenty-two years end her struggle with an inoperable cancer. He has written several books, the latest titled *Final Exit: The*

Practicalities of Self-Deliverance and Assisted Suicide for the Dying that contains how-to information on suicide.

Living Wills
Rose Gasner, director of legal services of the Society for the Right-to-Die, says most people want control over their fate. There are three main variations of right-to-die laws:

- **Living Will:** Allows individuals to specify in writing their wishes regarding life-prolonging treatment.
- **Durable Power of Attorney:** Allows individuals to designate another person to make medical decisions for them.
- **Statutory Surrogate Provision:** Authorizes certain individuals, such as a spouse or court-appointed guardian, to decide for the patient, if the wishes have not been specified in writing.

A Living Will is an example of an instructional advance directive in which you instruct others on how you want your care handled; a Durable Power of Attorney for health care is an example of a proxy advance directive giving others the authority to direct your care.

In Minneapolis, a man is fighting with doctors because he refuses to let his wife die. The doctors say that while such sentiment may seem heroic, it isn't helping anyone, including his wife, who has been in a coma for seventeen months. The doctors want him replaced as his wife's legal guardian because he refuses to let them unplug the respirator that keeps her breathing.

The doctors say he just doesn't understand that his wife is in a persistent vegetative state. The case is believed to be the first in the country in which doctors have gone against the wishes of a family in an attempt to terminate life-sustaining medical care.

But a member of the Anti-Euthanasia Task Force argues, "We've heard over and over that families should decide, and now doctors are saying there ought to be limits."

The National Hemlock Society, The Society for the Right-to-Die, the Anti-Euthanasia Task Force, The Cryogenics Society and supporters of the suicide machine confront each other daily, looking for answers where there are none, looking for truth where there is no absolute truth.

How You Might Use This Material
For you as a writer, these emotional issues surrounding death and dying that are filled with conflict make fertile ground for plot. You may choose

to write about the internal conflict the dying person experiences, whether to end it quickly or struggle at all costs to survive. Or, you may focus your story on the problems that care-givers must face; these can include the clergy, nurses and doctors, as well as family members. Here are some scenarios you might consider for your story:

- A mother can't bear to allow doctors to turn off the respirator that keeps her little boy alive, while she clings to a fragment of hope.
- A lawyer sees his elderly mother tormented as doctors and nurses struggle to keep her alive; it is against the law in his state to order withdrawal of life support, and to do so might be considered murder and result in his disbarment.
- A nurse gives a fatal dose of morphine to a suffering young woman with a terminal disease and is charged with murder.
- A wife, the only person who knows of a second will that leaves the vast majority of her husband's estate to charity, moves ahead quickly through the courts to withdraw life support from him and "allow the man she loves to die in peace." For her the motive is greed; the act is murder.

And so the struggle of life and death continues in a war with no victors. We fight against death, against that day when life will be smothered out by a dark nothingness. We hope to have a say as to how we die by inventing "living wills." We read magazines like *Longevity*, *Prevention*, *Health*, *American Health*, *In Health* and *Men's Health*. We smear on anti-aging creams, gulp down vitamins and think up new and inventive exercises.

But death always wins.

Chapter Eight

How the Body Is Handled

by Keith D. Wilson, M.D.

from *Cause of Death: A Writer's Guide to Death, Murder and Forensic Medicine*

H ere is a chronological account of procedures followed after the discovery of a dead body or immediately after someone dies.

Sequence of Events After Death

1. A body is discovered.
2. The body is pronounced dead by the appropriate person, usually a physician, but sometimes by a nurse or a paramedic.
3. The body is sent to the morgue or funeral home, identified by family or friends and tagged.
4. Either the attending physician determines the cause of death, or the coroner evaluates the death and determines if an autopsy is required to establish the cause of death.
5. If indicated, a medical-legal autopsy is performed.
6. The death certificate is filled out, stating the cause of death after determined by the autopsy.
7. All of the materials obtained (autopsy report, photographs, toxicology test results and opinion) are turned over to the authorities and become a part of the corpus delicti, or "body of evidence."
8. The body is then turned over to the family and becomes the property and responsibility of the next of kin for either cremation or embalming and burial.

Various Possibilities Following a Death
Unattended Death in a Nursing Home or Death Following Chronic Illness
Sample cases:

- An elderly person dies unattended in a nursing home.
- A person with a known fatal illness dies in a hospital.
- A young mother with a long-standing chronic illness dies unattended at home before the hospice nurse arrives.
- An eighty-three-year-old man apparently dies in his sleep in bed and is discovered two days later.

The procedure following these deaths would be:

1. The body is pronounced dead by a physician or registered nurse.
2. The cause of death is presumed by circumstances and requires no further investigation.
3. A death certificate is signed.
4. The body is sent to a funeral home.
5. The body is turned over to the family for burial or cremation. If the family elects cremation, they must wait at least forty-eight hours after the person died in case there may be any investigation into the cause of death.

Sudden, Unexpected Death Following Trauma
Sample cases:

- A farmer's tractor rolls over on him and he is crushed to death.
- Four teenagers are killed in an automobile crash.

The procedure following these deaths would be:

1. The body is pronounced dead by a physician, police officer or paramedic at the scene.
2. The coroner's office is contacted and an investigator is sent to the scene.
3. The body is taken to a funeral home or morgue.
4. Blood is drawn to test for alcohol and drugs for initial assessment.
5. A medical-legal autopsy is usually required.
6. A ruling is made and a death certificate completed and signed.
7. The body is released to the family for burial or cremation.

A Sudden, Unexpected Nontraumatic Death
Sample cases:

- A healthy man of fifty falls over dead of a presumed sudden heart attack.
- A teenage girl is found drowned in a bathtub.

- An elderly woman is killed from a fall down the cellar steps.
- A farmer is found dead in the barn from a gunshot wound to the head, possibly self-inflicted.
- A forty-two-year-old man dies on the operating table while undergoing coronary bypass surgery.
- A man is seriously injured in a boating accident; although attended to by paramedics, he is dead on arrival at the ER (DOA).
- A person is found dead lying beside the highway.
- A known alcoholic who lives in back alleys is found dead late one night.
- A sixteen-year-old boy is shot to death during the robbery of an all-night convenience store.

The procedure following these deaths would be:

1. The body is pronounced dead by a physician or police officer at the scene.
2. The coroner's office is contacted and an investigator sent to the scene.
3. The body is taken to a morgue designated by the coroner.
4. A complete medical-legal autopsy is performed.
5. A ruling is made and a death certificate is completed and signed.
6. An opinion is given and all the evidence is turned over to the court. This material constitutes the corpus delicti.
7. The body is only then released to the family for burial or cremation.

Although every type of death is not covered, you should now be able to place any death used in your plot into one of the three categories and then appropriately "handle the body" in the subsequent scenes.

Disposal of the Body
Historical and Religious Background

After the body has been declared dead and a death certificate signed, the body is turned over to the family for burial or cremation. Varying attitudes around the world toward death and dying are reflected in the many ways that the dead are disposed. Most burial customs reflect two factors: a belief in life after death and a belief that death brings a close contact with evil spirits.

Since primitive times, people have been afraid of the dead. Deep-seated fears, superstitions and religious beliefs govern how the dead are handled. Magic, prayers, sacrifices and varied religious customs developed because of the belief that death and the dead body were somehow linked with evil demons and angry gods, that even in death the deceased would have to do battle with evil spirits and demons. Even today, burial customs reflect this belief. All cultures have devised ways of dealing with their dead and the perceived evil spirits associated with them.

Ancient Aztecs believed that life is a dream from which Death awakens us. They respected death as an integral part of life. On All Saints Day and All Souls Day, Mexicans still celebrate and honor the dead with flowers and food for the graves; some don Devil's clothing or wear skull masks; some hang skeleton mobiles in storefronts. The celebration mixes respect for and fear of death and always ends with dancing in the streets, laughing, drinking, singing—as if the celebration of death could eliminate it.

Many burial customs throughout the centuries indicate a concern with life after death. The dead have been buried with possessions, weapons and food, all pointing to a belief in an afterlife.

Everyone alive must face the same inevitable fact "from dust we came, to dust we shall return." But how different cultures choose to get the dead back to dust varies greatly. Each has developed a unique set of laws or customs relating to the handling of the dead and the preparation of the body for the grave.

Archaeology suggests that cremation was first used during the Stone Age. In Tibet, bodies are sunk in water. The Sioux Indians of North America put their dead on high platforms. And a religious group in India, the Parsis, took their dead to enclosures and let birds pick the body clean.

Cremation

The use of fire to dispose of the dead is not new. Prehistoric people used fire, a miracle from the gods, to cremate bodies as far back as the Stone Age. The Greeks began using it around 1000 B.C., and the Bible reports the cremation of Saul in the book of Samuel: ". . . and took the body of Saul and the bodies of his sons from the wall of Beth-Shan, and burnt them there."

The Vikings, Romans, people of ancient India and Buddhists all used cremation for the dead. Cremation is the almost exclusive method used by Hindus of India. Traditional Orthodox Jewish culture forbids cremation, but the Catholic Church recently removed its ban and many Catholics now choose church-sanctioned cremation.

Cremation in the United States has grown steadily. In 1884 there were forty-one cremations in the U.S., but now there are several hundred thousand cremations annually. Great Britain and Japan lead the world in the number of cremations annually. In Great Britain, less than a third of all corpses are buried.

Requirements: Most crematories require a rigid, combustible container for the body (usually wood). It is important to remove pacemakers (an electrical device to trigger and regulate the heart rate) from the body before cremation, since the lithium batteries can explode and pollute the environment.

Many states require a person be deceased for forty-eight hours prior to cremation. This is to ensure that any investigation of the cause of death can be instigated if needed. Obviously, once the body is cremated, it cannot be studied further.

Once the casket is rolled into the cremation chamber, incineration occurs at temperatures of 1800° F or higher. Crematories most commonly use natural gas to produce the intense heat, but oil, propane gas or electricity can also be used as fuel. The combustion chamber, big enough to hold only one coffin at a time, is lined with fire bricks that can withstand heat up to 3500° F.

Cremation is usually performed at 1800° F; total time for cremation takes sixty to ninety minutes, depending on the weight of the body. When the cremation is complete, the white-hot brick furnace must cool down before the remains of ash and pieces of bone (weighing three to seven pounds, depending on body weight) are removed. Bone fragments are then collected and pulverized in a grinding machine to the size of granulated sugar.

The cremains are then collected in an urn and delivered to the funeral home. The ashes may be mailed but must be shipped registered mail. More than eight thousand Americans die abroad each year, and cremation (with the remains mailed back to the U.S.) is a convenient way of handling the body. There are no restrictions regarding the handling or resting place of cremains.

Similar to the celebrations and dancing on All Souls Day, some people in America have found new ways to honor the dead. In California, funerals have become more of a celebration of living than a mournful cry for the dead. Some choose to drop the cremated remains over the side of boats into the bay, followed by a handful of flowers that bob on the waves. Everything has been tried, from picnics to wine-tasting parties to garden parties with hors d'oeuvres and valet parking. In the mountains of Idaho, some choose to load ashes into cartridges and fire the remains into the sky to be scattered by the winds.

Embalming

Egyptians began embalming the bodies of the wealthy as early as 4000 B.C. The bodies were soaked in carbonate of soda, the intestines and brain removed, and salt and herbs packed into the body cavities.

In early nineteenth-century America, embalming also served to assure that no one was buried accidently "while in a trance." There was no doubt that the body was dead after embalming. The Civil War brought embalming to most funeral homes in this country, a custom that remains even today. It prevented decomposition and smell until the bodies could be sent back to their families for burial. Sanitation to halt the spread of disease was also a consideration at the time.

Today embalming serves to postpone decomposition and allows the body to be transported and viewed by the family before burial. It preserves the body, eradicates the smell of decomposing flesh and helps restore a somewhat lifelike appearance. However, since the Civil War, embalming remains almost exclusively an American tradition—it is rarely used in Europe.

Methods: Embalming methods have not changed in the past one hundred years. On a table, the limbs are massaged to counter rigor mortis, then an artery and vein beside each other (in the armpit, neck or groin) are cut open. The process consists of draining the blood, then filling veins with a preservative—a formaldehyde-based, blood-colored fluid. A large-bore needle is inserted in the naval (umbilicus) through which blood and waste are pumped from the abdominal cavity. Then it is filled with about eight to ten pints of preserving fluid.

Embalming takes about an hour and a half, and the effects are dramatic. The deathly pallor and greenish discoloration disappear, and there is no longer the odor of death.

Funeral directors make every effort to improve the rapidly declining appearance, to give the impression of peaceful sleep instead of death and decay.

After bathing and embalming the body, the beard will be shaved (on males). The eyes that have sunk back because of loss of vitreous fluid will have small pads placed under the eyelids to restore a lifelike bulge. The mouth is stuffed with cotton and stitched shut. The lips are smoothed to give the impression of relaxation with a faint smile. Makeup is applied, and finally, the body is dressed.

The fingers of the hands are gently tugged until they assume a pose suggesting peace and rest. It is the dead person's hands that most people are likely to touch during a wake or funeral service.

Burial

Burial is the most common method of disposal of the dead for Christians, Jews and Muslims. Burial developed from the belief that the dead will rise again. Like a seed, the body is planted in the earth to await rebirth.

Regulations: Unlike cremation, which has no laws regarding the handling and disposal of cremains, there are rigid laws concerning burial. These laws reflect both religious customs as well as health considerations and the prevention of spread of contagious diseases. Cemeteries require that a grave liner (concrete slabs) or coffin vaults be used. In the United States, the inside of the coffin is lined with copper or zinc, and the lid is screwed shut before burial.

Home burial is possible in some rural areas, depending on local laws. Burial must be some distance from a water supply, and graveyards become permanent easement on the property and may decrease the value of the land at sale. That prevents a family from burying grandpa in the backyard of the farm, then selling the property and allowing someone to farm over the grave. The home grave-site must remain a grave-site. In those circumstances when construction must proceed over a grave-site, the body must be removed and placed in another appropriate grave.

There are no laws concerning embalming prior to burial, and it is now performed almost by custom in the United States. But embalming still remains an option that family members may elect not to use prior to burial.

Funeral Director (Mortician)

Being a mortician is one of the oldest professions in the world. But who becomes a mortician? Interesting enough, more than 95 percent of those who choose to become morticians had significant personal contact with funeral directors prior to considering it as a way of life. The contact could be anything from mowing their lawn to knowing them in church.

But recruiting for the mortician industry is definitely a grass-roots phenomenon.

That is because most people have heard myths about funeral directors and mortuaries and focus only on the aspect of dealing with dead bodies. Other duties include comforting the bereaved's family and marketing caskets. While starting salaries average about $25,000 a year, six-figure incomes are possible after building up the business.

Requirements: Almost all states require funeral directors and embalmers to complete a course in mortuary science, which ranges from nine months to three years, followed by an apprenticeship of one to three years. This varies greatly from state to state: Ohio demands four years of college, but in California you don't need any formal education to become a funeral director. Colorado has virtually no funeral home regulations but does require a certification of competency in mortuary science.

The American Board of Funeral Service Education accredits and oversees more than forty mortuary schools nationwide. The students learn how to embalm, how to restore damaged faces using wax and makeup with details obtained from photographs, how to market caskets and how to comfort the bereaved family.

The Coroner and Medical Examiner

There are two types of medical-legal investigative systems currently in the United States: the coroner and the medical examiner (ME). Approximately twelve states currently have a coroner system, twenty-two have medical examiners and sixteen have both a coroner and medical examiner. The trend is for the coroner system to be replaced by the medical examiner.

There is confusion between the terms coroner and medical examiner. While under certain state's laws they may be synonymous, they are in fact separate titles. In some states the medical examiner is also the coroner, but in other states the medical examiner is appointed by the coroner to conduct the medical autopsy and to offer an official opinion for evidence.

The Coroner

The coroner is an elected public official whose duty is to oversee the mechanics of obtaining a medical-legal investigation of death. In some states, anyone may run for the office and be elected coroner—even without any formal education of forensic medicine. In some areas of the country, in fact, the coroner can be a funeral director.

A coroner with no formal education in forensic medicine will appoint a forensic pathologist who then functions as medical examiner. Or, if the state has both a coroner and medical examiner, the ME will examine a case and give the findings to the elected coroner, who will then render a coroner's report.

An elected coroner may appoint a deputy coroner to assist in the medical-legal investigation and to perform autopsies. The deputy coroner is almost always a qualified forensic pathologist, the same as a medical examiner.

Medical Examiner

A medical examiner is a physician who has specialized in a specific branch of pathology called forensic medicine and is trained in the legal investigation of death. The medical examiner is appointed either by the court or a coroner. The ME has the authority of the appropriate court officials to perform a medical-legal autopsy and render an opinion as to the cause, manner and mode of death.

Most states have now changed the law so that anyone running for the office of coroner must also be a forensic pathologist (and in this instance, the coroner and medical examiner will be the same individual).

This change is happening across the country and now almost all coroners are trained forensic pathologists, and the terms coroner and medical examiner are the same in qualification and training.

CORONER: A county or city official elected by popular vote. May or may not be a qualified forensic pathologist, depending on local laws.

DEPUTY CORONER: An appointed position, usually selected by the coroner.

MEDICAL EXAMINER: An appointed position, usually by the court.

Note: While the deputy coroner and medical examiner are qualified forensic pathologists, the coroner may or may not be, depending on local laws.

The Autopsy

by Keith D. Wilson, M.D.

from *Cause of Death: A Writer's Guide to Death, Murder and Forensic Medicine*

D r. Sally Rice, deputy coroner, adjusted the microphone attached to the front of her green surgical scrubs, snapped on a pair of sterile latex gloves, then picked up the chart and started to dictate. "This is Case Number 99-3760, Bobby Hicks. The body is that of a well-developed, well-nourished sixteen-year-old Caucasian male with brown hair and blue eyes. The body is 74 inches long and weighs 170 pounds." She put the chart down and moved beside the body.

X rays, multiple photographs, measurements and weight had all been obtained earlier. It was now time to proceed with the external examination and internal dissection of the body. Bright overhead lights blazed down onto the table.

"Rigor mortis is present in the extremities," the deputy coroner said. "The skin of normal texture; there is a single scar in the right lower quadrant of the abdomen from previous appendectomy."

She picked up a plastic ruler and held it against the chest. "There is a one cm gunshot entry wound on the right anterior chest wall with no burn or gunpowder residue present. There is a 32-gauge chest tube exiting from the mid-axillary line."

The autopsy was now under way on Bobby Hicks, who had been killed only sixteen hours earlier in a convenience store by a single .45-caliber round.

Category of Autopsies

Medical autopsy: A scientific postmortem examination of a dead body, performed to reveal the presence of pathological processes and to determine the cause of death.

Medical-legal autopsy: A specialized type of autopsy authorized or ordered by the proper legal authorities (usually the medical examiner) in cases of suspicious deaths, including suicide, homicide and unattended or unexpected sudden deaths in order to ensure justice for the purpose of determining the cause of death.

If a person dies without having been attended by a doctor in the past fourteen days, or under suspicious circumstances, or during a surgical operation, the coroner may rule that an autopsy is required. A medical-legal autopsy is required in all homicide cases.

Approximately 1 percent of the population in any given city dies each year; about one-fourth are investigated by the coroner's office. For example, in a city of 100,000 population, 1,000 people will die each year, and 250 will be reviewed or investigated.

A person brought to a hospital emergency room dead on arrival (DOA) is automatically reported as a coroner's or medical examiner's case. The coroner will investigate for possible foul play and determine if a complete postmortem examination is needed. All DOA cases will be initially investigated, but not all will automatically require an autopsy. Only those warranting further investigation or those suspected of foul play will have blood drawn for toxicology tests and to determine drug and alcohol levels.

This general category list shows the types of deaths usually investigated for cause of death:

- Murder
- Suicide
- Accident
- Sudden death in someone who seemed in good health
- Deaths under suspicious circumstances
- Prisoner or inmate who dies in custody
- Abortion (both legal and criminal)
- Deaths unattended by a physician
- Poisoning
- Death during/following medical procedures
- Before a body can be cremated or buried at sea
- A discovered body

Included here is a *complete* list of all reportable deaths that must be investigated by the coroner's office. This list is from the Coroner's Office in Lucas County, Ohio:

Reportable Deaths
All Homicidal Deaths
All Suicidal Deaths

Accidental Deaths
- Anesthetic accident (death on operating table, or prior to recovery from anesthesia)
- Blows or other forms of violence
- Burns and scalds
- Crushed beneath falling objects
- Drowning
- Explosion
- Exposure
- Fractures
- Fall
- Firearms
- Carbon monoxide poisoning
- Hanging
- Insolation (sunstroke)
- Poisoning (food, occupational)
- Suffocation (foreign object in throat) by bed clothing or other means
- Vehicular accidents
- Animal or insect bites (spiders)
- Therapeutic complications
- Airplane accidents

Abortions
- Criminal or self-induced

Deaths at Work
- All deaths at work, or work-related deaths
- Cassion (bends)
- Industrial infections (anthrax septicemia following wounds, including gas gangrene, tetanus)
- Silicosis, asbestosis
- Industrial poisoning
- Contusions, abrasions, fractures, burns

Sudden and Suspicious Deaths
    When in apparent health or in any suspicious or unusual manner including:
- Alcoholism

- Sudden death on the street, at home, in public place or at work
- Deaths under unknown circumstances whenever there are no witnesses
- Bodies found in the open, in shelter or at home alone.
- sudden infant death syndrome (SIDS)
- Death where abuse of the elderly is suspected
- Death of persons where the attending physician cannot be located or death of persons which have not been attended by a physician within two weeks prior to death
- All deaths occurring within twenty-four hours of admission to a hospital unless the patient has been under the continuous care of a physician for a natural disease that is responsible for death.

To report a death above, contact the coroner's office or call the police and ask to speak to the coroner's investigator.

Not all cases that come to the attention of the coroner's office will necessarily require a full medical-legal autopsy. The particular case may only require a blood test for alcohol and drugs or blood testing plus a superficial examination of the body before a cause of death can be determined.

When a case is brought to the coroner's attention for a ruling as to the cause of death, there are several options that the coroner or medical examiner can take, depending on the circumstances:

- Make an immediate ruling based on the circumstance with no further examination.
  Example: An elderly person who lives alone is found dead in bed. The coroner may rule "death from natural causes."
- Take blood tests for alcohol and drugs, review the corpse, then make a ruling. (This type of limited exam would only be performed in rural areas of the country where a medical examiner is not available.)
  Example: Victims of auto accidents, industrial accidents.
- A limited autopsy, where only a portion of the body is dissected and examined before a ruling is made as to the cause of death. This may be done to accommodate certain religious restrictions, or the coroner may decide that only a particular part of the body needs to be examined.
  Example: Industrial accident with a pipe through the brain.
- Complete medical-legal autopsy for homicide, sudden death, suicide or cases requiring a ruling for legal purposes.

A medical-legal autopsy by a coroner is much more involved than a general autopsy performed in a hospital. It requires special training and skill and must provide adequate evidence for either defense or prosecution and must differentiate "natural cause of death" from external causes.

A MEDICAL-LEGAL AUTOPSY INCLUDES:

- Identification of the body and tagging.
- Photography of body dressed and nude.
- Measuring, weighing and X raying the body.
- External examination of the body.
- Accurate detailed description of all wounds such as gunshot wounds, stab wounds or ligature bruises.
- Dissection and internal examination of the body.
- Toxicological examination of body fluids and organs (for evidence of drugs, poisons, alcohol, carbon monoxide).
- Opinion rendered and the "cause of death" added to the death certificate.

After a death is determined to be a coroner's case, the body is sent to the morgue. The body is identified and photographed, then given an accession number. This number, along with the name of the deceased, is recorded on a tag which is tied to the big toe. The body is identified through family members, friends, dental records or fingerprints.

Needless to say, establishing proper identification is the first priority.

Body in Casket Has Extra Leg; Family Sues
MIAMI—The family of a one-legged man whose body had to be dug up after it was learned a corpse with two legs was in his grave has sued the funeral home over the mix-up.

The funeral home "failed to check the toe tag of the body" when it collected a two-legged corpse at the medical examiner's office, according to the suit.

Instead, they accepted a "John Doe" body that went unclaimed for a month. A funeral home spokesperson said the medical examiner's office "gave us the wrong body."

After the mistake was discovered, the "John Doe" corpse

Sample toe tag.

had to be dug up and another funeral and burial held for the correct dead man.

Identifying corpses is not an easy task. Some are decomposed, some mutilated. When a body is left in the wild, maggots and animals devour it. Insects will finish off the last and leave a skeleton. In such cases, X rays of the body, dental X rays and bite molds may help establish an identity.

There are four specific things the autopsy should try to establish:

- **Cause of Death:** The instrument or physical agent that was used to bring about death (gun, knife, speeding car, poison, electrocution).
- **Mechanism of Death:** The pathological condition within the body that resulted in death (bleeding into the brain, torn heart muscle, lacerated liver).
- **Manner of Death:** The means of death. There are four possible manners of death:
  - natural
  - accident
  - suicide
  - homicide
- **Time of Death:** At best, the time of death can only be determined within a range of hours and usually within days.

There are two things that an autopsy cannot determine with 100 percent certainty: the time of death and the manner of death. Both can be stated as an opinion with a degree of probability that depends on the available evidence and circumstances.

For example, if a man suffered a fatal heart attack during a robbery, the autopsy can only prove that the heart attack was the cause of death. The manner of death was in fact homicide, but without other evidence, the manner of death will be listed as "natural causes."

When a person is found dead inside a burned building, the question is whether the person was killed by the fire or was already dead when the fire started. Soot discovered in the windpipe at autopsy means a high carbon monoxide level in the lungs, and *that* means the person was alive and breathing when the fire started. The cause of death: smoke inhalation.

Determining the *manner of death* is difficult, and in areas of the country without a highly trained medical examiner, many cases are incorrectly determined. Sometimes there has been fatal violence without any external signs of trauma. Examples are: poisoning, asphyxiation by placing a pillow over the face, or a blow to the body or head with an internal bleed.

Other Information to Be Determined by the Autopsy

In addition to knowing what weapon was involved, the coroner should try to determine which wound was the fatal wound. If there are multiple stab or gunshot wounds, this may prove impossible.

In most suicides, the instrument of death will be nearby. But the absence of a weapon is not conclusive evidence that the death is a homicide. For example, if a person shoots or stabs himself and doesn't die immediately, he will have time either to dispose of the weapon or to travel some distance from it before he dies.

Questions the Autopsy Will Try to Answer

- What was the cause, mechanism and manner of death?
- What was the time of death?
- How long did the victim live after the assault?
- What weapon (if any) was involved in the death?
- Which was the fatal wound?
- Was the body dragged or dumped?
- From what direction did the injury occur?
- What was the position of the deceased?
- Is there evidence of sexual assault (rape or sodomy)?

- Was the victim under the influence of drugs or alcohol?
- Is there evidence of a struggle?

The Autopsy, Step by Step
External Examination of the Body

The coroner must carefully examine the body: first fully clothed, then naked. Blood stains, semen, glass particles, paint, powder or dirt on the victim's clothing may supply valuable information. The entire clothed and then naked body, including the injuries, must be photographed to document the findings.

It may be necessary to X-ray certain parts of the body (X rays of the skull to determine the presence of bone fragments or of the chest to determine the bullet track). X rays can also determine the direction of blows to the head and body by the type of fractures, show bullets inside the body that have traveled far from the point of entry, reveal knives, needles and other embedded objects that may otherwise be overlooked.

Every external feature and mark should be noted, including scars, eye and hair color, height, weight, skin lesions, tattoos, moles, dental work, age and general condition of the body.

Hands and fingernails should be examined carefully for any foreign material such as blood, skin or clothing fibers that would indicate a violent struggle with the assailant. This material might provide evidence as to the identity of the killer.

Gunshot entry wounds are measured, the angle of entry determined and the gun's distance from the body determined. A near-contact wound (with the gun's barrel within 1″ from the body) will cause a burn from the short flame that bursts from the barrel. A close-range shot (from 2″ to 4″) will cause gunpowder soot that can easily be wiped away. An intermediate shot (from 12″ to 16″) will cause carbon stippling or "tattooing" that is imbedded into the skin in a ring pattern around the bullet entrance wound and cannot be wiped away. At this range there will be no gunpowder residue. A long-range shot (greater than 16″) will only have the bullet hole wound, with no burn, gunpowder residue or stippling present.

Dissection and Internal Examination of the Body

The order of internal examination of the body is basically from top to bottom. First the neck, spine and chest are examined, then the abdomen, pelvic organs and genitalia. Finally, the head and brain are examined.

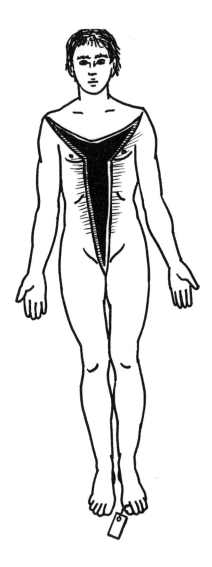

The "Y" Incision: The "Y" incision extends across the chest from shoulder to shoulder, then continues down the front of the abdomen to the pubis. All the internal organs are removed from top to bottom and examined.

The head is examined last in order to allow blood to drain from it to facilitate the examination.

The chest: First, the chest is examined for rib fractures. Then a thoracic-abdominal incision is made across the chest from shoulder to shoulder, crossing down over the breasts; then from the xyphoid process (lower tip of the sternum) a midline incision is extended down the entire length of the abdomen to the pubis. This is commonly referred to as a "Y" incision of the body.

Next, the ribs and cartilage are cut through to expose the heart and lungs. A sample of blood is taken from the heart after opening the pericardial sac to determine the blood type of the victim.

The heart, lungs, esophagus and trachea are removed en bloc; then each organ is weighed, its external surface examined, and then it is sliced into sections to evaluate the internal structure or damage. Any fluid in the thoracic pleural cavity is aspirated for analysis. Microscopic slides of tissue from the organs are prepared for examination of cellular changes.

The abdomen: The abdomen is examined in general, and any glaringly visible injuries are noted and traced before organs are removed. Fluids in the abdomen are aspirated for analysis. Each separate organ is then removed, weighed, grossly examined and sectioned. The stomach's contents are measured and recorded, with a sample sent for toxicology.

Usually the liver is removed first; then the spleen, the adrenals and kidneys (together); and finally the stomach, pancreas and intestines en bloc.

The pelvis: The genitalia are examined for evidence of injury or foreign matter. Vaginal swabs and anal swabs are obtained during the external part of the autopsy. In cases of fatal sexual attack (in which rape has occurred with murder), information useful in establishing the identity of the assailant, may be obtained by testing the seminal fluid found on the body or clothing of the victim.

Blood, semen and hair are collected and sent to the FBI lab or one of a few DNA labs for DNA typing. The DNA typing is *very* specific for one individual and can be accurate for purposes of identifying the individual to greater than one-in-a-million.

After the urinary bladder is taken out, the urine is removed and sent for toxicology. Many drugs (such as salicylates, barbiturates and Valium) are excreted by the kidneys and will be concentrated in the bladder, making the urine in the bladder a convenient place to detect the presence of drugs.

The head: Finally, the head and brain are examined. The eyes and eyelids are examined for petechiae in the conjunctiva (the mucous membrane that lines the inside of the eyelids and the forepart of the eyeball). Petechiae are tiny hemorrhages in the form of dark red specks seen on the mucous membrane and may be caused by increased pressure in the head from strangling, choking or hanging.

The skull is examined for fractures, punctures or other injuries. Then an intermastoid incision is made across the top of the head. The incision through the scalp starts behind one ear at the mastoid region (see illustration) and extends across the top of the head to the back of the opposite ear. The scalp is then peeled forward and away to expose the skull. Using a saw, the top of the skull is sawed through and removed, exposing the brain. The brain is examined, then removed, weighed and sectioned for microscopic review.

I've included autopsy scenes here from several authors to show how some of the terminology and details are incorporated into their scenes.

The huge "Y" incision that opens up the entire front of the body creates a very memorable, sometimes shocking sight to the nonprofessional and has often been described in literature. Here are a few excerpts from novels showing how these authors chose to describe the "Y" incision or the autopsy in general.

> "Autopsy's going on now, but the evidence looks like suicide. No note, but an empty bottle of"—he looked back at his little notebook—"imipramine." His unpracticed tongue put the emphasis on the wrong syllable. "Mixed it with alcohol. Pretty lethal, I'm told, low LD-50."
>
> Part of me heard his analysis of the amount of antidepressant Karen would have needed to ingest to have had a 50 percent chance of being consumed by a lethal dose, the LD-50. Mostly, I was transfixed by the image of Karen's beautiful body slit from chin to pudenda on a stainless-steel autopsy table somewhere across town.
>
> Stephen White, *Privileged Information* (Viking)

Examination of the Brain

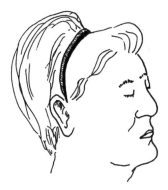

1. First, an intermastoid incision is made over the top of the skull, cutting all the way through the scalp down to the bone.

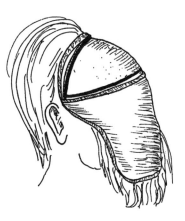

2. Then the scalp is pulled down over the front of the face, and the front quadrant of the skull is cut away and removed.

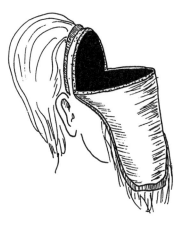

3. Then the brain is removed through the frontal craniotomy and examined.

One of the men moved around to the other side of the autopsy table and Ryan was looking at the whole body, cut open from breastbone to groin and seeing the man's insides, his vital organs and a slab of ribs, lying in a pile on the table.

Like dressing a deer.

The opened body seemed less human than the ones upstairs. It was a carcass with no face, or a face without features, a store mannequin. Ryan stared at the man's head and realized he was looking at the bare skull. The skin and hair had been peeled, pulled down, and lay inside-up over the man's face. That's why he seemed featureless. The attendant with the power saw had been cutting into the man's skull. He removed a wedge-shaped section. The brain was exposed for a few moments before the attendant pulled it out of the skull and placed it on the autopsy table.

Ryan, staring at the tag, let his gaze move up the yellowed legs, past the man's darker-shaded organ and thick pubic hair to the violent red opening. The assistant was doing something, scooping Robert Leary's stomach and internal organs into a clear plastic bag. He dropped the bag into the open cavity, working it in to make it fit, and laid the slab of ribs on top.

Elmore Leonard, *Unknown Man No. 89* (Avon Books)

I was making a Y incision on Cary Harper's body.

I removed the breastplate of ribs and lifted the block of organs out of the chest cavity while Marion looked on mutely. Water drummed in sinks, surgical instruments clattered and clicked, and across the suite a long blade rasped against a whetstone as one of the morgue assistants sharpened a knife.

Patricia Cornwell, *Body of Evidence* (Charles Scribner's Sons)

I described an autopsy in my novel, *Life Form*, by giving the reader a vivid description of the scene, then showing an internist's reluctance during an autopsy to face the death of his patient:

The autopsy room was cold. Like death. Air conditioning hummed from the ceiling. Torrents of icy air poured out of large vents onto the scene below.

Yost glimpsed at the waxy pale body; naked, lifeless-grey,

and already completely gutted through one massive ventral incision extending from the top of the sternum to the pelvis. Chile's body gaped open to reveal an empty cavity. His lungs, heart, intestines, and liver had all been removed. Spine showed through the thin fascia in the back.

The casual manner in which this morbid ritual of death was being carried out made Yost uncomfortable. This was not his territory. He did not belong here.

Keith Wilson, M.D., *Life Form* (Berkley Publishing)

Issues Concerning the Cause of Death

It is important to determine the cause of death. Even for historical figures long dead, we have a peculiar fascination with knowing the *causes* of their deaths. In order to do this, a body must be exhumed (or disinterred).

Exhume: (v). To remove from a grave. The Latin derivation is from *ex*, meaning "out of," and humus, meaning "earth." A body can only be exhumed by authorities, such as police, court-appointed individuals, or county government officials, and only by permission of the county authorities, usually through the coroner's office.

Dead men tell no lies—but they do leave clues. Forensic anthropology is the science that studies the remains of the dead for details of their past lives, as well as the cause of their death. By studying the bones, these scientists can tell age, sex, race and height. They can even tell the type of diet; vegetarians' bones contain more manganese, whereas meat-eaters have more zinc and copper.

While the body may have decomposed almost entirely, examination of the bones may provide clues to the cause of death. Head injuries can be determined by examining the skull, and fragments of tissue or bone can be analyzed for heavy-metal poisoning (arsenic, mercury, lead). DNA analysis also provides important details to the past. Bone, hair and nail fragments give DNA information to diseases, blood type, poisonings and genetic background. Even the blood types of mummies have been studied using the DNA of bone fragments.

The following article on the death of Amadeus Mozart more than two hundred years ago appeared in the *Tampa Tribune*:

Head Injury, Not Fever, May Have Killed Mozart
NEW YORK (UPI)—A new analysis of a skull believed to be Mozart's indicates the death of the composer may have stemmed

Secrets From the Grave

Skull: The skull in males is
thicker, heavier and has more
prominent brow ridges. Older people have thinned, osteoporitic
bones.

Face: The shape of facial bones
can tell race and regional background. The teeth can tell age,
general health and diet. In modern medicine, teeth are important
for identification by means of
dental records.

Arms and legs: The length of long
bones indicates the height,
weight, muscle development and
kind of work or activity
performed.

Nails and fingers: May contain
DNA for genetic background and
determination of blood type and
presence of certain diseases.
Bones in fingers and toes show arthritis, or give indication of repetitive activity or work during life.

Pelvis: A female pelvis is wider
and lower. The pubis and sacrum
tell whether she gave birth or not
during life.

The spine can also indicate arthritis
or wear from work such as carrying
heavy loads. Bones of skull, ribs
and pelvis may give clues to the
cause of death of the individual
(such as bullet holes, arrow or spear
wounds, or blows to the head or
chest with fractures).

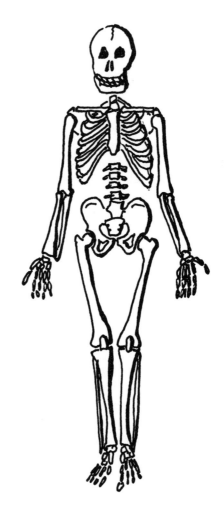

from a head injury rather than rheumatic fever.

Mozart died on December 5, 1791. French scientists recovered a skull from a Viennese cemetery and studied it in all proportions to previous paintings.

The French team found a healed fracture on the left temple of the purported skull of Mozart.

And this article questioned the cause of death of President Zachary Taylor, who died July 9, 1850, just sixteen months after taking office:

President Taylor: Was He Victim of Poison Plot?
WASHINGTON—A coroner plans to open the crypt of President Zachary Taylor to test the controversial theory that he was assassinated with poisoned fruit more than 141 years ago because of his opposition to the spread of slavery.

An author believes she has uncovered evidence that Taylor did not die a natural death, as most historians believe, but was poisoned by arsenic.

The coroner hopes there is enough left of Taylor to examine. If Taylor did get a lethal dose of arsenic, his remains may be well preserved.

The results of tests on the exhumed body of President Taylor showed that he died of a stomach ailment and in fact was not poisoned. But the same day that the results of the tests on Taylor were announced, it was reported that the remains of Huey Long's assassin, Carl Weiss, would be dug up to determine if the young doctor was actually killed by Long's own guards. Long was a U.S. senator when he was killed at the age of forty-two.

Forensic scientists recently began looking into a famous murder case:

Forensics Expert Looks at Lizzie Borden Case
FALL RIVER, Mass.—Almost a century after Lizzie Borden was accused in the ax murders of her parents, a forensics expert scanned their graves with radar Monday for clues in one of America's most celebrated mysteries.

Lizzie was acquitted in court but convicted in verse: "Lizzie Borden took an ax and gave her mother 40 whacks. When she saw what she had done, she gave her father 41."

If the skulls are there, scientists plan to exhume them, hoping modern science might shed light on the case.

Knowing the exact cause of death of those who have died remains a high priority in our culture. Maybe it is our need for a sense of order in life or perhaps the occasional thought of our own death that haunts us.

Although we may be interested to know the cause of death in others, their loved ones may have a need for privacy. Consider both possibilities when you write such a scene. On one side, a detective is determined to discover the true cause of death in an elderly man; on the other side is his widow, who may wish to protect her husband's privacy and blocks the detective at every opportunity.

This unusual "Dear Abby" column appeared recently in the papers:

Dear Abby:

How lucky we are to be living in West Virginia. The newspapers here, as a matter of policy, do not publish the cause of death in their obituaries. I understand that in some states the cause of death is required. A friend who works at the local mortuary told me that a newspaper editor in another state refused to print an obituary unless "cause of death" was disclosed.

Abby, why would this information be important to the general public? The friends and relatives of the deceased know the cause of death without having it in the print for all the world to see.

N.J.G.

Dear N.J.G.:

The cause of death is not the business of the public, but some newspaper editors feel that no obituary is complete unless it is included.

When the cause of death is a suicide, some obituaries disclose the details: "suicide by hanging," "suffocation," "overdose," "shotgun to the head," "slashed wrists," etc.

Bless those sensitive editors who show compassion and report deaths without disclosing the facts that may have been painful to the survivors. The good Lord knows they have already suffered enough.

The Autopsy Protocol

The autopsy protocol is the legal document file presented in court for evidence. It is a folder containing results of the autopsy along with the opinion, photographs, toxicology test results, X rays and fingerprints. The report includes:

1. External Examination:
   - Description of clothing
   - Description and identification of the body
2. Evidence of Injury:
   - External
   - Internal
3. Central Nervous System (head and brain)
4. Internal Examination of Chest, Abdomen and Pelvis
5. Toxicology Test Findings
6. Opinion

Opinion

The opinion comes at the end of the report and states the official cause of death. It is stated in simple terminology, giving the nature of injury, the cause of death and any other factors.

A portion of Bobby Hicks's autopsy report is included here to show how a typical report is worded:

> The body is opened by the usual "Y" incision extending across the chest and continuing ventrally down to the pubis. The pericardium is opened and the heart is removed. Gross examination of the heart and review of sections through the heart show normal myocardium and coronary vessels. Over 1000 cc's of bloody pleural effusion are present in the right thorax, and a chest tube inside the chest is seen extending toward the apex. The inferior branch of the right main pulmonary artery is transected and the right lung near the hilum shows extensive parenchymal hemorrhage. There is extensive damage to the right lung along a bullet track, extending superiorly and laterally toward the right scapula. . . .

A long, detailed autopsy report would continue, including a complete systems review. The autopsy report would conclude with the *opinion*:

Opinion: It is my opinion that Bobby Hicks, a sixteen-year-old male, died as a result of a gunshot wound to the chest. The bullet, a .45-caliber, passed through the right chest and avulsed the pulmonary artery, causing massive internal hemorrhage. The cause of death was a .45-caliber gunshot injury to the chest. The mechanism of death was loss of blood and shock secondary to traumatic hemorrhage of the lung. The manner of death was homicide.

Autopsies of the Fetus or Newborn Infant

Special rules apply to examination of a fetus or an infant that dies after delivery.

1. A fetus weighing 500 grams or less (less than 1.1 pounds) is considered nonviable. That is, even if it is alive for a brief period of time after delivery, it is considered medically nonviable. In this instance the fetus is considered a surgical specimen, and therefore no autopsy permit or death certificate is required. This varies according to state laws.

2. If the fetus weighs more than 500 grams and is born *dead*, then a special fetal death certificate is needed. The cause of death is prematurity and nonviability. No manner of death is ruled.

3. If the fetus weighs more than 500 grams and is born *alive* (even if only momentarily) and then dies, it must be registered as a live birth and a regular death certificate filed. An autopsy is not mandated by law, however, and can only be performed after permission is obtained from parents or legal guardians.

If a pregnant mother is killed and the fetus weighs more than 500 grams, two death certificates must be issued: a regular death certificate for the mother and a second for the fetus. If the fetus is born alive (even if it lives for only a very brief period following the death of the mother), a regular death certificate will be issued. A fetus born dead will require a special fetal death certificate.

Summary of Medical-Legal Autopsy

1. Body arrives at the morgue.
2. Body is identified, assigned a number and toe-tagged.
3. Body is photographed and examined, both clothed and nude.

Anatomical Nomenclature

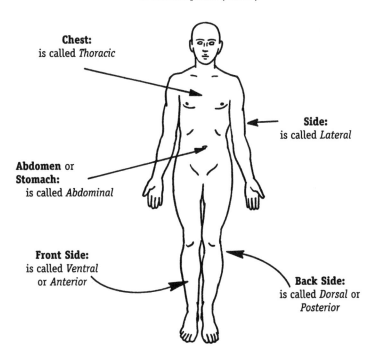

Top:
is called *Cephalic* ("head")

Chest:
is called *Thoracic*

Side:
is called *Lateral*

Abdomen or
Stomach:
is called *Abdominal*

Front Side:
is called *Ventral*
or *Anterior*

Back Side:
is called *Dorsal* or
Posterior

Bottom:
is called *Caudal*
("tail")

4. The body is weighed, measured and X-rayed.
5. Fingerprints are taken.
6. External examination is carefully performed:
   - Clothing is thoroughly examined; fiber samples and stains are examined.
   - Scars, wounds, tattoos, moles and other identifying markers are noted.
   - Fingernails, hair and skin are examined. Skin of arms and legs is checked for needle marks.
   - In females, a careful external examination of the genitals is performed to diagnose rape or sexual assault.
7. Fluids are withdrawn and toxicology tests performed.
8. Dissection and internal examination performed:
   - A body-length "Y" incision opens up the entire front of the body.
   - The lungs, heart, esophagus and trachea are removed.
   - The abdominal organs (liver, spleen, kidneys and adrenals, stomach and intestines) are removed.
   - The genitals are carefully examined; for a female, the uterus and vagina are examined for signs of pregnancy, rape or other sexual assault.
   - The pelvic organs (bladder, uterus, ovaries) are removed.
   - The contents of the stomach are carefully analyzed in cases of drowning, suspected drug overdose or poisoning.
   - The number and direction of bullet wounds are noted, along with estimated distance of gun as judged by the entrance wounds. Bullets are removed and placed in plastic bags for ballistics and evidence.
   - The skull is cut away with an intermastoid incision and the brain removed and examined.
9. Organs are returned to the body cavities.
10. The autopsy protocol with a final opinion and all photographs are turned over to the authorities and become a part of the corpus delicti for evidence in a court of law when indicated. The folder containing all the evidence is the case file.
11. The cause of death is determined and the death certificate completed.
12. The body is turned over to the family for disposal, usually by burial or cremation.

The Case File

The case file is simply a large 12″ × 14″ envelope that contains all the paperwork, photographs, legal identification records, fingerprint cards, property receipts, complete autopsy report with the opinion, newspaper articles, medical records, police reports, telephone calls and other pertinent material that could be used in legal proceedings.

The preceding illustration lists specific terminology to describe position or location during examination and autopsy of the body. This may be helpful to you as a writer when you wish to note something anatomically.

For example, a "ventral wound of the abdomen" is more accurate than "a hole in the front of the belly." However, whether or not to use the correct terminology depends on which character in your story is talking. A medical examiner might say a ventral wound to the abdomen, whereas a cigar-chewing detective might say "a hole in his gut." Read any of Elmore Leonard's books to see how he handles dialogue that varies according to the character speaking. The dialogue creates the character and brings them to life for the reader.

Chapter Ten

Larceny, Burglary, Robbery and Assault

by Russell Bintliff

from *Police Procedural: A Writer's Guide to the Police and How They Work*

F our types of crime against property and persons create most of the day-to-day work for police patrols and the detective division. Larceny (theft) is the wrongful taking of property with the intent of maintaining permanent possession of that property. Burglary is breaking into and entering the building of another with the intent to commit a crime inside that building. Robbery is the taking of a person's property while in his presence, by force, violence or intimidation. An assault happens when someone attacks another person in some way and the attack results in bodily harm. These crimes often are linked to more serious crimes involving drugs, arson and homicide.

Crimes fall into two criminal justice categories: misdemeanors and felonies. A misdemeanor in each state brings a maximum jail term of one year and normally a maximum fine of about $5,000 (fines vary in each state while the jail term remains consistent). A felony brings a minimum jail term of one year and fines above the lower court levels. Felonies also include capital crimes. The process for determining whether a crime will become a misdemeanor or felony depends on state or federal statutes. Normally, the value of property stolen will determine if a larceny will be a misdemeanor or felony. Most states set misdemeanor value limits between $500 and $2,500. Armed robbery and most burglaries are felonies because the crimes themselves are separate from the value of the theft. An armed robbery, for example, that nets $.50 will qualify as a felony because value of items or money stolen has no real bearing on the crime. The same rule normally applies in burglaries. Assaults, like larcenies, can fall in either the misdemeanor or felony categories depending on seriousness, injuries and whether or not the assailant had a weapon. Some assaults can happen without contact, and they normally go to court as a misdemeanor.

Larceny

Larceny is one of the most frequent crimes confronting the police and police detectives and is responsible for a large part of the detective's daily workload. Larcenies create difficulties for detectives assigned to investigate them. Often, discovery or reporting of the theft is delayed. Victims may be unable to accurately describe the property taken or prove it's theirs when police recover it from a suspect. All of this adds to the detective's investigative headaches.

Legal Considerations

The crime of larceny includes several different offenses that police detectives have to consider before starting their investigation. The detective must consider that all larcenies have in common a wrongful acquisition of (or assumptions or exercise of dominion over) the property of another coupled with the offender's intent to permanently deprive the owner of the property. The element of intent will prove the greatest challenge for the police detective during his investigation of this crime. Detectives attend to the following guidelines:

Common Law Larceny. This offense is defined in common law (as opposed to statutory law) as a taking by and felonious carrying away of property belonging to another, with the intent to deprive him or her of that property permanently.

False Pretenses (Fraud). This offense contains all the elements of larceny, plus the taking of property must happen by a designed misrepresentation that causes a victim to transfer custody of his or her money or property to the perpetrator. This can involve lawyers, accountants or con persons who gain control of a person's property, money or possessions.

Embezzlement. This larcenous act happens when a person lawfully receives the property of another through his or her position of trust and then intentionally withholds that property unlawfully. For example, a bank teller receives money to pay customers, retains part of the money and then alters the records to cover up the amount he has taken for personal use.

Elements of Proof for Larceny. Whenever a police detective begins any investigation, he needs to know firsthand the elements needed to prove the crime happened, and when a suspect becomes known, to prove that the suspect committed the crime under investigation. To prove the crime of larceny, the detective must satisfy the following elements of proof:

- The offender wrongfully took, obtained, or withheld from the possession of the true owner or any other person the property described in the complaint. Generally, any movement of property or any dominion over it with the intent to deprive the owner of the property without the owner's consent will establish this element of proof. However, not included in this element are the offenses of receiving, buying or concealing stolen property or otherwise being an accessory after the fact.

- The property belongs to a certain person named or described in the complaint. The offender might have taken, obtained or withheld the property from the true owner or from a person who had greater right to possession than the offender.

- The property reported stolen has the value alleged or had some value. As a rule, determining the value of stolen property stems from its legitimate market value at the time and place of theft. For example, a television set may have cost $500 new, but when stolen three years later might have a value of $150. Although stealing something with no value (like a common rock from the yard of a neighbor) might have moral implications, no larceny has been committed unless the owner of the rock can establish legitimate monetary value.

- The facts and circumstances of a larceny case show that by taking, obtaining or withholding, the offender clearly had intent to permanently deprive or defraud another person of the use and benefit of the property involved or to take it for his or her own use or the use of any person other than the true owner. These intents collectively establish the "intent to steal." Establishment of an "intent to steal," in most crimes, often arises from an inferred or implied intent developed from proven circumstances of the crime or the behavior of the offender before, during and after the crime.

Basic Investigative Techniques for Larceny Cases

Larceny takes many different forms, ranging from the once-in-a-lifetime theft by a person who needs money to safecracking and theft by professional thieves. The police detective knows that effective investigative techniques vary with the type of larceny they confront, the geographical area of their jurisdiction and a variety of other circumstances. However, many basic investigative techniques apply to all types of larcenies and are discussed in the following sections.

Initial Investigative Actions

Before a police detective leaves the station house for a larceny crime scene, she obtains all the available facts from the complainant, the person receiving the complaint, and the report written by the desk sergeant or patrol officer. Using that information, the detective can formulate an investigative plan and select, as applicable, the equipment needed to process the scene from the list of items shown in chapter two. When approaching the crime scene, the police detective always stays alert for any suspicious persons hanging around or among onlookers. Often, especially when a larceny involves neighbors, employees, juveniles or amateurs, a perpetrator may stay in the area to see what actions the police take. Detectives also know that witnesses will join other onlookers, wanting to tell what they know but uncomfortable about coming forward. That crowd of people can often supply valuable information otherwise overlooked.

Procedures at the Crime Scene

After following the general procedures of photographing, developing latent fingerprints, and other crime scene processing, the police detective will question the victim to find out the following information:

- Detailed description of the stolen property, including serial numbers, make and type of model, size and color, and personal marks such as initials and alterations.
- Names and addresses of persons able to verify ownership or possession of the items and corroborate the location of the property as stated in the victim's complaint.

- Nature and location of documentary evidence (for example, sales slips, invoices, or other proofs of purchase or acquisition) that will help the detective establish ownership, possession and value of the stolen property or aid in its identification when recovered.
- Description of situations, conditions, incidents or statements that may tend to cast suspicion on any persons including:
  - Names and addresses of possible witnesses
  - Names and addresses of persons having access to the stolen property
  - Any other relevant information the victim can furnish
  - Names and addresses of persons at or near the scene so that the detective can question them to find possible witnesses

The type of articles taken may provide a lead to the offender. For example, if the theft involved only toys, the offender may be a child or a person who has children. To aid in identifying the offender, the detective asks the following questions:

- What was stolen? The detective obtains complete descriptive information.
- From where were the articles stolen? A detective demands the exact location, avoiding generalizations. For example, department time and money may be wasted if, in the end, an alleged victim realizes the property wasn't stolen after all, just borrowed by a friend or misplaced.
- What valuables were present but not stolen? For example, the alleged thief stole a typewriter but did not steal a diamond ring and gold bracelet or valuable coin collection in plain view within the same room as the typewriter.
- How could the offender change, alter or disguise the stolen items to permit their resale, reregistration or open use? When an offender steals items to resell them, he will try to make them untraceable.
- What required materials, equipment or facilities would the offender need to disguise the stolen articles?

Investigative Procedures After Leaving the Scene

After leaving the scene of the crime, a police detective must create leads from definitive descriptions of the stolen property, find the property and link the suspect to the offense. The following information may supply those leads:

- Description of the property by the owner or witnesses. This description is strengthened when owners or witnesses can point out peculiarities, modifications or adjustments made by or known to them.
- Photographs or sketches of the stolen items.
- Serial numbers, laundry and dry cleaning marks, jeweler's marks, monograms or other personalized markings.
- Manufacturer's data labels and peculiarities of manufacture or design.
- Trace materials placed by the owner on items believed targets of theft. In cases of repeated thefts, materials or objects may be marked in ways enabling subsequent positive identification.
- Presence on stolen items of identifiable contaminants or materials from the scene of the offense; for example, traces of machine shop dust inside cracks on a piece of expensive stolen equipment.

When the owner of stolen property has insurance, the amounts, policy number, names and addresses of the insuring companies and beneficiaries of the policy or policies. Often, an insurance company may be able to furnish a detective with a detailed description of the stolen property, including sketches and photographs obtained from the victim when insuring the property.

Questioning Witnesses

The police detective makes every effort to find witnesses and question them to get additional information, leads and corroborating proof of ownership and theft. The common guidelines used by police detectives when questioning witnesses are as follows:

- Verification, by documents or statements, of the victim's ownership or possession of the property stolen and its location before the theft. Often, skilled detectives find witnesses in unlikely places or positions that can supply valuable information in this category. That information comes from the detective asking the right questions and remaining consistent even when logic would dictate that the interviewee would not have such knowledge. Much of that acumen stems from experience and instinct. Sometimes, informants have told police of a person who planned to obtain money by reporting a theft and using the police report to file an insurance claim. Later, the person might sell the same items to a backstreet dealer or fence.
- Presence at the crime scene of any persons acting suspicious. These

persons often seem to be suspects at first observation. Detectives often learn that suspicious behavior stems from nervousness about having information and apprehension about revealing this knowledge to the police and becoming involved.

- Presence at the crime scene of any persons known to have committed or been involved in larceny. This information is particularly important if the stolen property is of the same or similar type as property taken in other cases involving the known suspects. Often, detectives find that former offenders know the perpetrator of the crime under investigation or may have in some way participated in the crime.

- Presence at or near the crime scene of a motor vehicle and a description of the vehicle from witnesses, security or police patrols who noticed it before learning about the larceny. This information often comes from a note in a beat patrol officer's logs or from field intelligence furnished by a neighborhood watch or informant.

Other Investigative Actions

- Detectives regularly notify other law enforcement agencies about a larceny and supply a detailed description of the stolen property.
- Detectives check modus operandi files when available at their department and adjacent jurisdictions. This step often leads to valuable information, especially when the larceny appears to have been the work of a professional thief. Depending on what items were stolen, the detective might be able to discover probable perpetrators.
- Detectives make inquiries about any unusual activities at or near the crime scene before or during the estimated time of the larceny. An observant mobile canteen operator, for example, might have noticed two men in the area of a major commercial larceny during the days before the crime and may supply excellent descriptions.
- The detective checks possible and likely places of disposition of stolen property including:
  - Pawnshops.
  - Secondhand stores.
  - Known fences (dealers in stolen property—often, police allow some of these people to continue in business, and in return for the police looking the other way on minor deals, the "fence" agrees to serve as a reliable informant, especially on major larcenies).

- When a detective finds stolen property in the above locations or elsewhere, he will try to obtain added leads with a detailed description of the person who sold or pawned the items.

Evaluating Evidence

An evaluation of collective evidence may lead the detective to a suspect or suspects. Logical suspects include:

- Persons having a motive for taking the property or professional thieves who deal in a particular type of property.
- Persons having easy access to the property.
- Strangers or loiterers at the scene about the time the offense happened.
- Unusually inquisitive or solicitous individuals (this is often a masquerade).
- Individuals who have large gambling losses or excessive spending habits.
- Drug users.

Establishing the Motive

Establishing the motive for the offense will help the detective solve the crime. The motive may not be solely the desire to possess the stolen property or professional interests. Motives often include spite, vandalism, lucrative opportunity or the desire to deprive a person of his property. The stolen articles may suggest an obvious motive instead of the actual motive. The offender, failing to find the property he or she planned to steal, may take other items instead. When certain of the motive, a police detective tries to identify persons who probably had that motive and fully investigates their activities.

Questioning Suspects

When a police detective interviews the victim and witnesses, makes an evaluation of the evidence collected and develops the identity of a suspect, the next step is usually to question the suspect. A skilled detective will not approach a certain suspect until there's almost no need to question him. A novice detective tends to move too fast and approaches a suspect early on. Suspects, having intimate knowledge of what they did when committing the larceny, will quickly recognize the detective either has them cold or is fishing for a confession. I always approached suspects by first explaining that it made no difference to me if they wanted to talk or confess, that I already had sufficient evidence against them. I also showed them the evidence (verbally) and then told them what they did at the scene and later. After this explanation I would advise them of their rights and offer them an opportunity to tell their side of it. During three decades of criminal investigations, I can recall only five or six, out of hundreds of criminals, who didn't confess. It seems to be human nature to confess, especially when the perpetrator believes there's a chance that cooperation might ease the penalty later. However, a detective should not approach a suspect for a confession unless it's not needed. Suspects may try to beat the charges against them in court; their defense attorneys may attack the credibility of the confession and allege coercion or failure to advise the suspect that he or she did not have to say anything, etc.

The detective attempts to obtain the following information:

- Where was the suspect when the larceny happened?
- Who can verify the suspect's statement and whereabouts? The detective must decide if these persons do corroborate information received from the suspect.
- Is the suspect believed or proven involved earlier in larceny?
- Is the suspect employed or working recently in the establishment where the offense happened?
- Did the suspect have access to the place where the offense occurred?
- Does the suspect have friends employed in the establishment where the offense was committed?
- Is the suspect friendly with persons known to have committed or are suspected of having committed larceny?
- Does the suspect have any grudges against the owner or management of the establishment where the offense of larceny was committed?
- Is the suspect living above his or her normal income?

Searching a Suspect's Premises

When circumstances warrant, the detective may legally search the premises of a suspect with a warrant. The detective must obtain proper search warrants before conducting a search, and only that property specified in the warrant can be seized. If the detective finds stolen property on the premises controlled by a suspect, some prima facie evidence to associate the person with the offense may exist. This may involve questioning the suspect, witnesses, and the persons who supported or confirmed the suspect's original statement about his whereabouts when the offense was committed. Also, to strengthen evidence of identity and motive, it may be desirable to conduct a more intensive investigation of the suspect's background to uncover a previous involvement in larceny or evidence that he's engaged in activities or circumstances that need more funds than his normal income provides or special requirements for use of the goods taken.

Study of Security Measures and Supply and Accounting Procedures and Records

A study of security measures and supply and accounting procedures where offenses happen may help the detective's investigation. Weaknesses in security measures and accounting procedures may provide leads about the offender, as well as about the methods used to commit and conceal the offenses and to remove, transport and dispose of stolen items.

Background Investigation of Supply Handlers, Clerks and Custodial Personnel

Persons having access to or custody of property will be investigated by the police detective, especially when repeated larcenies happen at the same location. Complete investigations into their backgrounds may reveal who has a motive for the offenses.

Check of Welfare Agencies

A police detective might find leads in information from welfare agencies concerning persons who have recently sought aid for personal or family financial problems or who have recently repaid loans to the agency. Persons whose financial circumstances provide motives for offenses may become suspects. However, the detective must avoid casting suspicion on persons simply because they have financial difficulties.

Check of Personnel and Financial Records

The detective might find important leads through investigation of personnel and financial records. An individual may have no legitimate income or be financially committed beyond the limits of his or her income. While checking these records and during follow-up investigations, a detective needs to be discreet to avoid discrediting innocent persons.

Use of Evidence

Evidence the police detective gains through questioning persons or from other leads must be thoroughly evaluated. Investigative evidence, properly handled and thoroughly evaluated, may help accomplish the following:

Place a Suspect at the Crime Scene. This might happen by establishing that the suspect or his vehicle was observed at the scene by a witness or the victim, that he left fingerprints, palm prints or footprints, or that his vehicle left identifiable tire tracks. Other techniques for placing the offender at the scene include identification of soil or rock particles found on the suspect's clothing or vehicle that correspond to the type of soil or rock present at the crime scene, identification of property or tools left at the scene and traced to the offender, or the determination that other materials found at the scene can be traced to the suspect.

Find the Stolen Property. Finding the property or evidence of the property in the possession, custody or control of a suspect is not sufficient to convict an offender of a theft. The detective must obtain evidence to show the suspect knowingly and illegally deprived another of the possession of the property. One way to prove this is through evidence—often a witness—that the suspect sold or attempted to sell the stolen property without the permission of its true owner.

Show That a Suspect Profited by the Offense. It helps the case to show that the suspect benefited from the larceny or came into money under suspicious circumstances directly related to certain facts of the offense, especially if the suspect cannot show that the funds or credits were obtained in a legitimate manner. Such information may lead to the identification of offenders, receivers of stolen goods or associates of an offender carrying out a felonious scheme.

Specific Larceny Offenses
Motor Vehicle Thefts
Motor vehicle thefts have become a common problem and often call for special sections and teams working out of the detective division. Reasons for the thefts including joyriding, use in a crime or professional auto theft to supply "chop shops" where newer cars are disassembled and their parts sold or entire cars are shipped intact out of the country.

When investigating a motor vehicle theft, the police detective uses nine key elements to develop leads:

- Obtains a full description of the vehicle, including vehicle identification number (VIN), motor and body numbers.

- Determines the time and date of the theft and the vehicle's location when stolen (first assuring the vehicle wasn't repossessed by a finance company).
- Notifies and gives all pertinent information to the FBI, especially when near a state line or when there's indication the vehicle crossed a state line or was stolen for shipment to a foreign country.
- Determines who had access to the place where the vehicle theft happened. These persons are interviewed to determine if any of them were involved in the theft.
- Determines what personnel are missing who may have had a motive or cause for stealing the vehicle. The detective checks to determine if these persons show involvement in the theft.
- Contacts municipal, county and state law enforcement agencies for help in finding the vehicle and offender.
- Gives data, including VIN to the National Crime Information Center (NCIC). This step is important because it allows law enforcement officers throughout the country to determine whether a stopped or abandoned car was stolen. When police want to check a license number, VIN or a serial number on any other stolen property, they routinely conduct a computerized search through the NCIC.
- Conducts necessary investigative actions after recovering the vehicle, such as searching it, trying to develop latent fingerprints, taking photographs of interior and exterior and other actions as needed.
- The National Automobile Theft Bureau (NATB) supplies law enforcement with guides to help detectives with information about vehicle ID numbers and their location on a variety of motor vehicles.

Larcenies Involving Safes

When a larceny involves a safe, a police detective performs the following procedures:

- Determines the modus operandi used in opening the safe (often identifies methods of known professionals).
- Forwards samples of explosive residue, if applicable, and of the safe dust to the department, state or FBI crime laboratory for analysis. (Use of certain types of explosives may also identify the professional.)

- Sends safe, when feasible, to a law enforcement crime laboratory for examination. When removal of the safe is not possible, the investigating detective photographs it and makes casts or molds of toolmarks to send to a laboratory. Often, amateur and professional safecrackers alike will "peel" the door of a safe using distinguishable techniques. When possible, examination of the door or the entire safe by laboratory technicians will identify the type of tool used and what the detective should look for during an investigation. If the detective later finds the same type of tools in a suspect's possession, the laboratory can match those specific tools to the marks and provide expert testimony in court.

- Sends suspect's clothing to the crime laboratory to have it examined for explosive residue or safe dust. When a police detective finds suspicious clothing during a legal search of the suspect's home or vehicle, crime laboratory technicians may match residue from clothing to that from the safe.

- Questions known safecrackers and checks their alibis thoroughly. The "breaking" of a safe requires skills limited to a few persons. Investigation of the crime scene and other information often leads a detective to persons with a record of safecracking larceny. The development of intelligence on known "rings" of professional thieves is important in investigating safecracking cases. Such professionals may have the help of apprentices; younger people may also aspire to reaching professional status by undertaking jobs a professional might not try. The modus operandi of known professionals in the area, coupled with an evaluation of techniques applied in any given instance, can greatly help detectives during their investigation.

Burglary

Burglary is a crime of stealth and calls for meticulous investigative procedures to identify and prosecute perpetrators. Unlike assaults and robbery or other crimes of violence, burglary often is discovered long after it happens. However, burglaries are often linked to other crimes, including crimes of violence such as murder or arson. The Uniform Crime Report produced by the FBI each year discloses that victims report about five million burglaries each year, of which only about 18 percent are solved. Of burglaries solved, few lead to successful prosecution because evidence collected often cannot prove complicity in the crime. Many victims never report burglaries to the police, especially businesses or persons who have no insurance or victims of previous unsolved burglaries.

Key Points About Burglary

Every burglary contains the signature of the perpetrator; the police detective's job is to find it. That signature includes a variety of clues extracted from the crime scene, witnesses, motives, actions of suspects and other aspects that a skilled detective pieces together to bring about a successful conclusion to the case.

A common myth about investigation involves gathering evidence that taints public opinion about law enforcement capabilities and performance. In television and motion picture portrayals of law enforcement efforts, crime laboratory technicians play an important role, swarming over a crime scene of any kind and supplying detectives with a wealth of information leading to immediate arrests. In reality, there are few crime laboratories and limited technicians, and those existing have the same budget problems as departments. Detectives largely must process the crime scene, develop leads and investigate this crime, often single-handedly in most departments.

Important Definitions

In common law, the crime of burglary is the breaking and entering of a dwelling house of another in the nighttime with the intent to commit a felony therein. Modern statutory definitions of the crime are much less restrictive. For example, laws now commonly require no breaking and specify no time of day or night, nor do they exclude other kinds of structures. Also, certain state statutes classify the crime into first-, second- and even third-degree burglary to provide latitude for prosecution efforts.

Burglary and Lesser Included or Related Offenses

Included in the crime of burglary are lesser offenses. Depending on a state's statutes for this crime, a variety of different circumstances might apply. Besides the offense of burglary, some lesser included or related offenses are:

Breaking and Entering. There must be a breaking, either actual by physical force or constructive by trickery. To enter through a hole in a wall or an open door does not establish a "breaking." Removal of any part of the structure, such as a screen or window glass, does establish "breaking." Entry is accomplished when any part of the body enters the structure (building). An instrument such as a pole inserted into the structure to extract property from the dwelling also is entry.

Unlawful Entry. Entry upon lands or structures thereon that is effected peacefully without force and done through fraud or some other willful wrong is usually unlawful entry. It's closely related to burglary and breaking and entering. It is an entry accomplished through fraud or willful wrong by the offender. The intent to commit an offense within the place entered is unnecessary to establish this offense.

Housebreaking. Generally, housebreaking is a burglary, calling for breaking and entering a dwelling house with intent to commit any felony there. Under some statutes, housebreaking may include "breaking out" of a house after access was gained without breaking.

Criminal Trespassing. Criminal trespass occurs when a person enters or stays on or in any land, structure, vehicle, aircraft or watercraft when he or she is not authorized or privileged to do so. The crime involves entering or staying in defiance of an order not to enter or to leave the premises or property that is personally communicated by its owner or other authorized person; or entering such premises or property when posted in a manner likely to come to the attention of intruders or when fenced or otherwise enclosed.

Constructive Breaking Into a House. A breaking that might happen over time. For example, a yard worker removes screws from door hinges over time or uses his position to enter the building and create a situation making breaking into the house easy. Also when a burglar gains entry into a house by threats, fraud or conspiracy.

Types of Burglary

The two basic types of burglary include commercial and residential. Both have an alarming rate of increase and create serious concern to both police patrol and detective divisions. Often, the burglary rate determines the amount of confidence the police department can expect from its community. When beginning the investigation into both types of burglaries, the police detective always considers the possibility of an insurance fraud. Often, the victims of commercial and residential burglaries are also the perpetrators.

Commercial Burglary. Because commercial establishments often have better protection than residences, burglars may become expert in many methods of entry. He or she may also breach elaborate burglary alarm systems. Sometimes, information a police detective receives from an informant alerts the police to a burglary that has yet to happen. That type of information often leads to a surveillance of the building slated for burglary.

Residential Burglary. Expensive homes are the primary targets for residential burglaries; however, every home is a potential target. Beside the millions of dollars taken in residential burglaries each year, the potential for personal harm, even homicide, to inhabitants exists each time a family home is burglarized.

Profile of the Burglar

Because most burglars prefer to commit their crimes under cover of darkness and not to meet the victims, many people believe that burglars are cowards. Although a burglar may lack the outward confidence of an armed robber, never underestimate the capability of harm or threat he poses. Kidnappings, rapes, serious assaults and homicides often supply the motive or conclusion of a burglary.

When investigating a burglary, the police detective always deals with the intelligence of the burglar, which can vary from one extreme to the other. The higher the intelligence of the burglar, the more difficult the investigation confronting the police detective.

Intent and the Essential Elements of Proof

The crime of burglary, like all criminal offenses, calls for proving clear intent by the offender. Some crimes, by their commission, establish clear intent by the offender, such as robbery and assault. Burglary, however, is not as clear-cut.

For example, a former maid or gardener who received a key to a house during employment and was not required to relinquish it upon ending employment returns two weeks later and enters the house while the owners are absent. The offender's defense to the charge of burglary is probably that he or she returned to the house to retrieve personal items. The owner may allege the former employee stole items from the house. Though the employee claims to own the stolen property, the employee may insist that the owner gave him or her the items earlier. Since entry was gained with a key, and the owner made no effort to change the locks or recover the employee's key, clear intent might be difficult or impossible to prove, depending on the items removed from the house.

It is also possible the former employee did not take all the items claimed. In such cases detectives determine how many others have keys, including current employees who may be taking advantage of the confusion.

Burglary Scene Investigative Procedure

Initial actions in burglary investigations include the following:

- Recording the location and description of the structure or area entered.
- Determining where the owners or occupants were during the crime.
- Finding out when the owners or occupants left the premises and whether all the doors and windows were secured.
- Determining who has keys to the structure.
- Trying to find out the time of entry by the offender.
- Photographing, sketching and processing the scene for fingerprints, which must have priority before and during the search. Entry points, pieces of furniture and other miscellaneous household items (or office or commercial building items) possibly handled by the perpetrator(s) should be dusted for latent fingerprints.

Approach and Entry Investigations

After completing the initial investigative steps, the detective must also:

- Look for evidence to determine whether the offender walked or rode to the crime scene (footprints or tire tracks showing the route or means of entrance to the real property involved). Make casts of tire tracks and footprints found at the crime scene.
- Determine who had approached the crime scene earlier. Security or police patrol and area residents or workers often have seen something that can identify persons in this category.
- Collect toolmarks made by the burglar from forcing entry into the building or office in original form if possible (for example, by cutting out parts containing the marks or taking a door from its hinges and

retaining it as evidence or sending it to the crime laboratory for analysis). When it is impossible to collect original toolmarks, a detective makes casts or molds of them.

- Determine what equipment, if any, such as ropes, ladders or digging tools, was used in the breaking and entry.
- Establish where and how the offender gained entry. Examine the property carefully for broken or unlocked doors, windows, skylights or gates. Determine whether locks or fasteners were forced, picked, or if holes were sawed or hacked through walls, floors, partitions or roofs. Laboratory examination of wood, glass or metal evidence found at the crime scene may disclose the direction of the breaking force or determine the general type of instrument used.
- Exercise caution to ensure he's not following a trail of misinformation established by the offender to mislead the investigation (for example, the suspect breaks a window to conceal entry with a key or lock picks). Examine all the possibilities without jumping to a conclusion about entry.
- Determine the size and shape of openings, if they're large enough to fit the offender or to permit removal of the stolen property, and the height of the openings from the ground or from where the offender stood.
- Establish whether bodily entry to the premises occurred or if only the offender's arm or some instrument was used to gain his or her objective, or whether it appears that someone inside the building may or must have helped in the offense by passing articles to the offender.

Reconstructing the Offender's Activities at the Scene
Often, a detective can simulate the offender's search of the scene. The detective's simulation may show whether the offender was familiar with the premises and if he or she knew in advance the location of the object or objects stolen. The manner of the simulation may show the detective the key characteristics of the offender's modus operandi.

A close examination of fingerprints and other evidentiary items at points where the offender searched the premises may reveal important information. An attentive study of evidentiary facts may suggest how long the offender spent in the premises, whether interrupted, the level of burglary skill and how secure the offender felt during the crime. Detectives try to answer the following questions:

- Did the offender go directly to the objects he or she stole? This could show advance information and would suggest whether the detective needs to explore how the burglar obtained that information.
- Does the offender's search show signs of systematic, thorough, selective or haphazard characteristics? The manner of search may indicate the work of a professional or amateur.
- Did the offender replace objects after examining them?
- Did the offender close doors, windows and drawers? Such actions may show his or her choice of articles and motive, as well as his or her presence of mind and consciousness of detection. Items stolen may also aid a detective in determining whether the offender will sell stolen items or use them for personal or business use. For example, a professional burglar might "take orders" for specific items of jewelry or business or professional equipment (for example, medical items, computers, dental equipment and the like).
- What did the burglar do to guard against detection while searching the scene? Did the offender close the window shades or blinds or lock the inside door? Did he or she plan alternate escape routes?
- Was the scene rearranged to delay discovery of the offense?
- Was evidence destroyed?
- Were fingerprints wiped off, gloves worn, toolmarks defaced or footprints and tire tracks obliterated?
- Was evidence damaged by the offender, the victim or witnesses before police arrival?
- Were records in order, or was there an attempt to falsify, destroy or misplace them?
- Were added offenses, such as arson, committed to hide the offenses?
- Was the crime scene or evidence intended to be misleading or to draw suspicion from the offender?
- Is there reason to suspect the victim is the perpetrator?
- Was the crime staged in an attempt to collect insurance or make other kinds of claims?

Transportation

Evidence of the type of transportation used and the specific vehicles involved is important to the investigating detective. He or she will make casts of suspicious tire tracks found at the crime scene. Tire tracks and casts often enable the detective to determine the type and number of vehicles, direction of travel, places parked and materials dropped (gas, mud, oil or water) or picked up (soil or rock). Once a suspect vehicle is found, the crime laboratory can examine it and compare it with casts made at the scene.

Exit and Flight

Suspects sometimes leave clues during their exit and flight. Detectives consider the following:

- Did the offender prepare or use an existing escape route or break out?
- Did the offender unlock a door or window?
- Were toolmarks, footprints or fingerprints left at the scene?
- At what time was the exit made?
- Did the offender make more than one trip to remove stolen items?
- Was help needed to effect the removal of the stolen items?
- How many persons needed to handle the equipment used in committing the offense?

Burglary Investigation Profile and Pattern Guide

Police detectives find the following evaluation points helpful to create a profile and pattern (modus operandi) of a burglar or burglary ring when a series of burglaries happens systematically.

Location.

- Of the house, office or structure.
- Type of area (urban, suburban, rural).
- Of the owner before the burglary.
- Of the owner during the burglary.

Offender's Actions.

- Does evidence establish the offender's point of entry?
- What means or methods were used to enable the offender to gain entrance?
- How does the obvious entrance point relate to the size of objects stolen?
- Does the crime scene show ransacking or selective search?
- Were measures taken to guard against detection?
- How was the scene left?
- Does evidence show a definitive point of exit?

- What means did the offender use when exiting?
- Is there evidence of the offender returning to the scene to relock doors, close windows, etc.?
- What were the means of approaching (walking or riding) and leaving (escape route) the scene?

Property.
- What type of property was stolen?
- Can the owner supply identifying features of the property, such as serial numbers, damage, peculiar markings, etc.?
- Is there evidence of specific objects being taken, such as guns, TVs, stereo equipment or professional items?
- Were some valuable items present but not stolen?
- What means were used by the offender to carry the property off the premises?

Physical Evidence.
- If a vehicle was used, can casts of tire marks be made?
- Are there toolmarks at the point of entry or elsewhere?
- Was any glass broken? Does it provide any trace evidence?
- Are there any fingerprints, palm prints or footprints?
- Is there any other evidence of equipment used in the burglary?
- Is there evidence that the offender tried to destroy any physical evidence?

Armed Robbery

The crime of robbery is a serious offense that detectives confront many times in their careers. In common terms, robbery is the taking with intent to steal anything of value from a person against his or her will, with force, violence or fear of immediate or future injury to his or her person or property—or the person or property of a relative or a member of his or her family or of anyone in his or her company during the robbery.

Essential Elements of Proof

Investigation of robbery relies heavily on the elements of proof. The public perception of robbery varies, and often elements vary in state statutes. However, the following elements are usually called for as a minimum:
- A theft happened at a specific place and either personal or commercial property was stolen. This includes money or other property of value.

- The theft was from a person who would not otherwise surrender possession of the property of value. It is unnecessary for the property taken to be within any certain distance of the victim. For example, a perpetrator enters a house and forces the owner by threats of serious bodily harm with a weapon of some kind that is recognizable as having the capability to do so, and the owner discloses the hiding place of valuables in an adjoining room. If the offender leaves the owner tied, goes into that room and steals the valuables, he or she has committed armed robbery.
- The property was taken against the victim's will by force or violence—the actual use of force or violence or engendering fear in the victim for personal safety. For example, a perpetrator may threaten with a gun, knife, club or other weapon capable of causing serious bodily harm. Any amount of force is sufficient to establish robbery if the force overcomes the actual resistance of the victim or causes him or her not to resist.

When a police detective investigates an alleged robbery, she must be alert to the possibility that robbery might not have happened, although a lesser included offense or different offense might have been committed. What appears to be a robbery could be only theft. Theft by taking is an integral part of robbery and may be the offense if there is insufficient evidence to prove the requisite force or engendered fear. Conversely, if proof does not support a charge of theft, and the force element is present, a charge of assault may be made.

Multiple offenses, such as when a group of people is threatened and property is stolen from each person, establish as many robberies committed as there are victims. The offense against the person (the assault element) is more serious than the offense against the property (the theft element). Therefore, each instance of taking becomes a separate offense. However, when several people are threatened but property is taken from only one victim, only one robbery has legally occurred, although all the others might be victims of assault with a deadly weapon.

Detectives use caution because sometimes victims were not robbed as reported. Victims may have reported a robbery as part of a scheme to defraud an insurance company. Robbery, like burglary and arson, is often falsely reported as prerequisite to insurance claims or to cover the negligent loss of property. For example, an employee entrusted with a costly item of equipment decides to use it at home to do company work over the weekend. After leaving it in his unlocked car to run an errand, he returns to find it stolen. If the employee reports the crime truthfully, the company will allege the employee was negligent and might fire him. Instead, the employee decides to report that during an armed robbery, the assailant took his money and jewelry plus the company's equipment. The company will be sympathetic to the employee, but this creates headaches for the police who begin investigating an armed robbery. During a detective's thorough investigation, she may discover the hoax simply through attentive questioning. It's always a good idea to interview a victim more than once and a few days apart. It's difficult to remember an exact detailed description of a fictitious perpetrator and circumstances, especially when the victim doesn't know the detective will return for later interviews. If the robbery is real, the information will remain consistent, and a real victim may provide additional leads later. Certain information cannot change if it's accurate. For example, if a victim first says the perpetrator was bald and later describes his short brown hair, a detective can reliably assume that no robbery occurred.

Armed robbery can be difficult to investigate for other reasons, too. A robbery can involve intricate planning or be carried out as a spur-of-the-moment whim. In either event, a perpetrator is usually difficult to identify. Most robberies happen at night or under conditions where the robber's features are hard to distinguish. Often, a mask or disguise increases the difficulty of identification and creates significant problems in prosecution efforts even when the perpetrator becomes known. In situations where a robber directly confronts the victim, the emotional state created often intimidates the victim enough to prevent her from furnishing a detailed description.

The technique for theft investigation and many techniques for assault investigation are applicable to the investigation of robbery because elements of both offenses are lesser included offenses in the act of robbery. Normally, victims of a robbery will report it to the police soon after it happens. Law enforcement officers and investigators must respond immediately, because the possibility of finding the offender is often directly related to the length of time taken to begin and follow through with an investigation. Failure to identify a perpetrator immediately after a robbery reduces the probability of a successful prosecution.

Assault

Law enforcement officers deal regularly with assault. Each state has a statute addressing assaults. To help understand this crime and its relationship to the others in this chapter, a quick review of key court decisions and the model penal code follows. Although some statutes define assault with a deadly weapon as aggravated assault, the following information supplies a general overview of the various criminal aspects involved in these crimes and how police detectives investigate them.

- **Assault:** "Any willful attempt or threat to inflict injury upon the person of another, when coupled with an apparent present ability so to do, and any intentional display of force such as would give the victim reason to fear or expect immediate bodily harm, is an assault. An assault may be committed without touching or striking, or doing bodily harm, to the person of another." (*State v. Murphy*, 7 Wash. App. 505, 500 P.wd 1276, 1281)
- "Often used to describe illegal force which is technically a battery. For the crime of assault, victims need not be apprehensive of fear if the outward gesture is menacing and defendant intends to harm, though for tort of assault, element of victim's apprehension is called for." (*People v. Lopez*, 271 C.A. 2d 754. 77 Cal. Rptr. 59, 63)
- **Aggravated Assault:** "A person is guilty of aggravated assault if he: (a) attempts to cause serious bodily injury to another, or causes such injury purposely, knowingly or recklessly under circumstances manifesting extreme indifference to the value of human life; or (b) negligently causes bodily injury to another with a deadly weapon; or (c) attempts by physical menace to put another in fear of imminent serious bodily injury." (Model Penal Code, 211.1)
- **Assault With a Deadly and Dangerous Weapon:** "An unlawful attempt or offer to do bodily harm without justification or excuse by use of any instrument calculated to do harm or cause death. An aggravated form of assault as distinguished from a simple assault, e.g., pointing a loaded gun at one is an assault with a dangerous weapon." (*State v. Gregory*, 108 Ariz. 445, 501 P. 2d 387, 390)

Generally, the crime of assault with a deadly weapon or other means of force (such as a hammer) requires that the weapon used will probably produce death or grievous bodily harm. It is unnecessary, however, that death or grievous bodily harm be inflicted. Almost any instrument or object can be considered deadly or dangerous. Courts have held that items such as a bottle, beer glass, rock and a piece of pipe could probably inflict death or grievous bodily harm. However, it's held that an unloaded pistol, when presented as a firearm and not as a bludgeon, is not a dangerous weapon or means of force able to produce grievous bodily harm, and this would be so whether the assailant knew it was unloaded or not. This is an important consideration during investigation of this crime. The underlying key element of proof is that the person responsible must be capable of committing the crime. In other words, if he threatens with a gun, it must be loaded. Or, for example, if a person threatens another with a large knife, if the assailant is on crutches and cannot walk without them, and if the victim remains capable of moving about or escaping and is not trapped in any way, the knife is probably not considered a deadly weapon because the capability of using it for assault is absent.

Assault Investigation Checklist
This checklist spans the entire spectrum of assault. Assault with a deadly weapon is usually the most serious form. Other lesser assault offenses are probably applicable when the police detective cannot prove the more serious offense.

Substantiate the Allegation. Upon receipt of information alleging an assault happened, first establish that the offense did happen. Detectives normally do that by questioning the victim, an attending physician and any available witnesses.

Question the Victim. Usually, police procedure calls for questioning the victim at least twice. Color photographs of the victim (with his permission) offer a true picture record of injuries. Another set of photos taken about three days later will often show the full effects of the injuries.

During early questioning, besides establishing the probability that an offense happened, the detective tries to determine the type of weapon used, if any, and whether the victim knows or suspects the identity and motive of the assailant.

The detective's first questioning is brief, particularly when a victim is seriously injured or if questioning delays the search of the crime scene. When a physician believes the victim may die from the injuries, the detective must quickly obtain as much information from the victim as possible. A skilled detective will use a tape recorder to record any dying statements or declarations.

After a search of the crime scene, subsequent interviews may provide investigative leads. Most assaults stem from clear motives. The detective's discovery of a person with a motive and the opportunity and capability to commit the assault may lead to the possible identification of the assailant. Detectives also know victims may have a reason for withholding the truth about the assault, especially when they claim to know the assailant or any reason for it to have happened. For example, a man assaulted by the husband of a woman with whom he is involved may deny any knowledge of why the assault happened and may conceal the identity of the assailant. Also, detectives understand that a victim may not know why the assault happened. In seeking investigative leads, a detective considers the possibility that the assailant made a mistake in identity or the victim unintentionally or unknowingly interrupted some unlawful act of the assailant.

Search the Crime Scene. Detectives search the crime scene for evidence as soon after the incident as feasible. The search may often begin while the victim is still on the scene in cases where no immediate medical treatment is necessary. The crime scene search and collection of evidence will often make use of a well-planned field investigation kit selected from those items shown in chapter two. The detective gives special attention to objects, footprints, fingerprints, scuff marks and other traces that show activity or presence of persons at the scene. A commonplace item such as a button or piece of thread found at the scene may be of evidentiary value and provide a lead to the identity of the assailant. Detectives always look for physical objects that might have served as a weapon. If the victim was not present during the search, detectives usually revisit the scene with the victim after their initial crime scene search. This technique provides a better understanding of how the assault happened and may lead to the discovery of additional evidence and valuable leads.

Question Witnesses. Police detectives promptly find and question available witnesses to the assault. There is no legal requirement to caution witnesses of their rights. However, if, during the interview of a person a police detective considers a witness, that person says something that may make her a suspect, a prudent investigator stops the interview and informs her of her rights immediately. Although the Miranda decision (interpreting the constitutional Fifth Amendment rights by the U.S.

Supreme Court) calls for rights to be explained to an "arrested person" or "person in custody," a prudent detective who wants to win in court will discuss the rights with suspects not yet arrested.

When detectives question a suspect not under arrest or otherwise in custody, the suspect's rights, although based on the Fifth Amendment, become a "noncustodial" caution. For example, until a suspect is taken into custody, the government has no obligation to provide an attorney. Before arrest a suspect can leave at any time and refuse to answer questions or cooperate with the detective. Police detectives always keep the following points in mind:

- Be aware that witnesses may be reluctant to answer direct questions because they fear they may have to appear in court, or because the assailant is a friend or acquaintance, or from fear of the assailant retaliating against them.
- Develop all information about any unusual activity in the area by questioning persons living, working or near the scene about the identity of the persons who were seen or believed to have been in the area.

Question Suspects. Detectives seek answers to the following questions when questioning suspects:

- Did the suspect have a motive, opportunity and capability to commit the assault?
- Was the suspect near the crime scene before the assault?
- Does the suspect own or have access to the type of weapon used in the assault (if known)?
- Can the physical evidence found at the scene be linked to the suspect?
- Does the suspect have a sound alibi?

Get Background Information. When a police detective's investigative effort does not identify the assailant, she often checks the victim's background, associates and activities; she reviews law enforcement and other records to determine the victim's involvement in any previous incidents; she questions relatives, fellow employees, neighbors and associates. Information from these sources may show the victim has a motive for withholding information.

Often, the detective must confer with the victim's attending physician to determine if the injuries sustained could have happened by the

circumstances the victim claims. The detective wants to know the estimated age of the injuries and any related information that might show
if the victim gave police an accurate account of the assault.

The physician responsible for the care of the victim may help the
detective determine the type of weapon used to create the injury, the
approximate time it happened and the incapacity of the victim because
of alcohol, drugs or physical disabilities that might affect the victim's
accurate recall of the circumstances.

Chapter Eleven

The Con

by Fay Faron

from *Rip-Off: A Writer's Guide to Crimes of Deception*

"If it looks like a duck and quacks like a duck, it's a duck."
—Old Law Enforcement Saying

When I was a little girl, I had the notion that the entire world centered on me, a concept I still, on occasion, attempt to promote. In this fantasy, I'd determined that Earth was created solely for my benefit and that streets, houses and amusement parks were merely sets that someone went along and assembled before I arrived and tore down as I passed. Every mirror was a camera where my fellow man watched my every move, so amusing was I. These videos were then televised continually, much like the soap operas my grandma watched. The sleeping episodes, I'm sure, must have been particularly entertaining.

This theory evaporated in time, and eventually I was able to go to the bathroom without throwing a towel over the mirror. My mother in particular assured me such things just don't happen. During the middle of a hissy fit, as I recall.

Or do they?

Unbelievably, my little narcissistic world is just the sort of fantasyland created during the perpetration of a good con game. Whether the set is actually fabricated or the confellow's glibness sets the tone, the result is an altered reality in which the mark feels free to fall in with a new set of rules that he might otherwise question.

We see "legitimate" examples of this sort of sales every day. In multi-level marketing seminars, enthusiastic recruits often find themselves purchasing gallons of dishwashing detergent, convinced their neighbors will not only want to take it off their hands but anxiously join the soap crusade, as well, while across town, otherwise astute investors acquire time-share properties sight unseen and without comparing land values.

Much of what passes for business deals, telephone solicitations and mail-order offers are actually scams, carefully worded to stay just inside the law, proclaiming much but promising nothing. But in all cons, this altered reality exists, and everyone but the mark is in on the gag. Rarely does the pigeon consider the scenario was created solely for him. And why should he? Everybody knows that kind of paranoia can land you in the loony bin.

Why Should a Writer Care About Confidence Schemes?

OK, so say your thing is murder, and the genre demands a body on the floor, not a pigeon left holding a *mish roll*, that real-looking stack of phony ones. So why am I bothering you with all this? Well, because

1. Killers don't just drive over to the gun shop straight from delivering turkeys to the poor. Nope, they had a long life of dirty tricks where they've been honing their sociopathic skills with things like pigeon drops, boiler-room antics and insurance fraud.
2. A good story often demands that the perp fool the reader, which means he needs to be, almost by definition, a good con man.
3. Novels are not about folks who arbitrarily "go postal" for no good reason, but about people with motives. And what better motive than being betrayed?

Who Falls for Scams?

Quite simply, all of us fall for scams. Because as long as there is a lottery, we the people of the United States must believe in getting something for nothing. It's the law. And why shouldn't we? Because not to believe is simply not an option for anyone worth his weight in denial.

And so those who dream of stardom are especially susceptible to glamour scams. And those who fancy themselves entrepreners are tempted by biz-op schemes. And even the single welfare mom, who you might think has nothing to lose, has been known to invest $100 in a chain letter.

The Big Con and the Short Con

There are basically two kinds of cons, and they are defined not so much by a time limit but by whether the victim is left alone or not or is taken for the money that he is carrying rather than sent to the bank for more.

If you intend to write about cons, it's likely your story will center on one long con with a bunch of shorties as setup. Most any short con in this book can be elongated and its components exaggerated to give it the depth and breadth necessary to turn it into a big con.

The Big Con

In the far-fetched tale of trickery, *The Sting*, Robert Redford and Paul Newman effected a big con, so defined not just because it took several days to execute, but due to the extensive fictional setup necessary for its execution. Such elaborate schemes seldom happen in today's world, but our agency witnesses big cons every day, primarily in the form of sweetheart scams. These elderly victims are fleeced for years, their assets systematically drained and their hearts resoundly broken. More often than not, the con ends only when the victim has nothing left to give.

The Short Con

Most modern schemes are deemed short cons. The old quick in-and-out is the crime of choice because
- It's simpler to pull off.
- There's less chance of getting caught.
- The victim can seldom identify the perp.
- There's less time invested should the project fail.
- It doesn't take a whiz kid to do it.

Why the Con?

Our client was considering hiring a consultant who promised to peddle their undervalued stocks to eager offshore investors. His fee was 20 percent, plus a $2,500 retainer. Our client's request was simple: Was "Jerry Lane" legit?

In short order, we discovered: Lane's address was a mail drop, and his phone was issued under another name. His references were all phony, and the companies they worked for didn't exist either. Under a list of aliases, Lane had a long list of unsatisfied clients who all reported the same thing; once the retainer was paid, Lane's job was over.

In addition, we learned the Vancouver Stock Exchange had issued a general fraud warning regarding Lane, and the Royal Canadian Mounted Police were interested in his whereabouts, as well. Suddenly our fax lines were clogged with documentation from Lane's past customers and present detractors.

One such client said Lane became abusive when he'd declined to invest. "We received your call," Lane scrawled in a note. "Since you're not faxing us back a signed agreement or paying us a retainer, you are not serious—" To someone else, he wrote, "Thank you for your letter. I'm afraid we don't understand it, however. What is the problem with our proposal?" Even as we were compiling our report, Lane continued to harass our client to send off his up-front retainer. Often and obscenely.

Obviously, our client passed, but with his permission we alerted the local FBI. The San Francisco bureau shuttled the case to Marin County, who tossed it back again. Both police forces passed, as well, declaring it a civil dispute and a small-claims one, at that. Our argument that hundreds, perhaps thousands of folks had been swindled nationwide, as well as in Canada, fell on deaf ears.

Then one cop mentioned that Jerry Lane had received some press under another aka, his true name. Given that, we accessed Lexis-Nexis's extensive news file again, this time with better luck. "Stop Me Before I Steal Again," read the headline from a 1995 magazine article.

The article quoted Jerry Lane as admitting he had conned millions of dollars from hundreds of companies over the last decade. Unable to live with his compulsion to swindle any longer, he wanted to make a clean slate of it all—with the media, with authorities, with his victims. The mag itself declared that Lane stole "nothing to yelp about," and the scheme was "not particularly clever." In a press release to the magazine and others, Lane readily acknowledged what we already knew. That via telephone, mail and fax, he promised to bring eager, deep-pocketed investors to his clients' doorsteps, yet after receiving their up-front money, he simply did nothing. He'd fax his marks phony references and fake investors he claimed to represent. If victims checked his references, they'd reach Lane via a forwarded phone.

Claiming he decided to come clean after his young son heard him using a phony name, Lane now wanted to turn himself in—and, oh yeah, sell his story to Hollywood. He proceeded to fire off a host of press releases, figuring this would lead to well-paying talk show gigs. Then, of course, there was his book (mostly written) and screenplay (already optioned) both waiting in the wings.

Trouble was, Lane found, as we had, that he couldn't get himself arrested. And further, that an inconsequential con is basically a man without a book deal. In the end, when there proved no percentage in going straight, Lane simply went back to what he did best—perpetrating his creatively challenged scams.

A funny story. Except, of course, that Lane's victims were very real; their numbers were growing, and no law enforcement entity was the least bit interested—even after the self-proclaimed culprit had not only confessed but practically presented himself jailside, carrying the evidence in his own hip pocket.

Criminal vs. Civil Charges

OK, say your character has invested in a doughnut franchise across the street from a police station, figuring no way can he lose. The former owner tells him the cops come by daily, but doesn't mention it's because drug dealers inhabit the back booth. Your fellah gets robbed twice, and when the cops come to raid the joint, all the decent doughnut eaters beat feet.

So what is this? A mugging?

Nope. No violence.

A con?

Yep. Well, maybe not so much. Did the owner willfully, maliciously lure your character into this bad business deal or was it just a case of let the buyer beware?

Yeah? Think so?

OK, that makes it civil. So your guy sues. For fraud, since the former owner neglected to disclose the presence of drug dealers, nor did the Food and Drug Administration (FDA) designate doughnuts as their own food group as he'd intimated they would. But since fraud is by its very nature a criminal act, then why is it even possible to sue civilly for fraud, as well as embezzlement?

In the end, after many frustrating years in this work, I've decided that whether a con is considered a civil or a criminal matter has less to do with malicious intent than with the size of the district attorney's workload and his budget. No matter what the elements, take away the violence and most DAs will encourage the victim to go *civil*, as in *go away*. Why? Because they already have ten times more cases than they can handle, and this one, simply put, has not been chosen.

Determining Factors

So if a con can go either civil or criminal, what are a DA's deciding factors?

Caseload. A bad-check charge might not get a mention in *The New York Times*, but in Peculiar, Missouri, it's undoubtedly fodder for a six-week jury trial.

Dollar Amount. Most DAs have a dollar cutoff. San Francisco's, I think, is $150,000. Anything under that, and the perp skates. Think they know that? You betcha.

Number of Victims. Now, normally nobody's going to track down the perp of a $20 shortchange, but if a school of elderly people keeps getting ripped off, it just might behoove the DA (especially around election time) to close down that bingo parlor.

Evidence. Remember O.J. Simpson? Discussions as to why he was deemed "guilty" in the civil trial and "not guilty" in the criminal trial will continue long after Sydney and Justin publish *their* books, but pundits agree the defining factor was the obtainable goal of "preponderance of evidence" versus the sly "guilt beyond a reasonable doubt." Since nobody thus far has explained the latter so that anyone with an IQ under 180 can understand it, a criminal conviction in America remains as elusive as product endorsement contracts for the aforementioned Simpson.

Bottom line: When the DA does not have the evidence, he simply passes on the case. Which is why you always hear them bragging about winning every case they ever prosecuted.

The Victim. Many DAs won't take sweetheart cons, for example, since it's unlikely the jury will feel sufficiently sorry for a sixty-year-old woman who was silly enough to consider that a twenty-seven-year-old Antonio Banderas look-alike really thought she was swell. Who's to say it wasn't a mutual exchange of love for money? Perhaps she's just angry that he's now moved on. OK, he used her yacht to move in, but still.

Media Attention. DAs turn down cases every day for nasty schemes that wipe out people's life savings, rob them of their dignity and future security and leave them unsure of their own decision-making capabilities. Most times this goes down quietly, and only the victim and his friends know there'll be no justice. But then along comes a fat juicy news story, and suddenly the DA makes a giant leap into the pool of human kindness. Actually, prosecuting authorities cannot *not* be interested in the light of even the slightest media attention. What are they to say to their constituents? "Yeah, awful thing, old Doc Miller's falling for a pigeon drop, but 'scuse me, we're a little busy getting reelected around here—"

Chapter Twelve

Elements of the Con

by Fay Faron

from *Rip-Off: A Writer's Guide to Crimes of Deception*

"All good stories must have a beginning, a middle and an end."
—My high school English teacher

I f you think of a con as a play, which it is, it's easy to see how the confellow and victim are both "actors," although the latter, of course, is completely unaware of his role in the improv. In the detective agency, we use this concept all the time. Our "con" is called the *pretext call*, and its purpose is to elicit information, usually by phone, that will allow us to continue our investigation. Using our powers for good and not for evil, the usual scenario is to confirm someone's location. The gag must be carefully thought out: If I say this, and they say that, then what do I say?

One common ploy is to ask, "Is Stephi there?" when looking for a Stephanie Burke. With a wrong number, the return volley is almost always, "Sorry, fellah, wrong number." But if we've reached the right party, most scoundrels cleverly inquire, "Stephi? Uh, um . . . who wants to know?" At that point, it's easy to back out of the conversation with, "I'm sorry, is this the Capwell residence?" leaving no one the wiser. Had the pretext not been carefully thought out, and instead the initial question was, "Is Stephanie Burke there?" then it would have been necessary to tell Stephanie why we wanted to talk to her, perhaps blowing the entire investigation.

One inexperienced investigator tried a pretext call on *our* office, and when he didn't get the desired response (to elicit our physical address), his only rebuttal was, "Well, then, you can just die—" That, in my opinion, was not a well thought-out pretext call.

Now, like all good works of art, this "play" demands a beginning, middle and end. So the confellow carefully plots his script, taking into account that he does not have total control over the other actor and allowing for contingencies. The happy ending he seeks, of course, is the successful transference of the victim's assets into his own.

The Pigeon Drop: A Three-Act Play

ACT ONE

Late afternoon. Supermarket parking lot.
MOOCH, an old man, shuffles along, carrying his bag of oranges. CON
approaches, offers to tote his heavy load and makes small talk as they progress
toward MOOCH'S car.

CON
Hey, look—Somebody dropped their wallet—

MOOCH
We should turn it in to the supermarket office.

CON
Let's see if there's identification. . . . *(CON opens the wallet.*
Close-up of a wad of bills that would choke a dalmatian. He flips
through and finds at least a hundred $20 bills.) There's no ID—

MOOCH
Well, the person who lost it will surely go back to the supermarket and ask.

BYSTANDER
(Approaching.) Hey, what's hanging?

CON
We found this money and don't know who it belongs to.

BYSTANDER
Let me see that. *(He takes the money from CON and examines*
it.) Why, I'll bet this is drug money!

MOOCH
Why do you say that?

BYSTANDER
Look at all this cash! Nobody but drug dealers carry this much
cash!

CON
Drug dealers won't go back to a grocery store and ask about
their stash!

BYSTANDER
And even if they did, they don't deserve this money.
It's ill-gotten gains!

MOOCH
So what do we do?

CON
I say we split it between the three of us!

MOOCH
Is that legal?

BYSTANDER
Well, friend, as it turns out, I'm an attorney, so I know about
these things. The law says we must place the money in a safe-
deposit box for three months. If nobody shows up by then, we
can legally split the money!

MOOCH
How can we be sure one of us won't just steal it?

BYSTANDER
Do you have a safe-deposit box?

MOOCH
Yes, I do.

BYSTANDER
Well then, that's where we'll keep it! We trust you. But for all
our safety in this matter, we should all put up some kind of
good-faith bond—say, $150 each—to make sure none of us
steals the money.

MOOCH
(*Eyeing the loot.*) That sounds fair.

BYSTANDER
Do you have that much on you?

MOOCH
No, I don't, but I can get it.

CON
(*Pointing.*) There's an ATM right over there!

BYSTANDER
Let's go!

ACT TWO
The ATM a few minutes later.
MOOCH withdraws $300 (the limit) while CON and BYSTANDER busy
themselves behind him. MOOCH gives CON and BYSTANDER $150 each,
and they hand over the wallet. All exchange good-byes and promise to meet
back in three months.

ACT THREE
Inside the bank, the next day.
MOOCH opens his safe-deposit box and counts the money. The outside bill's
a twenty, but inside it's just cut-up newspaper. Close-up of MOOCH's sad
face.

Fade to black.

THE END

Seven Ingredients of a Con

So why does this classic still work almost six hundred years after its inception? Specifically, because it contains all seven ingredients necessary in a successful sting.

1. Too good to be true. Free money for doing nothing. What's not to like?
2. Nothing to lose. The old man thought he was holding the loot, so he felt in control.
3. Out of his element. This hasn't happened to Mooch before, so he knows no protocol and defers to the others' expertise.
4. Limited-time offer. Some decision has to be made by the time the three part company. There's no opportunity to consult family or friends.
5. References. Bystander appears as a rational third voice who just happens along. As a bonus, he's also a "legal expert."
6. Pack mentality. Both Con and Bystander seem in agreement on a viable course of action. Even if dubious, who is Mooch to disagree?
7. No consequences to actions. Since this is "drug money," nobody will report it missing and they certainly can't be accused of stealing it.

Insuring the ''Happy'' Ending

And so Con and Bystander just made three hundred dollars between them for ten minutes of blah-blah in a parking lot. Altogether a better living than mugging, you'd have to agree.

Will the old man report this incident to police? Not likely, since

1. To do so would be to admit he planned to keep drug money, which any honest citizen knows should have been reported to the authorities. Mooch might even be named an accomplice, thereby initiating his own criminal record at age eighty-nine. (Or so he thinks.) Furthermore, he'll undoubtedly be on probation until he's ninety-three.
2. Mooch can't identify the suspects and can't even report their names. So, even if the cops don't arrest him, they'll probably just ridicule him and he won't get his money back anyway.
3. If his family finds out how stupid he is, they'll undoubtedly put him in an old folks' home.

Anatomy of a Con

Just as successful sales techniques can be analyzed and learned, so can the components of a con. Since this is, after all, still just a transaction between two parties, the subtleties of those dynamics often determine the success of the entire exchange.

The Motivation
It can be the lure of getting rich quick, a willingness to lend a helping hand or even help in catching a thief. Whether the incentive is money, peace of mind or a warm fuzzy feeling, there simply has to be something in it for the victim or he just won't play. The incentive for Mooch, of course, was the money.

The Come-On
This is where the confellow encourages whatever the victim's incentive happens to be, assuring him there'll be no negative repercussions for his actions. He might flash some phony credentials or simply override objections with the sheer force of his personality. Here the come-on was declaring the cash "drug money," thereby insinuating nobody was ever going to claim it.

The Shill
Seemingly a stranger, this third party reinforces the victim's participation. In this case, Bystander be thy name.

The Swap
Out with the genuine, in with the gyp. Most often the switch is made during a diversionary tactic, in this instance while Mooch was busying himself at the automatic teller.

The Stress
To work, this now-or-never proposition must always be completed before someone with judgment happens by. Usually it is presented as a limited-time, one-time offer, or they might insist another taker is waiting in the wings. Here the very setting, a parking lot, demanded the deal be completed within a short span of time. Traditionally nobody spends much time in a parking lot.

The Block
The victim must be dissuaded from reporting the con to the coppers. Usually shame, embarrassment, fear, culpability or a combination of these concerns does the trick. Mooch, of course, was concerned that his advanced age would render him a candidate for the old folks' home.

The Emphasis

Since the purpose of a con is to get something from someone who wouldn't give it up if they knew everything, the con artist relies largely on smoke and mirrors to work his magic. For examples of this, we've only to explore much of the copywriting that lands, magically, in our mailboxes every day. Now, I'm not suggesting all mail-order offers are frauds, but since both cons and sales depend on persuading someone to part with their dough, sales and cons contain many common elements.

FAY FARON
IS GUARANTEED TO BE PAID THE NEW
$1,000,000.00
PRIZE—

What's not to like? A check is enclosed, and it's got my name right on it. They tell me a financial officer is standing by to help me invest my impending fortune so I will never again have to listen to some sorry pigeon relate how she spent $5,000 for tar that fell like rain from her roof. And all because I am the luckiest, most special person in the world, I know, deep down, I've only to go to my mailbox to have good things happen to me.

But wait. What's this small print right above it?

...if you have won, and return the winning number by the deadline, we'll officially announce that

FAY FARON
IS GUARANTEED TO BE PAID THE NEW
$1,000,000.00
PRIZE—

And this other stuff underneath?

> Odds of winning at a random drawing are determined by total number of eligible entries received. Distribution of printed forms is estimated not to exceed 120,000,000.

A truer representation might have read,

> THINK YOU,
>
> # FAY FARON,
>
> HAVE A SHOT OF WINNING
> THIS MILLION $ PRIZE?
>
> # THINK AGAIN
>
> —SINCE YOUR ODDS ARE ONE IN 120 MILLION, WHY
> EVEN BOTHER LICKING ALL THESE STAMPS?

Now that's clear! Instead, this copywriter chose to announce the odds in pint-size print and even changed the form of the numbers so that the $1,000,000.00 prize ($1 million) looked bigger and the 120,000,000 (no decimal point) looked less overwhelming.

It's called emphasis. Call attention to the bounty and downplay the reality. It's what a con is all about: Show the prize, describe the prize, discuss delivery of the prize and then mention in teensy tiny letters that the pigeon's chances of actually winning the prize are one in, roughly, none.

PART III

HARDWARE

Chapter Thirteen

Crime Tools Guide

by John Boertlein

Anything can be used as a tool in the commission of a crime. A human voice utters a robbery demand. The end of a knitting needle can be used to pry into closed car windows, hit the latch and open the door. A computer hacker fraudulently obtains someone else's password for Internet access and e-mails thousands of pornographic ads to others on the net. Guns, knives, bombs, tools and gimmicks—anything can be used. In this chapter, we'll discuss at some of the things you need to know when writing about crime issues or solving a case.

First, let's look at some of the most popular crime tools along with a few twists and variations. Then we'll go into what every writer should know about confronting a crime scene or using the tools of a crime as evidence.

Guns

When somebody hears a term like "crime tools," guns are probably the first things that come to mind. Why? Because they were originally invented for one reason: to kill people. You can bring self-defense, hunting or target shooting into the argument, but the bottom line is that guns are designed for homicide.

Handguns are the source of most of the gun controversies. It's difficult to justify the number available simply for their use in hunting or the widely popular sport of target shooting. Rifles, shotguns and any other types of firearms are also part of the gun controversies.

Political and moral debates aside, there are significant differences in the types and functions of firearms. You need to be aware of these differences when describing how a gun looks, how it's used and what its limitations or capabilities are. Let's take a "Guns 101" look at what might interest writers.

The following descriptions appear in "Anatomy of Firearms," a helpful page on the Web site for The Internet Pathology Laboratory for Medical Education (http://medstat.med.utah.edu/WebPath/webpath .html MENU). The information will help you write about circumstances involving firearms.

Revolvers
From "Anatomy of Firearms:"

The revolver has several advantages and unique features. Importantly, they are less expensive, simpler in design and more reliable than semiautomatics. A revolver is easy to master, even for novices. Revolvers, for whatever reason, seem to be more accurate than semiautomatics. On the negative side, revolvers are limited to six shots, are relatively slow to reload, have a gap between the barrel and cylinder that makes them less efficient and have a greater trigger pull.

Barrel length is smaller for concealability and longer for accuracy or energy. The ejector rod under the barrel is used to eject fired cartridges before reloading. Sights on a revolver are usually a blade in the front and a notch on the rear. The frame is the largest part, and all other pieces attach to it. Frames are

Simplicity, availability and reliability make the revolver one of the criminal's favorite tools.

Bullets are inserted into the revolver's cylinder, which then rotates when the trigger is pulled.

usually made of blued or plated steel, stainless steel or lightweight alloys.

A revolver may weigh less than one pound to more than four pounds. The cylinder contains five or six holes for the cartridges and can be swung out for easy reloading. This must be a conscious act, so that no empty cartridge cases will be found at a crime scene unless the assailant stopped to reload.

Semiautomatic Pistol

From "Anatomy of Firearms:"

This is a more recent development than the revolver, originating late in the nineteenth century. The advantage of semiautomatics is the use of the recoil generated by the fired cartridge to eject the empty cartridge case, load the next cartridge and cock the hammer. This is more conducive to firing multiple shots, so many are designed to carry fifteen to nineteen rounds. Disadvantages include a more complicated mechanism, they require more practice to use and the cartridge cases must be short to work well. Revolver cartridges are more powerful than semiautomatic cartridges for this last reason.

Even on open ground, ejected cases may be difficult to find, as they typically roll into hiding places such as grass or small depressions in the ground. Thus, ejected cases are usually left behind at the scene and must be searched for diligently.

The semiautomatic pistol has a complicated mechanism but offers up to three times the available ammunition before reloading becomes necessary.

Semiautomatic pistols actually eject spent cartridges through the port, shown here with the slide locked open. The accompanying magazine is replaced to reload the weapon.

Rifles
From "Anatomy of Firearms:"

Rifles differ from handguns in the length of the barrel and the presence of a buttstock. They are harder to carry, poorly concealable and more loosely regulated than handguns. However, they are much more accurate and shoot more powerful cartridges than handguns. Rifles may be manufactured as single shot, but most commonly are bolt action, which is used for large caliber hunting rifles. Military rifles are semiautomatic or automatic and have a detachable magazine holding five to fifty rounds. Pump action and lever action rifles, usually of lower caliber, have magazines below the barrel.

A semiautomatic rifle offers the speed and convenience of clip loading along with long barrel accuracy.

Shotguns
From "Anatomy of Firearms:"

Shotguns have a similar external appearance to rifles, but differ in the lack of rifling inside the barrel, which is the basis

The break action shotgun opens to load a single shell between shots.

The double barrel shotgun functions in a "break action," too, but offers two shots between loading.

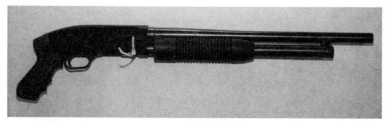

The pump action shotgun holds shells in a tube below the barrel. Reloading requires the user to "pump" the handle, which ejects the spent shell and reloads the shotgun.

This shotgun is semiautomatic, meaning it's reloaded on the same principle as the semiautomatic rifle or pistol.

for their legal definition. A shotgun shell may contain one large projectile (called a slug), a few pellets of large shot or many tiny pellets. Shotguns are available in single shot (break action), double barrel, pump action and semiautomatic.

The types of guns used for illegitimate purposes in the United States every year are countless. A 1998 FBI survey showed that in 1998, 670,500 victims of serious violent crime (rape/sexual assault, robbery and aggravated assault) faced an offender with a firearm. Additionally, 65 percent of the 16,914 murders in 1998 were committed with firearms. In your writing, you

It looks like a sawed-off rifle, but it's really a pump BB gun.

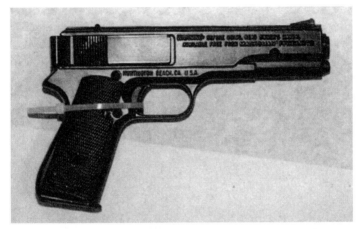

This spring-action BB gun could pass as a "fooler" for victims or law enforcement alike.

may want to consider several firearms tests available to crime investigators:

- Comparison: Matches bullets, cartridge cases and shot-shells to the weapon that fired them.
- Prediction: Determines the caliber and probable manufacturer of a fired bullet. Also predicts the type and brand or brands of weapons it may have been fired from.
- Function Check: Determines if a weapon is capable of firing or accidentally discharging or if the weapon can be restored to firing condition for test-firing.
- Distance Determination: Determines the presence or absence of gunshot deposits around a hole in clothing and the range of fire producing the deposits.

This BB gun operates using gas provided by the CO_2 cartridge you see inserted into its handle.

Cheap, easy to use and often deadly, the "Saturday Night Special" is readily available on the street. Shown here are examples of a semiautomatic and revolver.

- Toolmark: Identifies the tool that produced the toolmarks.
- Serial Number Restoration: Restores stamped serial numbers in metal or plastic items.

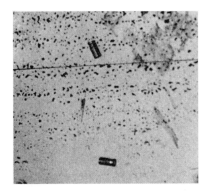

These spent cartridges were ejected from a pistol used to shoot a convenience store clerk. They are valuable evidence to tie the suspect to the scene of the crime.

Here's an example of an obliterated serial number on a pistol. The number was restored by criminalists using a chemical process.

- Open Check: Compares submitted firearms, bullets or cartridge cases to evidence in an unsolved shooting file.

Common Weapons of Assault
Knives/Edged Weapons

For the purpose of discussing knives, we'll include any sharp object that requires physical force to use it as a weapon. We'll concentrate on items someone would *personally* attack with, or up close edged weapons. Swords, hatchets, ice picks and machete-type objects certainly apply, but the street cop usually encounters variations of knives and sharp pointed objects on a more regular basis.

The most difficult part of dealing with an edged object as a weapon is the perpetrator's willingness to get close to his victim. Violence be-

A variety of knives.

comes more personal when bone cracks, blood spatters and vomit and spit go everywhere. Unlike the perpetrator who shoots from across the room or any other distance, knife fights are different, more intimate. You can use the intimacy involved in these types of fights in your work. The possibilities to produce drama in these situations are endless.

I experienced a knife attack as a uniformed officer on foot patrol at an outdoor shopping plaza near the University of Cincinnati. There were only three weeks until Christmas and the weather had grown increasingly colder. As I watched a couple of workers string red and green lights around lampposts, the only thought on my mind was to end the workday and meet my girlfriend for dinner and a visit to the holiday display at the Cincinnati Zoo.

I heard some loud commotion coming from in front of a supermarket that was around the corner, and my daydream ended. As I approached, I noticed a crowd of twenty or thirty people watching a huge man in a blue and gray flannel shirt crawl aimlessly around the pavement. Getting closer, I recognized the guy as a police officer. His face was purplish-blue and he was gasping for breath. Heart attack was the first thing to cross my mind as I rushed forward to help. I knelt down next to him. He was semiconscious and struggling to get to his feet.

A lady's voice in the crowd yelled, "He did it," and I turned around to see a huge man pull a knife from his back pocket. The man lunged forward from about five feet away and, in two quick motions, slashed me across the forehead and stabbed me in the right cheek. After the stabbing, my assailant continued to push at me until I lost my footing and we both fell to the ground. The guy was now on top of me and I was

It takes a distance of twenty-one feet for a cop to recognize a knife threat and react in a defensive manner. Here we see a bad guy at a distance of five feet and the necessary twenty-one feet.

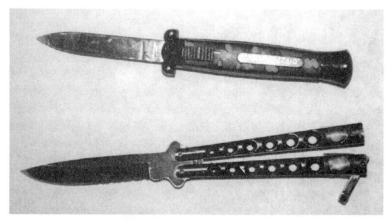

Here are two easily accessible, deadly knives commonly seen on the street. The switchblade opens with a simple push of a button and the butterfly knife requires only a flick of the wrist to be ready to use.

blinded by blood running into my eyes. There wasn't any pain, only the salty, bitter taste of blood from the stab wounds. I tried to pull my pistol from its holster, but my opponent apparently knew my intention and jammed the knife into my right elbow.

A couple of brave bystanders distracted the bad guy with punches and kicks long enough for the plainclothes cop to regain his senses. (It turns out the fighter had hit him in the face with a knockout sucker punch.) The other cop came up on his knees, drew his handgun and literally shot the assailant off of me.

As you can see, an assault with an edged weapon can be very dramatic. Here are a couple of details you can use in your writing about edged weapon attacks:

- It's been determined that in order for a person to recognize a knife threat, draw her weapon and react, the assailant must be at least twenty-one feet away from the target. If you pace off twenty-one feet, you'll see that the target must be pretty far away to keep from being cut by an assailant in a knife encounter.
- There are essentially two ways of attacking with a knife:
  - Slashing—drawing the blade across a target area and cutting open the skin in a straight line or forcing the knife's point across the target area and cutting open the skin in a straight line or jagged fashion.

- Stabbing—Puncturing the skin with the knife's point and forcing the blade into the target area, which could damage bone, internal organs, arteries, etc.
- A cutting victim may not immediately feel any pain. If they die, they may never feel any pain. From a writer's perspective, don't assume that once a knife assault occurs, the fight is over.

Here's something different for a ladies' purse. It looks like lipstick, but a twist of the bottom produces a razor-sharp, two-sided knife.

Blunt Objects

Any number of items can be used as offensive (or defensive) weapons, such as billy clubs, baseball bats, ax handles, "asps" or clubs. Whatever type of blunt object is used in an assault, the target area is more important in determining the damage to the victim or the intent of the assailant. For instance, striking a blow to the head with a tire iron could prove fatal for the victim, striking the knee area could prove painful and cause the victim long-term damage and striking the thigh area could cause bruising but have little or no pain or lasting effects.

If you're writing about a blunt object assault situation, consider the "vital and vulnerable" striking areas as described by Monadnock, Inc. in their training program for police baton use. Each level escalates the potential trauma for the portion of the body receiving the blow.

- Minimal level of resultant trauma. Injury tends to be temporary rather than long-lasting; however, exceptions can occur:

- Shoulder
- Forearm
- Lower abdomen
- Thigh
- Shin
- Instep
- Shoulder blade
- Upper arm
- Inside of wrist
- Buttocks
- Calf
- Achilles tendon
- Moderate to serious level of resultant trauma. Injury tends to be more long-lasting, but may also be temporary:
  - Collarbone
  - Rib cage
  - Upper abdomen
  - Groin
  - Knee joint
  - Elbow joint
- High level of resultant trauma. Injury tends to range from serious to long-lasting and may include unconsciousness, serious bodily injury, shock or death:
  - Temple
  - Ears
  - Eyes
  - Bridge of the nose
  - Upper jaw
  - Lower jaw
  - Throat
  - Solar plexus
  - Hollow behind the ear
  - Back of the neck
  - Spine
  - Kidney
  - Tailbone

Your character may be skilled, angry or simply defending himself, but blows to the various areas mentioned here can have predictable results.

Tools of Property Crime

Burglary (or breaking into a premise) and theft offenses come to mind when we mention property crimes. In this section, we'll discuss police technique in matching whatever hardware your characters use to the scene of the crime. The list of items one could use to commit any crime is long, so it's important to use "trace evidence" whenever possible in solving crimes. Based on the age-old theory that "every criminal leaves something and takes something from a crime scene," here is a list of tests used to pinpoint the tool with the crime:

- Microscopic and chemical comparisons of paint from breaking and entering offenses
- Glass particle comparison
- Microscopic comparison and identification of human hairs
- Shoe print and tire track comparisons
- Wood identification and comparison
- Chemical comparisons of inks and dyes
- Soil and debris comparisons
- Physical comparisons (such as matching the ends of wires, broken-off knife tips or torn clothing)
- Microscopic examination of samples collected from persons to determine if they fired a handgun (Gunshot residue)
- Microscopic comparison and identification of fibers

Alarms

No discussion of burglary tools would be complete without mentioning alarm systems. This is not because an alarm is a criminal tool; rather, the criminals have to deal with alarms when perpetrating crimes. Alarm systems can be as sophisticated or simple as one desires. We'll look at four of the most popular systems to give you an idea of how they work. Once you understand how they operate, you can come up with methods to defeat the systems.

- **Contact alarms** work on a continuum principle. Simply put, think of a wire maintaining the energy flow. A break in the wire causes one end to lose power. It's the same with contact alarms. They're usually placed on doors, windows or ordinary access points, for example, one contact is placed on a door, the other on the doorjamb. One contains

The contact alarm works using a mercury switch activated by magnetic contact. It's effective on windows and doors.

a magnet, the other a mercury (liquid metal) switch. When the door is closed, the mercury switch activates because of the magnet, completing the circuit. When the door is opened, the circuit breaks and causes one end to lose power, which activates the alarm.

- **Temperature alarms** work via a thermometer. If the temperature of the alarmed area rises above or falls below the selected temperature, the alarm activates. These are often used as fire alarms.
- **Light beams** work on the continuum or "wire" principle mentioned above. An infrared light beam is transmitted from one source to another, creating a continuous "wire." When something or someone walks through or interrupts the beam, the circuit breaks and the alarm activates.

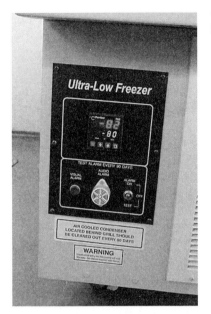

Temperature alarms work by monitoring changing environmental levels.

• **Motion detectors** operate using microwaves, infrared light or both. A source actually "reads" transmissions into an area. If the transmissions are interrupted by movement or change in temperature, the alarm activates.

A motion detector actually "reads" movement in a particular space, activating when the pattern is disturbed.

- **Local vs. Central alarms.** If you see these terms, it means the alarm either:
  - Activates on-site (local) usually with noise or flashing lights.
  - Activates at some other source (central) like an alarm company, police station or other alerting agency.

A combination of any of these alarms is often the most effective. I remember an incident several years ago when a young man broke into a local pharmacy. It was February and the temperature was well below zero. The guy spent most of the early morning hours clawing through the pharmacy's roof with a hammer, finally making a hole large enough to drop into. The motion detectors sensed his presence and set off an alarm at the central alarm company, which notified police dispatch, and my partner and I were sent to the scene.

When we arrived, the contacts were all in place and everything seemed secure. We were about to chalk it up as a false alarm when my partner fortuitously noticed a ceiling tile missing. At that point, we secured the building's perimeter, eventually catching the burglar when he tripped the contacts on the back door as he tried to get out. He'd managed to bypass the contact alarm by going through the roof, but he didn't make it past the motion detector set up behind the pharmacy counter. His only complaint: "Why in the hell didn't you guys catch me five hours ago before I froze my ass off on that roof?"

Automobiles

Cars can be used as getaway vehicles, as weapons to run someone over or as transports for illegal contraband. However, by and large, automobile crime involves theft, either of the car itself or the contents of the car. Your awareness of the items used in the theft of an auto, thefts from autos and the investigation of either will help when writing about the issues. Here are a couple points of interest.

Breaking Into Cars 101

There are the tried-and-true methods of breaking into a car, such as using coat hangers, baseball bats and large rocks, but here are some lesser known techniques:

- The "slim jim" or "lock jock" is a tool made from sheet metal that is machined to work a lock mechanism from inside a car door. The slim jim fits into the space between the car's window and the outside

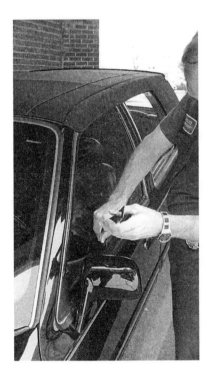

A "slim jim" is a thin piece of metal inserted into a car door, which manipulates the lock mechanism opening the door.

door panel. It has a hook to either pull or push the locking mechanism, unlocking the door. With a little practice, one can use the lock jock faster than a key.

- One of the newest ways to quickly, and relatively silently, shatter a car window is to break the ceramic section of a spark plug into little pieces. One small fragment flicked against auto glass does the trick.

Starting a Car (Without a Key)

Okay, you're in the car. Now how do you get it started? First, crack the steering column in the area of the ignition. (Most cops look here first on *any* vehicle they come into contact with because a broken column

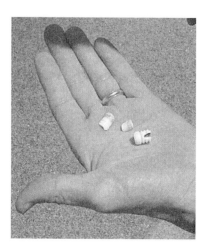

Small pieces of the ceramic part of a spark plug can be tossed against a car window to break the window in a quick, relatively quiet manner.

By cracking the steering column and pushing the ignition rod, even a novice criminal can start a car without a key.

usually equals a stolen car.) Next, locate the linkage rod, which should be located near the underside of the switch. Finally, push the linkage rod until you hear the ignition start and voila! You're driving!

Now it's all over except for a solution, providing your car didn't go to a chop shop (a place where stolen cars are dismantled and then sold in pieces) or your character didn't get caught inside the hot vehicle. Your best bet on the seemingly cold trail of an auto-related theft is fingerprints. The following is one law enforcement agency's standard outline for latent print examination of a vehicle.

- Record the exact time, date and location where the vehicle was found and the examination was conducted.
- Record the license number, VIN number, type, model, year and color of the car. (The VIN, vehicle identification number, is located on the front dash on the driver's side next to the windshield on cars made from 1968 to the present. Prior to 1968, the VIN number was located on a metal tag attached to the door frame.)
- Photograph the auto from both sides and from the front and rear,

making sure the license plates are visible in the photographs. Be alert to different plates being used on the front and back of the vehicle and newer bolts attaching older-appearing license plates (indicative of recently switched plates).

- Initially examine the door handles for latent prints. By "sidelighting" reflective surfaces with a strong light source, latent prints can be more readily located. After being photographed, latents may then be powdered and lifted.

- After the door handles have been examined, open all of the doors to the vehicle. Check the door frames for any service station stickers. They may provide a clue as to the owner of the auto or the locale where the auto was stolen.

- Photograph the interior of the auto. Take at least one photograph from each side. (This is important for establishing a permanent record of where different objects were located.) After taking the photographs, record the mileage of the suspect vehicle.

- Record on a worksheet where each lift is made.

- Note the position of the driver's seat in relation to the steering wheel. This can suggest the size of the person driving the vehicle.

- Logical nonporous surfaces to be processed for latent prints in the interior include:
  - Front and back of the rearview mirror and any visor mirror. It is recommended to detach the rearview mirror for processing
  - Seat adjustment controls and seat belt buckles
  - Bottom of an arm rest
  - Steering wheel and gear shift lever
  - All interior glass surfaces
  - Push buttons on the radio
  - Door and window handles
  - Dash of the auto including the light knob, cigarette lighter, ashtray and glove compartment button
  - Tape deck

- Logical nonporous surfaces to be processed for latent prints on the exterior include:
  - Sideview mirror
  - All outside glass areas
  - License plates
  - All exterior painted areas of the car including the roof, trunk, doors, hood, hood release, gas cap, door handle and underside

of any latch
- The engine of the car, the air cleaner and other areas that may have been touched if the suspect tampered with the engine. Be alert for latent prints in grease or oil on the engine area.
- Logical areas of the interior and exterior should be checked for contraband. A search log should be maintained reflecting what was found, who found it and where it was found. Areas to consider:
  - Above the sun visor
  - Underneath the seats
  - In the trunk of the car
  - Glove compartment interior and exterior on the outer shell underneath the dash
  - Engine area
  - Inside the hubcaps
  - Cigarette butts from the ashtray

Computer Crime

The computer explosion of the past decade offers law enforcement an entirely new high-tech crime tool to contend with. Criminals use computers for a number of illegitimate reasons including:
- Insider crimes
- Support of criminal enterprises
- Malicious hacking and phreaking
- Telecommunications fraud
- Espionage

Insider Crimes

Motivated by greed, opportunity, a grievance against the company or corporate espionage (trade secrets), "insiders" have legitimate access to an organization's information but exceed their authority in its use. Few statistics are available regarding the costs or damage incurred by insider crimes as they're seldom reported to law enforcement.

Support of Criminal Enterprises

Computers provide criminals with excellent record-keeping capabilities. More and more traditional criminal activities are being automated. Areas where computers are now being used include:
- Gambling
- Narcotics

- Prostitution
- Child sexual abuse and pornography
- Forgery
- Rape
- Abduction
- Terrorism

Malicious Hacking and Phreaking

Hackers (people who break into computers) and phreakers (people who break into phone systems) consider themselves the "warriors of the underground community." Their potential for reeking havoc is endless. They usually fall into one of these categories:

- Anarchists—they are antiauthoritarian
- "Carders"—they commit credit card fraud
- Viriists—they code and distribute computer viruses

As a tool for solving hacker and phreaker related computer crimes, consider the following Malicious Hacker/Phreaker Profile. These individuals:

- Are predominantly teenage males
- Possess poor interpersonal skills
- Are focused on technology
- Substitute their computer for interpersonal relationships
- Have an insatiable curiosity
- Are antiestablishment (nerds with an attitude)
- Desire to possess "forbidden knowledge"

Other terms you may need in writing about hackers or phreakers:

- Worm—A computer program that, once installed, continually re-creates itself, ultimately filling your computer's hard drive with useless information.
- Virus—A computer program containing a damaging payload. It spreads when individuals exchange programs that have been altered or infected and can cause loss of data.
- "Trojan Horse"—A program that looks like one thing when, in fact, it's something else. For example, you may receive a free offer to download a game onto your computer. You decide you'd like to give it a try. The game is loaded and you play away. But it's not only a game; it's also a "Trojan Horse." While you downloaded the game, another part of the program downloaded all of

the information on your computer to the game's source. Now you have a game, and the game's provider has everything they ever needed to know about you.

Telecommunications Fraud

Unauthorized use of ESN (electronic serial numbers) and MIN (mobile identification numbers) is the number one cause of loss in the cellular phone industry, representing a multibillion dollar cost. Telephone system computers comprise the largest computer network in the world. As such, they're a target for a variety of criminal activities including:

- Access Code Fraud—the illegitimate use of someone else's access code to make long distance calls.
- Call-Sell Operations—the illegitimate sale of someone else's calling card number to another for making long distance calls. For example, you're at an airport and need to make a long distance call. You take your calling card and set it on the top of the phone while entering the numbers. You don't even notice the guy standing next to you as he dials his pal's pager and touches in the number he's reading off of your card. The buddy, at some other location, proceeds to "sell" long distance calls to customers, some of whom really like the idea of talking to mom in Brazil for twenty minutes at the low low price of $10.
- Social Engineering Scams—occur when someone fraudulently obtains another's password or access to confidential or valuable computer information. For example, a criminal calls an executive's secretary, purporting to be a scared employee in fear of losing her job if "I don't get that information right away." The secretary, taking pity, discloses the access information to help out. The con then has access to all of the boss's goods.

Espionage

The Federal Bureau of Investigation estimates that there are 120 foreign governments actively working intelligence operations against the United States. With a focus on high technology and business systems, computers play an integral role.

The Crime Scene

Any successful investigation and prosecution requires precise crime-scene management and evidence processing. This became painfully apparent in the midnineties during the physical evidence portion of the O.J. Simpson trial.

As a writer, you need to be acutely aware of the basics of crime scene investigation to accurately portray any character who is involved in crime or criminal justice. For example, you may want your story to involve a criminalist or criminalistics squad. These people can make or break a case every time.

I recall a particularly brutal rape perpetrated against a young coed. It occurred in a house that a group of women shared near a large college campus. The victim was sleeping in her third floor room when the thug climbed a fire escape, stuck a pistol in her mouth, committed the act and left. This occurred before DNA evidence was available. The young woman didn't know her assailant, who had fled the scene prior to our arrival. Fortunately, we were able to preserve the scene and a criminalist managed to get a fingerprint off the window sill leading into the woman's room.

The offender was identified and arrested. He plead not guilty and took the case to a jury trial. A career criminal, he was prepared for his defense. He had an alibi, witnesses to the alibi and a hard-luck story to bring the jury to tears. The traumatized victim had difficulty with an identification. But there was one problem—the bad guy just couldn't explain how *his* fingerprint ended up on her third floor window sill on the night of the offense.

The defense attorney's only obstacle was a criminalist who was articulate, well-trained and experienced, and covered all the bases. I believe the convict is still a penitentiary resident.

If you choose to use a criminalist or criminalistics unit in your writing, they should be able to provide expert service and testimony in a number of areas.

Your criminalist needs to be able to develop, determine the value of and identify latent fingerprints. That is, he has to be able to use proper techniques to develop a print from its "invisible" form into something viewable. Once a print is visible, the criminalist must be capable of determining its value for comparison to other prints. Part of this comparison is the identification of specific, unique traits of a particular print.

Criminalists must be capable of giving expert testimony in court as to the identification of fingerprints. The term "expert" implies that the criminalist possesses the necessary knowledge, skill and training to render a credible, provable observation or opinion. Cases can be won or

One well-equipped van provides mobility for all the criminalist's needs.

lost based on a criminalist's credibility, skill and ability to articulate his findings.

Criminalists must be able to do plaster castings of things like shoe prints in mud or tire prints in soft surfaces or silicone castings of things such as toolmarks on surfaces for comparison purposes. Once while working the night shift, my partner and I saw a guy leaving the foyer of a doctor's office. It was two o'clock in the morning and had just started raining. The guy was dry, and although it was a relatively mild April night, he was wearing gloves. After checking the man, who said he was "just out for a walk," we found a pry bar and screwdriver in his pockets. An examination of the doctor's office entry door showed pry marks around the lock. We had interrupted a breaking and entering in progress. Our man was handcuffed and, while I sat in the police car with him, we called a criminalist to check for fingerprints and see if a silicone cast could be made to compare the pry marks with the suspect's tools. There really wasn't enough to get a solid comparison cast. But, when our genius burglar saw the criminalists doing their check, he protested. "They won't find nothin' of mine in there. I was wearin' gloves the whole time!" When his defense attorney heard the statement in court, he told me he'd wished we would have used the silicone on his client's mouth.

Your criminalistics team will also need to be skilled photographers, capable of photographing night scenes and photographically enhancing images of fingerprints and footprints, as well as developing black-and-white or color film and producing quick copies.

Your team should have expertise in collecting physical evidence and making sketches and drawings to scale. They must collect specimens for

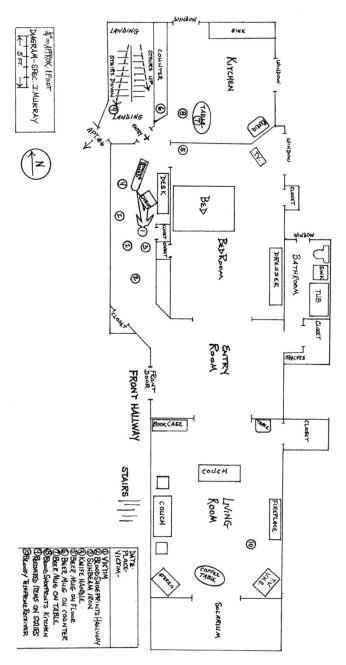

This detailed crime scene sketch is the culmination of the criminalist's work.

Where would you start on this crime scene?

scientific examination such as blood, semen and body fluid specimens or deposits on the hands of individuals to determine if the subject fired a handgun.

Your team should be capable of test-firing weapons.

Your criminalist needs the right equipment to do the job. Some of the items available for immediate use by the Cincinnati Police Criminalistics Squad include:

1. Light equipment
   - Power supplies/generators—gas and electric
   - Long extension cords (at least one hundred feet)
   - Large area lighting
   - Alternative light source (Luma-Lite)

Inside the lab—a fuming cabinet and dusting hood.

2. Tools—general hand tools and ladders
3. Metal detectors
4. Measuring instruments
5. Evidence vacuum cleaner
6. Boots, helmets, gloves, coats and other protective gear
7. Special camera equipment
8. Casting equipment
9. Fingerprinting equipment
10. Evidence collecting equipment

Protecting the Crime Scene

Protecting the crime scene is arguably the most important part of an investigation. Reasoning this as "most important" lies in the fact that once evidence is destroyed or contaminated, it's either lost forever or useless in court. Imagine the potential for blowing a court case because things weren't handled right at a crime scene.

A particularly ugly experience happened to me one day when, as a uniform supervisor, I received a call to a large apartment complex for a dead on arrival (DOA). I pulled into the parking lot and noticed a fire truck, an ambulance and the police car that belonged to the veteran officer who was also dispatched on the run.

A crowd of onlookers was gathered by the apartment entrance, curious to find out what was going on. As I approached the entry, the other officer came through the door and headed for the parking lot. Stopping him, I asked for information. All he could say was, "She's in there! She's in there!" Taking him with me, I found the apartment building's common hallway crowded with crying and upset people. The doorway to the apartment was open and inside it were people who were shouting, crying and pacing around. As I entered, I noticed a man and women, who were crying and agitated, sitting on a couch. Down a hall, half a dozen firemen scurried over something slumped on the floor. One tried to push past me with a blanket to "cover her up."

What I eventually found was a badly beaten and bloodied eight-year-old girl, naked and dead on the hallway floor. The crime scene? The most dreaded and horrible kind. Crime scene protection? None. As you can imagine, managing the crime scene became a nightmare. The first officer there had become too emotionally charged to do anything right and so had done everything wrong. One of the people on the couch was the victim's mother. After much confusion, it turned out that the mother had made a full confession to the first officer on the scene. You know his reaction.

As I mentioned, the officer involved in this scenario was a seasoned veteran. As such, he seemed a little resentful when I gave him remedial instruction on crime scene protection. But I quoted to him right "from the book" the way crime scenes needed to be handled. So for you to be factually correct in your writing, I'll do the same here.

HOW TO HANDLE A CRIME SCENE

The following procedures are recommended for effective and efficient crime scene investigation. They are cited from the *Cincinnati Police Division Crime Scene Manual*.

Protecting the Crime Scene. The first officer to arrive at the scene of the crime automatically incurs the serious and critical responsibility of securing the crime scene from unauthorized intrusions.

Dimensions of a Crime Scene. Obviously, there is no definite rule or set of rules that can be applied to defining the dimensions of a crime scene. However, the best physical evidence is found at or near the site of the most critical action taken by the criminal against the victim or property. Thus, one is more likely to find important physical evidence in the immediate area surrounding the body in a homicide case than at some distance away. Similarly, the site of forcible entry into a building or the area immediately surrounding a cracked safe normally has the greatest potential for yielding evidence. While it is possible the dimensions of a crime scene will be large, there will usually be apparent priority areas that should be given immediate protection. On first report of a crime, determine areas to be protected: (1) place of occurrence; (2) place of apprehension; (3) course of chase; and (4) observation point.

Initial Actions on Arrival at the Scene of a Crime. The success of an investigation that involves a definable crime depends heavily on the initial observations and actions of the first officer to arrive at the scene. This statement is generally applicable regardless of the type of crime. While the circumstances of the particular case will naturally govern the actions taken by the officer to protect and preserve the physical evidence, the following are considered to be generally valid guidelines:

HOW TO HANDLE A CRIME SCENE continued

- If injured persons are discovered at the scene of a crime, rendering aid is our first priority.
- If sufficient police personnel are available, the immediate steps necessary to protect the crime scene should be taken simultaneously with giving aid to injured persons.
- Because these procedures basically deal with collection and preservation of physical evidence, it is well to note that arresting suspects, detaining witnesses and requesting assistance, if needed, would all be integral to the actions that would be taken by the first officer or officers on the scene of a crime.
- Immediate protection measures include roping off certain critical entrances or exits and posting guards to control spectators around areas expected to have high potential for physical evidence.
- In *extreme* cases, it may be necessary to move objects that seem to have evidence potential from areas where they would otherwise be destroyed or drastically affected by the elements. *However, movement of evidence prior to the time it has been fully examined and processed should be avoided whenever possible.*
- The underlying intent of all actions taken to protect the scene of a crime is to preserve its physical aspects so that it may be reviewed in detail by the investigator or laboratory examiners assigned to the case. Thus, the major task of the officers preserving the scene is to prevent certain actions, specifically:
    - Unnecessary walking about. Particular precautions must be taken to avoid walking in areas that are likely to bear the impression of foot or tire prints.
    - Moving items or disturbing the bodies of deceased persons.
    - Touching items of surfaces that are likely to yield latent fingerprints or hinder the reconstruction of the crime (e.g., handling or unloading any firearm or weapon). **Only Exception-Officer Safety**.
    - Allowing any item to be removed from the scene without the specific permission of the officer or laboratory examiner who is in charge of the search.
- A responding officer should attempt to collect and protect the clothing of the gunshot wound and/or stabbing victims when clothing is penetrated. Hospital personnel should be advised that these items

HOW TO HANDLE A CRIME SCENE continued

are physical evidence. These items should be retrieved if possible or notification made to the follow-up investigator as to the disposition of clothing or projectiles removed during surgery.

Note-Taking at a Crime Scene. Good written records should be made and include the following information:
1. Who found the crime.
2. Notation of the basic facts:
   - The dates, times and location
   - Who was at the scene on arrival and their names
   - Who entered the scene
   - Where you have been
   - What you have touched
   - Weather conditions if appropriate
   - If the lights are on or off

Normal areas of a crime scene are:
1. Approach: the area forming the perimeter or any way into the scene
2. Entry: the exact location the perpetrator entered the scene
3. Offense: the precise spot the offense was committed
4. Exit: the exact area the perpetrator used to leave the site of the offense
5. Escape: the area potentially used by the perpetrator to leave the scene of the crime

Valuable evidence may be discarded or inadvertently deposited by the criminal some distance from the apparent immediate scene of the crime. Thus, the area to be protected may be expanded beyond the limits of that which is considered to have the highest priority.

The officer first assuming responsibility for the crime scene must cooperate with the investigators, laboratory examiners and other specialists who may later search and process it. The officers who secured the scene should make all their information immediately available to any officers who subsequently arrive to take charge of the investigation.

Details are important. It should be emphasized that once the criminalistics squad arrives, they will take charge of the crime scene. The evidence technician will control the crime scene.

We've seen the way it's supposed to be done. Depending on your story, your character might do a good job or totally bungle a crime scene. Let's go back to the first officer arriving on the scene of the reported DOA and, from your character's point of view, give them a textbook response.

You receive a radio call to an address you know to be a large apartment complex. The dispatcher tells you the fire department is on the scene reporting a DOA. You're only two blocks away and arrive in a couple of minutes.

You notice a crowd gathered around the entrance to the building and a fire truck and ambulance parked in the lot. A supervisor was dispatched with you, so you know he's on the way. You enter the common hallway to the apartment and see a group of people standing outside the open apartment door where the call originated. You walk into the apartment and see a man and woman crying in the living room area. A fire lieutenant meets you and says, "She's dead. There's nothing we can do." He points to the woman and continues, "That's mom. She told me she didn't mean to do it." *Now* is the time to react.

You see the body and it's determined she's dead. Immediately, you order the firefighters out of the apartment. You advise the dispatcher you'll need additional help. The fire lieutenant wants to leave, but you tell him he can't and ask him to stay by his truck. You clear the apartment up to the front door since that's your best bet to keep anyone out.

You take the two people from the living room, one of whom told the fire lieutenant she did it, to the apartment door and have them stay put. The crime scene is secured and help is on the way. When the supervisor arrives, you tell him what you've got. He makes notifications regarding who needs to respond and what they need to do. You contain the scene until criminalistics arrives. It's almost too easy.

Whatever the case, writers need to understand that, despite unpredictable twists or angles, your subject from the criminal justice system has some type of guidelines to refer to.

Chapter Fourteen

Crime–Scene Search

by Anne Wingate

from *Scene of the Crime: A Writer's Guide to Crime-Scene Investigations*

There is little probability of finding anything of importance if the attention be confined to safes, beds, boxes, stoves or chimneys. Absolutely everything must be examined, for there is no place where important objects cannot be hidden. The following for example are a few of the hiding places discovered by the author or his friends:—the horsehair stuffing of a sofa, a birdcage, the space between the back of a picture and its protecting board, the hole of an old key, the manger in a stable, a pot in which soup was actually boiling on the fire (it contained 28 gold coins), a prayer-book, old boots, a dog kennel, the space between two upright millstones, wine barrels, a spectacle case, a pill-box, old newspapers, a cuckoo clock, a baby's clothes; and on one occasion the criminal himself was discovered in a dung heap, a small opening having been made to give him air in the side nearest to the stable wall.

—Hans Gross, *Criminal Investigation*

Dr. Hans Gross, professor of criminology at the University of Prague, has the distinction of having written the very first book of criminology that was a major influence in the Western world. Originally titled *Handbuch fur Untersuchungsrichter als System der Kriminalistik* (A *Handbook on the Criminal Sciences for Examining Magistrates*) and published in the last quarter of the nineteenth century, it went through countless translations and new editions; the 1934 English translation of the third edition, which I quote here, was a very late version. Although almost everything in it is now outdated and superseded, it is still well worth reading because it was the first solid attempt to systemize investigation and turn it into a science.

The situation Gross describes in the preceding passage has not changed in the slightest. Some of the unlikely places my friends and I have found evidence include a hole in the outside wall of a house on the escape route of a robber, a residential garbage can in the alley two blocks from where the crime occurred, the inside top of a lipstick tube (an Avon special, made for holding solid cologne as well as a lipstick), inside sugar and flour canisters, inside refrigerators and freezers, inside an ornamental clock and inside curtain rods. Narcotics officers once searched a house for marijuana and hashish without success, but totally missed the six marijuana plants growing in small pots on the kitchen counter. (Dell Shannon—in real life, Elizabeth Linington—put that one in a book after I told her about it.)

Secret documents, jewels and drugs have been smuggled inside baby's diapers, inside corpses being returned home for burial, in balloons swallowed or thrust up the courier's anus, inside linings or hems of clothing, in cameras and film containers, inside ballpoint pens or fountain pens. Disassembled weapons have been smuggled disguised as camera components; assembled and disassembled weapons have been shipped in bags of flour, meal or powdered milk, in barrels of missionary clothing, in crates of tools and hardware. In fiction, hide contraband anywhere you like. You can be sure some real criminal has thought of it before you.

Collecting evidence deserves a special chapter—or more—of its own. In real life, it is critical that evidence be collected and treated correctly, if it is to tell what it can tell. In fiction, you have to know what you can and can't do with evidence—but bear in mind that this is something that changes. Keep track of court decisions and technical developments to keep your writing current.

A person searching a crime scene is less likely than someone searching a suspect's house to find evidence deliberately hidden, unless the scene also involved narcotics, smuggling, the concealment of stolen property or something like that. Also, a person searching a crime scene doesn't need a search warrant if someone who has control over the area is willing to sign a consent-to-search form. If no one is willing, or legally able, to sign a consent-to-search form, then a search warrant is essential.

Searching With a Warrant

For clarity, let's assume again that you are your fictional investigator. Here is how you get and use a search warrant:

1. You must be a law-enforcement officer. No search warrant can be issued to anyone who is not a law-enforcement officer.
2. You must prepare an affidavit, in duplicate, describing the area to be searched, the items you intend to search for and why you expect to find those items in that location (*probable cause*). Prepare a search warrant in triplicate. Take the affidavits and warrants to a judge and swear to the affidavits. At that time, if the judge thinks your cause is probable enough, the judge signs the search warrants. The judge keeps one copy of the affidavit; you keep the other, along with all three copies of the search warrant.
3. You and however many more people you need go to the scene. Unless the scene is already under the control of the police, as it usually is when you're searching the scene of a crime, or unless you have a no-knock warrant—which is issued only if there is strong reason to suspect evidence will be destroyed in the time it takes for someone to open the door or strong reason to fear for the safety of the officers serving the warrant—you knock on the door, announce yourselves as police officers and wait for somebody to come to the door.
4. Usually one officer (or more, if necessary) will corral all people on the scene and keep them confined to one area. It is courteous and good public relations, though not a legal requirement, to avoid frightening children or other innocent people unnecessarily.
5. Search for the items on the list. Make a list on the warrant itself—in triplicate, because that's how many copies of the warrants you have—of everything seized whether or not it was on the original list of items sought for.
6. You are not responsible for restoring the premises to their presearch condition. However, you should avoid unnecessary damage and take all reasonable precautions for safeguarding property that belongs on the scene.
7. Leave one copy of the warrant, complete with detailed list of items seized, with the people in control of the place you searched. If nobody is there, leave a copy of the warrant displayed in a prominent place. Keep one warrant for your files, and return one to the court that issued the warrant.

Be aware that when officers are searching with a warrant (and remember that your private eye or your brilliant amateur cannot get a search warrant), the warrant must describe the places they may look and the items they may look for. Among other things, this means that unless the warrant mentions "the house and all outbuildings" instead of just "the house" nobody may search the garage or the lawn mower shed. Unless the warrant also mentions vehicles, officers may search the garage but not the car parked in the garage. If the smallest item mentioned on the search warrant is a refrigerator, no one may search the junk drawer in the kitchen—and if someone does search the junk drawer in the kitchen and finds a pistol, that's tough. It is tainted evidence, not admissible in court, even if it is the weapon that was used to kill that officer's closest friend. However, an officer looking for a pistol who finds a stolen refrigerator may use that evidence, because there is no place the refrigerator would have fit that it would not have been reasonable to look for the pistol.

Furthermore—and this comes directly from the Constitution's Fourth Amendment, part of the Bill of Rights—the search warrant may be issued only on the basis of probable cause, listing what officers expect to find there and why they expect to find those items, and suspicion isn't probable cause. If an officer saw fifteen known drug wholesalers and twenty known dealers and thirty other people carrying cash and packages entering and leaving a suspect location in twenty minutes, chances are a judge will issue a search warrant. But if all the officer has is the fact that the owner of the house looks scruffy and there has been a lot of coming and going there in the middle of the night, almost certainly a search warrant will not be granted.

In the case of a crime scene, a crime is known to have occurred in that location and officers are looking for all evidence having to do with the crime. Generally, this is sufficient probable cause unless a judge rules otherwise. Judges are highly unpredictable.

The most common basis for issuing a search warrant in a situation not involving an obvious crime scene is the word of an informant. Although courts have ruled that the warrant, and the affidavit given in applying for the warrant, do not have to list the informant's name, the paperwork should specify that this is an informant whose information has in the past proven accurate. (This means that the first time or two that a particular informant is used, there must be some other source of the same information.)

An officer working with an informant should try to get the informant to list as small an item as possible because, remember, the smaller the smallest item listed is, the greater the scope of places the officer may look.

Exceptions to the Rule

There are exceptions to the rule requiring search warrants. If there is strong probable cause and the place to be searched is highly portable—a car, a boat, an airplane—in some situations the officer may reasonably search without a warrant. But if the situation is such that the vehicle can be impounded while a warrant is issued, then the search may not proceed without the warrant. I wrote a novel, *The Eye of Anna*, in which an officer searched a house without a warrant because he had strong probable cause to believe that a murderer had been holed up in the house, a hurricane was in progress, and the officer had reason to believe the house might be blown away before he could finish the search. (It was.) In real life, could he have gotten away with that? Danged if I know, but it was fun to write.

The other main exception is that if an officer has grounds to fear for his own personal safety, he may immediately search any area within the immediate physical control of the suspect for weapons. Often, officers stopping a car and searching the glove box under this exception find drugs instead of a weapon. Almost invariably, an immediate court battle ensues, arguing whether the officer had actual and reasonable cause to search for a weapon or whether the search for the weapon was merely an excuse to search for drugs. Courts have ruled differently in different situations, so this is a wide-open area to consider in writing fiction.

In real life, it is essential that no officer conduct a search alone. There should always be at least two people to testify as to what was found and who found it. Furthermore, the two people must always search together; it won't do any good, later in court, for Mel to testify that he was there when N.E. Boddy found the murder weapon, if Mel was outside or in another room and Boddy is accused of planting the weapon.

But this isn't a law book. Let's get on to what your character might find, how he should treat it and not treat it at the scene and what can be done with it later in the lab. Always, always, always remember that this information changes fast, so check with your real jurisdiction, or the closest real one to a fictitious one, at the time you are writing as to what can be done there at that time. Identification and crime-scene officers are genial souls, almost always happy to tell you what they're doing and show you around, provided they don't have a call at the moment. (But do be aware that even if you have an appointment, you can't count on the officer being there. Crime takes precedence.)

Evidence Collection

For now, let's get on with evidence collection. How do officers collect different items of evidence? What do they do with them after collecting them? In this chapter, we'll discuss collecting and packaging the evidence.

Expect the Unexpected

The only way an evidence technician can be prepared for anything is to be prepared for everything. Murder happens fast.

At the very least, an evidence collection kit must contain large, medium and small paper and plastic bags. If they are not preprinted with evidence tags (we'll get to those later), evidence tags can be attached with string or tape. The kit must contain paper coin envelopes, small vials of the type used by pharmacies to dispense tablets and larger plastic or glass containers with airtight lids. Anything meant to contain liquids should be made of an inert material so that the eyedropper and/or container will not leave its own chemical trace in the liquid, unless of course the lab already knows about and plans for the chemical trace, as in the case of some prepackaged kits. There should be a supply of cardboard boxes that can be set up to hold larger items; prepackaged kits for gunpowder residue, blood samples and rape analysis; vials with disposable eyedroppers fixed in the lids; dental casting material and equipment (the same stuff the dentist used to get the exact shape your bridge needed to be); and plaster casting material and equipment. Tweezers and scissors are essential. Obviously, the kit must contain evidence tags and the long, yellow preprinted evidence tape to keep people out of the immediate crime scene (although it's usually necessary, if it's a major crime, to post a few patrol officers on the perimeter also).

Rubber gloves are critical; I once caught pneumococcal pneumonia from a corpse, and in this day of AIDS, anybody who handles bloody items without wearing gloves is clearly suicidal. Of course you already know your character will need notebook, pens, pencils, tape measures, a camera and strobe and plenty of film and batteries.

It is useful to have several heavy-duty cardboard boxes with pegboard bases and a number of long, heavy nails to put through the bottom of the pegboard so that oddly shaped items may be securely immobilized.

This kit should be kept at all times in the vehicle that will be used. Each time the kit is used, it must be *immediately* restocked to be ready for its next use. Obviously, if the vehicle must go into the shop, the kit must be moved to the substitute vehicle. Murder happens fast and it doesn't give the unprepared person time to say, "Oops, let me get my stuff together." An officer who isn't prepared to go with no advance warning whatsoever and spend the next ten hours working a major crime scene, photographing, measuring, charting and collecting upwards of five hundred pieces of numbered and labeled evidence, without sending a patrol officer out to an all-night drugstore to get something he forgot, isn't prepared at all.

That doesn't mean your fictional character really has to be that well prepared. Sometimes a lack of preparation may add to the drama of the story—but remember that it also must be consistent with your character or story line. Either the character is perennially forgetful or lazy (like Joyce Porter's Dover), or the character has just finished with one major crime and is too dog-tired to remember to restock instantly.

Each Item Packaged Separately

When collecting evidence, the technician must package each item separately. This includes, for example, putting each shoe in a separate labeled evidence bag if a pair of shoes is being collected. If a victim's clothing is being collected, each item of clothing goes in a separate bag. (Yes, that includes each sock. It is appropriate to handle them with tweezers.) It is critical to label each item the moment it is collected and to make corresponding notes in the technician's notebook immediately. Trusting it to memory and planning to write it up later is extremely stupid; memory cannot be trusted that far, especially by someone who has other things on her mind.

Paper or Plastic?

How does your character decide whether to use paper or plastic to collect the evidence?

If the item is likely to be even slightly damp, it must be packaged in paper so that the moisture can continue to evaporate; otherwise, the item is likely to begin to rot. Clothing with blood on it is a special problem. It should not be folded in on itself; rather, it must be spread out and allowed to dry. In Albany, Georgia, where I worked for nearly seven years, this was a big problem for a long time; there were times when we had no usable interrogation rooms because they all were full of bloody clothing drying out. (And one rather hysterical day, one detective ushered a suspect into an interrogation room another detective had just put a suspect shotgun in. Fortunately, the suspect was a rather mild-mannered burglar, and on seeing the shotgun he backed out in a hurry.)

But we had one unexpected and somewhat serendipitous stroke of luck. One day a city commissioner walked through the city parking garage and saw Doc Luther, head of the crime-scene unit, and me fingerprinting a suspect vehicle. He stopped short. "Don't you have a better place to do that?" he demanded.

"No, sir, we do not," Doc told him. "Not unless we want to do it outside." (The day was rainy. Fingerprint powder and rain do not combine well.)

The commissioner asked more questions, and Doc let him have the situation: We had already lost one case in court because we were fingerprinting a car full of stolen property when the suspect walked by. Although in fact the suspect did not touch any of the stolen property at that time, he managed to convince a jury that he did and that was how his fingerprints got there. Even Doc and I had to admit that the suspect had been close enough that he *could* have touched the property. He mentioned the problem with bloody clothing—which should have been our responsibility, but we had no place to deal with it—drying in interrogation rooms. He explained that the problems were getting worse, as crime in the city expanded at a geometric rate.

"I'll take care of that," the commissioner said.

A few months later, we had a nice building at the bottom of the parking lot. It was big enough for us to fingerprint even a large suspect vehicle and to process and store other large evidence. From then on, bloody clothing was dried and stored there.

If your officer is working in a small jurisdiction, by all means use the problems of small departments. Things can't be done exactly right, and there are tremendous fictional opportunities there.

Nothing with blood on it should ever be packaged in plastic or glass or anything else airtight, unless it is the blood itself and it is put in special vials that already contain a known blood preservative. The laboratories can work easily with dried blood or with properly preserved blood, but not with rotted blood.

Dry items may be packaged in plastic, although no particular harm is done if they are packaged in paper. Something that may need to be repeatedly examined, such as a pistol, should always be in transparent plastic, so that it can be examined without the police seal being broken. Obviously, any time the seal is broken—for fingerprinting or test-firing—notations should be made on the evidence tag, so that the defense attorney can't question later why there are two or three sets of staple holes.

Learning to pick things up without damaging fingerprints that might be on them is an art. It generally involves using only the fingertips to pick up items and holding them by edges that are too small to hold prints; there is really no way to learn without practicing. Try it yourself, so as to know the problems your character is facing.

Let's go on, now, talking for a few paragraphs as if you are your character.

Once you have succeeded in picking up the item, the next problem is packaging it without rubbing out the fingerprints. If the item is absorbent, there is no problem at all. Those prints aren't going anywhere. They are in the substance, not just on the surface, of the item. However, you must be extremely careful not to touch the items yourself, as even the most casual touch will add more prints. These things are best handled with tweezers at all times.

If the item is irregularly shaped, there's really little problem, because the protrusions will hold the paper or plastic away from the rest of the surface and keep it from rubbing out prints. But when you have something regularly shaped—a drinking glass, a pane of glass—you may have problems, because plastic will tend to mold around the item and rub out prints. Paper works better, especially ordinary brown paper grocery-type sacks, because they are too stiff to rub out prints unless the item is badly mishandled. In actual practice, Doc and I tended to print small items on the scene whenever possible, and then transport them (if necessary— often the prints were all we needed, and the item could be left at the scene) with fingerprints already protected by tape. With larger, heavier items, there is no problem, because these items will be transported in boxes and there is no chance of the boxes' rubbing out prints.

Of course, with extremely large items, there may also be a problem, because it may be impossible to move the item without touching areas that might hold prints. In that case, it is essential to print the areas that must be touched, then move the item, and then finish the work in the lab. What if the item is outside and it's raining? Then you go crazy for a while. Honestly—I can't provide advice. You just assess the situation and try to do whatever will be least harmful to the evidence, then hope you haven't missed something vital.

For dramatic purposes, you may decide instead to have your character do whatever is *most* harmful to the evidence, either by accident, deliberately or because the situation is so bad it cannot be redeemed.

Often, detectives brought us pieces of broken glass, holding them carefully by the edges, to have the surfaces printed. In a case like that, generally the detective would lay the glass on the seat beside him in the car on the way in and hand it to us with a separate evidence tag for us to attach later. This worked well; the car's seat covers were too stiff to damage any prints, and it would take us only minutes to print the item and attach the tag.

This Glass is Full of—Something

Now suppose you need to fingerprint a container that is full of an unknown liquid. You will eventually have to get an analysis of the liquid, so you can't just dump it. You can't fingerprint the container with the liquid in it, because examining an item while fingerprinting it involves turning it in different directions to get the light on it at different angles.

Being able to pick up a glass, cup or bottle by the rim and the angle where the side and the base join—using only your fingertips—and pour the contents into another container takes a lot of practice. But that is the only way to do it. After that, the glass or cup must completely air dry before fingerprinting begins. (No, you should not use a hair dryer on it. The resultant heat and rapid moisture evaporation could harm any remaining fingerprints.) This in turn means that very often it must be transported into the police station with the dregs of the liquid still in it—which means that it must be packaged and transported right side up.

For collecting some evidence, there are special kits you can buy from suppliers or, sometimes, obtain from the crime lab. To collect blood samples in the preservative jar, simply unscrew the lid, collect the sample with the enclosed eyedropper and screw the lid down again. The directions that come with the kit tell you which items do and do not need to be refrigerated. (After we got a refrigerator in the lab, many a day Doc, Butch and I stored our lunches in the same refrigerator that might be containing biological samples waiting to be transported to the lab. We were, of course, careful that everything—including lunches and samples—was properly packaged.)

A rape kit has to be kept refrigerated after use, and it should be transported to the lab as soon as possible. The officer or evidence technician does not personally use the rape kit; rather, she takes it to the hospital and turns it over to the examining physician, who will use the kit. (Preferably, the examination will be performed in the officer's presence, to cut down on the chain of evidence, unless the officer's presence is too distressing to the victim.) Following the examination, the physician turns the kit back over to the officer. The rape kit contains fine-toothed combs, tapes and vials to collect swabs from several pubic areas, vaginal washings and combings, and loose hairs that might be those of the suspect. These critical bits of evidence are the reason police ask the victim not to bathe until after she has been medically examined; very often the victim will then shower right in the hospital before putting on the fresh clothes she has taken with her. All the clothing she was wearing at the time of the assault and immediately after it will be turned over to the police in hopes that some hair, fiber and/or semen from the assailant remains on it.

Shoe Prints, Tire Tracks

Shoe prints and tire tracks are first photographed with a special camera on a frame that points directly down. Because the camera is on a frame, the ratio of the negative to the original (that is, the relationship in terms of size) is known, and the original track can be exactly reproduced in size. After that, the officer should make casts, often called moulages, of them. She begins by spraying the surface with a fixative; ordinary hair spray or shellac will do in a pinch, but a special fixative available from supply houses is preferable. Then a portable frame—metal or wood—is placed around the track. Using the bucket and stirring stick that is part of her equipment and following package directions on the bag of plaster, the officer mixes the plaster with water obtained at the scene. (Someone who habitually goes places where water is not readily available should carry several gallons of water in the trunk of her car.) Very carefully, pouring onto the stirring stick held just above the print in order to break the flow and diffuse the plaster mixture and keep it from damaging the print, the officer pours the plaster into the frame. The plaster is reinforced with twigs, straw and so forth from the scene; an officer who customarily goes places where she cannot expect to find twigs and straw should carry Popsicle sticks, available in bulk in craft stores under the name of "craft sticks," as a substitute. It is important to avoid using twigs and straw from a different location, as that might confuse scientists who are studying the shoes and tires and the casts.

Waiting for the plaster to dry may take anywhere from ten minutes to two hours, depending on the quality of the plaster and the atmospheric conditions. When it is nearly dry, a twig or even a finger is used as a stylus to put the officer's initials, the date and the case number in the back of the plaster. When it is completely dry, the casting is carefully lifted and put into a cardboard box upside down to finish drying. The officer should not try to clean it; that is left for the lab to do. This procedure accomplishes two things at once: It provides a cast of the shoe or tire, and it provides an exact sample of the soil, with its associated leaves, twigs and debris, in which the print was made, for comparison to the soil adhering to the shoe or tire.

Toolmarks

An officer should never attempt to fit a suspect tool into a toolmark; doing so would damage the evidence. If at all possible, the item the toolmark is on should be collected and packaged for transmittal to the lab. The crime-scene kit should contain a small saw so that officers can, if necessary, saw out a section of the door frame where the pry mark is located. (I once moved into an apartment and noticed immediately that a section of an interior door frame had been sawed out and neatly painted over and several circles of carpet had been taken out and replaced with carpet almost, but not quite, matching in color. That alerted me that a major crime of some sort had occurred in that apartment.)

If removal of the area is absolutely impossible, dental casting material can be used to obtain an exact cast of the print. The officer must follow directions on the container, as there are many different types of dental casting material.

Fibers, Soil, Hair, Leaves, Pollen, Fireclay

Any piece of small evidence that is big enough to see, no matter what it is, should be collected with tweezers and put into coin envelopes (if there is the slightest possibility that it is even slightly damp) or into small plastic bags.

But what about the ones that are too small to see?

This is when an *evidence vacuum*, a small, extremely powerful vacuum cleaner equipped with filters, is useful. The vacuum cleaner is first cleaned, even if it is always cleaned after use, just in case somebody else forgot to do it last time. Then the officer inserts the first filter, and choosing a small, easily definable section such as the floorboard, passenger's side, front seat, she vacuums up *everything* in that area. Then that filter with its entire contents is placed in an evidence bag, the vacuum cleaner is cleaned again, the second filter is inserted and the work continues.

If the same area is going to be fingerprinted, it is essential to use the evidence vacuum before fingerprinting, to avoid contaminating the vacuum sweepings with fingerprint powder. Obviously, it takes something of a contortionist to vacuum an area without touching it, but ident people learn to do such things.

Soil and Leaf Samples Outdoors

Samples are collected from every area the perp would have contacted. Each one is packaged separately; both the evidence tag and the officer's notes should tell *exactly* where each sample came from. Triangulation is crucial in case someone else should have to locate the exact same spot again.

Broken Glass

You already know how glass is collected without damaging fingerprints. Your officer will be sure to identify, in notes and on the evidence tag, exactly where each fragment came from. The lab needs that information.

Blood Spatters

Blood spatters can be few and widely scattered; they can be widely dispersed over a large area. Totally accurate photography and measurements are critical. In a case in Cincinnati, a man was stabbed in the lung. Blood in the lung mixed with the air and sprayed through the exit wound so that a fine, almost imperceptible mist of blood covered the immediate area. Detectives observed that an area of floor was *not* sprayed; from that they were able to ascertain the shape of the perp's jacket and to deduce that when they found the perp's jacket, it would have blood on it. In other cases—these involving stabbing or bashing—detectives have been able to determine from the pattern of blood spattering the height and even the hand preference of the perp and—again—to know that certain items of clothing will have blood on them.

Not all blood is red; not all blood tracings are visible. Large amounts of blood, after being exposed to air for several hours, turn to a very glossy black and tend to dry in stacks and then crack so that the floor will appear to be covered by irregular stacks of glossy black tile. In other situations, blood may turn pinkish, brownish or even greenish. It is very difficult to scrub all the blood up; even after the walls and floors appear immaculate to the naked eye, spraying the area with a chemical called luminol (which is available in several different trademarked packagings) will cause all areas where blood has been to fluoresce. In such a case, taking up the floorboards, tile or carpet will usually disclose puddles of blood lying on the subflooring. It may also be necessary to take apart the plumbing and look for blood traces in the sink traps.

Smaller spatters of blood should be allowed to dry naturally, even if that involves keeping the scene sealed and guarded for several days. Then each one should be measured, rephotographed, traced in complete detail and carefully triangulated not only in location, but also in exact position within that location (is the spray coming from up or down, left or right?). Then, if possible, the surface containing the spatters should be removed to the lab.

Chapter Fifteen

Interviews and Interrogations

by Russell Bintliff

from *Police Procedural: A Writer's Guide to Police and How They Work*

T he best sources of information about people are the people themselves. Probably the best way of getting information from people is to ask them for the information. Effective police officers and detectives have learned to become proficient in the art of interviewing people. There are two basic methods for getting information:

Interviewing. The questioning of a person who has or is believed to have information of interest to the police officer or detective. The person interviewed is usually a victim or witness but may be an informant or someone else who can provide information, even if not always directly related to the crime under investigation. During an interview, the police detective will encourage the interviewee to give his or her account of an incident or crime. "Probing" is a good way to describe the technique of interviewing. A skilled interviewer will "probe" a person's memory to draw out key information, even information the interviewee doesn't realize he has.

Interrogation. An interrogation involves questioning a person suspected of having committed a crime, having complicity in the crime or having direct knowledge about the crime but who is reluctant to supply the information to police. "Prying" is the best word to describe an interrogation. The person being interrogated is normally unwilling to part with the information the police want or need, including confessions, location of a murder weapon or victim, names of others involved in the crime, who hired the suspect to commit a crime and other incriminating information.

The Decision to Interview or Interrogate

The distinction between interviewing or interrogating is not as clear-cut as it might seem. An interview may become an interrogation or vice versa, and the police detective has to remain alert to which will be appropriate at the time. Interrogation conjures up images from the past of hot lights, the rubber hose and a horde of detectives—ties loosened, sleeves rolled up and shoulder holsters in clear view—hovering over a sweating suspect. That's where the term "sweat it out of him" originated. However, in this age of computers, fax machines and sophisticated crime-solving techniques, as well as strict court rules and aggressive defense lawyers, the traditional methods are now mainly of historical interest.

Note: A common myth supports the idea that a confession resulting from an interrogation closes a case. However, a confession without corroborating testimony, physical and circumstantial evidence does little to solve a case. I learned early in my career that interrogations can often create more trouble than good. For example, a tainted interrogation that discloses information leading to collection of solid evidence can destroy a case in court if a good defense lawyer can persuade the court not to admit the suspect's confession or any of the evidence gained from his confession. I always wait until the last investigative step to interview or interrogate the suspect. Then I do it only to let the suspect "tell his side" of the story should he choose to do so.

Legal Considerations of Interviews and Interrogations

The police question a wide variety of people, most of whom are not criminal suspects. They interview victims, witnesses, informants, complainants, interested participants, disinterested parties, women, men, children of both sexes, professional people, blue-collar workers, white-collar workers, no-collar workers, people who arouse their curiosity, people who behave in a lawful manner and people who do not. In each category, the police officer and detective must have an intricate knowledge of the law, the crime and what information they need.

When interviewing children, for example, parents or guardians normally must remain in the room. Depending on the situation, another person—normally a nonpolice female—can suffice. Some children don't want to talk in front of their parents because of potential repercussions; some parents coach or answer for their children. Whenever police interview a child, especially on sensitive topics, the prosecutor should advise them legally on the procedure before the interview begins.

Male officers interviewing females must also consider legal aspects, especially when the interview involves references to sexual matters. A male officer or detective interviewing a female victim or witness should always have a female officer present; often, but not always, a female officer can conduct a more productive interview.

Every citizen is protected by the Fifth Amendment of the Constitution. The Supreme Court's 1966 ruling regarding the *Miranda v. Arizona* case clarified the protection and set forth certain guidelines of police conduct that have become famous as the Miranda Warning. However, the Miranda Warning applies legally only upon the arrest of a person or for those already in custody for another crime. The Fifth Amendment does not specify that a person only gets this protection after he's been placed under arrest or taken otherwise in custody. It leaves a gap that most police fall into unless they apply the noncustodial rights warning to any person the officer suspects or any person who "might" become a suspect. Noncustodial rights follow the language of the traditional Miranda Warning with this difference: The suspect does not have the option of having a lawyer appointed for him and is advised he can leave anytime he desires. Suspects must know and understand that they are not under arrest. If the police suspect a person of a crime but only later gather enough evidence to arrest him, the noncustodial rights may subsequently establish that the police gave the suspect every opportunity to exercise his constitutional rights.

Other legal aspects the police officer and detective must cope with involve the witness. A cooperative witness may consent to giving a detailed description of what she knows but refuses to testify in court or changes her story in court. Many cases never reach the courtroom because of these problems. Detectives should always obtain a written statement of the interview and have the interviewee sign it with a witness. Doing that will not ensure the witness won't recant or refuse to testify, and since the statement cannot be admissible in court as evidence, why bother? When the police detective depends heavily on the interviews to create other evidence and later establish probable cause for arrest and search warrants, the witness may back out with an excuse that she never told the detective the information he says she did; the detective can quickly lose credibility and get into legal trouble as well. He can be sued for false arrest, illegal seizure and a variety of other charges brought against him and the department. In rare situations, the officer might face criminal allegations, suspension or dismissal. Taking the time to obtain a written statement from this type of witness protects and supports the detective's actions.

Importance of Human Factors

Human factors affect a police detective's success in stimulating an interviewee to talk and influence the accuracy or truthfulness of the information she receives from the interviewee. The detective evaluates each interviewee and the information furnished, attempting to understand the person's motivations, fears and mental makeup, then uses her understanding of the interviewee to gain useful information.

When selecting an interview or interrogation technique, a police detective must consider perception or memory, prejudice, reluctance to talk and personality conflicts.

Perception and Memory

The validity of the information disclosed during an interview or interrogation depends on the interviewee's ability to correctly perceive what happened in his or her presence, to recollect that information and to communicate the information correctly to the detective. A mistake made in recalling a particular incident is often due to one or more of the following:

- Location of the interviewee relative to the incident at the time it occurred. Rarely do two people give the same account of an incident they both have witnessed.
- Weakness in the interviewee's ability to see, hear, smell, taste or touch.
- Lapse of time since the incident occurred or lack of reason for the interviewee to attach much importance to the incident when it occurred. The account given of an incident later is often colored, consciously or unconsciously, by what the interviewee has since heard or seen regarding the incident. Further, an interviewee may bridge gaps in his knowledge of a particular incident by rationalizing what he did see or hear; he may repeat the entire mixture of fabrication and fact to the investigator as the truth.
- A police detective should interview witnesses and victims as soon as is practical after an incident occurs. Even then, all the detective's skill is required to discover what the interviewee observed and can

recall accurately. A suspect who is interviewed immediately has less time to formulate alibis with potential conspirators or to establish an otherwise viable sequence of events that could minimize his responsibility in the incident.

Reluctance to Talk

The detective may encounter a person who is reluctant to divulge information and must overcome this reluctance—in a legal manner—to secure the information she needs.

The most common reasons for reluctance to talk are:

- **Fear of Self-Involvement.** Many persons are not familiar with police methods and are afraid to aid the police. They may have committed a minor offense they believe will be brought to light upon the least involvement with the police. They may think the incidents that occurred are not their business or that guilt lies jointly on the victims and the accused. They may fear publicity. They may fear reprisal by the suspect or the suspect's associates against them, their family or property.
- **Inconvenience.** Many persons disclaim knowledge of incidents because they do not wish to be inconvenienced by being subjected to questioning or required to appear in court.
- **Resentment Toward Police and Police Methods.** This resentment may be particularly prevalent among persons who have no loyalty to the organized community. Sometimes the resentment manifests itself as sympathy for the accused person, who is regarded as the underdog pitted against the impersonal, organized forces of society and their chief representatives—the police.
- **Detective-Interviewee Personality Conflicts.** Lack of success in an interview or interrogation may be due to a personality conflict between the detective and the interviewee. For example, racial and gender factors will often create personality clashes. When that is the case, the detective should voluntarily withdraw in favor of another investigator before all chances of success are lost. An interviewee may feel compelled to talk to a new detective after his experience with the first detective whom, for one reason or another, he found objectionable.

Witnesses to Interviews and Interrogations

There is usually no requirement to have a witness attend a nonsuspect interview; however, it is advisable to have witnesses to an interrogation.

The written statement serves as the best witness to an interview, especially when its signing is witnessed by another officer or other credible person. With suspects, however, someone should be present to witness the rights warning, oath-taking and signing of any written statements obtained from the suspect.

Nothing prohibits a police detective from excusing a witness to the interrogation after obtaining the waiver of rights when the detective prefers certain psychological advantages that come from a "person-to-person" encounter with the suspect. The witness should return to hear a suspect confess to the crime and witness the signing of any statements.

Normally, no more than two detectives should be present in the interview room, since interrogating a suspect in the presence of many law enforcement officers has been held by the courts to suggest duress and coercion. Guns and handcuffs should not be visible to the witness, victim or suspect during an interview or interrogation because this also suggests coercion.

The officer who witnesses the rights warning should be the same person who witnesses the signing of statements; this prevents having more than two detectives or officers appear in court to testify.

Female Interviewees

The police detective should be sensitive to the fact that a woman may be reluctant to talk in other persons' presence about intimate topics. However, when it is necessary to question a female, the male detective should, for his own protection, have a female witness within hearing. The use of a two-way mirror and concealed microphone is also appropriate in such a case. The fact that the interviewee believes she is alone with the detective may assist in overcoming her reluctance to talk. Whenever possible, a female detective should interview or interrogate female suspects, witnesses and victims.

Types of Persons Interviewed and Interrogated

During criminal investigations, police detectives may question a variety of people as noted earlier in this chapter. In the following sections, I'll discuss what the police detective must consider about each category of persons before tailoring his or her technique to gain the most from the effort.

Victims

A victim is normally interviewed to develop the facts of an incident. This interview may take place in a hospital, at the victim's home or at another location not of the detective's choosing.

A victim is not always a reliable or cooperative witness, sometimes due to fear of retaliation from the perpetrator or his associates; a state of mental or physical shock; poor memory; possible involvement of relatives or friends; or fear of publicity.

Also, a victim may be too eager to please and, in an attempt to cooperate, may exaggerate and distort facts. It may be necessary to interview a victim several times before all facts are correctly and accurately disclosed.

Occasionally, it is necessary to interrogate a victim. Victims commonly inflate the value of property to obtain large insurance claims or to win sympathy from bill collectors. Victims may also attempt to hide their involvement in an offense, a common ploy of victims in drug-related investigations.

Witnesses

A witness is a person, other than a suspect, who has information concerning an incident or crime. A witness may also be the victim, complainant or accuser who first notified the police of the incident or crime. Although some witnesses are eager to tell the police what they know or think they know, others remain elusive or uncooperative.

The police detective often has to search out witnesses who do not voluntarily come forward to present their knowledge of a crime. A witness to a crime may be:

- A person who observed the crime being committed.
- A person who can testify as to the actions and whereabouts of the accused at the time the crime was committed.
- A person who knows facts or heard the accused say certain things that would tend to establish a motive for the commission of the crime.
- A scientific specialist who has examined the physical evidence and can give impartial testimony in court concerning the collected evidence.
- A person who by his or her knowledge of certain facts or occurrences can contribute to the overall knowledge of the case.

A witness is usually interviewed, but may be interrogated when sus-pected of lying or withholding pertinent information. It is not necessary to warn a witness of her rights under the Miranda decision unless she has said something to the detective that makes him believe her status as witness has changed to that of suspect. Under these conditions, all questioning should cease, and the suspect must be informed of her consti-tutional rights.

Informers

The success and efficiency of investigations often depend to some extent on persons who, for pay or for other reasons, furnish information about criminals and their activities. This source of information is protected by the police detective, who often interviews the informer under conditions of the informer's choosing.

Complainants and Accusers

During an investigation, one person may report on or accuse another. The complainant or accuser is usually interviewed. In some cases, how-ever, the detective may have to interrogate accusers or complainants suspected of lying, of distortion, of concealing the fact that they pro-voked the accused or of attempting to divert suspicion from themselves.

Others

To understand the motives and actions of persons involved in a crime or incident, the police detective interviews persons acquainted with the victim, suspect, witness or informer. These interviews are regularly con-ducted in the office, home or place of business. Rarely do these interviews result in an interrogation.

Distracting Persons

The police detective may encounter persons who have no real connec-tion with a crime or possess no knowledge of it, but who nevertheless present "information" to the police. They may claim to be witnesses or victims—or even perpetrators. Despite the lack of any real basis for their statements, the prudent detective will listen to their stories, evaluate what they say in relation to the known facts and take the necessary action.

Sensation or Publicity Seekers

Persons in this category are not often encountered during investigations. Emotionally disturbed persons, however, occasionally present themselves as witnesses, as additional victims of known suspects or as accomplices to suspects who have received considerable publicity. The investigator must make every effort to handle publicity seekers in such a way that neither the investigation nor the reputation of the police department suffers. Detectives must be aware of "attention-seeking" behavior. Police regularly encounter people who confess to crimes after reading about them in newspaper accounts. The best way to protect against these persons and to judge the legitimacy of other persons who do come forward is to withhold some key details that only a person who was actually involved would know about.

Grudge-Bearing and Lying Witnesses

Because of previous conflict with an accused or suspected person or to settle an old score, a person with no real knowledge of a crime or incident may volunteer information about or profess to be a witness to an event. A thorough familiarity with the known facts and details of the event will often enable the detective to detect inconsistencies in the story of such a person.

The testimony of the grudge-bearing or lying witness may closely parallel the accounts of the incident released to the media or allowed to circulate through other channels. What the real motives of these persons are remain obscure to the detective. However, he or she will check their background information to disclose the untruths and the motivation for their statements.

False Accusers

A false accuser may make a charge that later investigation will disclose to be groundless. Sometimes, such a charge will persist until a trial is conducted. False charges are, at times, exaggerated versions of actual crimes of lesser nature, but sometimes they are made when no offense has been committed. False charges are particularly prevalent in sex cases and are not uncommon in other crimes.

A false charge may represent the sincere though erroneous thinking of the victim or may rest on the victim's reaction to previous ill will, suspicion or jealousy. All the detective's skill is required in the first interview with an accuser to separate truthful from unfounded accusations. This must be done in a diplomatic manner. Anything the detective does to slight a person who volunteers such information or to make him feel that his reporting of the matter was foolish may cut off a possible future source of reliable information.

Conducting Interviews

There are four basic objectives of an interview and interrogation:
1. Secure complete and accurate information.
2. Distinguish fact from fantasy.
3. Proceed according to a well-thought-out plan.
4. Have truth as the objective.

Information

It's important that a police investigation reveal the real truth. The police detective may be able to verify the statements of one person by interviewing several other people who witnessed the same event. Not everyone sees the same things through the same set of eyes or experience. Any number of factors may influence the perception, memory and articulation of those observations in a later interview with a police officer. When two eyewitness accounts differ, it does not necessarily mean that one person is lying, nor is it impossible for two witnesses to tell stories that sound quite similar. The police detective should also test the information that a witness shares by personally visiting the crime scene and location of the witness's reported observation. The detective places himself at the exact spot described by the witness and observes (or hears or smells) for himself if it is possible for the witness to have perceived what was reported.

Fact Versus Fantasy

The skilled police detective checks the witnesses for honesty and reliability. She checks records and finds out what other people who know them have to say about the witnesses' sobriety, emotional state and reputation for truthfulness. She compares statements of several witnesses and walks through the event as it was described to determine what could have happened and what could not have happened. People who remember events have "landmarks" in time because they actually happened. The detective will remember the sequence, the people present and attendant items that tend to verify a witness's statements. For example, the witness describes an event, names other people who were present and may even be able to tell the detective what show was on television at the time. The witness will remember these things even if asked to recount what happened in reverse or to skip around and go back and forth among his various observations. A fabricated story will sound different every time and will probably fall apart when the witness is asked to recount certain observations out of sequence.

Plan
When the police detective has examined the crime scene and learned all she can about the crime and the person she is to interview, she will have a good idea about questions to ask the witness. Detectives often make an outline of their questions and keep police reports, sketches and pictures of the crime scene handy to help prepare them for the interview.

Truth
This is the ultimate focus of every investigation the police detective conducts. Although the detective may have certain information that leads her to believe she knows what the suspect, witness or other inter-viewee is going to tell her, she has to keep an open and nonjudgmental mind. A preconceived notion that certain people are innate liars or that others speak nothing but the truth will get an officer into trouble.

Interviewing Techniques
Preparing for an Interview
The police detective prepares himself adequately to maximize the effec-tiveness of his interview. Often it's hasty, maybe no more than a mental review of his knowledge of the case or a quick briefing by the patrol officer who first arrived at the crime scene. When time permits, however, a more formal preparation takes place. The police detective's six key elements of preparation include:

Familiarity With the Case. The detective must fix in his mind what he currently knows about the crime following the "who, what, when, where, why and how" guide. He needs to give special attention to the specific details, especially those that have not become public knowledge.

Familiarity With the Background of the Interviewee. The police detec-tive must acquire some background knowledge about the interviewee before the interview. Normally, he obtains that information during a preinterview session. The detective also attempts to develop a rapport with the person interviewed. One of the best "warm-up" techniques includes having a person talk about himself. The detective should ask the interviewee for the following personal information:

- Name and address.
- Age, place of birth, nationality and race.
- Educational background.
- Present and past occupation, skills, places of employment.
- Habits, hobbies and associates—how and where leisure time is spent.
- Information about past problems with police or other legal troubles.

The detective should ask these questions and others that come to mind in a casual manner, taking an interest and trying to find some common topic he can talk with the person about. For example, maybe the interviewee was born in Wyoming and the detective is from northern Colorado, or they might have attended the same college or have similar hobbies, such as boating. These important techniques can create an environment that enables the interviewee to remain at ease. Often they will reveal far more information than they would have in a cold, traditional police setting. This "warm-up" precedes advising them of their rights, since none of the identifying information is incriminating.

Estimate of Information Sought. The police detective must have an objective for the interview, yet remain attentive to added information. All known information, plus information obtained from each interviewee, has a cumulative effect and the skilled detective uses this to his advantage. Each interview he conducts should be reassessed in light of any additional information that can be gained from each person.

Establishing Physical Environments. Whenever possible, the police detective arranges to have a private area for the interview, free from outside interference such as telephone calls or other interruptions. The best location is a specially furnished interview room at the police station.

The traditional interview room at a police station will be austere and sterile; these "police" environments rarely produce the desired interview or interrogation results. Much of the reason these facilities remain stark stems from traditional thinking, especially among the older police officers who normally have control of how the station house operates. As time, education, training and new thinking spread throughout police ranks, many of the old ideas, customs and traditions will be replaced.

A skilled, successful interrogator will choose or create an environment that has a moderate "official" feel but will also try to put the interviewee into a setting he doesn't expect, a setting that's more like a business office instead of a police station.

Note: I've created several interview rooms over the years at police stations. My technique transforms the standard austere and "official" interview room into a pleasant environment with fish tanks, pictures on the wall, lamps and other furnishings so that it resembles a business office. When an interviewee enters this pleasing, businesslike environment, she has temporarily left or "escaped" from the "police environment." I found that interviewees coming into police stations were tense and uncomfortable and wanted to provide just enough information to satisfy the detective and then get out. Other interviewees would become hostile and refuse to talk or would say they didn't know or see anything, even when the detective knew those persons might hold the key to investigative success. Hostile witnesses often make more trouble for the detective than no witnesses, especially in court, where a person testifying might say the opposite of what she said to a detective or become evasive and make the court doubt her testimony.

Establishing the Right Seating Arrangement. Depending on the effect the detective wants to create for the interview, the seating arrangement in an interview often plays a key role. For example, the detective may choose to have a table or other barrier between him and the interviewee and sit in a bigger chair for psychological advantage. Size and design differences in furniture indicate relative importance or superiority. The same concept plays an important but unspoken role in offices of government officials, business executives and others. The skilled detective plays off that unspoken sense of superiority when necessary to impress or ensure that interviewees clearly understand their role.

However, the detective doesn't want to take advantage of his superior position, so he moves away from the desk and big chair to one of the same size as the one occupied by the interviewee, demonstrating an air of openness and trust between them.

Often, a detective will arrange the seating so the two sit face to face, knee to knee, and assume the attitude of a "concerned uncle." After first creating an impression of authority and distance, the detective uses this casual seating to give the interviewee a sense of closeness to the detective, somewhat like an old friend, someone to whom he can tell all he knows without fear.

Ensuring Comfort and Social Necessities. The police detective has a responsibility for the safety, health and comfort of the person she interviews if it takes place where she controls the environment, such as in the police station. The detective must ensure availability of restroom facilities, water or other refreshments when the interview is prolonged. The detective must also ensure that the interviewee experiences no psychological abuse or duress beyond normal nervousness. Statements made under stressful conditions will probably be recanted. Witnesses or suspects may claim they said what the detective wanted to hear just to get out of there as soon as possible (which could also be true).

Interview and Interrogation Strategies

A successful interviewer or interrogator must learn to do some acting that satisfies the situation and the personality of the interviewee. The type of image the detective wants to project to the interviewee depends largely on the background information available plus the preinterview discussion noted earlier. The following "roles" will normally cover any interview or interrogation situation the police detective might encounter and includes those used by seasoned investigators.

Personality

To become truly proficient at interviewing or interrogation, a police detective learns the importance of portraying a variety of personality traits. She must adjust character to harmonize with, or dominate, the many moods and traits of the interviewee, becoming so involved in the part that she begins to feel the emotions and attitudes she's pretending to display. The detective must be able to feign anger, fear, joy and other emotions without allowing that to affect her judgment or reveal any personal emotion about the interviewee.

Sympathy

A police detective soon learns that people like to complain and gossip. He can use that knowledge to considerable advantage in most interviews. Depending on the interviewee, the detective finds the right opportunity to begin his act of sympathy for the interviewee who has to endure the situation, such as a victim of a crime, or for a witness having to endure the responsibility of possessing valuable knowledge. During interrogation of a suspect, the detective might project sympathy and a seemingly genuine understanding of why the person committed the crime.

Note: Over twenty years ago, in an advanced criminal investigation school, I received some good advice from a salty old instructor. He said: "What you want to do is develop a strong preinterview rapport, then advise the person of his rights, and when you do it right, the person will say, 'Why do I need a lawyer? I have you.' " The sympathy approach has rarely failed me over the years, and there are many criminals still in jail because of it. Many "hardened" criminals—including rapists, murderers, professional arsonists, burglars and armed robbers—confessed when I used this approach, proving that even they wanted to tell *someone* and, when taken from the "police" environment and traditional attitudes, told all they knew despite understanding they would go to jail for it. I've even had criminals come out of the courtroom on the way to prison for ten, twenty, thirty years or life, and shake my hands as they passed, thanking me for my fair treatment and understanding. Although it has happened many times, I'm still amazed, especially in those cases where the suspects provided me with evidence I probably would not have found without their confession. I've also never had one of the suspects I've interviewed or interrogated challenge or recant their statements or confessions.

Sincerity

Sincerity plays a large role when detectives interview children and the elderly. The detective must convey a sincere sympathy, and normally that's easy to do. Children and elderly people can sense when a detective lies to them, even when it doesn't involve words. They see through an act that's insincere. Once the image shatters, all the techniques known to a veteran detective won't salvage the situation, and rarely will another detective or officer fare better, because the suspicion will remain. Even when it's difficult to feel sincerity toward the interviewee, the police detective must project sincerity effectively.

Impartiality

A skilled police detective conducting interviews or interrogations must appear totally impartial, neutral and open-minded about the situation and the person. Police detectives are traditionally portrayed as becoming "involved," but in real life involvement is the fastest route to failure during interviews. It often leads to interviewees saying whatever they perceive the detective "wants to hear." Whenever the detective cannot project the neutrality he needs, he should not participate in the case investigation, especially in the interviews of suspects, victims or witnesses.

Empathy

Empathy differs somewhat from sympathy. The successful detective knows she must project the understanding needed to draw out important information. The skilled detective approaches these techniques by placing herself in the interviewee's position and asking how she would react in that situation. When the detective can do that, she will know how to obtain the total cooperation of the interviewee.

Firmness

There are times when the police detective must be firm with the interviewee, and often that technique serves to emphasize the importance of the information sought. Most people like to feel needed and important; they want the detective to tell them firmly just how important they are to the successful outcome of an investigation. Certain people the detective encounters during interviews will be indecisive and may signal that they would like the detective to be firm. The projection of firmness often supplies the "excuse" that interviewees are looking for to tell what they know or confess to a crime.

Note: The traditional portrayal of police detectives hovering over a suspect or witness or using "macho" treatment went out with the rubber hose and the hot lights. Certainly, instilling fear in the heart and mind of an interviewee or suspect will bring desired results eventually. The "tough" approach of earlier years led to the Miranda Rule decision and others regarding treatment of people by the police. Today only the unskilled, untrained or plain stupid law enforcement personnel force testimony or confessions from people with these techniques. They are easy to spot—they're the ones who lose all the cases in court. Courts across the country have taken a strong stand on interview and interrogation techniques used by the police. The purpose of investigating a crime and bringing the perpetrator to prosecution in court is to win a conviction. The greatest percentage of cases lost in court result from shoddy investigation including inept interviews and interrogations.

Techniques of Taking Written Statements

Earlier I mentioned that the smart police detective or officer always obtains a written statement from the interviewee and suggested how important that document could be to the credibility of the officer and outcome of the investigation. However, understanding the techniques of "taking a statement" is important. The idea of "getting the facts" and putting them in a report can backfire; putting them in the report and supporting them with the person's written and signed statement can make all the difference.

Who Writes the Interviewee's Statement?

The detective should always write the interviewee's statement based on information revealed during the interview. The detective must define the focus of the statement and cover elements of proof. The written statement should contain the "relevant" information an interviewee is prepared to testify about in court. Most interviewees will ramble on about all types of things related and unrelated to the crime. During the interview, the detective listens, takes notes and shapes a written statement from what he hears that has importance to the case. For example, a typical interviewee will digress into all sorts of suppositions, guesstimates and anecdotes. The detective, the prosecutor and the court are only interested in the narrow parameters of the crime under investigation. The written statement must emphasize information that establishes "elements of proof," identifies other relevant aspects, and focuses on the credible knowledge of the interviewee. Only a rookie would have an interviewee write his own statement. However, after three hours of talking, the interviewee might expect a long multipage statement and be confused or disappointed when the detective hands him a one- or two-page written statement to read and sign. The detective must explain the reasons to the interviewee. This will have the additional benefit of helping the interviewee understand what might be expected of him later when testifying in court.

Recorded and Verbatim Statements

Police detectives often record the interview on tape or have a stenographer in the room taking down everything said. Both have advantages and disadvantages for the detective.

Tape Recording the Interview

Tape recording an interview will supply an absolute record of what went on and what was said by whom during an interview or interrogation. However, many interviewees don't consent to being recorded, and often the interviewee becomes very uncomfortable in the presence of a microphone or tape recorder. It affects what they say and when they talk; they may appear to measure each word. Normally, the interviewee must be told the interview is being taped. Most detectives use their judgment about using a tape recorder on a case-by-case, interviewee-by-interviewee basis.

Verbatim Statements

Few police departments have the budget necessary to provide stenographic personnel for each interview; however, high-priority cases such as murder will normally require a stenographer in the interview room. Verbatim statements place great demands on the skill and experience of the stenographer. For example, when the interviewee begins to ramble about how she doesn't like chocolate cake or ice cream, the stenographer must stop until the detective gets the interviewee back to the relevant information.

Note: One common problem of verbatim or recorded statements results from the ramblings of interviewees, often going into guesstimates, supposition, hearsay and other matters that have nothing to do with the case at hand. Interviewees also tend to name a variety of people, some perhaps relevant but most not so. A defense attorney has the right through "discovery" to obtain the tapes or transcripts and might win approval to have the tape played for the court. If the interviewee expressed a variety of opinions and mentioned names that the detective discarded as irrelevant to the case, a skilled defense lawyer could make it sound as if the police had run a shoddy investigation, picking and choosing evidence to frame the defendant. Although untrue, the jury might begin wondering and that could lead to "reasonable doubt" and acquittal.

Closed Circuit Television (CCTV)

CCTV has come into widespread use in police departments and serves a valuable purpose, both in patrol functions and for the detective. Many departments now have a mobile version of CCTV mounted in police vehicles to record stops and activities of patrol officers or detectives and the occupants of stopped vehicles. Most departments now have CCTV in the booking area of the police station to record the activities and conduct of officers and arrested persons from the point of entry until booking processes end. This prevents accusations of brutality or improper behavior by police officers and records belligerence or intoxication of persons brought in. Jails and prisons also use CCTV extensively to monitor and control inmates.

The CCTV is also of value to detectives for recording their interviews and interrogations. But just as recorders and stenographers pose problems, there are a variety of pros and cons associated with CCTV use. Often the CCTV will not be used by the detective until after the preinterview session and perhaps the interview itself is completed. When the information has critical importance or the suspect wants to confess, the CCTV is turned on to record that part. Each situation has its own requirements, but with discretion and skill, the officer or detective interviewing or interrogating can take advantage of a CCTV system.

Use of Lie Detectors

One of the largest myths in law enforcement concerns polygraph systems, often called "lie detectors." The reality of the polygraph is that they're unreliable. Polygraph and voice stress evaluators both operate on the same principles; neither "detects lies," but both might or might not detect stress, and that's much different from a conclusion that a suspect or witness has lied about some information. This weakness of the system also works in another way as well. If a person takes a polygraph test and, although guilty of a crime, does not perceive or believe his or her acts created a crime, the polygraph or voice stress test will not indicate any deception characteristics.

Note: During my thirty years as a law enforcement officer, the last twenty as a criminal investigator, I've caused suspects, witnesses and victims—about twenty-five in all—to take a polygraph test. Despite using highly trained and skilled polygraph operators in various places throughout the United States and in a few foreign countries, I've received the wrong information from the tests every time. I stopped asking for polygraph tests, as many detectives who gain experience over the years believe they waste time and rarely show guilt or innocence accurately.

The Interrogation

Interrogation techniques come into play primarily with a suspect of a crime when the objective is a confession. Normally, a suspect will ask for a lawyer when the Miranda warning is given them at the time of arrest and that prevents questioning until a lawyer talks with them or is present at the interrogation. A smart lawyer will tell the suspect not to answer any questions, especially if she knows or suspects the person is guilty of the crime. However, the exception that leads to an interrogation is the suspect who says he's innocent and doesn't need a lawyer and agrees to questioning. When that situation happens, the following key elements guide the police detective.

When to Interrogate

A person should be interrogated only if she definitely and with good reason is believed to be guilty of a crime, to be an accomplice to a crime or to be withholding information directly pertaining to a crime. A person who can be successfully interviewed is never interrogated.

Planning the Interrogation

The police detective bases her plan for interrogation on the facts of the case and on the background information she's able to develop on the person interrogated. Statements of the victim and witnesses, added to information derived from the physical evidence of the case, enable the detective to reconstruct the crime mentally and to anticipate some of the facts she may obtain from the suspect during the interrogation.

Time of Interrogation

The time of interrogation depends largely on the crime, when the suspect is identified and who the suspect is. I personally leave talking to the suspect to the last step in my investigation when I have all the facts. I try to be in a position where I don't need the suspect's cooperation. Instead I give her an opportunity to tell her side of the story or express her denial of involvement.

It's important to note that a suspect, even when waiving her rights and consenting to an interrogation (or interview), has no obligation under the Fifth Amendment to tell the truth if it incriminates her. A witness, for example, might be guilty of a crime for lying or giving false information; however, a suspect can legally lie, give deceptive information or sign false confessions or proclamations of innocence and she cannot be charged with a crime for doing those things.

Place of Interrogation

Normally, an interview room or detective's office in the police station provides the best environment for an interrogation. There's little basic difference between the interview and interrogation in this respect.

Categorizing Suspects

Suspects are categorized according to the approach most likely to induce a successful interrogation. The categories are:

- Known offenders whose guilt is reasonably certain because of evidence available. This category may be further divided into suspects more readily influenced by sympathy or understanding and suspects more readily influenced by logic.
- Suspects whose guilt is doubtful or uncertain because of the lack of essential facts or because of weaknesses in the available evidence. Persons in this category are interrogated to determine truth, falsehoods and distortions of facts.

Note: Some suspects cannot be placed precisely in any of the above categories. The accuracy of the detective's efforts to classify a suspect depends upon his own ability and experience and upon the availability and accuracy of information developed about the suspect or the case. An incorrect classification may lead to an unsuccessful interrogation if the approach based on the original classification is not skillfully and quickly changed before the suspect becomes aware of the detective's error.

Introduction and Warning in the Interrogation

Even though the suspect was advised of his rights at the time of arrest, a prudent detective will readvise him before starting an interrogation. In the stress of arrest, a person might not understand or even remember if the officer told him his rights. If the suspect confesses and supplies much information about the crime—for example, where money or weapons or bodies are hidden—and his attorney can later have the confession ruled inadmissible, probably none of the evidence collected from the confession will be admissible (fruits of the poison tree). Detectives always need to ask suspects if they can read and write English; sometimes they cannot, and that can negate the Miranda warning and any confession or admission in a written statement they sign. The prudent detective having any doubt about a suspect's ability to read and write English must have him read something (not the Miranda warning) he could not possibly have memorized and make that remark in the notes. Once the suspect agrees to continue, the detective can begin to interrogate.

Police Detective's Approach to Interrogations
Several approaches are available to the police detective when questioning a suspect including direct, indirect, psychological or other means. Each of these techniques is explained below.

Direct Approach
The direct approach is normally used to interrogate a suspect whose guilt is reasonably certain. The detective assumes an air of confidence concerning the suspect's guilt and stresses the evidence or testimony indicative of that guilt. Two modifications of the direct approach are:

Sympathetic and Understanding Attitude. A person who is a first offender or who has committed an offense in the heat of passion, anger or jealousy is normally responsive to a sympathetic and understanding attitude. The detective should treat the suspect as a normal human being who, under the stress of circumstance or extreme provocation, has committed an act that is alien to his or her true nature. The detective should strive in every way to gain the confidence of the suspect and to minimize the moral implications without giving any intimation about the penalties of the crime.

When dealing with such a person, the detective should, in a confident manner, emphasize the evidence against the person. Signs of nervous tension should also be pointed out to the suspect as evidence of his guilt. The suspect is repeatedly urged to tell the truth; the use of words with sinister meanings or connotations must be avoided. The question design enables development of a complete and detailed account of the crime from the moment it was first conceived by the suspect until it happened.

Logic and Reasoning. The habitual criminal who feels no sense of wrongdoing in having committed a crime must normally be convinced by the detective that his guilt can be easily established or is already established by testimony or other evidence. The detective points out to the suspect the futility of denying his guilt. The suspect should be confronted at every turn with testimony and evidence to refute his alibis. When the suspect admits to commission or complicity in another crime or to any act or motive connected with the crime under investigation, the admission can be used as a wedge to help secure a complete confession.

Indirect Approach

The indirect approach is exploratory and used normally when interrogating a suspect whose guilt is uncertain or doubtful. Detectives check the suspect's alibis to determine their truthfulness. Facts definitely known to the detective that suggest the suspect's guilt will formulate questions to test the person's reactions and determine whether he or she is inclined to lie.

When evidence is lacking or weak, the detective must proceed cautiously to place the suspect in a position where he or she will be forced to distort or alter facts definitely known to the detective. The suspect should then be requested to explain satisfactorily any discrepancy or distortion of information. The detective may at times imply that much more is known by making statements or by asking questions that lead the suspect to believe that the answers are already known.

After this situation has developed, the detective may revert to direct questioning to obtain an admission or confession. In the indirect approach, the question design develops a detailed account of the suspect's activities before, during and after the time an offense was committed.

Psychological Approach

This approach is designed to focus the thoughts and emotions of the suspect on the moral aspects of the crime and bring about in the person a realization that a wrong has been committed. Great care is taken in employing this approach to ensure that the suspect does not become so emotional as to render any statement made as inadmissible.

The detective may begin this type of interrogation by discussing the moral seriousness of the offense, by appealing to the suspect's civic-mindedness or to responsibilities of citizenship or by emphasizing the effects of their acts on their spouse, children or close relatives. From this beginning, the detective may proceed to such matters as the sorrows and suffering of the victim and the victim's relatives and friends.

The suspect may tend to become emotional when discussing his mother or father, his childhood and childhood associations, his early moral and religious training and persons he holds in high esteem, such as school teachers, religious instructors, athletic coaches, neighbors or friends. This tendency is particularly true when a suspect is guilty of a crime that he feels violates the moral values he associates with these people. Often, the emotional appeal of some person or personal relationship increases in intensity with the passage of time and with the distance separating the suspect from his former environment. By emphasizing the contrast between the suspect's present and former ways of life, the detective may intensify the suspect's emotional response, especially when he has deserted his family, has become orphaned or otherwise separated from his family or when he has forsaken the way of life prescribed in his early moral and religious training.

The psychological approach is often successful with a young person and with a first offender who has not had time to develop a thinking pattern typical of a hardened criminal.

Skill is required in utilizing this approach. The basic emotions and motivations most commonly associated with criminal acts are hate, fear, love and desire for gain. By careful inquiry into the suspect's thinking, feeling and experience, the detective is likely to touch upon some basic weakness and thereby induce in the suspect a genuine desire to talk. The detective should make every effort to establish a common ground of understanding. She should help the suspect to construct a face-saving rationalization for his motives for committing the criminal act and thereby make talking about the crime easier for him.

Other Approaches

After all other interrogative methods and approaches have failed to produce an admission of guilt or confession, techniques of a more subtle nature may be employed. Detailed planning and realism are prerequisites to the successful use of these techniques. The detective should plan the use of these techniques carefully so that the approach will not be obvious to the suspect. Furthermore, the detective must be careful not to jeopardize the success of further interrogative effort by disclosing to the suspect just how much or how little information has been obtained by the police.

The Cold Shoulder. The suspect is invited to the detective's office. If the suspect accepts the invitation, he is taken to the crime scene. The detectives accompanying the suspect say nothing to him or to each other; they simply await the suspect's reactions. This technique permits the suspect, if guilty, to surmise that the detectives may have adequate evidence to prove his guilt, and this may induce him to make an admission or confession. If witnesses whose identities are known to the suspect are available, they may be requested to walk past the crime scene without saying or doing anything to indicate to the suspect they are aware of his presence. This procedure serves to intensify the impression that the facts of guilt have already been established.

Playing One Suspect Against Another. This technique may be used if more than one person is suspected of having been involved in the commission of a crime. There are many variations of this method. In all variations, one suspect is played against another by purposely encouraging the belief of one suspect that her companion in the crime is cooperating with the police or has talked about the crime and has laid the blame on her.

Suspects are normally separated and not allowed to communicate with each other. Periodically, they may be allowed to glimpse or to observe each other from a distance, preferably when one is doing something that the other may construe as cooperation with the police and as prejudicial to observer's interests. The detectives may sometimes confront the stronger suspect with known facts that have been allegedly furnished by the weaker suspect. Known details of the crime may be mentioned in the presence of the stronger suspect under conditions that compromise the weaker suspect. One suspect may be cordially treated or even released, while the other may be given the "cold shoulder." This method is most successful when investigators infer rather than assert that one suspect has confessed to the crime.

Evaluating the Information

The police detective has ample opportunity during the interrogation to observe and evaluate the physical mannerisms and the emotional state of the suspect. The detective must remain alert for any signs of emotional disturbance or nervous tension that may indicate deception or guilt. The detective should evaluate the information given by the suspect in light of known facts, the testimony of the victim and witnesses and the physical evidence available. The detective should verify by other investigative means every pertinent statement made by the suspect.

Telltale Body Language

During interviews and interrogations police detectives must watch for telltale body language. The seven areas considered most important are:

1. Eyes. No matter what their mouth says, the interviewees' eyes will tell the detective what they are thinking. If the pupils widen, they have heard the detective say something pleasant to them. The detective made them feel good by what she said. When pupils contract, the opposite is true. If eyes narrow, the detective has said something they don't believe, and a feeling of distrust is setting in.
2. Eyebrows. If one eyebrow is lifted, the detective has told them something they don't believe or that they perceive to be impossible. Lifting both eyebrows indicates surprise.
3. Nose and ears. If they rub their nose or tug at an ear while saying they understand the detective, it generally means they're puzzled by what she is saying and probably don't know at all what the detective wants them to do.
4. Forehead. If the interviewees wrinkle their forehead downward in a frown, it means they're puzzled or don't like what the detective has said. If the forehead is wrinkled upward, it indicates surprise.
5. Shoulders. When interviewees shrug their shoulders, it usually means they're completely indifferent. They have no interest in what the detective is telling them.
6. Fingers. Drumming or tapping fingers on the arm of a chair or top of a desk indicates either nervousness or impatience.
7. Arms. If interviewees clap their arms across their chest, it usually means they're trying to isolate themselves from the detective or they're actually afraid of the detective and are trying unconsciously to protect themselves.

Chapter Sixteen

The Art of Forensic Psychology

By Katherine Ramsland, Ph.D.

T wo elderly women are found murdered. One is a pawnbroker, the other her stepsister. The former was killed with several severe blows to the back of the skull by a blunt weapon; the latter was hit on the top of her head with what appears to have been the sharp side of an ax. No weapon was found at the scene, but there is evidence that the murderer cleaned himself there. Although some money and a few small items were taken, robbery does not appear to have been the motive.

The detective in charge of the case interviews everyone who had business with either of the victims. In order to screen for potential suspects, he must devise a profile based on both the crime scene and what he knows from his experience with human psychology. Not only must his profile include a range of characteristics but also a strategy for approaching and questioning suspects. Such is the task faced by Inspector Porfiry in one of the earliest examples in fiction of criminal profiling, Dostoevsky's *Crime and Punishment*.

In fact, Porfiry does interview all business associates, but also investigates their lives. He discovers that a student named Raskolnikov has recently been ill, has failed to pay his rent (so he needs money) and has published an article on the idea that extraordinary men are not held to the laws of common people and such men can commit crimes without moral accountability. He's a likely suspect. Porfiry figures that if Raskolnikov *is* the murderer, he will have to approach the young man with some cleverness. When his attempts to trick Raskolnikov fail, Porfiry subtly pressures him into believing that he is a primary suspect and under surveillance. It works. Eventually, Raskolnikov breaks down under the strain of guilt and paranoia and confesses.

Forensic psychology is growing more popular as a subject for contemporary writers, showing up in novels like James Patterson's *Kiss the Girls* and Thomas Harris's *The Silence of the Lambs*, as well as television shows like *Law & Order*, *Cracker* and *Profiler*. In an episode of *Law & Order*, for example, a psychiatrist used by the district attorney was asked to evaluate a young boy to see if he was capable of killing his infant brother. If so, then they would proceed against the boy, but if not, then their suspicions would go to the parents. Authors who create a forensic psychologist for their stories need to know the range of specializations and methods in which these professionals engage.

Overview

So what exactly is forensic psychology? Most people don't really know. They can't quite figure out what psychologists do with corpses, but that's because they misunderstand the word *forensic*, which has more to do with the legal and judicial process than with the morgue. This discipline involves psychology *in* the law, *by* the law and *of* the law. Wherever the legal system and psychology intersect, you have forensic psychology. Such professionals use their expertise with human behavior, motivation and pathology to provide psychological services in the courts, play key roles in criminal investigations, develop specialized knowledge of crimes and motives and conduct forensic research.

Most forensic health professionals work either in a correctional setting or psychiatric hospital. Contrary to popular notions, they don't tend to be active investigators, although that's not altogether implausible. They usually perform the more ordinary roles of assessment and treatment or therapeutic intervention. They need a good background in abnormal and social psychology, along with experience in psychometric testing. Personality theory and criminology is a plus, as is an area of specialization such as juvenile aggression or psychopathy.

Psychological assessment in the forensic arena is relevant to a broad spectrum of cases, from juvenile delinquency to criminal competency to sexual allegations. By virtue of additional training in law and criminality, behavior specialists can assist in the fact-finding process involved in arriving at just decisions in court. They may also assist in civil matters, such as child custody, disability, sexual harassment or claims of emotional suffering.

Assessments can be done for the court, the government, insurance companies or any other decision-making fact finders involved in legal issues. Psychologists may also consult on investigative work. Yet for the most part—and of most interest to crime and mystery writers—mental health specialists with forensic background use their expertise in an adversarial arena. A forensic behavior specialist may serve as an expert witness for the defense or prosecution, or may simply present findings as ordered by the court and be impartial to either side. When a psychologist is hired by one side, generally she is viewed as an enemy by the other, and cross-examination aimed at diminishing witness credibility can be intense.

For the most part, psychologists are there to present findings from test data and clinical interviews, specifically in terms of whether a defendant understands the charges and the legal process, or what his mental state was at the time he allegedly committed a crime. One major difficulty for psychologists—and a source of stress in the courtroom—is that they are trained to help, so they want their findings to make a positive difference. However, as with other types of forensic scientists, psychologists must remain neutral, present their findings to the best of their ability and let the lawyers decide how to use the information.

Try as they might to avoid it, they may be there strictly as a "hired gun." A psychologist was hired by the defense in another episode of *Law & Order* who specialized in dissociation. Because he made a good living at being a court witness and had a heavy investment in defending his theory and expertise, he worked hard to help clear a woman charged with murder. When his own theory began to undermine his testimony, his conflicted response betrayed him as a man with a personal agenda exploited by the defense, not an objective professional. Such experts are all too readily available, although their reputations among their peers usually suffer.

Psychiatrists, Psychologists and Neuropsychologists

Any of these professionals, with additional training in forensics procedures, may be utilized as expert witnesses in the courtroom, but there are differences in the way they approach theories of criminality, use of medication and types of assessment tools. There are also differences in their education and training. Thus, using a psychiatrist as a courtroom consultant or investigative character in fiction would involve a different approach than using a psychologist or neuropsychologist.

Psychiatrists have medical degrees in addition to their clinical training in psychology and tend to make diagnoses based on the *Diagnostic and Statistical Manual of Mental Disorders—IV*, which lists and describes various mental and behavioral syndromes. Writers would need to understand how the manual is used and presented in court. Psychiatrists can also evaluate drug reactions and prescribe drugs, so a writer developing a psychiatrist would need some education in psychopharmacology. A psychiatric approach tends to be either neurological or Freudian. If they do therapy, they tend to assess the causal factors of a person's behavior from past influences—particularly the parents. If they believe strictly in physiological manifestations of mental illness, they tend merely to prescribe drugs and engage in little or no psychotherapy. Forensic psychiatrists are often employed in psychiatric hospitals and prisons, and with the arrival of managed care, psychiatrists are more often used in psychological diagnosis, in part because of their access to hospitals.

Writers will need to know where their character went to school, where they got additional training in psychiatry, how they make interpretations from assessments specific to psychiatry and whether they are board certified in forensic psychiatry.

Likewise, psychologists can do personality assessments for use in diagnosing a case, but their range of theoretical approaches is often greater than that of psychiatrists. They may emphasize cognitive, behavioral or even existential criteria. They may have a preference for behavior modification procedures or for therapies that address deviant behavior via some broad-range context that includes family systems, environment and sociological factors. In other words, they tend to deal with patients on a more individualized basis and to figure out treatments or therapeutic tools that seem relevant to the unique aspects of the case, rather than relying on a strict catalogue of traits. Psychologists cannot prescribe drugs, but are familiar with psychopharmacology. They tend to work in a consulting partnership with psychiatrists or physicians so that they can get drugs prescribed.

A neuropsychologist, on the other hand, tends to focus on the brain and the neurological system to make assessments of mental disorder. In recent years, with increasing evidence of mind/body interaction and the cellular imprinting of emotions, many clinicians have had to include some knowledge of neurology in their repertoire of clinical skills. For example, schizophrenia appears to have a greater physiological component then was previously believed, so neurological studies have become more relevant in its treatment. There is less emphasis than was once the case on blaming the mother or some disruptive element in the environment. Sociopathy is gaining the same status, particularly with new studies on the relationship between brain injuries and antisocial behavior. Neuropsychologists can administer the full battery of tests that psychologists ordinarily do, but they add tests for such things as vision, emotional processing, sleep disorders and organic brain conditions. They tend to have more knowledge of the way the body and its disorders influence the mind than the average psychologist, which has greater scientific impact in a courtroom procedure. They cannot prescribe drugs, but they are expert in assessing drug-related manifestations in behavior. They may also utilize hypnosis more readily than psychiatrists and tend to have better training in it.

Steps in a Typical Case
1. Referral
Psychologists generally get drawn into a court case through an attorney. They may have done some networking to notify attorneys of their availability, but they might also be called upon because of expertise in some area, such as women who kill their babies or children with crime-related trauma. An attorney (or the court) will call, describe the case and offer to set up an appointment with the client. The psychologist must then inform the client that anything said or written down is for the court and may be entered into the legal process. They should not get caught up in confidentiality issues, because they are there as court officials, not as therapists. They should also restrict their client encounters to the referral issue.

Most people think that mental health experts are only used in cases where the insanity defense is being considered and that such situations become a matter of dueling experts, with each side paid to say whatever that attorney wants him to say. While it is true that attorneys may pressure psychologists to enhance or downplay certain psychological ramifications in order to strengthen their case, the psychologist is better off giving an impartial report of what she has found.

Most often, this referral will be for a competency hearing or a "mental state at the time of the offense" (MSO) determination. Unabomber Ted Kaczynski, for example, was evaluated for his ability to defend himself and was found mentally unable to do so. If a person suffers from schizophrenia, as with a man who pushed a woman onto a subway track, then he must be assessed for his mental state at the time—could he conform his actions to the law?—and whether or not he was taking medication. It actually is rare that anyone gets an NGRI ("not guilty by reason of insanity"), but these are the cases that get media scrutiny, so they seem more numerous than they are. And when used, they rarely convince a jury.

2. Building a File

The first thing psychologists must do is collect information. Fortunately, they have the attorney's resources at their disposal, so they provide a list of what they need, such as school and hospital records, work appraisals, military records, crime scene photos, autopsy reports and witness statements, and the attorney must do his best to get them. They also gain information from their own clinical interviews on family background. The kind of information that must be avoided is that which is known to have been illegally acquired, because it will jeopardize the admissibility of the entire report.

Then psychologists perform tests. Forensic assessment involves intelligence, personality, projective and motor skills assessment tests. The most common battery includes the Wechsler Adult Intelligence Scales, the Minnesota Multiphasic Personality Inventory (for evidence of defensiveness, lying, malingering, schizophrenia and psychopathy), the Rorschach, the Thematic Apperception Test, the Millon inventory and, when organic damage is suspected, the Bender-Gestalt and the Halstead-Reitan neuropsychological test.

One important function when testing a defendant using any sort of diminished mental capacity or insanity plea is to check for malingering—the faking of symptoms for amnesia or psychosis. Several tests, such as the MMPI, include scales that indicate lying, exaggeration, faking bad and faking good. Psychopaths are con artists and can fool even the best behavioral expert. However, they often get caught on the tests because their ideas about the symptoms of psychosis are based on popular misconceptions rather than a real experience with it.

Another factor in diminished capacity cases is to check the state law. New York has a defense labeled "extreme emotional distress" (which does not have a clear definition), while other states make no provision for diminished capacity whatsoever, except in the case of insanity. Whatever the defense, writers should always check the state laws and proceedings. Often there is little uniformity from one district to another.

3. Psychological Report

This must be a written summary of the psychologist's findings specific to the referral issue, which will include the referral source, the reason for the referral, the sources of the data on the client, a confidentiality waiver, the test scores and interpretations, significant client background, collateral information, a mental status examination, a DSM-IV diagnosis, observations during sessions, a summary and recommendations. Anything that goes into this report is discoverable and open to cross-examination, although there is a certain amount of lawyer/client privilege on the defense that extends to the psychologist's examination.

4. Protocol

Like any expert witness, psychologists must be fully prepared when going into court. Generally, they have done an assessment for the court based on psychological tests, crime-scene photos, clinical interviews, public records, witness interviews and hospital or prison reports. Whatever they have written has been made available to the other side and they must be prepared to defend or explain their opinions. In addition, if they have published other material relevant to their testimony, e.g., a book or article on situational homicides, then they may have to defend or explain any statements in those reports as well.

The idea is to be credible, confident and competent, i.e., trustworthy. Court etiquette demands that they dress conservatively, have all relevant data on hand, act professionally and address either the judge or the jury, depending on the type of legal proceeding (bench or jury trial). They answer only questions they are asked and if they feel that something should be brought out in the trial that has been neglected, they make that suggestion to the relevant attorney (unless hired specifically by the court as a neutral witness). Impression management is the key. The more clear (free of jargon), composed and convincing they are to a jury, the more likely it is that their testimony will make a positive difference.

5. Making Recommendations

Although psychologists try to avoid making a judgment on the "ultimate issue" of guilt or innocence, they are often asked to give an expert opin-

Competency hearings.

These legal procedures take place in both criminal and civil cases. Most often, we hear about competency to stand trial—whether or not a defendant understands the legal process and can contribute to his defense. However, there are other competencies relevant to the criminal process: the competency to waive one's Miranda rights (right to silence and to legal counsel), to confess, to understand the nature of the crime committed, to testify, to refuse an insanity defense and even to be executed. Charles Singleton murdered a sixty-two-year-old store owner in 1979 and was given the death sentence. At some point during his many years of appeals, he developed paranoid schizophrenia and had to be given psychotropic drugs to relieve the symptoms. His psychosis went into remission, but he decided to stop taking the drugs, making it difficult to carry out his sentence: We don't execute the insane. The issue then became an ethical dilemma: Do we force him onto medication to make him sane enough (competent) to be executed?

In civil cases, competency screenings cover such things as parenting capacity in child custody suits, guardianship and consent to treatment.

Insanity.

Most people believe that this is a psychological term, but it is, in fact, a legal definition. It means a lack of responsibility for one's actions due to mental disease or defect, which reduces criminal intent. Admittedly, there is room for interpretation, and various states have differing responses to the idea of cognitive or volitional impairment. Substance abuse and brain damage assessment are generally part of the screening process.

---

ion on the chances of an offender repeating his offense. Historically known as the analysis of "dangerousness," it is now referred to as risk assessment.

Gary Gilmore had spent much of his life in prison for delinquent activities. After being released and then committing armed robbery in 1973, he went to trial again. He asked permission to address the court, saying that he had experienced only two years of freedom since he was fourteen. He argued that "you can keep a person locked up too long" and that "there is an appropriate time to release somebody or to give them a break. . . . I've got problems and if you sentence me to additional time, I'm going to compound them." The judge had a tough decision. He might have asked a psychologist to give him some guidance about Gilmore's future, and in fact, in prison and out, Gilmore proved to be dangerous. He was released in April of 1976 and by July, he was back for the cold-blooded murder of two men.

It was once the case that mental health experts used their best clinical judgment to try to determine whether someone was going to repeat his violent behavior if let out into the community. However, they were right in only one out of three cases. That means that there were many "false positives"—people committed who would not be violent—and "false negatives"—people allowed to go free who then committed violence.

In the eighties, a number of studies were undertaken to develop instruments that would improve the percentage of correct assessments of dangerousness, and instead of focusing on dangerousness itself, they emphasized what they called risk factors.

Interviews and inventories were developed to determine whether a defendant was a psychopath (which had a high correlation for recidivism), whether he was sexually deviant (another good predictor), how impulsive he was, whether he had a character disorder or mental illness, whether he had paranoid delusions, what his school record was and what his history of violence was. (Gilmore would have had a poor showing on all counts.) Out of these studies came guidelines for making predictions based on facts and logic rather than on intuition or psychoanalytic assumptions.

According to risk assessment expert, John Monahan, such research must meet seven criteria: (1) "Dangerousness" must be segregated into component parts: risk factors, harm and likelihood of occurrence; (2) a rich array of risk factors must be assessed from multiple domains; (3) harm must be scaled in terms of seriousness and assessed with multiple measures; (4) the probability estimate of risk must be acknowledged to change over time and context; (5) priority must be given to actuarial (statistical) research; (6) the research must be done in large and broadly representative samples; and (7) the goal must be management as well as assessment.

The above criteria are met in a study done by the MacArthur Foundation. They examined the relationship between mental disorder and violent behavior directed against others and devised a comprehensive list of risk factors. Experts developed risk assessment instruments, such as the Psychopathy Checklist-Revised (PCL-R), to assist with measurement and prediction. The PCL-R proved to be one of the best predictors of repeat violence because psychopaths seem not to learn from punishment.

The PCL-R was devised by Robert Hare. He listed twenty items to be evaluated by a clinician. The instrument, with items grouped around two basic factors (narcissistic personality and antisocial behavior) was tested extensively with prison inmates. Psychopathy was defined as a disorder characterized by traits such as lack of remorse or empathy, shallow emotions, manipulativeness, lying, egocentricity, glibness, parasitic lifestyle and the persistent violation of social norms. The perfect image of a psychopath was depicted in a character played by John Larroquette on several linked episodes of *The Practice*—and he *did* recidivate!

Risk management, i.e., devising programs that would help a person avoid repeating his crimes, focuses on those factors that yield to intervention, such as substance abuse, delusions, social support and living arrangements.

Other Applications

Outside the courtroom, psychologists have some presence in emergency service fields such as fire control, corrections and law enforcement. They may be asked to consult with police departments on hostage negotiations; provide assessments on preemployment exams for police officers, fitness for duty evaluations and special unit (SWAT, Tactical Response Team) evaluations; or offer investigative assistance with unsolved crimes. Of most interest to writers is (1) the art of profiling, (2) psychological autopsies, (3) investigative psychology and (4) investigative hypnosis.

Profiling

Within the past two decades, there has been increased use of profiling, although it remains a controversial tool. Not everyone believes that devising a hypothetical portrait of a suspect makes a contribution to solving crimes, but some profiles have been surprisingly accurate. The problem is that it's difficult to know when you're working with a good one until the suspect is caught and compared against it. Hitler was profiled to try to determine his vulnerability and plan of action, and profiling was used (ineffectively) with the Boston Strangler. Thomas Harris includes this device in *The Silence of the Lambs* and *Red Dragon*, and Faye Sultan offers female profiler Portia McTeague in *Help Line*. Even the earliest fictional detectives like Sherlock Holmes and Poe's Auguste Dupin offer some sense of what's involved in the process, in that the finest details of a crime scene must be noted and perhaps examined in ways that no one expects. Intuitive thinking is essential, coupled with logic.

Outside fiction, profiling has been developed in the FBI's Behavioral Science Unit (a.k.a. Investigative Support Unit) by such people as John Douglas (*Mindhunter*), Robert Ressler (*Whoever Fights Monsters*) and Stephen Michaud and Roy Hazelwood (*The Evil That Men Do*). However, it is also used by police departments all over the country as a tool in their crime-fighting arsenal. The basic idea is to get a body of data yielding common patterns so that one can give a general description of an UNSUB (unknown suspect). Profiling involves the psychologist using his expertise in human behavior, motivation and patterns of pathology to create a multidimensional report. Contrary to popular belief, it's not necessary that the offender be a serial criminal. Profiling can be done from a single crime scene, and since 70 to 75 percent of murders are situational, developing a way to profile without reference to repeated patterns is useful.

A good profile is an educated attempt to provide investigative agencies with parameters about the type of person who committed a certain crime, based on the idea that people tend to be slaves to their psychology and will inevitably leave clues. Male or female? Organized or disorganized? Geographically stable or transient? Impulsive or compulsive? They work best if the offender displays some evidence of psychopathology, such as sadistic torture, postmortem mutilation or pedophilia. Some killers leave a "signature"—a behavioral manifestation of a personality quirk, such as staging the corpse for the most humiliating exposure or tying ligatures with a complicated bow. This helps to link crime scenes and alert law enforcement officers of the presence of a serial rapist or killer. It may also help, if a pattern is detected, to predict future possible attacks, the most probable pickup or dump sites and victim types.

Profiling is not just a personality assessment, but includes other types of data. Assessing an UNSUB's age, race, sex, occupation, educational level, social support system, MO, type of employment and other sociological factors are just as important as evidence of a personality disorder. It's also important to include a geoforensic analysis of the kind of place a killer might chose as a body dump site, such as Ted Bundy's preference for heavily wooded mountains outside Seattle.

The best profilers have gained their knowledge from experience with criminals and have developed an intuitive sense about certain types of crime. Their knowledge base is developed from both physical and non-physical evidence. Generally, profilers employ psychological theories that provide ways to analyze mental deficiency such as delusions, personality characteristics like hostility, criminal thought patterns and character defects. They also need to know about actuarial data such as the age range into which offenders generally fall and how important an unstable family history is to criminality.

One of the most astounding profiles ever developed was done in 1957 by psychiatrist James Brussel in the case of New York's "Mad Bomber," George Metesky. Brussel studied photos of the bomb scenes, analyzed letters written to the newspapers and concluded that the bomber was paranoid; hated his father; was obsessed with his mother; worked at Consolidated Edison; had a heart condition; lived in Connecticut; was heavyset, middle-aged, single, Catholic; lived with a brother or sister; and would be wearing a double-breasted suit, buttoned. Although investigators found Metesky in his pajamas (at the Connecticut home of his two sisters), when they requested that he get dressed, he came out wearing a double-breasted suit, buttoned.

Caleb Carr picked up on this technique in *The Alienist* with his turn-of-the-century psychologist, Dr. Kreizler, who follows the idea of creating "an imaginary man"—the sort of person who might commit the murders—and initially establishes that the serial killer of young male prostitutes is organized (makes a plan), does not like what he is doing (conflicted), is triggered by something that the boys represent (compulsive) and wants to be caught (possibly dissociated). As the clues come in, he adds more details to the portrait, and in the end, is proven correct in his extrapolation from the crimes to the criminal's personality and circumstances.

As exciting as this process is, crime writers should realize that it is not universally respected, nor is its success rate analyzed or documented.

Psychological Autopsies
A medical autopsy determines cause and means of death by examining the body. In cases where the manner of death is unexplained, such as someone hit by a car, and it's not clear whether it was a suicide or homicide, natural or accidental, a psychological autopsy may be needed

to assist the coroner or medical examiner in clearing up the mystery. The idea is to discover the state of mind of the victim preceding death and the results may be used to settle criminal cases, estate issues, malpractice suits or insurance claims. First used in the 1950s in Los Angeles, psychological autopsies are now a more standard resource, although still questioned as a rigorous scientific technique for use in court.

The investigator examines numerous factors to make the proper determination. In a suspected suicide, for example, it's important to rule out accident and such unfortunate incidents as autoerotic asphyxiation. The database generally consists of an examination of the death scene; a study of all documentation pertaining to the death, such as witness statements and police reports; interviews with family members and associates; medical autopsy reports; and all relevant documents pertaining to the individual's life history, like school or employment records. A close examination of the death scene may indicate degree of intent and lethality—a secluded place and the use of a gun indicating a higher degree than using slow-acting pills in a place where the victim is likely to be discovered.

In a suspected suicide, questions would be asked about the victim's stress level and any major changes in his or her life, such as marital separation, unemployment or a significant death in the family. One of the most famous psychological autopsies was done by Dr. Raymond Fowler following the death of Howard Hughes. He practically wrote a biography, and in fact, the methods are not dissimilar. Arthur Bahr, in his first novel, *Certifiably Insane*, made his protagonist, a forensic psychiatrist, a specialist in this technique.

Psychological Investigator
This is a hybrid between a psychologist and detective, although not quite fully either one. Such professionals might help the police to interpret a crime scene. They don't necessarily have a graduate degree in psychology, nor a license, but get involved in applied projects in police work. Specifically, they help to gather information that then gets interpreted within a scientific framework, which involves background in sociology, geology and psychology. They cannot testify in court, but might make for an interesting character in a novel.

Investigative Hypnosis
A landmark appellate case in 1968, *Harding v. State*, involved a request to allow the admission of court testimony that had been "refreshed," or

enhanced, through hypnosis. Prior to that, hypnosis had been considered too unreliable for lawful admissibility. With the *Harding* judgment, testimony was admitted, but jurors were instructed to evaluate its credibility. More such cases followed, and soon courts were forced to devise guidelines. However, a number of courts opted for the *Frye*-based decision in *State v. Mack*, in which the Minnesota Supreme Court ruled that hypnosis had not been generally accepted by the scientific community and, therefore, recall from hypnosis is inadmissible. Today, courts are still divided on the subject.

Yet the state courts may not have the last say. In 1987, the U.S. Supreme Court challenged an Arkansas law that prohibited *per se* the testimony of witnesses whose memories had been hypnotically refreshed.

Due to the foibles of human memory, hypnosis has been utilized as a tool to try to fill in gaps, add detail and ensure accuracy in eyewitness testimony. The most popular techniques involve past-memory regression and memory enhancement, as was seen on the "Mind Over Murder" episode of *Cracker*, where the abrasive police psychologist, Fitz, helped an officer to recall details when his partner was killed. A psychological hypnotist exploits the subject's suggestibility in order to induce a trance that produces a relaxed mental state. The subject becomes attentive, focused and less prone to critical judgment that can block memory. Going into a trance purportedly allows the heightening of imagination, with the hope that some detail, such as a license plate number, might be recalled that would otherwise remain inaccessible. Hypnosis was used in such high-profile cases as the Boston Strangler and the Sam Sheppard murder investigation. Even Ted Bundy was convicted in part with hypnotically refreshed testimony, which was the subject of one of his appeals. (He lost.)

Problems with using hypnosis include the possibility that a recovered memory is incomplete, inaccurate or based on some leading suggestion. There also might be hypermnesia—exceptionally vivid recall of the past—or confabulation—filling in the gaps with false material that supports the subject's self-interest. In addition, hypnotized subjects may experience hypnotic recall, in which a posthypnotic suggestion of something that did not happen gets retroactively integrated into the subject's memory as if it did. Also, personal beliefs and prejudices may influence how an event was initially registered and/or how it is interpreted by the person during recall. More problematic is "memory hardening," which occurs when a false memory brought out through hypnosis seems so real that the subject develops false confidence in it. All of these problems have been documented in experiments, along with the realization that a false memory, once articulated, can be difficult to distinguish from genuine memories. Unfortunately, jurists are generally unaware of these errors, and one study with college students showed that they attributed a higher rate of accuracy to hypnotically refreshed testimony than was warranted by evidence.

Conclusion

Fitz on *Cracker* has something in common with Inspector Porfiry in *Crime and Punishment*: Both know how to decipher criminal offenders and employ psychological pressure points to get results. A good grasp of how psychology works in forensic situations can enrich any crime novel and heighten suspense—but only if it's credible. Knowing how psychologists work is not sufficient; forensic psychology involves an entirely different type of perspective, training and experience. Writers who do their research will be rewarded with satisfied readers not only among the lay public but among those in the profession as well.

Chapter Seventeen

Profiling the Criminal

by Sean Mactire

from *Malicious Intent: A Writer's Guide to How Murderers, Robbers, Rapists and Other Criminals Think*

From 1940, with a patriotic pause for World War II, to 1957, New York City was terrorized by an unknown subject who came to be known as the "Mad Bomber." The police were baffled and up against a stone wall until they consulted Dr. James A. Brussel. Dubbed by the press as the "Sherlock Holmes of the Couch," Brussel is the founder of the art of psychological profiling of criminals. After one interview with the police, Brussel, with almost psychic ability, provided a detailed portrait of the Bomber. But it was not magic nor was it pure science that led Dr. Brussel to his conclusions. He simply zeroed in on a single subject by combining identifiable behavioral characteristics with statistical probability, the skills of modern psychiatric examination and good intuition.

While this new "art" of criminal investigation was successful and pioneered the field of modern forensic psychology, the technique used by Dr. Brussel was limited and prone to error because it focused on individuals. For the next seventeen years, this technique rested in the shadows until, in 1974, the FBI's Behavioral Science Unit based at Quantico, Virginia, debuted its new system of "profiling" based on the pioneering work of Dr. Brussel. To the ever expanding world of law enforcement and criminal detection entered the "psychological profiling team."

The Development of Profiling

Prior to 1974, profiling, the development of a psychological mug shot of an unknown suspect, was a very haphazard effort. Even though Dr. Brussel had earlier successes with his technique, it was not highly accurate, and when used as part of a team effort, the technique was totally off target. When Dr. Brussel was asked to join a team of experts to assist with the Boston Strangler case, the team concluded that there were two murderers: one a loner, who worked as a schoolteacher, and the other a homosexual with an intense hatred of women. In fact, this profile never led to the Strangler's arrest. He was apprehended by good old-fashioned police work. Once in custody, the profile proved to be dead wrong. Albert DeSalvo was a married man with children and a former soldier. He did not hate women and he did not hate his mother, as the Freudian theories put forth by the team suggested. He was a rapist who killed only when he became enraged over his own impotence. When he discovered that his impotence was "cured" after the last murder, he stopped murdering and returned to committing only rapes. But this failure to correctly profile the Boston Strangler did not cause law enforcement to throw the baby out with the bath water. Profiling was a good idea that only needed work to improve the technique's accuracy.

With a grant from the National Institute of Justice, the FBI set up its special project for profiling at the FBI Academy in Quantico, Virginia. The bureau began by compiling a library of known cases and defined psychological studies and interviews of murderers. (Coincidentally, such a project had been suggested by crime writer Colin Wilson in 1960.) This was the beginning of a new weapon in the war on crime.

This new system of psychological profiling focused in on reading *the crime scene* for behavioral clues in order to identify the *type* of criminal responsible for the crime. This was an advance over the method used by Dr. Brussel and his peers, which focused on the individual and greatly depended on the guidance and reputation of the psychologist or psychiatrist offering the professional assessment. Since most of Dr. Brussel's contemporaries had their own theories on criminal behavior, the old "profile" method was flawed by personal bias and the whims of chance. The new FBI method was highly systematic, allowing law enforcement professionals the flexibility of combining their years of investigative experience and intuitive judgment with the behavior clues deduced from the crime scene evidence, coroners' reports and statistical probability. The central component of the system was the classification of unknown subjects into two types: the organized or the disorganized offender. However, this relied too much on experience and intuition, so a further component was added: the Criminal Personality Research Project. This began as criminal behavior surveys based on interviews with a series of imprisoned murderers and rapists that provided an ongoing database of behavioral characteristics. This component is now an encyclopedic data bank that is continually reviewed and updated.

In 1984, the system was enhanced by the establishment of the National Center for the Analysis of Violent Crime, also based at Quantico and run by the FBI's Behavioral Sciences Unit (BSU). NCAVC is a law enforcement clearinghouse and resource center for the collection and sharing of violent crime data. Together with the BSU, also known as the "think tank" of law enforcement, NCAVC uses the latest in cutting-edge computer technology to combat violent crime nationwide, especially serial crime. This includes specialized projects such as VICAP (the Violent Criminal Apprehension Program) and PROFILER (a computerized system that profiles serial murderers).

In 1973, the early system of the BSU was put into practice when seven-year-old Susan Jaeger was abducted and murdered while camping with her parents in Montana. When the FBI entered the case employing its new technique, it profiled the unknown subject as:

- A homicidal voyeur, who lived near the victim's campsite
- A young, white male, as statistics suggested
- An organized type, made evident by the use of a knife brought by the offender and taken away
- A loner of average or higher intelligence, also as statistical probability suggested

These behavioral jigsaw puzzle pieces were put together with the investigators' experience, which also said that since no ransom note or word had come forth, the girl was dead and the killer most probably mutilated the victim for souvenirs.

In January 1974, the murder of a local teenager was linked to a suspect who was identified by an FBI informant. However, no evidence could connect him to the crimes. The suspect was David Meirhofer, a twenty-three-year-old single Vietnam veteran who lived near the campgrounds. Despite the fact that Meirhofer had passed two tests, a lie detector and a truth serum interrogation, the experts from Quantico were sure he was their man. Aided by Susan Jaeger's parents, the FBI induced the killer to tip his hand, enabling them to obtain a warrant for the search of Meirhofer's apartment. As they had predicted, body parts—the grisly souvenirs of Meirhofer's crimes, which proved his guilt—were found, and while in custody, he confessed to the killings of the two girls and also two local boys whose disappearances and deaths were then unsolved.

Shortly thereafter, Meirhofer hanged himself in his jail cell. This was a breakthrough case, and David Meirhofer became the first serial killer to be caught by the new technique of criminal profiling. Within a decade, the system would be refined and would be known as the accurate, systematic profiling technique called CIAP (the Criminal Investigative Analysis Program).

While Dr. Brussel is credited with the founding of the art of profiling, the refiners of the technique to be known as CIAP were Howard Teten, Patrick Mullany, Robert Ressler and John Douglas. These pioneers of profiling put their careers on the line to advance the new technique, which included unofficial interviews with convicted murderers that could have wrecked their careers if there had been any problems stemming from the interviews. However, there were no complaints, and the risk paid off with invaluable answers to numerous questions about why these killers did such brutal acts.

The Elveson Murder

In 1979, their research, added to the infant technique, was put to the test to aid in the search for the killer of New York City schoolteacher Francine Elveson. Miss Elveson, 26, was the victim of a brutal sexual assault and mutilation murder. Her naked, maimed body was found on the roof of the apartment house where she lived with her parents. In this case, the FBI got an opportunity to examine a crime scene as that canvas of mayhem we discussed earlier. The killer literally arranged the body to create a portrait of murder and rage and to use as a challenge to police that he would never be caught. He had even written his challenge on the victim's thigh. All her personal effects were carefully placed to accent the portrait, and the mutilation was also carefully done to dehumanize the dead woman, with the removed body parts placed back on the body with artistic intent. A pendant in the shape of the Jewish symbol for good luck, the Chai, was taken as a souvenir, and the woman's body was bent and twisted into the shape of the Chai, an almost mocking replica of the pendant.

The case was extremely bizarre, and there was a lot of publicity. Over two thousand suspects were interviewed, but by the time the FBI was called in, the police were no closer to catching the killer than the day the body was found. The police felt they had no clues.

However, John Douglas, one of the pioneers of profiling, found a number of clues in this ritual killing that the police could not see. Agent

Douglas was looking for clues to the *type* of murderer, while the police were searching for the individual murderer.

The canvas the killer had created with crime science produced this portrait of the unknown subject:

1. The killer was both "organized" and "disorganized." The FBI called this a "mixed" crime scene; however, the killer was classified as a "disorganized" type because it was felt that the killer had acted out a fantasy ritual with a victim that he simply killed on the spur of the moment. There was no planning; the victim was not chosen and hunted. The victim was just unlucky enough to meet her killer by chance, and the killer took advantage of this meeting to act on his fantasy.

2. The portrait also indicated a white male, between twenty-five and thirty-five, of average appearance and who was familiar with the layout of the building and the habits of the tenants. The killer was confident that he would be uninterrupted during the ritual mutilation that he carried out.

3. Statistics pointed out that the killer was a school dropout and was unemployed, lived alone, and did not use drugs or alcohol.

4. The ritual and the sadistic rage involved in the killing indicated that the killer was sexually inadequate and could not relate to women normally, which was borne out by the fact that the victim was not raped but was object raped with a pen and umbrella thrust into her vagina. The semen found on the body showed that the orgy of mutilation gave the killer the sexual gratification he desired. These factors also indicated that the killer had a history of mental illness and possibly had been in a psychiatric hospital. The killer's implied desire to shock and offend, along with his challenge to the police, also indicated the presence of mental illness.

5. The way in which the crime appeared to have happened seemed to indicate that the victim knew her killer, that the killer was a regular visitor to the building, and that given another similar window of opportunity, he would kill again.

Armed with this profile, the police closed in on Carmine Calabro, a thirty-year-old, unmarried, unemployed actor, who was a high school dropout and who regularly visited his father, a neighbor of the victim. However, Calabro had an alibi that almost cleared him. He had severe mental problems, and he was undergoing treatment in a psychiatric hospital at the time of the murder. But it was discovered that the hospital's security was very lax, and Calabro was absent without permission on the day of the murder.

Calabro pleaded "not guilty," but dental evidence matched the bite marks on Francine Elveson's body, and he was convicted, sentenced to life in prison. This was another impressive demonstration of the art of profiling, and the profile was so accurate that the police jokingly asked why the FBI hadn't given them the killer's phone number too. The jokes stopped and soon the new investigative tool was warmly embraced by the country's law enforcement community.

The Murder Types

As a result of its research, the FBI lists five categories of murder:

1. **Felony murder**—a homicide committed during the commission of a serious crime, such as armed robbery, hijacking or arson
2. **Suspected felony murder**
3. **Argument-motivated murder**—a homicide that occurs during a domestic dispute and is distinct from criminal-motivated murder, the proverbial "crime of passion"
4. **Other motives**—homicides with identifiable motives that are separate from the first three types of murder
5. **"Unknown" motives**—homicides with no clear motive present. There are two categories of mass murder:
   - **Family mass murder**—This is the killing of four or more members of the same family by another family member, as in the case of John List. List was a New Jersey insurance salesman and Sunday school teacher who killed his mother, wife and three children in November 1971, then disappeared. He left behind a detailed confession that gave an exact account of how he carried out the murders, and the press implied that the motive was money. List was not arrested until June 1989 after an aged likeness and a bust were broadcast on *America's Most Wanted*.
   - **Classic mass murder**—This is the killing of four or more non-family victims in a single location at one time. This is a type of seemingly motiveless crime that is becoming more and more prevalent worldwide. The motive, if there is any, usually is only discovered well after the killings, but the pattern indicates that classic mass murderers are mentally ill men and women who vent their hostility against society in an orgy of

stabbings and/or shootings of victims chosen at random. Such was the case of Charles Whitman, the Texas Tower killer, who shot up the University of Texas in Austin, killing sixteen men and women and wounding thirty in ninety minutes in 1966. In 1989, Marc Lepine declared war on women and killed fourteen at the University of Montreal. He wounded nine others plus four men. He complained that "feminists have always spoiled my life," and he blamed all women for a "life filled with disappointments." Police later found a "hit list" of fifteen prominent Quebec women. Lepine's rage ended with the one mass killing and then killing himself. Other notables are Richard Speck, who killed eight nurses in their apartment in 1966; James Huberty, who shot up a California McDonalds in 1984 killing twenty-one men, women and children and wounding nineteen—the worst mass murder up to that time in modern American history; and Richard Farley, who shot up his workplace in 1988 after being fired for sexually harassing a female co-worker he was obsessively stalking and planning to kill for four years.

The FBI Behavioral Sciences Unit also lists two kinds of multiple murderers:

1. **Spree killer**—This is a person who commits murder in two or more locations, but the killings are linked by motive as a single event, as in the case of Michael Ryan, who killed sixteen people and wounded fourteen in 1987 in England. The Hungerford Massacre had two killing grounds nine miles apart, the second being the town of Hungerford itself, which is the reason that this is regarded as spree killing rather than a mass murder.

2. **Serial killer**—Sometimes, a serial killer will become a spree killer, as in the 1984 case of Christopher Wilder, a successful businessman who led the FBI and numerous state law enforcement agencies on a coast-to-coast manhunt. In seven weeks, Wilder kidnapped, raped, tortured and murdered as many as ten women in twelve states before being killed by a New Hampshire state trooper on Friday the thirteenth. It was this case that underscored the need for a national resource center that would help track and apprehend transient violent criminals. A little over a month after Wilder's death, NCAVC was established at Quantico.

Computer Profiling

With the enormous leaps in computer technology in the past six years, profiling is no longer being exclusively done by human minds. PRO-FILER is a computer-based expert system that uses a very sophisticated "if-then" program to determine the type of criminal that human profilers do. So, now the computer is part of the profiling team, but the humans have the last word on what the final profile report will say.

However, it must always be remembered that profiling is an art, not a science, and it is far from perfect. Since 1982, Seattle's Green River Killer has not only defied detection after over fifty murders, the killer has also never been successfully profiled, thus remaining an absolute enigma. Ted Bundy was another that would have defied profiling because he did not really fit any specific type. He was not a genius, but he was an intelligent overachiever, who is far from the "loser factor" that somewhat flaws the profiling system. He had been a good student, dated women, interacted with people well, had a good work history and been a modest success at the time he became a full-time serial killer. By the time Bundy was "profiled in a sense" and listed seventh on a list of ten suspects, he was already under arrest. By then he had killed as many as seventeen women, and after he escaped jail, he was suspect number one.

The Profile Matrix

In the same manner that crime-scene analysts outline a criminal, the practitioners of the art of profiling are governed by the same question outline utilized in journalism. So, to develop a portrait of evil, connect the dots by answering the following questions:

1. Who?
   - Who are the victims (women, children, gays, prostitutes, elderly or men)? Are they targeted specifically, or are the targets varied?
   - What type (organized or disorganized) of killer is involved? Is the killer:
     - Visionary
     - Mission oriented
     - Comfort oriented
     - Lust motivated
     - Thrill motivated
     - Power-control oriented?
2. What?
   - What was the cause of death?

- What kind of deviant sexual behavior is evident?
- What are the unusuals?

3. When?
   - When did the crime occur (time of day, time of month, time of year)?
   - Did the crime occur on or near a particularly significant event or date?
   - Did the crime occur on a religious-related date or occult-related date?
   - Is there anything special or unusual about when the crime was committed?

4. Where?
   - Where did the crime occur?
   - Where was the body or victim (if still alive) found?
   - Was the victim abducted from another place, and if so, where did the abduction occur?

5. How?
   - How was the crime committed?
   - Was the crime method specific, or does the method vary?
   - Was there anything unusual about the methods?

6. Why?
   - Does the crime appear to be sexual in nature?
   - Does the crime appear to be profit motivated?
   - Does the crime appear to be spontaneous?
   - Does the crime appear to be planned?

Other Factors

As we have seen, the FBI has proven that there is more to the crime and crime scene than just the physical evidence, which emphasizes the importance of looking beyond these factors. In doing so, the BSU has specified two main types of violent criminals. These types are the *organized* and the *disorganized*. In addition, the personal characteristics of the criminal and the behavior of the criminal after the crime have been defined for each criminal.

The personal characteristics of the organized violent offender may include:

- High intelligence (IQ 135+), may be college educated
- Social competence
- Sexual competence

- Living with a partner
- Being an only child or most favored child in family
- Having suffered abuse or harsh discipline in childhood
- Controlled moods
- Maintaining a stereotypical masculine image
- Being charming
- Having moods subject to situational cause
- Being geographically and occupationally mobile
- Following media coverage.

The behavior of this type after the crime may include:
- Returning to the crime scene
- Volunteering information
- Being a police groupie
- Anticipating being questioned
- Moving the body
- Disposing of the body to advertise the crime.

On the opposite side, the disorganized violent offender characteristics include:
- Having low to average intelligence (IQ 80–100)
- Being an unskilled worker (may be school dropout)
- Being socially immature
- Having had a rough childhood with a father whose work history was unstable
- Having suffered abuse in childhood
- Being anxious during the crime
- Using drugs or alcohol minimally
- Living alone
- Living and/or working near crimes
- Paying little or no attention to news media
- Being dominated by significant behavioral change
- Being a nocturnal person
- Having poor personal hygiene
- Having secret hiding places
- Not usually dating.

This type's behavior after the crime may include:
- Returning to the scene of the crime

- Attending funeral of victim
- Clipping obituary
- Turning to religion
- Keeping a diary and/or collecting news clippings
- Changing residence
- Undergoing a personality change.

How the crime scene is produced differs between the two types of offenders.

The organized criminal:
- Plans the offense
- Targets strangers
- Personalizes the victim
- Controls conversation with victim
- Controls crime scene
- Requires victim to be submissive
- Uses restraints
- Acts aggressively
- Moves body
- Removes weapon
- Leaves very little evidence.

The disorganized criminal:
- Acts spontaneously
- Targets people he or she knows
- Depersonalizes victim
- Keeps conversation with victim to a minimum
- Creates a chaotic crime scene
- Attacks victim with sudden violence
- Does not use restraints
- May have sex with corpse
- Leaves body at crime scene
- Leaves weapon
- Leaves a variety of evidence

PROFILE OF JACK THE RIPPER: A NEW PERSPECTIVE

Here's a little academic morsel to ponder. It was derived from actual events surrounding the notorious crimes that terrified Victorian London and related crime reports. Using the Profile Matrix as a guide and looking beyond the crime scenes, this information offers an alternative viewpoint on this infamous criminal who murdered six to eight prostitutes.

Who

Victims were all lower-class women forced to earn a living via prostitution. Crimes appear to be victim specific. Perpetrator could either be male or female. Crimes reflect *organized* type. Suspect presumed to be male because of sexual bias of the day, but female could have committed the same crimes.

What

There were multiple stabbings, mutilation, indications of cannibalism and necrophilia and some occult overtones. All the killings had the same modus operandi, or MO.

When

Two murders occurred prior to more famous mutilation murders that began in August 1888. It is possible that this first set of killings was experimentation. From then, five murders, the infamous "Ripper killings," transpired over a period of five months—four on very secluded streets, one in the fifth victim's home, all always at night. Two victims were killed in one night, probably because the killer was interrupted while committing the first crime of that night. Despite the belief that the Ripper had committed suicide, another identical murder occurred eight months later in July 1889.

Where

The crimes occurred in the back streets of the poorest, most crime infested, most severely neglected and ignored neighborhoods of London. Victims were attacked in secluded areas, but it was very common for the sound of screaming to be heard, so victim's cries, if any, would have been ignored. The fifth murder in victim's flat would have been ignored as a domestic dispute.

PROFILE OF JACK THE RIPPER continued

How

Weapon believed to have been used was either a bayonet or a surgeon's knife or a butcher's fillet knife. Blade was extremely sharp, long and narrow.

Why

There are many theories, including one that says a crazed journalist committed the crimes to bring attention to the plight of the poor of Whitechapel. However, the most feasible theory is the idea that the killer was driven insane by syphilis and that prostitutes were killed because the killer believed them to be the source of the disease. If the killer had a mission, it is possible that he or she believed that by killing whores, the disease would be eliminated. Another plausible theory suggests that a female drug addict did the killings, at first for money and then for satisfaction.

PART IV

PARTICULAR PROBLEMS

Chapter Eighteen

Street Gangs

by John Boertlein

I t seems that gangs have proliferated across the country in the last decade. But in fact, gangs came into existence in the United States in the early 1800s, and many of the street gangs known today originated in the 1950s and 1960s. When writing about gangs, you will need to be aware of the common traits among those involved in gang activity.

Let's begin by defining exactly what a "gang" is. There are many variations on the subject. The predominant theory concerning the cause of gangs and gang behavior is based on social, cultural and economic reasons. We'll touch on this later in this chapter and look at some common characteristics of a gang member. The state of Ohio recently established a legal definition of the term "gang" in an attempt to make participation in a gang a criminal offense in the state. Before we read the actual definition, let's consider the rationale associated with creating such legislation. This is from the Ohio Revised Code, section 2923.41, section 3A.B.C.:

> The General Assembly finds that it is the right of every individual, regardless of race, color, creed, religion, national origin, sex, age, sexual orientation or handicap, to be secure and protected from fear, intimidation and physical harm caused by the activities of violent groups and individuals. It is not the intent of this act to interfere with the exercise of the constitutionally protected rights of the freedom of expression and association. The General Assembly recognizes the constitutional right of every citizen to harbor and express beliefs on any lawful subject whatsoever, to lawfully associate with others who share similar beliefs, to petition lawfully constituted authority for a redress of grievances and to participate in the electoral process.

> The General Assembly finds, however, that the state of Ohio is facing a mounting crisis caused by criminal gangs whose members threaten and terrorize peaceful citizens and commit a

multitude of crimes. These activities, both individual and collectively, present a clear and present danger to public order and safety and are not constitutionally protected.

It is the intent of the General Assembly to eradicate the terror created by criminal gangs by providing enhanced penalties and by eliminating the patterns, profits, proceeds and instrumentalities of criminal gang activity.

Sociocultural reasons for gang development and the constitutional implications aside, let's consider a definition that specifically spells out what a street gang is:

- "Criminal gang" means an ongoing formal or informal organization, association or group of three or more persons to which all of the following apply. It has as one of its primary activities the commission of one or more of the following offenses:
  - A felony
  - An offense of violence
  - Corruption of a minor (eighteen-year-old having a sexual encounter with another who is thirteen to sixteen-years-old)
  - Criminal damaging
  - Trespassing
  - Failure to disperse
  - Interference with custody
  - Contributing to the delinquency of a minor
  - Intimidation of a witness or public official
  - Weapons violation
  - Trafficking in drugs
  - Ethnic intimidation

This is a simplified version. It illustrates, however, exactly what we're talking about with street gangs. Outlaw motorcycle gangs, skinheads, prison gangs and cults actually differ in motivation and structure. Street gang members pose a different twist as potential characters because, individually or collectively, we can expect certain things from them.

Gang Structure

The following terms may prove to be useful in writing about gangs:

- **National gang**—It has direct ties to West Coast or Midwestern gangs, including members and/or leaders from the parent set of the originating city. Some national gangs include local members recruited through drug trafficking connections.

- **Nation**—A nationally recognized faction or group of sets; the umbrella criminal organization. Examples include "crips," "bloods," "folks" and "people."
- **Set**—This term describes particular gang units. The members of a set are usually close-knit and tied to a certain school or neighborhood. You can use this term to describe a subgroup of any criminal organization.

The following are examples of national gang structures:

Nation	Set Name
Crips	116th Street Avalon Gangster Crips
	68 East Coast Crips
	Eight Trey Gangster Crips
	43 Hoover Crips
	107 Hoover Crips
	Rollin' 30's Crips
Bloods	Pasadena Lane Bloods
	Red Bloods
	Tree Top Pirus
Folks	Black Gangster Disciples
	Cold-Blooded Gangsters
	Insane Gangster Disciples
	Brothers of the Struggle (BOS)
	Spanish Cobras
	Latin Jivers
People	Conservative Vice Lord Nation
	4 Corner Hustlers
	Unknown Vice Lords
	Cicero Insane Vice Lords
	El Rukns
	Latin Knights

- **Clique, klicka**—Similar to sets, these terms are most often used by West Coast Latino gangs. A clique is a close-knit group within a gang.
- **Posse, crew**—These terms are also similar to set, however, they're

often incorporated as part of the gang name. The term "posse" is often associated with Jamaican gangs. Many street gangs have adopted the term, especially those with drug trafficking connections to Jamaican gangs.

- **Local gang**—A gang comprised of members from a specific vicinity. Generally, gang leadership is locally based. The influence of national gangs may be seen in graffiti and drug trafficking connections.

Graffiti, elaborate or simple, usually sends some type of message. In this case "It's a white thang."

Categories of Street Gangs

Street gang members generally fall into three categories, namely:

- **Leaders**—Often the senior gang members, the leaders ordinarily range in age from sixteen to twenty-two. The leader determines the nature and pattern of gang activity. Their power is related to their ability to recruit and control.
- **Hard-core members**—The gang's most serious, and often most violent, criminals. Most of the members in this category range in age from sixteen to twenty-two.

- **Fringe members**—Described in the past as "wanna-bes," these members participate in a gang's criminal activity. They're "initiated," but aren't proven in the membership.

  The ages can range from eight-year-olds to late teens. These members probably closely identify with a gang, have adopted the gang's philosophy and may frequently be in the company of gang members.

Several years ago, I worked as a police sergeant in a neighborhood experiencing the emergence of what amounted to juvenile street gangs. Graffiti announcing "O.G.'s," "Original Gangsta's" and "Miami Boyz" popped up everywhere. Kids wearing L.A. Raiders' and University of Miami hats and clothes took to the streets fighting, tearing things up and getting high. Because this was a fairly different phenomenon (or old problems with a new face), the situation received a lot of media attention. As an organization, we needed to identify and deal with the situation. Some of the gang-related techniques used by cops can be valuable to you when developing characters or situations. Consider these identification methods used by law enforcement:

- **Admission**—What better way to identify a gang member than by self-identification? Some "gangsta's" are quite proud of the fact. This information could be valuable, especially with the sentencing part of a criminal trial.
- **Association**—Association with previously identified members through arrest documents, etc., can help identify other members or affiliates.
- **Identified by others**—Identification by other gang members or informants is often a reliable indicator of gang affiliation.
- **Clothing**—Clothing of a particular color or style or the way it's worn (tilted to the right or left) can indicate gang membership or affiliation. Remember, although gang members do use these items to identify themselves, many are also fads followed by others. A combination is more indicative of gang membership. Below are a few examples:
  - **Caps**—Caps or hats are worn distinctly pointed to the right or left.
  - **Clothing type**—Starter jackets or team colors could indicate gang involvement. However, they're also popular among non-gang youth.

The manner in which clothing is worn can be an indication of gang affiliation. These drawings depict how the tilt of one's hat might indicate the wearer's tie to a particular gang.

- Belts—The gang's name or symbols appear on the belt or belt buckle, and/or the buckle is worn on the right or left side.
- Bandannas—Colors of bandannas have particular meaning (blue = Crips / red = Bloods). The bandanna is tied on the right or left side, or hangs out of a right or left pocket.
- Gloves—These are worn only on one hand, either the right or left.
- Pant leg—Members wear one leg rolled up, either the right or left.
- Pockets—Members may wear one pocket inside out, either the right or left side.
- Buttons—Buttons may display a gang's insignia, name or symbol.
- Colors—Some gangs identify with specific colors. The absence of a color may also be significant.
- Jewelry—Gang symbols can be used in jewelry. Another identification of potential gang involvement are earrings worn in particular locations or in one ear only.
- **Tattoos**—Gang tattoos often include the gang name or some type of gang symbol. Members sometimes put tattoos on their hands or shoulders in an attempt to make spotting them difficult.
- **Hand signs**—Some gangs have developed elaborate hand signals to communicate with each other or to represent their affiliation to other members or rival gangs.
- **Graffiti**—This involves spray painting or drawing on buildings,

A Folks hand symbol.

A Peoples hand symbol.

A Folks symbol.

A Peoples symbol.

clothing, books or personal effects using gang alphabets or symbols.

- **Slogans**—Many gangs have their own slogans or chants.
- **Haircuts**—Some gangs wear particular styles or have the gang's symbol or slogan shaved onto the members' heads.
- **Photographs**—Persons photographed with other gang members, especially when flashing gang hand signs or wearing formal colors, may be affiliated with a gang.
- **Family**—Having family members associated with gangs increases an individual's potential for gang involvement.

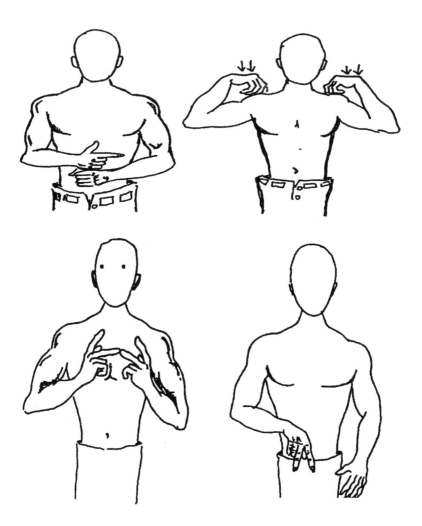

Symbols and hand signs take on different meanings, some of them deadly. Consider these examples of the secret language of gang life.

- **Writings**—Members will often write about their gang ties in school books, on clothing or in a journal or diary.
- **Different agencies**—Other sources of information, like schools, employers, social programs and recreation facilities, may be privy to information on gangs occurring in these forums. Likewise, these agencies may be experiencing gang-related problems.

- **Pattern of arrests**—If someone's criminal record looks like a trail of gang-related offenses, chances are good that he is affiliated with a gang.

Obviously, anyone who displays one of these traits isn't necessarily a gang member. When writing about a character's involvement with a street gang, it's a good idea to include multiple indicators to prove gang status. A gang's behavior will be similar individually or collectively. For example, our previously mentioned Original Gangsta's all wore L.A. Raiders' hats and jackets, and most had homemade "O.G." tattoos on their right hand between the thumb and index finger.

Everything we've discussed so far is visible. You can use these items in writing to portray your gang character. But, as we mentioned in the beginning of this chapter, gangs are a social phenomenon. It would be wise to consider some of the social factors or indicators leading to at-risk behavior when you write about what's going on inside a gang member's head. The following "Factors Leading to At-Risk Behavior" were developed by Reno, Nevada, police officer Craig Pittman:

- Low self-esteem
- Low grades
- Little extracurricular activities or school involvement
- Poor communication skills
- Lack of community-based programs
- Dysfunctional families
- Single parent families
- Philosophical or ethnic attractiveness of gangs
- Desperately seeking identity
- Truancy and poor school attendance
- Relative's or significant other's gang affiliation
- Socioeconomic factors
- Drug and alcohol usage
- Respect (or lack thereof)
- Environmental survival
- Psychological factors

Law Enforcement Response

Street gangs are a fact of life in the United States. We've looked at indicators, signs, social and cultural factors and legislative definitions. Let's conclude with the guidelines developed by the Cincinnati Police

The Hi-Point semiautomatic pistol and the Intertec-9 are popular favorites with gang members.

Division to deal with street gangs.

- **Patrol and observe**—Cops need to look for signs of gangs in the neighborhoods where they work. Watch for graffiti, "colors," flashing of gang signs and hand signals, fighting between groups (especially with weapons), traveling in packs, increased drug trafficking and drug use, widespread vandalism and information or complaints about gang activity from others in the community.
- **Document all contacts**—Gang legislation is only as good as an agency's ability to document and prove affiliations and membership. There needs to be a central repository for gang information. Cops should complete field interview report (FIR) cards, citations, arrest slips and/or offense reports whenever making a suspected gang contact. Copies of all documentation must be provided to the unit responsible for gang intelligence.

Finally, your cop character could use this guide for working with gangs:

- Your cop should be decisive, firm and fair. She should be aware that lenient treatment of gang members will be seen as a weakness to be taken advantage of.

- Intimidation of gang members by police usually escalates into a confrontation and seldom creates respect. Lectures to "scare gangsters straight" don't work and should be avoided.
- Media attention to a gang or its members tends to escalate gang violence. In dealing with the media, your character should always emphasize the negative side of gang involvement (arrests, convictions, prison terms, injuries, death). Your character should treat gang issues as serious, but caution the media against sensationalizing gang-related events, which can cause a problem to escalate or lead to direct retaliation by one gang upon another.
- Your character should be aware of graffiti. When she finds it, efforts should be made to record and remove it. If graffiti remains, it invites more "writing on the wall" and attracts rival gangs.
- Your character should treat each gang member or suspected member as an individual. A cop's treatment could affect an individual's degree of involvement in a gang or increase or decrease the chance of developing a source of information within a gang.
- Your character's primary goal should be to prevent conflict whenever possible. An incident, no matter how minor today, could cause any number of gang-related or motivated acts of vengeance or reprisals, even long after the original incident.
- Your character needs to document any and all information and forward it to a central coordinating resource.

Chapter Nineteen

Hate Crimes and Hate Groups

by John Boertlein

H ate crime is a relatively new term for an old problem. In this chapter, we'll take a look at the most recent definition of what a hate crime is as well as law enforcement techniques for identifying, reporting and prosecuting hate-related offenses. We'll also consider several examples of organized hate groups and the possibilities and implications of using the information in your writing. The following is one of the latest definitions of hate crime from the *Training Guide for Hate Crime Data Collection* (U.S. Department of Justice, 1990):

"A hate crime is a committed, threatened or attempted criminal act by any person(s) against a person or property of another individual or group that may in any way constitute an expression of racial, religious,

 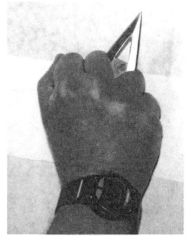

A "knuckle knife"—easy to hide and easy to use!

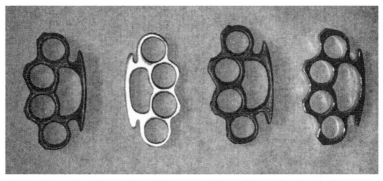

Old-time brass knuckles or "knucks" are used for packing a deadly punch.

ethnic or national origin, sexual orientation or other forms of bias. Motivated by prejudice, hate crimes may include but are not limited to:

- Threatening communications
- Physical assaults
- Vandalism
- Cross burning
- Destruction of religious symbols
- Firebombing or arson
- Homicide

"Single criminal acts like menacing, criminal damaging or telecommunications harassment may initially appear as less serious when viewed in the larger context of all crime. However, what might begin as a minor offense may escalate into a more serious crime, particularly if the crime was motivated by bias. Such criminal acts may generate fear and concern among victims and the broader public and have the potential to escalate, possibly causing counterviolence. Therefore, if an incident appears to be one of racial, religious, ethnic or national origin, sexual orientation or other forms of bias, it should be investigated as such."

Legislation in the state of Ohio provides for *enhanced* sentencing for those convicted of "ethnic intimidation." This means the penalty increases for conviction of offenses, for example, assault, if proof is established that the assault was committed for reasons of bias. The following hate/bias codes were established in Ohio for reporting purposes. The codes are entered on official bias crime police reports. They're used for keeping statistics on particular victim groups. They're fairly comprehen-

sive and may be of use in your writing:
- Anti-white, anti-African-American, anti-American Indian/Alaskan, anti-Asian/Pacific Islander, anti-multiracial group(s)
- Anti-Jewish, anti-Catholic, anti-Protestant, anti-Islamic, anti-other religion, anti-Atheist/Agnostic
- Anti-Oriental, anti-Arab, anti-Hispanic, anti-other nationality
- Anti-male homosexual, anti-female homosexual, anti-homosexual, anti-heterosexual, anti-bisexual

Similar laws exist around the country. Police, therefore, have the responsibility to investigate and verify bias and/or prejudice as motivation for crimes. Listed below are several items police officers are instructed to consider when determining if probable cause exists to believe an incident was motivated because of animosity toward the victim's race, religion, ethnic or national origin or sexual orientation. You may want to consider these same questions when writing about hate crimes.
- Were words, symbols or acts that are, or may be, offensive to an identifiable group used by the perpetrator or are they present as evidence?
- Are the victim and the suspected perpetrator members of different racial, religious or ethnic groups?
- Does a meaningful portion of the community perceive and respond to the situation as a bias-related incident?
- Is there an ongoing neighborhood problem that may have initiated or contributed to the act (e.g., could the act be retribution for conflict between neighbors or with area juveniles)?
- Does the perpetrator have a true understanding of the impact of the crime or the incident on the victim or other group members? Are the perpetrators juveniles?
- Does the crime or incident indicate involvement by an organized hate group (e.g., Ku Klux Klan, American Nazi Party, Black Muslims, 5%'ers)?
- Were objects that represent the work of an organized hate group (white hoods, burning crosses, hate graffiti) left at the scene of the crime?
- Has an organized hate group claimed responsibility for the crime?
- Did the victim recently move into the neighborhood? Is his or her family the only one, or one of just a few families, of their racial, ethnic or religious group in the area?

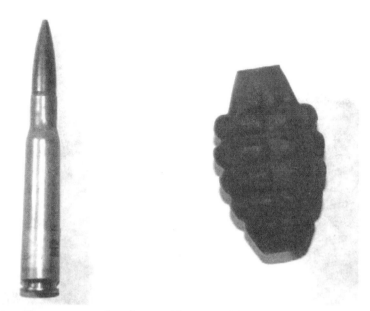

Pictured here are a grenade and a .50 caliber ammunition. Some hate groups get into bigger "military fare."

- What is the victim's relationship with his or her neighbors and/or local community groups?
- Has the victim experienced past or repeated incidents of a similar nature?
- Was the victim put in a state of fear by the incident and did the perpetrator commit the crime with the goal of creating such fear?
- Is there a connection between the date of the incident and holidays or special programs or events?
- Does the incident indicate a "copycat" syndrome that might be the result of media coverage of similar incidents?
- Were there any recent occurrences in the community or incidents reported by the media in which a member of the offender group was harmed by a member of the group to which the victim belongs?
- Was the suspect previously involved in a similar incident?
- Does the suspect claim membership in or associate with an organized hate group?
- Does the incident lack any other clear motive?

Get the idea? First, your situation needs a crime with the potential of being motivated by bias. Next, through one or any combination of the ideas offered above, bias is established as the motive. Then steps must be taken against the acts. Let's look at the Cincinnati Police Division's 2000 Procedure Manual's policy for taking steps against hate crime:

> All Hate Crimes will be treated seriously and the investigations of these crimes will be given priority. The proper investigation of racial, religious, ethnic or national origin, sexual orientation or other bias crime incidents, is the responsibility of all police officers. The Police Division will use every necessary resource to rapidly and decisively identify the perpetrators, arrest them and bring them before the court.
>
> The actions taken by the Police Division in dealing with incidents of racial, religious, ethnic or national origin, sexual orientation or other acts of bias, are visible signs of its concern and commitment to the community. Special emphasis will be placed on victim assistance and community cooperation in order to reduce victim and community trauma or fear.
>
> Officers must demonstrate sensitivity toward the feelings, needs and concerns that may be present in the community as a result of incidents of this nature.

Sound like overkill? No, I think it underscores the importance of the hate crime issue to our society in general and law enforcement in particular. When writing about hate crime situations, be sure to understand the serious weight the issue commands.

Consider the case of a man we'll call "Dave." Dave lived in a multi-family apartment in a low-income part of town experiencing an influx of members of a different race. Dave's reputation among his neighbors was that he was an avowed bigot who frequently expressed fear at the area's change. Plywood covered the windows in Dave's apartment, and he frequently shouted veiled threats and obscenities to the "different" residents as they passed by.

One afternoon, one of Dave's neighbors, an elderly lady of a race different than Dave's, had an asthma attack on the walkway near Dave's apartment. She fell to the ground gasping for air. Some bystanders came to her aid. Dave exited his apartment and, when he was about three feet from the woman, shouted, "Need any help [racial slur]?" He followed up with, "Go ahead and [obscenity omitted] die!"

The lady became more excited and, according to the witnesses, actually choked for air. She later said she experienced chest pains and felt faint. Dave kept at his badgering, and the longer he went on, the worse the woman felt. Paramedics arrived, eventually transporting her to the hospital. Dave finally shut up and ran into his apartment when a uniformed cop arrived.

The officer received the same information just presented. He had questions that he related to me. I'll pose the same questions to you. You be the judge. What occurred between Dave and the elderly lady?

    A. Nothing. Dave may have been discourteous and annoying, but the First Amendment guarantees Dave the right to express himself freely, despite the *biases* or opinions of others.

    B. Nuisance. Dave was only guilty of a "nuisance" charge, like disorderly conduct, for being an annoyance to his neighbor.

    C. Menacing. Dave alarmed the ailing lady by telling her he "would help her die," but that's it. Was he serious? Did the recipient of his crude remarks really believe he'd hurt her?

    D. Ethnic Intimidation/Menacing. Dave's apparent hatred of another race led him to exacerbate the situation. His only motive for causing a disturbance was his bias toward his neighbor's race.

    E. Attempted Murder. Yeow! Dave's racial remarks and his badgering that escalated the woman's condition could've killed her. It's all his fault!

What's your answer? Some might argue for "A," since every American is allowed to speak their mind. Others may contend it's merely disorderly conduct or, at the most, menacing because Dave wasn't responsible for the initial incident preceding his behavior.

We went with "D"—Ethnic Intimidation/Menacing. All, including the prosecutor, agreed with our assessment for the following reasons:

- Dave's behavior escalated from an annoyance to a threat when he asked the lady "if she needed help" dying.
- The witnesses' and victim's statements agreed that her condition became worse the more Dave went on. And the worse the victim became, the more Dave went on.
- Dave used racial slurs with the victim, who was essentially a stranger to him prior to the incident.

- Dave had a reputation among the witnesses for bigotry and bias.
- Dave ran off when the police officer arrived.

All of these points are arguable in court, but this case hasn't been argued yet. Dave skipped town when the warrants were signed. He calls once in awhile to see if "it's all gone away." It hasn't. Nonetheless, there's a pretty good case against Dave, if and when he returns.

We've discussed what a hate crime is and how that's determined. Now let's look at a phenomenon known as "hate groups." First, here's a recent definition:

> An organization whose primary purpose is to promote animosity, hostility and malice against persons belonging to a race, color, religion, gender, handicap, sexual orientation or ethnicity group that differs from that of the organization. Such groups have an organized hierarchy and chain of command (e.g., Ku Klux Klan, American Nazi Party).
> —Training Guide for Hate Crime Data Collection (U.S. Department of Justice, 1990)

In the early 1980s, some extremist organizations, particularly those most prone to violence, established paramilitary camps, which added a disturbing dimension to the organized hate movement in America. These mostly clandestine facilities provided advanced training in:
- Weapons
- Demolition
- Guerrilla warfare
- Terrorism
- Weapons of mass destruction
- Standard indoctrination identifying the racial and religious "enemies" that might someday be targets

Some of the causative factors attributable to the development of hate groups are:
- Periods of high immigration
- Attempts by disenfranchised groups to increase their political and economic power
- Periods of economic instability

A Nazi flag.

These groups often tend to break up because of arguing and internal dissension. Spin-off groups often take names similar to other hate groups, for example the *Neo*-Nazis.

Neo-Nazis identify themselves within the group and to the public by adopting names and general hate philosophies. An example is White American Skin Heads (WASH), a skinhead contingent that:

- Is identified by their shaved heads
- Sports Nazi regalia
- Preaches violence against Blacks, Hispanics, Jews, Asians and homosexuals
- Is armed with knives, chains, steel-toed Doc Maarten boots, handguns, shotguns, assault firearms and sometimes more powerful weapons
- Has engaged in everything from murder and violent assault to property crimes and vandalizing religious institutions, especially synagogues
- In many instances, has aligned itself with old-time hate groups and attended rallies and marches, especially with white supremacist groups like the KKK, Aryan Nations or White Aryan Resistance

Hate groups also support various ideologies and strategies. Ideologically, hate groups:

- Are primarily motivated to perpetrate crimes to obtain money to be used in the pursuit of a political agenda
- Are explicitly racist
- Consider people of color (and, recently, homosexuals) to be subhuman

- Often blame the government, communism and/or racial "conspiracies" for most of the problems in our country
- Use the most up-to-date versions of technology, such as the Internet, cable TV or computer bulletin boards, to spread messages of hate
- Sometimes try to follow a more mainstream approach to spread their messages, such as running for public office (like David Duke, the Grand Imperial Wizard of the KKK)

We've examined characteristics, philosophies and ideologies of hate groups in general. But the term hate group also covers groups that are extreme in their particular beliefs. "Extremists," often labeled as "far right" and "right wing" or "far left" and "left wing," have distinguishing differences and similarities.

Right-Wing Hate Groups

Right-wing hate groups are reactionary and tend to rehash problems of the past. To emphasize their point, they express strong beliefs in social order and the values of the past. The right wing believes the present social order is breaking down and, consequently, they desire to return to the "good old days." Typically, leaders of the far right strongly maintain these beliefs and are often well educated. The main body of a right-wing group is typically blue-collar workers with limited education. Right-wingers are easily exploited by economic fear and tend to "scapegoat" or blame others for their misfortune.

The right wing targets weaker groups. They rarely strike at government symbols, preferring to target Jews, Blacks, Asians and other minority groups.

Far-Right Hate Groups

The John Birch Society. A man named Robert Welch founded the John Birch Society in 1958, publishing *The Blue Book* to expose "the communist conspiracy." Avowed anti-Communists, the society also published *The Politician*, depicting President Eisenhower as a "dedicated, conscious agent of the Communist Conspiracy."

The Militias. Militias, being "Anarchy-Libertarians," find any and all government oppressive. They're hard-core extremists believing that the U.S. is in the grip of a powerful conspiracy. Militias view the United Nations, International Monetary Fund and ideas like globalism as mass conspiracies.

Recent examples of significant encounters with militia groups include Ruby Ridge in 1992; the Branch Davidian compound incident in Waco, Texas, in 1993; and the Murrah Federal Building bombing in Oklahoma City in 1995.

Jewish Defense League (JDL). Orthodox Rabbi Martin David Kahane founded the JDL in New York City in 1968 as a means of protecting the Jewish community from crime. The JDL works on the premise that Jewish rights should be defended by attacking Egyptian, French, German, Iranian, Iraqi, Lebanese and Palestinian targets in the United States.

Factions of the JDL include the Jewish Armed Resistance, who sent pipe bombs to Soviet, Iraqi and Polish diplomatic offices. Another spin-off group, called the Jewish Direct Action, started in 1984.

Neo-Nazis

The term "Neo-Nazi" encompasses various organizations generally advocating:
- Nazi symbolism (like swastikas)
- Use of terms such as "Nazi" or "National Socialist"
- Reverence for Adolf Hitler and the Third Reich

Examples of Neo-Nazi organizations include:
- The National Renaissance Party founded in 1949 by James Madole in New York
- The American Nazi Party founded in 1959 by George Lincoln Rockwell. The group changed its name to the National Socialist White People's Party in 1966 and again to the New Order in 1981
- American White Nationalist Party, founded in Columbus, Ohio, in 1972
- National Alliance founded in 1974 by Dr. William Pierce
- National Democratic Front founded in 1985 by Gary Gallo in Knoxville, Tennessee
- National Socialist Movement founded in 1975 in Cincinnati, Ohio, by James Mason

In your writing, you'll be able to find an extremist group to fit whatever situation you need. But let's not stop there. The 1980s brought several major Neo-Nazi organizations to prominence. They're worth mentioning to illustrate the finer points you can customize in your work.

Nontraditional Neo-Nazi Groups

These groups established doctrines described as "nontraditional" or what might be called "contemporary hate de jour."

Aryan Nations. In the 1980s, a man named Richard Butler founded the Aryan Nations in Hayden Lake, Idaho, with the goal of bringing together different hate groups through annual conferences in Northern Idaho. He recruited membership from the KKK, Posse Commitatus and other Neo-Nazi groups. "Nations" publishes two newsletters for the "hate community": *Calling Our Nation* and *Aryan Nations Newsletter.* Hate groups in the Aryan Nations include:

- **The Mountain Church of Jesus Christ.** This was founded by Robert Miles, a former Grand Dragon of the United Klans of America in Michigan. The members were sent to prison in 1971 for conspiring to bomb an empty school bus.
- **The Order.** The Order came to being in the early 1980s courtesy of Robert Matthews, who later died in a shootout with the FBI. The group committed robberies as a means of funding the organization. They gained notoriety by murdering a Jewish Denver talk-show host, Alan Berg. Today, many members reside in penitentiaries.
- **Posse Commitatus.** Founded in 1969, this group received attention in February 1983 when its member, Gordon Kahl, murdered two United States Deputy Marshals in North Dakota. Kahl himself died in a shootout in Arkansas in June of that same year. The Posse Commitatus's claim to fame revolved around their refusal to pay federal income taxes or even acknowledge the government's existence above the county level.
- **White Aryan Resistance (WAR).** WAR is one of the first Neo-Nazi organizations to use the Internet for hate purposes via their computerized bulletin board. They also publish a newsletter, *WAR*, in California. WAR promotes the skinhead movement, underscoring a 1988 attack by skinheads on three Ethiopians, one of whom died. As a result, the Anti-Defamation League teamed

with the Southern Poverty Law Center to sue WAR founder Tom Metzger and his brother John for vicarious liability. The ADL won the suit, which was still under appeal as of 1997.

Ku Klux Klan

Historically one of the most publicized hate groups in the United States, various factions merged in 1961 to become the United Klans of America. Through the years, the FBI has spent millions of dollars infiltrating and tracking the Klan. Other national organizations, like Klanwatch, have also formed to track Klan activity.

Two incidents in the late 1980s impacted the Klan. In 1987, the Southern Poverty Law Center won a court judgment against the UKA and six of its members for the 1981 slaying of an African-American teenager, whose body was left hanging in a tree. United Klans of America was forced to pay damages and, in the process, lost their national headquarters building in Tuscaloosa, Alabama. In 1988, the U.S. Justice Department charged thirteen members of the KKK and Neo-Nazi groups with sedition. As of 1996, Klan membership was estimated to be around four thousand.

Common-Law Courts

This group is the most radical and confrontational segment of extremists whose philosophy revolves around separation from government. In its latest survey, Klanwatch identified 131 known, active common-law courts in thirty-five states. Activities of common-law courts include:

- Staking claim to many of the powers of the American legal system
- Resolving disputes among "Freemen" (other separatists)
- Taking action against those in authority whom they see as "trampling" on "sovereign citizens" rights
- Filing invalid liens against individuals who oppose them
- Threatening, intimidating, assaulting and conspiring to kill public officials and law enforcement officers

Most of these courts identify themselves only with the county or city where they are located. Some assume more exotic names:

- The Truth Fellowship Order of Protection in Schenectady County, New York
- The House of Common Law School for Responsible Sovereignty in Santa Fe, New Mexico

- The Michigan Common Law Venue Supreme Court in Ottawa County, Michigan
- The Restoration Township Rural Society in Palm Bay, Florida
- Juris Christian Assembly in Modesto, California

You'll find these organizations coast to coast. If your writing includes common-law movement ("Sovereigns") activities, whatever the venue, you may want to use some of these common characteristics of "Sovereign Citizens":

- Their beliefs frequently lead to confrontations with law enforcement authorities, during which they're willing to use force.
- They separate their middle and last names with a comma or colon, for example, John William, Doe or Joe Thomas: Smith.
- When signing a legal document, Sovereigns often include the phrases "pro se" (for himself) or "sui juris" (of his own jurisdiction).
- Typically, Sovereigns refuse to carry a driver's license, claiming they have "a right to travel."
- If they carry a driver's license, Sovereigns will add the phrase "all rights reserved without prejudice" to their signature when signing the license.
- Sovereigns either have no license plates on their cars, a homemade license plate or one issued by a bogus, foreign-sounding government.
- Sovereigns might challenge the jurisdiction of a law enforcement officer or court official during a confrontation.
- Sovereigns refuse to acknowledge questions directed to them during a traffic stop or court proceeding.
- They refer to their state as a "republic" and call their U.S. zip code a "postal code."
- Sovereigns claim a court has no authority over them because the flag in the chambers has yellow fringe on it, making it an "admiralty court" illegally operating on land.
- They may file a document at the courthouse called an "asseveration" (a solemn declaration unaccompanied by an official oath).
- They may file an "alluvial" title that, supposedly, frees them from property taxes.
- Sovereigns refer to American currency as FRNs—federal reserve notes.
- They also may base their legal arguments on biblical passages, especially from the Old Testament.

We've looked at the right-wing extremists, but for every extreme there are two ends. The left wing is every bit as passionate as the right, but for different reasons. The following are some left-wing hate group characteristics:

- They possess a profound distrust of the social order.
- Left-wingers believe the social order is corrupt.
- Their ultimate goal is revolution and total societal change.
- The left wing believes in a Marxist-style state.
- They possess an elitist view of society at large.
- Typically, left-wing group leaders are well-educated and extremist.
- Membership is usually well educated.
- Membership in left-wing groups is typically younger than their right-wing counterparts.
- The left wing tends to be economically upper class.
- They believe they know "what's best for society."
- Left-wing targets are usually government personnel and property.
- The left wing's preferred activity is to engage in terrorism.
- Left-wing group members have similar political ideology, including:
  - The belief system explains and justifies their preferred political order for society.
  - The belief system is a convenient way of twisting facts, theories and information into a comfortable set of facts, which can be accepted by group members.
  - These interpreted values, opinions and beliefs are quite sensible.
  - Members view society in terms of "good guys" and "bad guys" who have "wronged me or mine."
  - "Bad guys" become an entity—THEM—which makes it easier to dehumanize the object of their hatred. They often use name-calling or labeling.
  - Both left- and right-wing groups recruit from military personnel in order to gain access to training and equipment.

Hate groups also have certain conspiracies they believe in. Here are a couple of examples:

- Many groups, on both sides, view Roman Catholicism as a conspiracy to control the world through Rome or the Vatican.
- There is a conspiracy among international Jewish bankers to economically control every country.

Here are some examples of contemporary left-wing hate groups.

Communist Party. The Communist Party gained notoriety in the 1970s when Angela Davis, a teacher at UCLA, purchased firearms that were later used in a hostage-taking/homicide at a courthouse in California. Davis eventually made the FBI's Top Ten Most Wanted list. She was eventually arrested in New York and later acquitted. The Communist Party began publishing a newspaper, *The People's Daily World,* in 1986.

Black Panther Party. Huey Newton, Bobby Seale and David Hilliard, three students at Merritt College in Oakland, California, founded the Black Panther Party in 1966. Their beliefs revolved around the writings of Frantz Fanon, Malcolm X, Robert F. Williams and Mao Tse Tung.

World Workers Party. The WWP organized in the early 1990s as an independent communist group supporting all Marxist nations. They also sponsor a youth organization known as Youth Against War and Fascism.

Having examined several hate groups and their philosophies, let's take a look at a couple of characteristics of convicted conspirator Terry Nichols, whose crime is infamous. Using the brief details below, see if you can determine Nichols's affiliation in the world of hate groups:

- In 1993, he filed an affidavit of sovereignty and declared his freedom from the federal government.
- He claimed in open court that the judicial system had no control over him.
- He attempted to pay off his credit card bills with bogus money orders he purchased from a Wisconsin-based sovereignty group.

Pretty easy exercise? You get the point about hate groups.

Chapter Twenty

Terrorists

by Sean Mactire

from *Malicious Intent: A Writer's Guide to How Murderers,
Robbers, Rapists and Other Criminals Think*

T errorists are often misrepresented by gross stereotypes and major misconceptions. Not all terrorists are ignorant, unintelligent, foaming-at-the-mouth Arabs. Of all the different types of criminals, terrorists are the most cunning. In essence, terrorists are the ultimate predator, the great white shark of criminals.

Contrary to popular belief, terrorism did not begin in 1964 with the founding of the Palestine Liberation Organization. The earliest foundations are those established by Hasan and his Order of the Assassins, but to understand the origins of modern terrorism, we have to go back 190 years to the Napoleonic Wars, when the French Army occupied Spain. The Spanish employed terrorist tactics, and from this point on, all national liberation movements would follow this illustrious example.

This was also the first time a doctrine of cooperation was established during a joint campaign involving an organized group of irregular resistance fighters and a regular army. It was used again during the American Civil War and found new life during World War II. In between those two wars, the first real "armies of liberation and resistance" were organized by the American Indians. In fact, the fathers of modern terrorism were Commanche Chief Quanna Parker, Lakota War Chief Crazy Horse and the Apache leaders Geronimo and Cochise. These great warriors organized one of the first campaigns of nationalist-ethnic liberation against an oppressive colonialist-imperialist government, which was the American government of 1866 to 1908. Other anticolonial liberation wars that followed, beginning in 1946, employed this pattern set by Native Americans.

Modern European and South American terrorism has its roots in the Nationalist and early proto-Communist agendas of the early nineteenth century, such as the Irish Fenian movement, the Italian Risorgimento movement; the Young Germany and Young Poland movements; the

Latin American Wars of Liberation of 1810 to 1817; and the Mexican Revolutions of 1812 and 1864. The First and Second Boer Wars in what is now South Africa are the only original standouts of nationalist movements. The Soviets of Lenin and Stalin and their successors did not invent terrorism; they only refined the activities of old political criminal groups.

The Boer Wars marked the third time Europeans fought Europeans using tactics of irregular warfare. There was no real Boer army, just organized bands of Boer farmers who conducted highly efficient raids, with large-scale battles in between. These wars saw the invention of several acts of criminal conduct that Western governments are now so familiar with. The Boers introduced the "terrorist bombing," the "hijacking" and the "commando raid." The British introduced "counterterrorism," "pacification" and the "concentration camp," which caused the deaths of twenty thousand Boer women and children. The Nazis only copied the British in both motive and operation. The only refinement the Nazis made was the addition of death camps, which were different from the concentration camps established in the 1930s to detain political prisoners.

What Is Terrorism?

There is no one definition of *terrorism*. A study of references on the subject written in the past sixty years will give you over two hundred definitions. However, there are only five major terms regarding *unconventional warfare* that are appropriate. These are:

1. Guerrilla warfare
2. Resistance-commando warfare
3. Low-intensity warfare
4. Insurgency warfare
5. Special operations warfare

In 1980, the U.S. State Department adopted a "description" of what terrorism is composed of, but it was not a definition:

> *Terrorism* is the threat or use of violence for political purposes by individuals or groups, whether acting for or in opposition to established governmental authority, when such actions are intended to shock, stun or intimidate a target group wider than the immediate victims. Terrorism has involved groups

seeking to overthrow specific regimes, to rectify perceived national or group grievances or to undermine international political order as an end in itself.

In 1987, the U.S. State Department published a more specific definition:

> Terrorism—premeditated, *politically* motivated violence perpetrated against noncombatant targets by subnational groups or clandestine state agents, usually intended to influence an audience. "International terrorism" is terrorism involving the citizens or territory of more than one state.

Since the key words in both statements are "political" and "audience," or "target group," in essence, terrorism can be defined as "political theater." It is the only type of crime and class of acts of human destructiveness that is so premeditated that there are a script, actors, a stage and an audience. Why do you think it was so easy to do a made-for-TV movie about the hijacking of the ocean liner *Achille Lauro* and the bombing of the World Trade Center? The terrorists already wrote the script, and the media gave these killers what every terrorist hopes for: *mass publicity*. Madison Avenue ad agencies would kill to get ratings like those that terrorists get. Ironically, the strategy that terrorists use to spread their messages is identical to those used to promote Nike shoes, Hanes underwear and Coca-Cola. There is no difference between the communications concepts, except that people get killed when terrorists advertise.

Still, there is no consensus on a real definition of what terrorism is. Politicians have their own definition, journalists have theirs, academians have theirs and psychiatric professionals have theirs. The public's definition depends on which side they support. It has often been said in the Middle East that a "terrorist is one person's hero and another's criminal." At one time, a majority of the Israeli government was wanted for acts of terrorism against the British, when Great Britain governed Palestine. This included Prime Ministers Begin and Shamir. Begin was the one who helped blow up the King David Hotel, killing a bunch of innocent British tourists. However, he condemned the Palestinians for similar actions. The former terrorist Shamir is now the peacemaker who has embraced his enemy Yassir Arafat, who is now the terrorist turned politician-peacemaker. So, as you can see, the business of terrorism is not just political theater, it is a political soap opera that can border on the absurd.

For our purposes in this chapter, we will use the following as a working definition: Terrorism—all acts of politically or religiously motivated violence intended to change, through fear and intimidation, public and/or government policy and which are justified to the perpetrators and are heinous crimes to the targets and victims.

This just about covers all types of terrorism from pro-life zealots who shoot doctors and burn clinics to Islamic fanatics to the IRA to the KKK and neo-Nazi Skinheads to the acts of our own government in retaliatory response to acts of terrorism by foreign groups or governments. All terrorists consider themselves soldiers. George Washington and his officers were patriots to the residents of the American colonies, but they were terrorists to the British, especially our guerrilla fighters like Ethan Allen and Francis Marion, the Carolina Swamp Fox. In a way, Begin and Arafat are George Washington to their people, but they were bitter enemies to each other. All violent religious militants, such as the Hezbollah (Party of God-Islamic Jihad), consider themselves to be "soldiers of God," though it is doubtful that God condones this behavior.

The Elements of Terrorism

Is terrorism a *crime*, an *act of war* or an *act of political necessity*? Since there is no way to realistically define or classify terrorism, it is best to identify terrorism as a special classification of human destructiveness delineated by its three main categories:
1. Goals
2. Strategies-objectives
3. Operations-organizations

All these characteristics make terrorism a special type of intentional trauma. Terrorism is the use of criminal actions as weapons and tactics of war, which makes terrorism different from other criminal activities. The crimes that are committed are part of the overall operations. Terrorism is an act of war, even though there is no apparent "war" being waged. And it is definitely an act of political necessity. So, simply put, terrorism is a highly premeditated act of intentional trauma.

Goals

Regardless of the motives, either social or religious, the goals of all terrorism are *political*. This sets the terrorist apart from the criminals and mentally ill to which the terrorist is often mistakenly compared. In the minds of the terrorists, they see themselves as victims who must right great social or economic wrongs, for which the ruling authorities are to blame. Terrorists see that only violence, as a tactic of last resort, will make target governments accede to righting the alleged wrong. For terrorists, their goals are the moral imperatives that justify the use of any means to attain these goals. However, it is important to note that terrorist acts are not justified by the doctrines that most terrorist groups subscribe to. All Muslims are prohibited from committing suicide; so, the suicide bombings that Shiite terrorists have committed are in direct violation of their fundamentalist Islamic beliefs—the same beliefs for which the Shiites are waging this "holy war against Western evil."

Strategies/Objectives

The objective is simple; it is to terrorize the enemy government and intimidate the public. Unlike conventional warfare, there is no intent to destroy the enemy, only to use the fear and public dissatisfaction created by terrorist violence as leverage to obtain the mandated political goals. Thus, the strategy and the tactics are the use of fear and publicity for maximum psychological effect.

In most cases, the fear experienced by the public is greatly unjustified and exaggerated. However, the threat that exists is overpowering, as exemplified by the hundreds of thousands of American tourists who were afraid to travel to Europe in 1985 and 1986. This fear is instilled in the public by both the terrorists' acts and the publicity that the news media is manipulated into giving. This is the heart of "terrorist theater."

No other weapons better serve the terrorist's cause than the reporter, the microphone and video camera. All victims, all target locations and the timing of violent acts are chosen in the same manner as an ad agency advertises a client product. The World Trade Center bombing and the subsequent TV movie had the highest global ratings of any media event in 1993.

Crucial to all terrorist operations is the component of the premeditated use of the threat of violence. Terrorist activity is composed of crimes—murder, assault, hijacking, kidnapping, arson, sabotage and other heinous acts—and are not legitimate acts of war, but we are not talking about conventional warfare. This is "unconventional" warfare that pits irregular troops against innocent civilians and the military and law enforcement agencies employed by the target government.

As a matter of operational organization, terrorist groups are paramilitary criminal gangs. In peacetime, there is no justification for terrorist acts. However, in wartime, as in the case of the Vietnam War, both sides employed terrorist tactics as part of their military operations. As Viet Cong irregulars carried out murder and sabotage, so did the American Special Forces as part of their antiterrorist campaign. This is what Operation Phoenix was all about. The only difference between us and them was the level of brutality and the constant use of mass murder that the Viet Cong embraced.

Operations/Organizations

Terrorists always work in predatory groups. Some individuals have acted alone in terrorist acts, but this is rare. Like organized crime groups, terrorists are a subcultural element. Members derive self-esteem from the group and not the cause. Thus, peer approval becomes the primary motivation for the individual to commit crimes, and the goals of the group take a backseat. They operate either in small groups or in small units directed by the central organization, such as the PLO or IRA, that are organized into brigades that are subdivided into cells. There is also no allegiance to any particular country. Terrorists are not only a subculture, they are a subnational element within a country. As in the case of the Tupamaros of South America or the Italian Red Brigade, terrorists are a cancer that grows with the body of a nation, with the exception of state-sponsored terrorism, such as in Libya, Iran and Iraq. All terrorist groups need sponsors, hosts or a parental relationship with a country or a larger group in order to operate and survive.

The Mind of the Terrorist

As stated earlier, terrorists are neither insane nor morally depraved. These gross misconceptions and stereotypes are a way of "dehumanizing the enemy." This is a typical defense mechanism that helps people cope with terrorist violence. It also helps the public avoid facing the real issues that drove these people to commit terrorism. In other words, as long as you think the enemy is a rabid dog, it's easier to kill it instead of trying to make peace with it.

It is very easy to slap on the labels of "antisocial," "psychopath" or "evil entity," but these overly simplistic descriptions of terrorist behavior ignore the political, economic and social environment factors that contribute to the creation of the individual psychopathology of the terrorist.

Like all intentional trauma, terrorism is a matter of medical ecology. Terrorists are a product of their own individual psychologies interacting with their environments. However, they are not victims of society, unless they are fighting to overthrow a tyrannical dictatorship or military junta, as was the case with Fidel Castro and his campaign to overthrow the government of Cuba's Batista in 1958, or in a war of liberation, as in the case of the Algerian FLN. In the case of any brutalized, impoverished populace, the use of terrorism to gain freedom is perfectly acceptable. To the British, the Boston Tea Party was a terrorist act; to the American colonies, it was an act of liberation from despots. As you can see, how the behavior of those who commit acts of unconventional warfare is viewed depends upon whose side you support.

The Typical Terrorist Profile

1. Most terrorists are male, but there is a large proportion of females in their ranks, and the women are often more cunning and deadly than their male counterparts.
2. Terrorists usually begin their careers around age twenty to twenty-five.
3. Terrorists are generally single and come from middle- or upper-class families.
4. The average terrorist has a college education and has a history of being a campus radical or of being involved in student protest movements. Many are college dropouts, which demonstrates their dissatisfaction with society. College campuses are where many terrorists begin their careers by joining or being recruited by terrorist groups. Some groups have started as college protest groups.

There is no terrorist personality type, but there are certain traits that are common to those prone to political violence:

1. Low self-esteem among follower types, not among the leaders
2. A desire to take high risks
3. Feelings of not being able to control one's life
4. Places unrealistic demands upon self
5. Tends to raise expectations, rather than lower them when confronted with failure
6. Unable to cope with rejection or failure
7. Feels life is controlled by external forces
8. Externalizes bitterness over failure and desires to take wrath out

on "the enemy" that is allegedly responsible for the problems in the terrorist's life

9. Deep feelings of weakness, self-denigration and self-hatred, which they project onto the society being attacked

10. Single minded; has same organized hunter-killer traits as most serial killers, especially mission-oriented killers

11. Sees society as the "bad enemy" that must be punished—especially common among terrorist leaders

12. Idealizes self; sees self as "good person who has been victimized"—especially common among terrorist leaders, who exhibit a grandiose self-image that projects confidence and purpose and attracts followers

13. Extroverted, narcissistic and aggressive behavior, more prevalent in leaders than followers, with a further disposition toward sadistic "appreciation of 'work' "

14. Followers usually drawn by leader's charisma, not the cause; tendency among followers to use group to compensate for feelings of inadequacy

15. Ability to control impulsivity and apply reflective thought to actions—a sign of mental stability

16. Restrained, able to suppress need for gratification until goals are obtained

17. Inconsiderate, self-centered and emotionally cold

18. Sometimes displays sociopathic traits, e.g., lacks remorse or is easily provoked to violence, but most often displays either ambivalence or abhorrence toward harming people, sometimes even going to great lengths to avoid killing people

The Group Mentality

Regardless of the psychological makeup of individual terrorists, terrorism is still a group activity which compensates for the individuals' lack of self-identity and provides these individuals with security and certainty. Basically, there is little difference between a terrorist cult and a religious cult. These groups tend to be countercultural, and the activities tend to be beyond the limits of behavior that society condones. This is why both entities tend to attract people who have a grievance or feelings of deprivation. In essence, one might describe terrorist groups as "violent political cults" that offer their members an explanation of the causes of their mutual problems and propose a remedy. In the case of many Islamic fundamentalist terror groups, terrorism is a family affair. The primary motive of the kidnapping of Westerners in Lebanon was to exchange them for Lebanese relatives who were being held in European jails.

An identity crisis can be the motive for people joining a terrorist group. Irish Catholics who join the IRA and adopt Marxist ideology are substituting Marxism for the Christian faith they are in crisis over. Basque separatists are searching for their own national identity, just as Palestinians are seeking political autonomy. In other cases, members look to the group as a substitute for the family that they are in crisis over. People join terrorist groups or cults to fulfill personal needs or because of social obligations to family or community or religion or ethnic identity. However, they stay in these groups and conform to group demands because of the individual's personal commitment and the pressure of peers from within the group. Many seek to enhance their self-image through dedication to a mission, a need to sacrifice and any self-justification that they can derive from the group. Others seek to enhance their standing within their own family or community. Admiration of peers and family is a key factor with many IRA members, as well as other ethnic terror groups. Other key factors are money and power. With the loss of outside support from the Communist bloc and some wealthy Arab nations, many terror groups are engaged in organized crime activities and drug trafficking. With the billions of dollars that members can have access to, monetary wealth and its inherent power are major motivating factors.

Another factor that is essential to group cohesion is the group ideology, which is holy gospel to each member, dictates what is good behavior for members and submerges and destroys the individual's identity. The individual's morality is drowned and is substituted by the group's morality. Killing may be abhorrent to the individual, but if the group says it's okay, that person will slaughter as many innocents as the group says to. Violence is seen by the individual as politically justifiable, strategically necessary for the group's goals and, therefore, morally essential.

Also contrary to popular belief, terrorism is an act of rational, sane choice. Since these groups are smaller than the enemy they oppose, turning to extreme violence is the most appropriate choice for the group to achieve its political goals. To gain independence for Algeria from France, the Arab FLN (Front de Liberation Nationale) had to resort to terror tactics to defeat the militarily superior French colonial forces. Thus, terror tactics are the wake-up call that is used to force the enemy to address the grievances of the group. Killing innocent civilians also puts pressure on the opponent to make a deal to stop the killing.

The idea that terrorist acts are compulsive is only partly right. Terrorism is part of the cycle of violence that relates to the problem as one of medical ecology. Once a group begins the use of violence, it sets in motion a cycle that continues in response to the actions of each side. If the opponent reacts to the first wave of terror acts by attacking the group or its supporters and resources, the next wave of attacks by the group is retaliatory. The harsher the crackdown, the more violent the retaliation used. However, this escalation of violence is gradual. Each wave of violence by both sides, including the decision to use violence initially, is preceded by intense planning, organization and a strengthening of group cohesion. Also, those who actually engage in violence are those members who have been with the group the longest. The rookies are generally given the nonviolent jobs of administration and logistics, such as bookkeeping, courier assignments, publication production, supply management and even secretarial duties. Once the escalation begins, the compulsion factor comes into play. This factor is controlled by the group's psychology and not by external forces or reality. The characteristics of the group's psychology are:

1. The illusion of invincibility
2. Excessive optimism
3. Excessive risk taking
4. Presumption of moral superiority
5. Single-minded view that the enemy is evil
6. Intolerance of any kind of opposition, from within the group and from without

David Koresh and his Waco cult were classic examples of terrorist group psychology. However, the environment that brought about their shift toward violence was not an oppressive one; it was an environment of liberal religious tolerance and policies of government noninterference. This is why other groups are growing and moving closer to another Waco-type conflict. They feel they can get away with murder because this liberal climate gives them a false sense of security and invulnerability. Thus, to fully understand the full spectrum of terrorist behavior, you have to appreciate the following motivational and contributory factors:

1. Social dissatisfaction
2. Political disaffection

3. Economic deprivation
4. Personal crises and conflicts

Strategy, Tactics and Victims

Currently, there are over five hundred terrorist groups in operation worldwide. Only the PLO has turned toward peace, but small splinter factions do not agree with the recent peace treaty with Israel and vow to continue the cycle of violence that Arafat and the majority of the PLO leadership have broken from. Within Israel, peace with the "old enemy of Zionism" has created Jewish factions that are threatening acts of terror against both Jews and Arabs.

Strategy

Terrorism is both a strategic initiative and a system of tactical operations. Terrorists do not undertake random acts. Consider the bombing of the World Trade Center in New York. This act was part of a global strategy that was planned for a long while and was timed to take place for maximum fear and publicity. The fact that the terrorists were caught is not a factor. It is highly likely that their arrests were part of the plan. This strategic element and threat to national security are what make terrorism different from random crime. The strategy involved depends on the political agenda:

1. The IRA is Marxist but is concerned with making money and liberating Northern Ireland.
2. The Marxist groups in Europe are interested in organized crime and perhaps initiating another Russian revolution or world Communist revolution.
3. The PLO is now a peacemaker, except for factions bent on the destruction of Israel.
4. Those with an agenda of ethnic autonomy are the ones to watch because they have the most to lose by not bringing worldwide attention to their cause.
5. The Islamic fundamentalist groups are just out on a "holy war" against *all* non-Muslims and those within their faith who will not conform, as in Egypt.
6. The neo-Nazis and right-wing extremists are out to destroy democracy for the "good" of the people.

In the 1990s, we have a major political void in the sponsorship of terrorism. The Soviet Union is dead and out of the terror game. The Soviet bloc countries are now democracies and are also out of the game. East Germany is gone and definitely out. Libya is more concerned about being bombed by America than bombing America through terrorism, so they're out, too. Kuwait is out because of the conflict with Iraq, the new alliance with America and its European allies and a distant relationship with Israel. So, with the New World Order firmly entrenched, the World Terrorist Network (WTN) has had to find new "friends" to help its various assorted causes. China is in; Iran is very in; Iraq is distantly in; Syria is still in, but may drop out soon; and some newfound friends among the Mafia and other organized crime groups are in for the money. They each have their own agendas, but only Iran, as a terrorist sponsor, has an immediate threat potential. The strategy we will see unfold in the coming years will be based on who is sponsoring, who needs the most exposure for their cause and the political situation of the time.

Tactics

The operational tactics of terrorists depend upon the group and the resources at its disposal. Generally, this will mean any act that intimidates innocent civilians is a good tactic. When ground to air missiles fell into the hands of the IRA, every airliner flying to Europe was at risk—and still is. But, so far, this tactic does not interest the IRA, as it may upset the applecart they are operating. They are more interested in parading machine guns in full view of British troops during IRA funerals, which demonstrates that even the strictest gun control laws, even those administered under martial law, are absolutely useless. Terrorists and criminals can get weapons of any type, anytime they want to. At one time, drug gangs here in the United States were supplied with weapons from Cuba that were made in the Soviet Union.

The most common types of terrorist tactics are armed attacks. Bombings, arson, murder, hijacking and kidnapping are the usual. Targets can be anyone or anything, but generally the targets have more of a "symbolic" value than as hard targets. At other times, the targets are hit purely to gain leverage, as in the taking of hostages. Extraordinary tactics are generally directed at increasing financial resources. These include bank robbery, extortion, blackmail, ransom and drug dealing. The IRA is very big on extortion, robbery and drugs. They also run a string of brothels in Holland and Germany. Tactics also depend on the operational environment or theater of operations, which is where the terrorists have concentrated their agenda, as in the PLO operating in areas close to Israel. With resources and sponsors closing down, future terrorist strategies and tactics will have a far greater potential for mass destruction. Such tactics would include:

1. Computer hacking and manipulation of computer services
2. Nuclear terrorism
3. Use of biological weapons
4. Use of chemical weapons

With the current instability of the Commonwealth of Independent States (CIS), the former Soviet Union, and their need for hard cash, the possibility of NBC (nuclear, biological, chemical) weapons falling into the hands of terrorists is very great. The future possibilities of terrorist tactics and strategies are only limited by the limits of the human imagination.

Victims

The majority of victims of terrorism are innocents. Only a small percentage of killing during the past thirty years have been hard-target assassinations, and most of these were local opponents of the IRA, PLO or Italian Red Brigade. The innocent majority, such as Christmas shoppers in downtown London, are *symbolic targets*. Almost every year, there is a "seasonal" attack designed to force the British to get out of Northern Ireland. However, the slaughter continues, because both sides are stubborn. To the terrorists, these atrocities assert the message of their cause: An armed struggle is a moral imperative against the oppressive order. The innocents are dehumanized into "the enemy." With these types of traumatic crises, the victims' circles are expanded to include the entire country. Almost everyone who visits New York or London wonders if a bomb is going to go off, and almost every airline passenger thinks for a brief moment about the possibility of hijacking. And let us not forget the Lambs of God, who terrorize innocent doctors, bomb and burn buildings and murder anyone that is opposed to their zealous views. They do this all in the name of God. In their minds, God and Jesus Christ are the precipitators of terrorism and are as motivational as Yassir Arafat. But God gave them a choice, and they chose evil.

PART V

VICE-RELATED CRIMES

Chapter Twenty-One

Vice Enforcement:

Gambling and Liquor Investigations

by John Boertlein

T he cliché that goes something like, "If it's fun, provocative and you really like it, it must be illegal," is not far from accurate when we talk about vice-related crime and its investigation. There are arguments all over the board on regulating "victimless crimes." And the added implications of organized crime's involvement in vice are well documented. But for the purposes of this chapter, we'll put moral arguments aside and concentrate on an investigative level applicable to the laws governing vice activity, even though those laws vary tremendously from state to state and jurisdiction to jurisdiction.

Drugs received a chapter of their own because they seem to be the most enduringly popular vice. Here we'll examine other favorites like gambling and liquor enforcement from an investigator's point of view. If you're using a vice investigation scenario in your writing, remember that your character's ability to blend in and mingle are the foundation of any effective investigation technique. Without this talent, vice investigation becomes a futile task.

Gambling

Regulations affecting gambling differ widely from venue to venue and with the advent of riverboat gambling, off-track betting and Internet gambling, the rules are changing all the time. Most legalized gambling is subject to strict government scrutiny and control, but the backroom poker game and street corner bookie still exist.

Essentially, gambling becomes a law enforcement concern for one of two reasons:

- It's a game of chance with winners and losers that is conducted in a public place.
- It's a type of bet, wager, scheme or game of chance where somebody makes a profit.

Whether it's sports betting, horse racing or any other event on which you can wager on the outcome, bookmaking is the best example of someone getting a cut of every participant's action. Let's take a look at the bookie's role in "playing the ponies" for fun and profit.

A lot of people believe that when a bettor wins, the payoff comes out of the bookmaker's pocket. This couldn't be more wrong. Sports books and racetracks work on the same principle as the percentage bookmaker, and a percentage bookmaker *cannot* lose. Back to our horse race bookie. In a percentage book, the odds given and the amounts accepted on any horse are determined by certain rules and conditions by which the bookie retains 20 to 30 percent of all the money placed with him on each race, no matter what horse wins. More simply, when you win on a race, the money you get comes from other bettors via the bookie, not out of his pocket.

Consider the following table showing how the odds and wagers are controlled in a 20 percent book:

Name of Horse	Odds	Percentage	Amount Wagered
Mean Mike	3-2	40	$400
Big Man's Dream	20-1	4.76	$47
Badge Girl	13-5	27.78	$277
Dizzy Lizzy	15-1	6.25	$62
MC's Lament	8-1	11.11	$111
Go Jackie Go	40-1	2.44	$24
Randal C.	30-1	3.23	$32
Goin' Broke	8-1	11.11	$111
Bones Buster	20-1	4.76	$47
Garibaldi	10-1	9.06	$90

Total Amount Taken In: $1,201

This particular book shows the bookmaker can accept $400 on the first horse, $47 on the second horse and so on, to stay within the limits of the 20 percent book. In total, he takes in $1,201. And no matter which horse wins, he won't pay out any more than $1,000. Using the 20 percent formula mentioned, no horse could win and cause more than $1000 to be paid out. Therefore, he's $201 to the good before the race is even run.

Suppose the first horse wins. The bookie took in $400 on this horse, or to simplify things, let's say he took in two hundred $2 bets. The odds were 3 to 2, and 3 plus 2 equals 5. So the bookmaker has to pay out two hundred times $5 or $1,000. Only one horse can win, so he's still $201 in the black.

Or say the second horse wins. The bookie took in forty-seven $1 bets. The odds were 20 to 1, so he pays forty-seven times $21 or $987, and he's $214 ahead of the game.

The arithmetic is simple. The odds on the first horse were 3 to 2. To find the percentage, the bookie simply adds 3 and 2, which equals 5, divides 100 by 5, which equals 20, and then multiplies the 20 by the amount of the wager—$2 in this case—which equals 40. So 3 to 2 odds equals 40 percent of the book.

The odds on the second horse were 20 to 1, which add up to 21; 100 divided by 21 equals 4.76; so 20 to 1 equals 4.76 percent of the book.

The odds on the third horse were 13 to 5, which add up to 18; 100 divided by 18 equals 27.78; therefore, 13 to 5 odds equals 27.78 percent of the book. And so on.

Obviously, these numbers can vary with the size of the book's bank, number of customers and "expenses." In the example we just used, if our bookie was working one track with ten races playing for 20 percent of a $1,000 payoff per race, he's taking home $2,000 a day, tax-free. Throw in some simulcasts or increase your volume, and he's got a pretty nice racket going. Bookmaking on sporting events can be engineered the same way.

Successful investigation and prosecution of bookmaking operations depends largely on surveillance and documentation. An investigator needs to create a detailed paper trail proving:
- Positive identity of those involved
- A continual pattern of profit from bookmaking
- An account of the profits

Remember, the difference between gambling and "for amusement only" is that somebody is enjoying a cut for facilitating the process. Video poker machines with automatic payout are one thing, but proving that someone is taking a percentage of the pay is the heart of gambling investigations.

Liquor Investigations

Since the Twenty-First Amendment to the U.S. Constitution abolished prohibition in 1933, liquor control has been a nationwide law enforcement concern. Although laws vary from state to state and venue to venue, most liquor regulations are founded in public health and welfare concerns, from driving under the influence (DUI) to underage consumption. Moral and ethical arguments aside, if you're using booze as part of your writing, consider these licensing and regulatory terms based on liquor laws in Ohio. Every state has similar regulations.

- **Beer:** "Beer" or "malt beverages" include all brewed or fermented malt products containing one-half of 1 percent or more of alcohol by volume, but not more than 6 percent by weight.
- **Intoxicating liquor:** Liquids and compounds, other than beer, containing one-half of 1 percent of alcohol by volume, which are fit for beverage purposes. Includes wine and mixed beverages, even if they contain less than 4 percent of alcohol by volume.
- **Wine:** Intoxicating liquor made from fermented juices of fruits or other agricultural products that contains not less than one-half of 1 percent of alcohol by volume and not more than 21 percent of alcohol by volume.
- **Mixed beverages:** Intoxicating liquor, such as bottled and prepared cordials, cocktails and highballs, where the alcoholic content is not less than one-half of 1 percent by volume and not more than 21 percent by volume.
- **Spiritous liquor:** Intoxicating liquors containing more than 21 percent of alcohol by volume.
- **Low-alcohol beverages:** Any brewed or fermented malt product, or any product made from the fermented juices of grapes, fruits or other agricultural products, that contains no alcohol or less than one-half of 1 percent alcohol by volume.

Examples of Liquor-Law Violations

- **Sales to underage persons:** The minimum age for consumption of alcoholic beverages is twenty-one. No person, permit holder or agent shall sell or deliver beer or intoxicating liquor to anyone under twenty-one years of age.

- **After-hour sales:** No person shall sell or consume on the permit premises any beer or intoxicating liquor between the hours of 1:00 A.M. and 5:30 A.M.
- **Sales to intoxicated persons:** No person shall sell, deliver or furnish beer or intoxicating liquor to an intoxicated person.
- **Gambling or gambling devices:** No holder of a liquor permit premises will permit gambling or gambling devices on the permit premises.
- **Solicitation of patrons:** No permit holder will permit solicitation of drinks or money on the permit premises.
- **Bootlegging/keeping a place:** No valid permit holder shall sell or deliver intoxicating liquor or beer.
- **Consumption in a motor vehicle:** No person shall sell or consume any beer or intoxicating liquor in a motor vehicle.
- **Obstructing/hindering:** The permit holder, an employee or customer of a permit premises shall not obstruct or hinder any law enforcement officer from inspecting a liquor permit premises. The law enforcement officer must be inspecting for liquor premise violations.

Chapter Twenty-Two

Prostitution

by Mauro V. Corvasce and Joseph R. Paglino

from *Modus Operandi: A Writer's Guide to How Criminals Work*

Prostitution has been defined by the law as the practice of offering your body indiscriminately for money or its equivalent. The President's Commission on Law Enforcement reports that there were over 50,000 arrests for prostitution and commercialized vice in 1985. In 1992, the figures were 76,400 arrests nationwide, which assumes that approximately 65,000 persons were engaged in such activity with a total yearly income of $322 million. Other studies have claimed that prostitution involves 100,000 to 500,000 men and women in the United States and that the profession itself grosses more than a billion dollars a year.

It is a simple fact of life that some people either prefer to or have to pay for sex, and as long as there are people willing to pay for it, there will be others willing to sell it. It is a classic case of supply and demand, just like any business.

Citizens complain that prostitution makes it impossible to carry on legitimate businesses in some parts of the cities. New Yorkers lament that prostitutes have caused a deterioration of Times Square; Hollywood merchants claim their area has become known as a hookers' paradise; officials everywhere point an accusing finger at court decisions that they say have made it almost impossible to control prostitution effectively. Boston has attempted to segregate vice areas of the city into red zones, while in Salt Lake City, police have taken to arresting the clients of prostitutes known as *johns*. In other cities cooperating news media publish the names of men picked up for soliciting prostitutes. Periodic vice raids are used to round up prostitutes in many cities, but in spite of these and other efforts, prostitution continues to flourish. Some officials have urged that prostitution be legalized as it is in Germany and other parts of Europe, which means not so much legalization as regulation. In the United States, Nevada has more or less adopted such a plan. But what works in Nevada might not work in other areas of the country, since those areas of the state where prostitution is legalized are very small towns, the inhabitants of which are fewer than those in a block of urban apartment buildings.

Today's brothel is likely to be right around the corner in the form of a massage parlor, a nude photo club, an escort service, dial-a-massage, a sauna house or some other thinly disguised market for sexual services. The motive for the prostitute's client appears to remain much the same: the craving for sexual variety, perverse gratification and intercourse free of entangling commitments. As for the prostitute herself, the evidence suggests that now, as in the past, her activity is voluntary, representing for some a considerable range of advantages including flexible work hours, contact with diverse people of power and influence, a heightened sense of activity and the opportunity to make substantial sums of money.

A Brief History of Prostitution

In ancient Greece the lowest prostitutes were street walkers and brothel inmates. Far above both were the *hetaerae*, who were distinguished by being educated in the arts and by serving only the wealthy and powerful. They provided entertainment and intellectual companionship, as well as sexual gratification. The *hetaerae*, drawn from the population, compensated for the fact that wives and daughters were not permitted to entertain, go outside the home or acquire an education. In fact, Demosthenes summed it up when he said, "Man has the *hetaerae* for erotic enjoyments, girlfriends for daily use and wives to bring up children and to be faithful housewives."

Similarly, Japan until very recently had three classes of women outside of respectable family life: the *joro* in brothels, the *jogoku* or unlicensed prostitutes on the streets or in bath houses, and the *geisha* or dancing girls. Trained in dancing, singing and other methods of entertaining guests in tea houses, geisha girls were an indispensable adjunct to Japanese entertainment. However, not all of them were open to prostitution, and if they were, they were selective in their customers.

In modern society about all that is left of prostitution is the commercial form, in which one party uses sex for pleasure, the other for money. To tie intercourse to sheer pleasure is to divorce it from both reproduction and from any sentimental social relationship. This does not mean that people feel as strongly about prostitution as they do about thieves or arsonists. A recent survey conducted by *McCall's* magazine found that only 7 percent of the respondents said they would clear the streets of prostitutes if they had the chance. The distaste for prostitution is manifested mainly by reluctance to have a bordello in the neighborhood or to be identified with the business or its personnel. Otherwise, it does not seem to bother the general population.

Causes of Prostitution

If prostitution offends the moral principles of people, why does it exist? And, if it denigrates women, how does it recruit its members? To explain prostitution in economic terms is begging the question. Since prostitution is defined as selling sexual favors, one might say that retail merchandising has economic causes.

Prostitution arises from the demand for the prostitute's services. This need for service arises out of the regulation of sex itself and the limited liability of a commercial sexual relationship. If the customer has money, he can obtain satisfaction with no further obligations. In the case of a female prostitute, the only clients that she needs to procure are men. A john, or client of the prostitute, does not become enmeshed in courtship, friendship or marriage. Let's face it, every male finds himself sometimes, and some males find themselves most of the time, in circumstances where sexual release through more reputable channels is impossible.

Our experiences have shown that, of course, not all males visit prostitutes, but those who do depend on them for a major portion of their sexual activity. About 30 percent of men have never had contact with prostitutes. Of the rest, most have had only one or two experiences. No more than 15 to 20 percent of men visit a prostitute more often than a few times a year. This still leaves a substantial portion of the adult male population. For them, what does prostitution provide that other outlets cannot?

The primary advantage of prostitution for these men is its impartiality, impersonality and economy. Attracting and seducing a woman can be costly. By its effort to contain sexual acts in a meaningful and enduring social relationship, society creates advantages for prostitution. For less than the cost of a single date with a girl who is not a prostitute, a male can engage in whatever sexual fantasies he desires with a prostitute. Additionally, the impersonality of prostitution makes it particularly suited to strangers. The man away from his wife or circle of girlfriends cannot, in a short time, count on seducing a respectable woman. Also, since certain sexual acts are considered immoral for wives and sweethearts, the prostitute has an advantage. That is, the prostitute, as long as she gets paid, will usually perform 99.9 percent of the services requested by the client. The demand for prostitution will not be eliminated or seriously altered by a change in the economic system. The underlying basis for the demand is inherent in human society.

Prostitute Categories

Now it's time to put on our hot pants, lipstick and high-heeled shoes and check out the action on the streets.

The Legalized Brothel

In some countries prostitution is a legal, commercial venture. Brothels are licensed and regulated by the government in an effort to minimize the negative impacts of venereal disease and organized crime. These two side effects of prostitution are generally present in situations where prostitution is illegal.

In Nevada, the practice of legalized brothels is accepted in almost all of the seventeen counties of the state. When it was open, the Mustang Ranch, one of the fifty or more licensed brothels, was the largest, doing an annual business of between $3 and $5 million. The house rules were not too strict. Drugs and sloppy clothes were not allowed. There were between twenty and twenty-five women working in this establishment at any given time. They were regularly inspected by physicians and required to hang their health certificates on the walls. The average income of the women was approximately $600 to $700 per week, of which $300 went for room and board. The women were free to accept or reject customers for any reason. They could, for example, discriminate against clients from different ethnic backgrounds. Whether or not the legal brothel has resulted in an increase or decrease in venereal disease or AIDS cannot be established. It has, however, decreased the activity of the police and courts in Nevada in dealing with prostitution.

The Illegal Brothel

In the United States most brothels that operate do so illegally. A common scene in New York City is luxurious east-side apartment houses, catering to New York and visiting businessmen.

Sue, the proprietor of the brothel, receives a minimum of $700 every few days tax free. A *trick*, which is a sexual act, costs anywhere from $35 to $75 and the money is divided equally with the hooker. Sue calls the hookers or prostitutes to work when they are needed. Sue is perpetually looking for new women to satisfy her customers. She usually hears of women from other hookers.

Sue considers her apartment a clean, respectable place that gentlemanly clientele can frequent. She avoids troublesome or aging hookers. Troublesome hookers are those who give out their home telephone numbers, which Sue considers stealing, and those who don't share the money that they have made from a client.

To prevent detection by the police, Sue pays off the doorman and the building manager, and the owners of the building seem oblivious as long as the rent is paid. Every two or three years, Sue changes her apartment and her telephone number, in the process dropping a few johns, who either showed violent tendencies or didn't pay enough money. However, Sue must always stay on the right side of the clients she drops because they can always go to the police.

The Street Walker

In many respects the street walker is at the bottom of the prostitution hierarchy. The most common scene that we have experienced is a young girl, either a runaway or a throwaway child, who drifts to the big city after leaving her home. She could be running away from sexual abuse by family members or friends. She often works as a waitress or clerk and for a time lives a rootless, disorganized life without friends and without ties to any social institutions. During this crucial period she is dissatisfied, tense, bitter and bewildered. She is far away from home and away from things that, even though they were uncomfortable, were her mainstay in her younger years. Her shiftless, alienated way of life brings her into contact with established prostitutes, who on the surface seem to be very well off and have good job security. Her morals are at a low, and she hungers for some kind of friendship and affection, so she will accept dates arranged for her by a prostitute friend or the prostitute's pimp.

What is a very common sight in New York City is for the pimps to be wandering around the Port Authority Terminal, which is the largest bus terminal in the United States. As these runaway or throwaway children enter the Port Authority, they are overwhelmed by the vastness and are easy to spot as new to the area. The pimps, who are male, frequent the coffee shops and rest areas of the Port Authority and attempt to strike up a conversation with these runaways. They offer them shelter for the night or possibly a part-time job or some money. They want to build up a friendship so that they can have this girl dependent on them. Some of them may actually come right out and request that they work for them as prostitutes. However, most of them state that they would be willing to have these women work as escorts for young men who need affection and attention at social events.

These young women, unaware of city life, enter into these relationships with pimps not knowing that it is really a front for hardcore prostitution. Eventually, the pimp moves from friendship to initiating the girl into prostitution either by raping the girl himself or having multiple members of his circle of pimps rape her repeatedly until she gets accustomed to rough sex.

The curious relationship between prostitutes and pimps, to whom they turn over a large part of their earnings, is seen as an attempt by the women to overcome loneliness and form a relationship with someone who seems to be lower than themselves.

Once the girl is degraded into this type of life, she becomes the pimp's servant and works for him where and when he tells her to. In return for these services, the pimp will give the girl free room and board, and, of course, she must have sex with him or any of his friends whenever they desire. Eventually, some street walkers will move from one pimp to another. However, if she moves, it will be a tremendous distance away from the original pimp, as pimps have certain territories and zones. The girl is only supplied with free room and board as long as she works for the pimp. Should she decide to go out on her own, she must work even harder to make money to have a place to stay. Some women who successfully do go on their own and escape from the pimps will arrange to live with other hookers so that they can share the rent.

Eventually, street walkers will move outside lawful society when they get arrested. After a time, the arrest experience is viewed as a simple occupational hazard, much like overstock in a regular retail business. Eventually, the prostitute becomes stabilized in her calling, finds her friends almost exclusively in this type of industry and acquires a recognized status as a prostitute.

The Call Girl

In the upper echelons of prostitution is the call girl who usually maintains her own apartment and keeps a book, in which she lists the names and phone numbers of her clients. Generally, she responds to calls, although she may also use her book of names to solicit. Most of the call girls encountered by the police have a deep hatred for men, demonstrate a pattern of lesbianism and have very strong suicidal tendencies. Additionally, most of these women are characterized by having been rejected by both parents or they have a history of being sexually abused; sometimes prostitution is used as an attempt to replace affection that was missing during childhood.

Currently, the typical call girl is equipped not only with a residence from which to operate, but also with a beeper and cellular phone. The call girl usually escalates to this level after working for a short time as a street walker. However, it should be noted that not many street walkers make it to call girl status. It takes a special kind of woman to elevate herself, gain enough money to go out on her own and operate this way without being attached to pimps who dominate her. In effect, they have the same spirit of entrepreneurship as do persons who open up their own business.

The call girls we have encountered have ranged from the street walker who elevated herself to housewives and college students desiring to make extra money. Recently there was a call girl arrested in Princeton, New Jersey. It was later discovered that she was a police officer's wife operating out of her home. She had an appointment booked for one particular businessman when another steady client requested the exact same time. After she accidently divulged the name of the first client to the second client, there was an altercation involving these two gentlemen, which they both ultimately reported to the police. Of course, neither gentleman disclosed that they were clients of the woman, they simply stated that they had information that she was a prostitute. The police officer, who worked the four to twelve shift, never knew that his wife was out of the house, as every time he called her, she answered the phone. She programmed her home phone to forward calls to her cellular phone so that she could pick up the phone wherever she went. She was home during the day when her husband was there but, while he was out on patrol, she was cruising the streets also, in a different type of business.

Massage Parlors

The massage parlor has come to be regarded as a type of illegal brothel and is often located within the neighborhood shopping district. Massage parlors are usually relatively inconspicuous. There's not much publicity or advertisement, and the outer facade of the building is not very ostentatious or enticing to the casual shopper. Frequently, these massage parlors advertise through small classified ads in local papers.

Police employ a method called the *duken* to close down massage parlors. The duken entails having a plainclothes police detective accost an unsuspecting victim about to enter the parlor. The officer will say something like, "We know who you are and what you are doing here, would you like your wife to find out about it?" Out of fear, the victim will introduce the officer to the employees of the massage parlor as a friend of his who wishes their services.

Once the detective gains entry, he plays the part of the customer coming in for the first time. The detective cannot carry a gun, identification cards, handcuffs or any object that would make the owner or employees of the massage parlor suspicious. Like the other patrons, the officer then receives a massage.

Smart prostitution houses always tell their clients to go into a room, remove all their clothes and wait for their girl. This is because most police departments will not allow their officers to remove their underwear when investigating houses of prostitution. And of course these prostitutes know all about this.

At no time may the detective suggest anything of a sexual nature to the masseuse. There must only be solicitation on the woman's part. The masseuse might attempt to sexually arouse the client while massaging his genitals, but at this point there is absolutely no cause for arrest. As an enticement to get involved in sexual intercourse or oral sex, many of these massage parlors will have televisions showing X-rated movies. Only after the masseuse suggests sexual intercourse or oral sex and states a monetary fee is she liable for arrest. At this time the officer may make an arrest even though no actual intercourse or oral sex took place. Massage parlors usually employ only a few women as masseuses. Approximately two women do the massaging and soliciting. Their ages range from the mid-twenties to the mid-forties.

The Drug Addict Prostitute

A relatively recent addition to the world of prostitution, particularly in the United States, is the drug-addicted prostitute. Like the male drug addict, the female addict finds that after a time she must turn to an illegal activity to support her expensive drug habit. As males turn to burglary and robbery, women turn to prostitution.

A large percentage of street walkers are addicts. Call girls are not generally addicted. It is estimated that 90 percent of female addicts engage in prostitution at one time or another because prostitution is a quick source of the funds necessary to support their drug habit and the drug habits of the men with whom they live.

The Male Prostitute

In many large cities, particularly New York, male prostitutes have emerged as street walkers competing not for the needs of women seeking men, of course, but for the needs of men seeking men. Unfortunately, these male street walkers are young boys called *chicken hawks*, sometimes as young as nine or ten. These boys are the throwaway, disposable children of this century. Faced with no way to survive other than selling their bodies, they cruise the streets along with other prostitutes.

You would expect that these boys would appeal to strange, deviant, homosexual men; however, the opposite is true. As with regular female prostitution, many of the clients for these chicken hawks themselves are married and have children. It is a type of sexual fantasy that they, of course, cannot get within their homes unless they sexually abuse the male children.

Many male prostitutes dress to appeal to both types of johns. Males cross-dress as transvestites and appear to be female. Depending on the type of john, many of the boys are beaten or sometimes killed when the male client finds out in the middle of the sex act that the prostitute is actually male. These types of injury occur hundreds of times in New York City alone over the course of a year.

Prostitution and the Mob

Prostitution is and has always been one of the steady money makers of organized crime. However, the mob has denied any major interest in this field ever since 1936, when Charles "Lucky" Luciano was sent to prison by a crusading New York district attorney. Luciano's operation included over two hundred prostitutes housed in at least ten, four- to six-bedroom apartments. His neighborhood managers directed the women to locations where the business was heavier than usual on certain nights. His bookers transported them between neighborhoods to achieve the consumer appeal inherent in new faces of prostitutes. His collectors and housekeepers made certain the prostitutes turned over the agreed percentage of their earnings. His icemen paid off in the police stations and court rooms. His strong arm men or enforcers maintained discipline and settled disputes. His bailbondsmen, attorneys and physicians administered to the needs of the enterprise handling an arrest or ill health. A linen firm, which Lucky had an interest in, supplied the towels and sheets for his prostitution business.

This enterprise was the first concrete example of wraparound organized crime operations and it made a great deal of money. However, it was also a landmark case that revealed the need to insulate top men from the operations of a criminal enterprise. Luciano, who did not participate in the daily workings of any prostitution house, was convicted because detectives unearthed evidence of his operation of the business and used the theory of conspiracy to prove his guilt.

It should be noted that prostitutes are frequently excellent informants and are very cooperative in dealing with the police. Since they work on the street, they witness many things and encounter many men over the course of their employment. It is also a bit surprising to find how many men will tell these women secrets they have never told anybody in their life. These prostitutes, like bartenders, are willing to listen and they keep an ear out for anything that may be able to help them should they be arrested by the police.

In the movies and television some prostitutes are portrayed as warm, loving individuals who can be saved by the right man. This is totally fictional. Our experiences have found that most prostitutes have, by the age of eighteen, lived more in their lives than most women forty to fifty years of age. They are hardnosed businesswomen, know the streets and know how to survive. Prostitutes are not easily swayed by emotion and sentiment. The longer a prostitute works the streets, the more she realizes that is all she will ever be.

Whether in brothels or in the streets, under bridges or in automobiles, prostitution remains at the bottom of the social scale. It is the most convenient sexual outlet for legions of strangers, perverts and physically repulsive people in our midst. It performs a role that no other institution performs. In view of the conditions and the continued historical presence of prostitution, it is highly unlikely that it will ever be eliminated as a vice in society.

There are several organizations actively engaged in efforts to protect prostitutes: COYOTE in San Francisco, which stands for Calling Off Your Old Tired Ethics; PONY, which stands for the Prostitutes of New York; PUMA, which stands for the Prostitutes Union of Massachusetts; and ASP, the Association of Seattle Prostitutes. Prostitution appears to be developing a higher profile.

Chapter Twenty-Three

Sexual Predators

by Sean Mactire

from *Malicious Intent: A Writer's Guide to How Murderers,
Robbers, Rapists and Other Criminals Think*

R ape and other sex crimes are the number one felonies in America.
For writers, this can be a complex and sensitive issue to deal with
because there are so many myths about sex crimes. Here we will
dispel the myths so that these crimes can be seen and portrayed by writers
in a realistic fashion.

Rape is the only crime in which the victim is regarded as the offender, and sex crimes are treated with indifference, often being white-
washed with the label "victimless." At this writing, a number of police
departments in Maryland are being condemned for the practice of using
polygraphs, which are totally unreliable, to check the credibility of the
victims. If the victims failed this test, they were branded liars and the
cases closed. However, in over 75 percent of these cases of so-called
"liars," perpetrators turned up years later who confessed to the cases that
were closed, proving that the victims had told the truth in the beginning.
Unfortunately, this treatment of victims is common all over the United
States. The implementation of special sexual assault units by police departments is a recent innovation, the first of which was pioneered in the
early 1970s; there has not been much progress in those twenty years.

Rape Defined

The best way to define rape and sex crimes is to define what they are
not, then define the reality. This will then be followed by some myth
busting to set everything in its proper perspective. Rape is not an act of
passion gone out of control, as many people believe. It is an act of destruction and degradation that is a symptom of a complex psychological
disorder. It is also a malicious, violent crime that defines the essence of
violence as a disease.

Sexual relations are usually achieved between individuals either by
means of consent (negotiation), through pressure (exploitation) or by

force (intimidation). The first is the basis of all healthy relationships, and the latter two are the basis of all nonconsenting sexual encounters, i.e., sex crimes.

Rape and *sex crimes* are defined as nonconsenting sexual encounters involving unwilling individuals who are either forced or pressured into sexual activity by persons in positions of power or dominance. In exploitative encounters, the victim is harassed and pressured into having sex. If he or she refuses, that person's social or economic or job status is placed in jeopardy. In forced encounters, the victim is threatened with physical harm or is subjected to physical harm with the accompanying threat of death or more serious injury or there is the implication of physical harm to the victim or others. There may be no visible direct threat, but the victim perceives a genuine risk. A forced encounter can also involve assaults on victims who are incapable of consenting or resisting, as in the case of people who are unconscious or physically or mentally disabled.

Rape is always the act of a psychologically dysfunctional person, but the offenders are rarely insane. This is why rape and sex crimes are such complex issues. It is also the reason that the myths are so appealing. The psychosocial issues are so frustrating to comprehend that the myth is easily more satisfying than reality.

First of all, the worst myth that has to be busted is that rape and sex crimes are about sex. Rape and sex crimes are only about power and anger. The majority of clinical studies of sex offenders reveals that these crimes are motivated primarily by hostile, aggressive retaliatory (not related to rejection reaction) and compensatory needs and not sexual needs.

Myth number two concerns the stereotypes about the perpetrators. The popular misconception of offenders frequently regards them as either lusty males reacting to rejection, sexually frustrated men trying to satisfy pent-up needs or demented sex fiends with insatiable and perverted desires. Again, the majority of clinical studies show that sex offenders are often either impotent or sexually dysfunctional. This explains why in many cases of rape, there is no evidence of semen. This does not mean that forced intercourse did not take place. Also, intercourse does not have to be part of the rape. The victim can be subjected to sodomy or oral sex, and even in those cases, semen may not be present because the rapist was sexually dysfunctional.

Rapists are also viewed as oversexed or unable to engage in normal sexual relations. Since rape and sex crimes are an expression of power and violence, sex is not a motivational source. So, the simplification that offenders are oversexed is a fantasy. According to federal statistics, one-third of sex offenders are married or have girlfriends (relationships that still do not satisfy power needs) and are highly active sexually with their spouses or partners at the times of the crimes.

Many people think that sex offenders are either insane or just healthy, aggressive young men out to sow some wild oats. Typical sex offenders are profiled as individuals with serious psychological problems that impair their ability to engage in healthy, intimate relationships with other people, male or female. They are usually suffering from personality disorders that make them incapable of displaying any warmth, trust, compassion or empathy. Any relationships that sex offenders do have are usually seriously lacking in mutuality (caring about things in common, likes and dislikes), reciprocity (caring about each other) and any genuine sense of sharing.

As to myths about victims, the worst is the public attitude that rape victims "ask for it" or provoke the assault. It is also a popular misconception that the victims can prevent an assault if they really want to. When you take into account that sexual assault victims include both males and females and range in ages from infancy to the elderly, the idea that the victims are at fault is absolutely without merit. A four-year-old boy or girl is in no way seductive or provocative and neither is an eighty-five-year-old woman in a wheelchair, but these are samples of the 1993 rape victims in the Washington, Baltimore, New York areas, and it is doubtful that they invited their assaults. Sexual assaults have been committed by doctors and lawyers in their offices, with a variety of victims. At this time, there are over a dozen school teachers up on sex offense charges on the East Coast alone. Sex crimes have been committed in the victims' homes, public parks, cemeteries, shopping malls, public rest rooms, churches, alleys and on main streets, side streets and beaches. Sex crimes have occurred in all places, in all seasons and at any time of the day, and the victims have ranged from male police officers to female soldiers to elderly hospital patients to severely mentally and physically disabled children. Since sexual assaults are committed using intimidation with either weapons or threats of harm or injury or by use of brute force, it is doubtful that child and elderly victims can prevent being attacked.

The last myth concerns the belief that pornography and sexual explicitness are the causes of rape and sex crimes. Several studies sponsored

by the Justice Department, including FBI profiles, show that sex offenders are generally less exposed to pornography and erotic materials than
average males.

Forms of Rape

The crime of rape is categorized into three forms:
1. Anger Rape
2. Power Rape
3. Sadistic Rape

In all nonconsenting sexual encounters, the components of anger,
power and sexuality are always present. In these crimes, sexuality is nothing more than the primary tool with which the perpetrator is expressing
his or her anger and/or power needs. Sex crimes are, therefore, patterns
of sexual behavior that are primarily concerned with status, hostility,
control and dominance. Sensual pleasure and sexual satisfaction are generally nonissues and nonexistent in these encounters. The acts of sexual
predators are violent, destructive sexual behavior in the service of non-
sexual needs.

Anger Rape

Anger rape accounts for 40 percent of violent sex crimes. The assault is
characterized by physical brutality. It either comes as a "blitz" attack (a
sudden, extremely violent attack) or is preceded by a ruse of some sort
that distracts the victim. Once the victim is off guard, the attacker sav-
agely overpowers the victim. The offender is fully conscious of his anger
and rage and vents his fury both physically and verbally. The intent is
to debase and injure the victim, and the rape becomes the ultimate
expression of his contempt. Vicious, brute force is often the attacker's
only weapon used to overpower the victim, after which sex is the weapon
of degradation. Other acts of humiliation include sodomy, oral sex and
urination or ejaculation or defecation on the victim.

The attacker is generally impotent during the attack. In fact, the
anger rapist often regards sex as "dirty," and this makes it appealing as
a weapon that he can use to defile and humiliate his victim. The sex act
itself is often disgusting to this type of offender; satisfaction and relief
are only gained by the discharge of the attacker's anger, not by the sex
act. These attacks are short in duration. The attacker strikes, assaults
and flees, and there is rarely any premeditation involved. The common

theme that appears in these crimes is that these incidents are often motivated by revenge. The attacker often feels that he has been wronged, hurt, put down or treated unjustly by some individual (often a woman), situation or event (often involving a woman). In most cases, the victim is an innocent who had no association with the attacker, but the attacker makes the victim a symbol and transfers his hate for the actual subject of anger to the victim. Since these attacks require a catalyst, they are often sporadic and have no pattern to them.

Power Rape

In these crimes, sexuality becomes a tool by which the attacker compensates for feelings of inadequacy, and the assault serves as an expression of mastery, strength, control, authority, identity and capability. The intent is to capture and control the victim, and only enough force is used to achieve this aim. Verbal threats, intimidation with weapons and/or physical force are used to this purpose. The sex act is only evidence of conquest to the attacker, and the assault often involves the victim being kidnapped or held captive, followed by repeated assaults over an extended period of time. These attacks are usually the result of obsessional thoughts and masturbatory fantasies (unrelated to sexual impulse) about sexual conquest and rape. This type of attack constitutes a test of the attacker's superiority, and the attacker often feels excitement, anxiety, anticipated pleasure and fear. This is part of the thrill of the fantasy, but in reality, the attack usually disappoints the offender, never lives up to the fantasy, and the attacker goes on the hunt again, continually in search of "the right victim."

In these crimes, a pattern is prominent. The attacks are repetitive and compulsive. Several attacks may occur in a short period of time, making this offender a serial rapist. The attacks are either premeditated or opportunistic. The victim generally is the same age as the attacker, and the choice of victim is determined by availability, accessibility and vulnerability. After the attack, the offender may feel so in control of the victim that the rapist may tell his name to the victim, drive the victim to the police station or do some other defiant act. These offenders feel so secure about their crimes that they feel they can get away with anything, and unfortunately, they often do. This further increases their sense of power and control. The intent of these criminals is to assert their competency and validate their masculinity. The latter is motivated by fears of homosexuality or conflicts with identity. They regard all types of sexuality as threatening, and their pursuit of heterosexual encounters is often driven and compulsive and serves to counter fears of being homosexual. Power rape accounts for 55 percent of sexual assaults.

Sadistic Rape

With this crime, we can find all the factors of power rape and anger rape. Sadistic rapes account for 5 percent of sexual assaults. The offender transforms his anger and desire for power into eroticized aggression that is then vented upon the victim in the form of acts of sadism. The intent is to derive intense gratification from injuring the victim and to take pleasure in the victim's torment, anguish, distress, helplessness and suffering. Usually, the victims follow a pattern in age, appearance and occupation, and they often symbolize to the attacker something he wants to punish or destroy. The crimes are deliberate, calculated and preplanned, with the offender taking great precautions to hide his identity. The victim is stalked, abducted, abused and sometimes murdered. The attacker usually ties up and tortures the victim, often in a bizarre or ritualistic manner, as in the case of the nomadic killer, Christopher Wilder, who blazed a trail of serial murder-rape from coast to coast in 1984. The attacker may cut the victim's hair or arrange it in some style; he may wash the body or dress the victim to suit some fantasy; and he may force the victim to behave in a certain manner. The victim may be subjected to biting, burns and whipping. Injury to sexual areas of the victim's body, such as breasts, genitals and buttocks, are common, and in some cases, the victim may be object raped with a bottle, stick, knife or other objects as a substitute for the offender's own sex organs. These crimes often accompany sexual homicide, and the offender will often mutilate the victim prior to or after death and have sex with the corpse.

For this type of offender, excitement and sexual gratification are associated with and derived from the infliction of pain and the exercise of power over the victim. Control is all-important, and the offenders often derive further satisfaction from their ability to hide their dark side and to be like chameleons, as in the case of Ted Bundy. For these perpetrators, there is a thrill factor to being an "invisible hunter." The intent is abuse and torture, the means is sex and the motive is to punish and destroy.

Patterns of Sex Crimes

As with other types of crime, sex crimes can be broken down into categories—patterns that experts have discerned through years of observation.

Gang Rape

The majority of sex crimes are committed by loners. However, there is an increasing trend toward assaults involving multiple offenders. If the attack involves only two, it is called a *pair rape*. The term *gang rape* is reserved for crimes with three or more attackers.

In the majority of gang rapes, the crime is committed against a single victim, though there have been cases of two and three victims in a single incident. Offenders are generally white and range in age from 16 to 34, with the majority being 17 to 27. Victims are generally also white and within the same age range. Contrary to popular belief, rape is a predominately white crime, with the majority of victims being white. Blacks make up a small percentage of offenders and victims, and rarely are the crimes interracial. Gang rape has the same characteristics as single-attacker rape involving power as a motive, but in the cases of multiple attackers, the assailants derive peer support and mutual respect from their acts. The attackers usually target strangers, and a vehicle is generally used in the crime. These crimes are usually premeditated.

Male Rape

This is a subject that little notice is given to because the public prefers to give a blind eye to men who rape men. Instead, the concentration is put on crimes committed against women and children. However, male rape is equally as important as sexual assault against women and children. There is an unfortunate myth that all males are safe from sexual assault once they become adults and that the only way a man gets raped is if he goes to prison. This is regrettably untrue. A male is just as much at risk as a woman. Approximately 2 to 6 percent of all rape cases reported to rape crisis centers involve male victims, and the victim population is most probably much higher; however, there is a far worse stigma attached to male victims than to female. This stigma usually discourages men from reporting being assaulted.

The only times the public becomes aware of male victims is when they are murder victims, as in the cases of John Wayne Gacy, Jeffrey Dahmer and Dean Corll. Unfortunately, the public automatically assumes that the victims were homosexual, otherwise they would never have been associated with their killers. In fact, most male victims are heterosexual and are usually attacked after they have been abducted and rendered incapable of resisting. It is also assumed by the public that men who rape men are homosexuals or bisexuals. However, the average offender is married or has a girlfriend and is sexually active with such at the time of the crimes.

It is generally believed that a man is more powerful than a woman in defending his sexual zones from invasion. However, since attackers employ the same tactics against men as those used against women, the victim's ability or inability to fend off attack is irrelevant. Attackers usually employ either entrapment, intimidation and/or physical force to control their victims. In most cases, a combination of all three along with the use of weapons, drugs and alcohol are used to subdue the victim. In the known cases, one-third of victims were attacked while unconscious, another third were coerced with a gun into forced sex, while the other third were the targets of blitz attacks and were raped after being beaten senseless.

Patterns of Violence

In a recent study of all known cases of rape, the victims were assaulted in the following manners:

- 22 percent were sodomized
- 19 percent were subjected to anal sex and forced to perform oral sex on their attackers
- 17 percent were sodomized and masturbated by their attackers
- 14 percent were subjected to both anal and oral sex
- 11 percent were forced to perform oral sex on the perpetrators
- 17 percent were subjected to oral sex and then forced to fellate their attackers
- 15 percent were subjected to oral sex only by the perpetrators
- 14 percent were forced to masturbate their attackers
- 17 percent were forced to have sex with other male victims while the offenders watched
- 14 percent were fondled and object raped.

The one major difference between attacks on men and attacks on women, other than the types of sex acts, is that male victims are ten times more likely to be subjected to multiple sex acts than women, who are usually assaulted with a single vaginal penetration.

In 30 percent of known cases of male rape, the victim was hitchhiking. This is the same high-risk activity that women victims were often involved in. Another 30 percent were assaulted while swimming and hiking alone. Seven percent were attacked on the street, while another

7 percent were attacked in their homes. Four percent were attacked by their employers at their workplaces. John Wayne Gacy lured his male victims to his home with job offers. Offenders are generally between 12 and 41 years old, with the average age being 21. As with the rape of females, the offenders and victims are predominately white. Only 8 percent of offenders and 4 percent of victims were black. Eighteen percent of assaults were interracial. The majority of offenders were strangers to their victims, but many cases also involved friends who raped friends and older relatives who raped younger relatives.

Offenders usually commit these crimes for five reasons:
1. **Conquest and control**—the same power dynamic as in the rape of women
2. **Revenge and retaliation**
3. **Sadism and degradation**—coincides with the murder of the victim
4. **Conflict and counteraction**
5. **Status and affiliation**—usually associated with gang rape

Child Rape and Rape of the Elderly

Rape crosses all boundaries of age and sex. Because of their vulnerability and helplessness, children and old people, both male and female, are often the victims of rape.

Children are the subject of power rape usually when an adult victim is unavailable. However, the majority of victims are targeted for sadistic rape and murder, as in the cases of Wayne Williams and Dean Corll. In cases of anger rape, the sexual assault is usually used as an additional punishment of an already battered child.

Again, this is predominately a white crime, and the offenders range in age from 12 to 72, with the average age being 35. In cases of power and anger rape, the victims and offenders are either acquainted or related. In sadistic rape, the victims are strangers to their attackers.

The rape of the elderly is almost the same in nature to child rape. Because of the myths about rape, the public believes that the attacks are motivated by sexual arousal and desire on the part of the offender combined with the victim being at fault for doing something that stimulated his or her attacker. Thus, we have this stereotype of a victim that is young, attractive and dresses and acts in a sexually provocative manner. This stereotype goes up in flames when it comes to child cases or cases of elder rape. The reality of rape is that children and old people are not chosen for their sex appeal; they are chosen because of their helplessness.

Offenders are predominately young, white, single males. The age range is from 12 to 38. As for victim preference, the choice of prey is white women ages 50 to 85.

Of all forms of rape, sexual assault of the elderly tends to be the most violent. In the majority of cases, offenders intentionally inflicted life-threatening injuries, and in many other cases, murder was intended along with sexual assault. In over a third of all cases, offenders clearly intended to injure as well as rape their elderly targets. Only a small percentage of cases shows that the offender only intended to rape. In clinical studies of offender motives, the reason why assaults of elderly women are more violent than of other age groups appears to be that these older women represent authority figures to the offenders, such as teachers, principals or employers. The victims also symbolize people the offender has come to resent and want revenge upon, such as a parent, stepparent or foster parent. The elderly, like children, are the most vulnerable in our society. However, the fact that the elderly are more isolated and, in many cases, in poor health makes them more at risk than children. No one is eager to keep an eye out to protect these defenseless members of society, and as the offenders know, the elderly have been left totally helpless.

Marital Rape

Other than the movie *The Burning Bed* and the Bobbitt case, there has been little attention paid to the issue of marital rape. While many people are acquainted with the brutal statistics of domestic violence in the United States, very few know or realize that many women are raped, as well as beaten, almost on a daily basis. Many of these victims are subjected to rape and sadistic torture up to two or three or more times a day. In other cases, women are subjected to beatings and rape by their husbands and boyfriends and then forced to prostitute themselves or else suffer worse abuse.

Many cases have come to light in recent years of men who forced their wives to engage in sex with friends, family and any other male acquaintance the husband would want to share his wife with. The attitude of these men is that a wife or girlfriend is a "sex slave," who can be treated like livestock. These men feel they have the power of life and death over these women. It used to be that a husband had spousal immunity from prosecution for "forcing his attentions" on his wife, but increasingly, states are abandoning these laws. Now a wife has a right to say "no."

As to motive, offenders generally hold the following views:

1. **Sex is equated with power**—Offenders feel that they have a God-given right to sexual relations with their spouses and that if a wife refuses, the offender sees this as a loss of control. Thus, rape is used as a means of "keeping her in line."

2. **Sex is equated with love and affection**—These offenders regard sex as the only means of expressing closeness. So to them, when their wives refuse sex, they are saying they don't love their husbands anymore. In response to this rejection, the rape becomes a perverse way of saying "I love you."

3. **Sex is equated with virility**—To these offenders, sex with their wives is an affirmation of their manhood. To be denied sex is to be emasculated. To avoid such damage to their egos, rape becomes the solution to their insecurities.

4. **Sex is equated with debasement**—Punishment is the intent of these offenders, and they use rape as a weapon for teaching their wives or girlfriends a "lesson." The sexual assault may be concurrent with a beating. The wife overcooks dinner, she gets raped. She doesn't do the laundry right, she gets raped. And so on.

5. **Sex is equated with marital success**—These offenders see the rape as a way of making a success of their marriages. Sex is used as a panacea, a cure-all, for a failing marriage.

Women Who Rape

Contrary to popular belief, a woman is just as capable of committing sexual assault as a man. While it is not heard of often, it is not uncommon. Just like few men are willing to report being sexually assaulted by other men, they are just as reluctant to report being assaulted by women. With these offenders, the motive is power. Since the law does not specify the sex of an offender, any form of "forced sexual encounter" is regarded as rape, regardless of whether the attack was committed by a man or a woman. Since society upholds the myth that a man cannot be raped by a woman, a man is perceived to be a "willing" sex partner. However, the reality of rape is that since the sex act is a physical one, a man can be sexually stimulated against his will. When a woman forces a man to engage in sexual intercourse or oral sex at gunpoint, this is rape. Women also rape women, but like men raping men, it is generally not motivated by homosexual desires.

The most common sex crime women commit is the rape of children. In the majority of cases, the offender is the mother of the victim, but there have been many cases of male children being raped by teachers, baby-sitters and health care workers. The motives are the same as with male offenders, and the crimes are usually ones of opportunity and availability of the victims. As to victim preference, boys are commonly the targets of rape because they are less likely to report the incident than girls.

Chapter Twenty-Four

Child Molesters and Child Murderers

by Sean Mactire

from *Malicious Intent: A Writer's Guide to How Murders,*
Robbers, Rapists and Other Criminals Think

To the public and to most writers, the term *child molester*, like *serial killer*, invokes the worst kinds of stereotypes. Many believe that these offenders are dirty old men in grungy raincoats hanging around playgrounds with bags of candy, waiting to lure children. Others believe that the offender is the dark stranger who takes advantage of the vulnerability of children. And finally, there is the belief that child molesters are perverts who expose themselves or fondle children without engaging in vaginal or anal intercourse. Behind all these stereotypes is the myth that says all child molesters are nonviolent offenders, an unwarranted idea that these offenders never physically harm their victims.

Ritual is the one word that best describes crimes against children. And contrary to popular belief, these rituals are the worst forms of violence because of the lifelong emotional and psychological wounds that are inflicted. This factor voids the belief that these criminals are "nonviolent."

The Child Molester

Crimes against children, especially sex crimes, are absolute proof that violent crimes do not have to involve physical injury, and these crimes are the very essence of what defines "acts of *intentional trauma*." Therefore, the definition of *child molester*, in medical and legal terms, that is used by the Justice Department is "any individual, male or female, who inflicts intentional trauma and engages in illegal sexual activity with children and nonconsenting minors under eighteen years of age." This is the true portrait of a child molester, and like the serial killer, this criminal can be *anyone*.

The Pedophile

In very recent years, the 1980s in fact, the term *child molester* has become passé, and now the media has popularized the term *pedophile*, which used to be exclusively a psychiatric term. *Pedophile* has been defined as "anyone sexually attracted to prepubescent children," and the term *hebephile* has been applied to those who are attracted to pubescent children. *Hebephile* is rarely used because it does not constitute sexual perversion in the view of the psychiatric community. On the other hand, *pedophile* has developed a broad public usage, even to the point of becoming cop slang, as in the terms *pedo case* for a child molestation case and *pedo squad* for the investigative team that tracks down pedophiles.

The *Diagnostics and Statistics Manual of Mental Disorders* (DSM-III-R), which is the clinical bible of the American Psychiatric Association (APA), defines *pedophilia* in the following medical terms, not legal terms:

> 302.20 PEDOPHILIA—The essential feature of this disorder is recurrent, intense sexual urges and sexually arousing fantasies, of at least six months' duration, involving sexual activity with a *prepubescent* child. The person has acted on these urges, or is markedly distressed by them. The age of the child is generally 13 years or younger. The age of the person (patient-offender) is arbitrarily set at age 16 years or older and at least 5 years older than the child (victim).

Note that the key word here is *prepubescent*. However, despite this definition, many mental health and social work professionals apply this overused term to people who have a sexual preference for teenagers. The other important factor is that the definition stresses both the *act* and *fantasy* of engaging in sexual activity with children. This is a psychosexual disorder of the first degree. However, misuse and overuse of the term, along with misperceptions about this disorder, have led to problems in recognizing, investigating and convicting offenders.

It is the "nice guy" syndrome, which is the same cause of misconceptions about serial killers, that clouds the minds of both victims and bystanders. It is also that recurring "label" problem. People make assumptions that a person cannot be a child molester because he or she is "such a good neighbor, church deacon, den mother, good worker, etc." So, these "nice people" escape detection and conviction for their crimes because people do not realize that these offenders can be anything from a convicted felon to a minister, rabbi or priest to a doctor or lawyer or teacher. It must also be understood that child molesters can also have "normal" sexual relations with adults, and the molesters often engage in sexual relationships with adults in order to gain or continue access to their preferred victims: children. It is not uncommon for a child molester to marry or have a relationship with a person who has children so that there is a source of victims.

Two important questions to consider: (1) Are all child molesters pedophiles? (2) Are all pedophiles child molesters? The answer to both questions is *no*. While the terms are used synonymously by the public and the media, there are major differences between the two, even though many pedophiles are child molesters and many child molesters are pedophiles.

The Types of Offenders

The medical model divides sex offenders who target children into two broad categories: situational and preferential. The law enforcement model, however, goes several steps further in an expanded definition of types that fits the needs of obtaining identifications, arrests and convictions. This model was developed by the FBI Behavioral Science Unit.

Situational Child Molesters

These offenders do not have a real sexual preference for children. Their motives for engaging in sex with children are varied and complex, with the frequency of such activity ranging from chronic to a one-time act. The numbers of victims are generally small and the molesters may, at will, change from child victims to defenseless, vulnerable adults and back to children. It is not uncommon for this type of offender to work in a day-care center and then leave that job in order to sexually abuse elderly patients in a nursing home.

Regressed. This type of situational child molester usually has low self-esteem and poor coping skills. He or she targets children as a substitute for a preferred adult sex partner. A stressful or traumatic event can often be a catalyst of child molesting behavior. Victim preference is based on availability. Often this offender will molest his or her own children. This molester usually coerces children into engaging in sex and may or may not collect pornography. If the offender does have a porno collection, it is the homemade variety, composed of videos and still photos of offender and victims.

Morally Indiscriminate. This is a very aggressive offender who lives to abuse others. The sexual abuse of children is part of a general pattern that also includes lying, cheating, stealing, and abuse of friends, family, co-workers and spouse or partner. These offenders molest children because they feel they have a right to do so. Victim criteria involve vulnerability and opportunity. The offender has the urge, sees a child, says "Why not?" and attacks. Force, lures and manipulation are the usual means of obtaining victims, with strangers being the main targets, but it is not uncommon for the offender to be an incestuous mother or father. A pornography collection may include detective and S&M rags and some child porn of teenagers. Impulsiveness makes this person a high risk to any child of any age.

Sexually Indiscriminate. This offender likes to experiment with sex. He or she is willing to try or do anything when it comes to sex. Again, the motive is experimentation, and there may be no real sexual preference for children. The offenders just molest children whenever they are bored. They may experiment with their own children. Sexual encounters with adults will tend to lean toward the bizarre, and it is not uncommon for children to be included in these activities. This offender is generally found among the middle class and upper class of society and will also have multiple victims. Offenders will collect porno and erotica, but kiddie porn will comprise a small portion of this collection. Offenders' sexual history will include sadomasochism, spouse swapping, bondage and use of the occult for sexual purposes only. They are never active Satanists.

Inadequate. These offenders may be psychotic, schizophrenic (eccentric and out of touch with reality to a minor or major degree), mentally disabled, senile or a combination of these factors. They tend to be misfits and loners. This offender usually becomes sexually involved with children out of loneliness and insecurity or curiosity and can be considered at risk of committing murder. Children are chosen as victims because the offender finds them to be nonthreatening objects with which to explore sexual fantasies. Victims can be either strangers or known to the offender or related to the offender. Sexual encounters with children are generally the result of expressions of anger and hostility that have built up to the boiling point in the offender. Sometimes the victim is a substitute for a specific adult. Cruel sexual torture is not uncommon, and these molesters may often abuse the elderly—whoever is helpless and encountered first. This offender collects adult porn. Most of the sexually motivated child murderers are this type of offender.

Preferential Child Molesters

These offenders are sexually attracted to and prefer children and fit the clinical definition of pedophile. Their behavior is part of a highly predictable pattern called sexual ritual. These offenders feel compelled to attack children and will do so even at the risk of discovery. They not only have a hunger for children, but they desire many children, which leads them to molest large numbers of children. They usually have age and gender preferences for victims, with boys tending to be the common targets. Among this category are three subgroups of behavior.

Seduction. Here the pedophile actually courts the victims with attention, affection and gifts, just like an adult would seduce another adult. After a while, the victim becomes willing to trade sex for these benefits. Seductive activity involves multiple simultaneous victims and a sex ring, a group of offenders that shares victims. The offender's ability to identify with and relate to children enables him or her to build rings within schools, day-care centers, churches or neighborhood institutions, such as scout troops. The offender's status as an authority figure is also a factor in the seduction. Children who have already been abused or neglected by others are at high risk of being targets of these offenders' seductions. Seducers are rarely at a loss for a source of victims. Often the seduction creates such a binding relationship that the offender has difficulty "dumping" a victim who becomes too old. The victim often threatens to disclose the relationship if the offender tries to terminate it, and this places the offender at high risk of discovery. At this point, the offender will use threats and/or physical violence to keep the "secret." He or she will also use coercion to hold onto victims to prevent them from ending the relationships before the offender is ready to.

Introverted. This is the source of the dirty-old-man stereotype. However, this kind of offender can range in age from 16 to 80. Generally, these offenders are found among the young. They engage in minimal conversation with their victims, preferring instead to wait around places children frequent and to target strangers or very young children. Sometimes these offenders will just watch the children; other times they will engage in brief sexual encounters. They will also tend to expose themselves at playgrounds and school yards or make obscene phone calls to children. Sometimes they will frequent child prostitutes and will often marry in order to beget children that they can abuse as early as infancy. These offenders definitely prefer children and are also very predictable.

Sadistic. These offenders are the most likely to commit abduction and murder. They only prefer children as victims, and they only gain satisfaction from the infliction of psychological and/or physical pain. There have been cases of seduction molesters who became sadistic molesters, and it is not known if this pattern of behavior is something that already exists in the offender and surfaces for some reason in the offender's criminal career or if the sadism is a need that develops later as part of the abuse pattern.

Combination Offenders

It is not uncommon for pedophiles to have multiple psychosexual or personality disorders or to be suffering from psychosis. A pedophile's sexual interest in children might be combined with other sexual deviations. These may include any or all of the following:
1. Exposure (exhibitionism)
2. Obscene phone calls (scatophilia)
3. Exploitation of animals (zoophilia)
4. Urination (urophilia)
5. Defecation (coprophilia)
6. Binding (bondage)
7. Baby role playing (infantilism)
8. Infliction of pain (sadism, masochism)
9. Real or simulated death (necrophilia)

This list, however, is not complete. We would need a book on this subject alone to cover all the sexual deviations. Also, the combinations of behavior disorders are only limited by the imagination. Preferential molesters may want to experiment with other sexual deviations. Indiscriminate situational molesters may desire to involve children in their chronic experimentations. Child molesters can be psychopathic or paranoid or serial killers of adults. The most dangerous are the indiscriminate preferentials. Having no conscience, it is not beyond them to commit abduction, sadistic torture and murder of children for the fun of it. These offenders can fit into a very broad pattern of multiple behaviors.

Sex Rings

In summary, while a lot of attention has been focused on day-care centers, keep in mind that sex rings may be found anywhere groups of children are being cared for. Hospitals, pediatric nursing homes (hospices), schools, churches, juvenile shelters, community centers and recreation camps can be the hunting grounds of employees who manifest any combination of sexually deviant behaviors. Religious cults and large religious sects are the most prone to harbor and, in several cases, even promote child sexual abuse. There is no conclusive evidence of Satanic cults involved in such abuse, but there are many cases involving Christian groups. There have also been a few cases involving New Age sects. Always remember David Koresh and his child brides. This type of case is typical of the rule, not the exception.

Incest

Of all child sex offenses, this is the hardest to prove. Also, there is no typical pattern of behavior that is specific to incestuous parents. The classic pattern involves the preferential molester who marries a man or woman with children of a desired age and gender. It is also common for the offender to just live with the children's parent, pretending to be a caring boyfriend or girlfriend. There is also the type that befriends a single parent, offering to help as a "parental figure" and as a financial resource. With the increase in single-parent families, this type of M.O. is becoming more common. It is not uncommon to hear of "uncles," and sometimes "aunts," who have no family connection to the child victims, sexually abusing children. Also, offenders may marry in order to be able to adopt or become foster parents. The least common practice is for an offender to beget his or her own children, but it happens.

Often, child sex abuse is not the primary factor in incest cases. These involve incestuous parents who just morally indiscriminate. Since they are devoid of a conscience, they are cunning, manipulative predators. If caught, they turn on the charm and deny any wrongdoing, or, if the evidence guarantees a conviction, they will plead that "they are sick and need treatment." This plea for help is generally an attempt to escape being put in jail, where these offenders run a high risk of being made victims of sexual abuse by their fellow inmates. These morally indiscriminate offenders are suffering severe personality disorders that are more serious than pedophilia. They are dangerous and are considered to be difficult or impossible to treat. To buy into their sympathy ploy is to give them a future license to hurt people.

Female Offenders

Two social stereotypes make female sex offenders very hard to identify and convict. The first concerns the position of women as care givers in our society. In this context, women who are in charge of caring for children can handle children in almost any manner without suspicion. This is reflected in several recent cases of sex abuse in day-care centers. The offenders were all women. In many cases of physical abuse involving mothers or "sitters," sexual abuse may be concurrent. Murder is also very feasible. The second stereotype involves the sexual double standard regarding age and gender that is inherent in our society. If a man has sex with a teenage girl, he is a pervert. However, a sexual relationship between an older woman and a teenage boy is regarded as an achievement of manhood for the boy.

While a number of cases concerned female offenders motivated by sex, other cases indicated a motive involving more serious psychological problems. It is considered rare, if not impossible, to find a woman who displays the behavior seen in male preferential child molesters. However, for a long time, the idea of women as serial killers was dismissed as an impossibility. Such an idea went against all those sacred social myths about women. And like all myths, this one was flushed when several women fitting the profiles applied to male serial killers were identified, arrested and convicted. Contrary to popular belief, any criminal and destructive behavior that a man is capable of can be committed by a woman. Personality disorders are also not gender specific.

Teenage Offenders

This is also a growing phenomenon. Teenage offenders can fit into any category of molesting behavior, but the majority are found to be of the morally indiscriminate preferential type. This group is growing at a very disturbing rate.

Most teenage child molesters are or were victims of sex abuse themselves. When a younger child is molested by an older child, it is common for the case investigation to lead to other older offenders who have abused the older child.

The Pedophile Profile

While there may be more situational child molesters than preferential, the number of victims is higher with preferential offenders. The situational may only molest a handful of children in a lifetime. However, a preferential may account for hundreds or even thousands of victims in a lifetime. Preferentials are also the main type involved with sex rings, child prostitution and child pornography. While all child molestation cases are hard to prove, the preferential offender makes investigation easier by his or her predictable and repetitious behavior patterns. The characteristics of these patterns are identified below. (NOTE: These factors mean nothing by themselves. Even all together, they do not constitute proof. But, the presence of a combination of these factors constitutes the grounds for more intense investigation.)

Long-Term and Persistent Pattern of Behavior
- Victim of child sex abuse
- Limited social contact as teenagers
- Discharged from military for child molestation
- Moves frequently and unexpectedly
- History of prior arrests
    - Sex offenses involving children
    - Nonsexual types of offenses
    - Attempts to acquire child victims
    - Impersonating a police officer
    - Violating child labor laws
- Multiple victims
- Planned, repeated or high-risk attempts to acquire victims

Personal Traits
- Over age 25, single and never married
- Lives alone or with parents
- Limited social life
- Rarely or never dates

- Married but with "specific intent" or has "special relationship" with spouse
  - Married to person with minimal sexual needs
  - Married to strong, dominant type
  - Married to weak, passive type
  - Marries as cover or for convenience
  - Marries to gain access to children
- Excessive interest in children
- Has "special friends" who are either teenagers or young children
  - Socializes only with children
  - Hangs around places children frequent
- Few or no relationships with peers. May have close adult friends who are also pedophiles
- Has victim pattern that indicates age and gender preferences
- Refers to children as clean, impish, pure, innocent, etc.
- Refers to children as objects, projects or possessions

Well-Developed Techniques in Obtaining Victims
- Skilled at identifying vulnerable victims. Almost like a perverted sixth sense, the "hunting sense" of offenders can single out, from dozens of children, that one child who comes from a broken home or has been the victim of physical, sexual or emotional abuse or is suffering neglect. These offenders can be compared with vultures and other scavengers that can sense weakness or death in other creatures that are miles away.
- Identifies with children. Unable to relate to adults, these offenders have been described as "master seductors" because of their ability to *listen* to children. Others have been described as "pied pipers."
- Has access to children. This is one of the most important factors, but has been the source of dangerous stereotyping and paranoia. Not everyone who works with children is a pedophile. Unfortunately, many pedophiles use either employed or volunteer positions involving contact with children to provide access to victims.
  - Holds parties for neighborhood children
  - Takes them on field trips
  - Pedophiles can be teachers, baby-sitters, camp counselors, school bus drivers, physicians, dentists, photographers, clergy, social workers, police, scout leaders, Big Brothers, foster parents, sports coaches, business people who employ teenagers or minors

- Those who would never be suspected but should never be ruled out, for example, nurses, Girl Scout troop leaders, private tutors and music instructors
- Other types of traditional care givers and adult supervisors of children
- Will use any opportunity to "get the adults out of the way" in order to isolate the children for victimization
- Seduces with attention, affection and gifts. The offender literally seduces the victims by befriending them, talking to them, listening to them, paying attention to them, spending time with them and giving gifts. This is a courtship process, and since the offender becomes a "lover" to the victims, it is easy to comprehend why these victims are not likely to report strangers who molest them. A teenage prostitute who is beaten and raped by her pimp may not leave her tormentor because she fears the likely repercussions, but these victims generally express that their main motive for staying is because the victimizer is "the only person who loves me." These victims have been seduced, which is an area of understanding that has been vastly ignored.
- Skilled at manipulating children. This is an essential factor in the operation of a sex ring. To have simultaneous sexual encounters with numerous victims, the offender will use seduction, competition, peer pressure, psychology, motivation, threats and blackmail. Not all pedophiles have the ability to manipulate children.
- Has hobbies, interests and/or activities appealing to children or teenagers.
- Shows sexually explicit material to children. May also use phone sex services and computers to lower the inhibitions of child victims.
- Sexual fantasies focusing on children
  - Youth-oriented decorations in house or room
  - Excessive photographing of children
  - Collects child pornography and child erotica.

Pornography and the Pedophile

Not everyone who has pictures of nude children is a pedophile or child molester. There are many innocent reasons why an adult may have such materials. Not long ago a famous portrait artist of children was charged with violation of child pornography statutes because she took "reference photos" of her own children to use in her work that hangs in many public galleries. Until just a few years ago, such photographs were perfectly acceptable. However, society's paranoia has changed its definition of *pornography* and *obscenity*.

Pornography is derived from the Greek *porne*, referring to anything akin to prostitutes. Generally it is written or pictorial material that describes or portrays the acts of prostitutes or any sexual activities. This is a description based on definitions from several major dictionaries, but the specific reference to the acts of prostitutes expressly limits the definition of pornography to materials that depict vaginal, oral or anal sex between men and women or men and men or women and women. "Anything of a sexual nature" cannot be included in the definition because it would have to include lingerie ads. To the perverted mind of a sexual deviant, even these ads can cause sexual excitement. To any other person, these are just ordinary photos.

Thus, the collection of a pedophile can include almost anything that will represent his or her most cherished sexual fantasies. They save books, magazines, articles, newspapers, photographs, negatives, slides, movies, albums, drawings, audiotapes, videotapes, video equipment, personal letters, diaries, clothing, sexual aids, souvenirs, toys, games, lists, paintings, ledgers, photographic equipment, etc.

Videotape is the current vogue. Computers are also popular. Already, pedophile rings have been discovered using the latest computer technology to "collect" and distribute sexual fantasy material. CD-ROM and Photo-CDs will most probably be the next tech craze for pedophiles. This will make the task of trying to discover "collections" much more difficult, as the perpetrators will be able to "hide" their collections on CDs. There is no limit to the nightmare scenarios for law enforcement.

Research has defined four categories of collectors of child pornography:

1. **The closet collector**—This offender keeps the collection a secret and is not actively involved in molesting children.
2. **The isolated collector**—This offender is deeply afraid of discovery and, therefore, generally keeps his child molesting activity and collecting a secret between him- or herself and the victims.
3. **The cottage collector**—This offender has a need for peer validation, so he or she tends to share the collections with other pedophiles. This person is also an active child molester and shares in this activity as well. There is no profit incentive.
4. **The commercial collector**—This offender is in it for the money

and the kicks. These persons are active molesters, but they also recognize the profit potential in selling pornographic and erotic material to other collectors.

Child Pornography

The working definition of *pornography* that we discussed earlier applies only to material depiction sexual activity between adults. The definition of child pornography is similar but must cover a broader scope. Child pornography is defined as any visual (not written) material depicting sexual activity between adults and children and sexual activity between children and children. It also includes photos and videos of naked children, but these depictions are only pornographic if they are sexually explicit, such as close-ups of sex organs.

This is a gray area that involves both a behavioral definition and a legal definition. Therefore, the intended use of photos of naked children is a very important factor. If an artist uses photos of children for anatomical studies in painting, these photos are not pornographic. However, several states may consider such photos as pornography under their obscenity statutes. This is an area where the law can be blind because it makes gross assumptions that can ruin the lives of innocent people. So, it must be kept in mind that the key element of intent to be aware of is "harm." If there is no depiction of harm to the child portrayed or if there is no criminal intent involving harmful victimization, then the photos or videos are not pornographic.

There are two types of child pornography:

1. **Commercial**—This is your black market stuff that is produced and distributed overseas for commercial sale. Wherever there is a large, active sex industry, such as in Thailand and other parts of the Pacific and Southeast Asia, as well as Latin America, you will find a large child prostitution and child pornography industry. American customers are the chief consumers for these foreign markets, but the smuggling of such materials into this country is usually conducted by pedophiles. Because of the risk, there is not enough profit incentive for American organized crime to be involved. However, Asian crime syndicates that control this market are apt to recruit pedophiles to carry the goods in for them. Because of their sexual and personal interests, these offenders are more than willing to take the risks. Often, pedophiles will disguise their commercially produced material to look like the "homemade" variety,

to avoid harsher penalties if caught. However, a good forensics lab can tell the two apart.

2. **Homemade**—This is material that was not originally intended for sale and distribution. However, the quality can be better or equal to that of the commercial grade material. This is because the pedophile has a personal interest in the quality of the product. It is also one of the biggest black market operations in North America. You won't find these materials in the X-rated shops, but they have been found by police in the private homes and offices of doctors, lawyers, ministers, teachers and other "nice people" who are the pillars of society.

While the overseas sex trade does involve a high degree of child slavery, and such a child sex trade is growing in this country, most victims involved in these films and pictures are victims of seduction or sex rings that used coercion. These are generally prepubescent victims.

Despite the growing number of missing children, abduction is not the general means by which children are involved in the pornography trade. Runaway children and throwaway children who become prostitutes are often involved in kiddie porn. A lot of pornographic materials are made with the knowledge of the victim's parents or are made by the parents for their own use or for sale. Because of the seduction factor, you see a lot of these victims smiling in pornographic materials. There are also more boys than girls involved in pornography because of the market's gender preference.

Another factor involved in child pornography is the long-term impact on the victims. These are hidden crimes that involve the victimization of a child. Many victims try to ignore or repress the knowledge of the harm done to them. However, they often find that they cannot escape the past. The pictures and videotapes are permanent records that are used over and over again, further compounding the victimization. It is not unusual for child victims to commit crimes—including murder—as teenagers or adults in order to recover and destroy the evidence of their molestation.

Child Erotica

This is another gray area. Because child erotica or "pedophile paraphernalia" can be *anything* that serves a sexual purpose for an individual, as in a carrot being perceived as a phallic symbol, such items are not generally illegal. For the pedophile, child erotica can be anything from books on children or children's books to toys to games to pictures of children cut out of women's and family magazines. However, collections of any of the materials noted in the following categories are indicators of possible pedophile activity:

- Published materials relating to children—books, videotapes, magazines and articles on the following subjects:
  - Child development
  - Sex education
  - Child photography
  - Deviant behavior: child sex abuse, sexual disorders, pedophilia, man-boy love, incest, child prostitution and missing children
  - Police procedures and detective magazines
  - Nudism, erotic novels and "men's" magazines
  - Newsletters from pedophile support groups and advocates of the legalization of pedophilia, such as the North American Man-Boy Love Association (NAMBLA) and the Lewis Carroll Collectors Guild
- Unpublished materials relating to children
  - Personal letters
  - Diaries
  - Fantasy writings
  - Manuscripts
  - Phone-address books
  - Financial records indicating purchases of kiddie porn or other materials
- Pictures, photographs and videotapes relating to children
- Souvenirs, trophies and miscellaneous items
  - Photos, tapes, video and photo equipment
  - Clothing from victims
  - Jewelry and personal items from victims
  - Sexual aids
  - Notes and letters
  - Charts and records of activities with victims (scorecards, etc.)
  - Computers and equipment
  - Toys, games and dolls
  - Costumes
  - Alcohol and drugs

Motivation for, Use of and Characteristics of Collections

Nobody really knows why pedophiles start and maintain collections, but theories do exist. Collecting may help satisfy compulsive, persistent fantasies about children or may validate the pedophile's behavior, which may explain why a lot of offenders have many scientific and academic books on the subject. Collecting may also provide a means of obtaining peer reinforcement, or it may be related to the need to cherish memories of the offender's encounters with children. The children may grow up and become unattractive to the offender, but the victims' youth and attractiveness are maintained indefinitely by the photo or tapes.

Since we are unsure of the pedophile's motive for collecting, we are also unsure how a pedophile uses the collection. Perhaps it is used for sexual arousal and gratification, sometimes as a prelude to an encounter with children. It might also be used to lower the inhibitions of victims or to blackmail and coerce child victims into continuing the relationship or even to break off the relationship and maintain the secret. Collections could also be used as currency between pedophiles.

A pedophile collection usually has six major characteristics:

1. The collection is the most important thing in his or her life.
2. It is constant. The pedophile can be compared to a pack rat that feels he or she never has enough.
3. The collection is organized, with tidy, well-kept records.
4. The offender has a desire to keep the collection as a permanent fixture in his or her life. Some offenders have willed their collections to other pedophiles to preserve their collections.
5. The offender will always want his or her activities kept secret, so the collection will be concealed. Secret hiding places can be anywhere in the offender's home or work but generally where the offender can get access, including safe deposit boxes. Hiding places are only limited by the imagination.
6. In seeking validation for his or her behavior, the pedophile will share the collection with other pedophiles.

The Computer

There have been many cases of criminals abusing advances in technology to their own ends, but none is more prominent than the pedophile's use of computers. It is an offender's best friend and helps achieve all the characteristics that facilitate collecting. A computer can be used for validation, organization, maintenance of permanent records and so on. It can also be used to produce and distribute porn and to network with sex rings to find new victims. Whole collections, along with records of thousands of victims, can be stored on a few diskettes that can be concealed anywhere. The computer is a communication tool that helps pedophiles contact electronic bulletin boards. NAMBLA has a very large bulletin board that is over ten years old. Recently, in Maryland, a sex ring operated by county government employees was caught using state computer facilities to transmit and receive child pornography. The abuse of today's technology is only limited by the imagination and skill of the offender. Software advances are moving so fast, especially in multimedia, there are almost no limits to the possibilities or applications for criminal abuse. This includes computer-generated interactive kiddie porn. If you look in any computer magazine, you will see ads for adult computer porn. The future may get worse as computers become less expensive, more sophisticated and easier to operate and the offender's intelligence, skills, economic means or employment access increases. This means the risk factor will become significantly reduced, thus making this criminal market more attractive to organized crime. There may already be a computer network that is smuggling in child pornography by means of computer communications links.

Child Murderers

Child murder is nothing new. As we previously discussed, several of the most notorious serial killers of the early twentieth century were child killers. Albert Fish was the only exception; he was a pedophile who killed one child. Peter Kurten killed both children and women, and Fritz Haarmann killed teenage boys. More recently, there are the cases of John Wayne Gacy, most of whose victims were teenage boys, and Wayne Williams, the Atlanta Child Killer. In a recent study of serial killers, over 25 percent killed at least one child and 8 percent preferred child victims. One of the most famous team killer cases, Myra Hindley and Ian Brady, killed children for kicks. Why children and teenagers? They're easy prey, but there are other motives:

- Sexual gratification
- Enjoyment
- Monetary gain
- Personal reasons—"an urge to kill"
- Perverted acts—child molestation and necrophilia
- Revenge
- Mental illness

In 1983, there was an explosion of hysteria over the issue of missing children. Numbers reported ranged from 20,000 to 1.2 million children abducted each year. This prompted an army of nonprofit organizations (NPOs) to pop up out of the woodwork. By 1988, there were so many NPOs that they were actually competing with each other for funding and sometimes fighting over cases. All these groups caused so much panic and confusion that the public became vulnerable to con artists and crooks who use the pretense of looking for missing children as a license to steal. There were even ex-cops who tried to hustle a buck in this new "child safety racket." In 1984, the government set up a nonprofit organization to help with this problem, and in the past ten years, despite ups and downs, such as being burned by the numbers game, the National Center for Missing and Exploited Children remains as one of a handful of nonprofit agencies that is reliable and reputable. In 1989, the Justice Department finally did a complete study of the problem and vindicated the FBI, who claimed all along that the number of victims was much smaller than the NPOs were claiming. The bottom line turned out to be that in five years, only about twenty thousand children disappeared and that the annual rate was only one to two per one million population. This means that only about 150 children per year are victims of stranger abduction, with teenagers 14 to 17 years old being at higher risk. Besides miscalculations of victim populations, there has also been confusion over the definition of victim categories. Missing and murdered children can be categorized as follows:

1. **Runaways**—These are children who voluntarily leave home or choose to leave because they cannot tolerate their home environments, mostly because of sexual abuse. These children soon become involved with drugs, prostitution and pornography. Once believed to account for 95 percent of missing children, the fact is they account for less than 50 percent.

2. **Throwaways**—These are children who have been forced out of their homes or have been abandoned. The numbers are estimated to equal runaways, and their fate is the same. However, they are more likely to be found dead. This is a very large and often ignored victim group.

3. **Parental and relative abductions**—These children are abducted by a parent or a relative, such as an in-law or aunt or uncle. This group accounts for over 50 percent of missing and murdered children. These children are at high risk of being murdered and/or

sexually abused by their abductors. Sex abuse is usually the motive for the abduction.

4. **Children murdered by parents or relatives**—Again, these children are attacked by a parent or relative. This group includes children killed in the process of physical abuse or even as victims of murder-suicides involving entire families.

5. **Stranger abductions**—These include two subgroups: short-term abductions and uncompleted abductions. This crime only accounts for 3 percent of all abductions, but it accounts for 64 percent of all abduction-murders.

On the average, 2,500 to 3,000 children are killed each year, with about 15 percent killed by their own parents or relatives. This fact, along with the 1989 Justice Department report, completely dispels the myth that thousands of children are being abducted and murdered by strangers. It is also not true that stranger abductions are on the rise. Children are more at risk at home, with black children at highest risk. Last year, a woman in Maryland burned her home down and killed her six children to cover up the child abuse she was suspected of.

Murderer s Profile
While parents and relatives account for most child murders, only 8 percent of all serial killers kill children exclusively. In general, these offenders sexually assault their victims before or after death. Most of the offenders are male, but over 25 percent are female. Male killers target strangers and females target family. As expected, women use quiet means, such as poison, while men are more apt to use brutal violence. The motive for males is generally sexual gratification, while women are prone to kill children for financial gain or just enjoyment, as many have admitted. In several cases, female killers have insured their own children, children of relatives and children of neighbors and friends, then killed them to collect the insurance. However, there have been other cases of nurses who killed or attempted to kill numerous children as a means of career enhancement or as "acts of mercy," and in one case, the killer wanted to justify the need for a new pediatric care wing and killed over twenty-five children.

Child Lures
In the majority of cases, the victims are "just snatched" when they are left unattended for a few seconds or a few minutes. In cases involving

teenagers, the victims were often overwhelmed by sudden, violent attacks or abducted at either gun- or knife point. However, lures commonly used by child murderers are somewhat similar to the methods used by pedophiles. These methods include:

- Coercion
- Bribery
- Asking for help in finding a lost pet
- Pretending to be a police officer, which is why many offenders prefer to use blue sedans.
- Pretending to be a talent agent
- Pretending to be injured and needing help (this is often used on teenagers)
- Offering employment, as in the Gacy and Williams cases

In the case of Myra Hindley and Ian Brady, two of their victims were abducted from their homes. While it is rare for abductors to break into homes to take victims, children have been abducted from inside and outside their homes, and there is an increasing trend toward this activity.

The modern child molester-child murderer defies the classic stereotypes. Today, these offenders may look like young church deacons or yuppie stockbrokers or someone like Arthur Gary Bishop. Bishop was a "good Mormon"—the product of a righteous Mormon family—an avid churchgoer, an Eagle Scout, a Big Brother volunteer and a missionary worker, and he worked as an accountant. Over the course of four years, this nice guy committed several serial rapes of children and killed five boys. The ages of his victims ranged from four to thirteen years old. Using his unsuspicious, upstanding appearance, Bishop found it quite easy to abduct victims in broad daylight in public places. One victim was taken from his home, another from a grocery store while he was shopping with his grandfather.

Chapter Twenty-Five

Drug Enforcement

by John Boertlein

T he illegitimate drug trade in the United States is a multibillion dollar industry. From top to bottom, our country's drug enforcement effort is complex to say the least. In this chapter, we'll look at the United States Controlled Substance Act (CSA), the federal law that "schedules" substances according to their potential for abuse, potential for physical or psychological dependence and currently accepted legitimate medical use. Secondly, we'll consider facts about some of the more popular drugs of abuse in today's society. Then we'll survey the international drug market. Finally, we'll take a look at several undercover techniques used to deal with mid- and street-level drug enforcement.

The Controlled Substances Act

Although the Controlled Substances Act (CSA) regulates drugs on the federal level, most drug-related individual state laws also use it in determining penalties or offense status. The CSA is designed to place substances into categories (referred to as schedules) based on their potential for abuse and addiction and their accepted medical value. Schedules are rated I (highest potential for abuse) through V (least potential for abuse) as follows:

Schedule I
- A high potential for abuse
- Has no medical use in the United States
- A high potential for psychological or physical addiction
- Examples: heroin, LSD

Schedule II
- A high potential for abuse
- Has a current accepted medical value in the United States
- A high potential for psychological or physical addiction
- Examples: morphine, methadone, amphetamines

Schedule III
- Less abuse potential than Schedule I or II substances
- Has a current accepted medical value in the United States
- A potential for moderate to low physical dependence but high potential for psychological dependence
- Example: ketamine

Schedule IV
- Low potential for abuse
- Has a current accepted medical value in the United States
- Limited potential for physical or psychological dependence
- Example: valium

Schedule V
- Low potential for abuse
- Accepted for medical use in the United States
- Limited potential for physical or psychological abuse
- Example: codeine

In writing about drug enforcement, it's important to know the hazards of your subject and the consequences of those hazards (e.g., a pound of heroin causes a much bigger stir in everybody's circle than a pound of Tylenol 4 codeine tablets). Keeping this in mind, let's consider some popular contemporary drugs:

Cocaine

Cocaine's legitimate medical use is as a local anesthetic for surgeries of the eye, nose or throat. The drug's other, and more notorious, use is as a powerful stimulant. By the time cocaine makes its way to the street, it's usually in the form of a crystalline powder or an off-white chunky material. It's probably "cut" or "stepped on" to increase volume (and profits) with similar-looking substances such as inositol, mannitol or lactose (sugars) or local anesthetics like lidocaine.

Users get cocaine into their systems through three routes:
- Snorting—inhaling cocaine powder through the nostrils where it's ingested through nasal tissues and absorbed into the bloodstream.
- Injecting—using a hypodermic needle to shoot the drug into a vein, releasing it directly into the bloodstream.

- Smoking—inhaling cocaine vapor or smoke into the lungs, where it's absorbed into the bloodstream as quickly as when it's injected.

If your story takes place during a certain era, you should consider the "pre" and "post" crack era as a determining line. The general "tone" of street crime changed in the 1980s when crack hit the scene. Lots of people were using, and the effects were noticeable. Consider cocaine's effects from the point of view of someone on the frontline:

- The initial effect of euphoria, or "anything goes!"
- Increased alertness and intellectual functioning, or "I know *exactly* what I'm doing!"
- Greater confidence, or "Yeah, I know exactly what I'm doing and nobody better argue with me about it."
- Increased energy, or "But if you want to argue, let's go!"
- Social inhibitions reduced—need we say more about this one?
- Top it off with an overall feeling of power and confidence, and what do you have to deal with?

That's the top side. Naturally, there's a downside to deal with, too. After thirty minutes to an hour, when the high wears off, a whole new set of problems sets in. The user experiences:

- Anxiety
- Apathy
- Insomnia
- A general sense of negative feelings
- Craving for more cocaine
- Paranoia
- Maybe even hallucinations

Whether your character is a cocaine user or a person interacting with a coke head, you may be able to establish behaviors or responses considering these facts.

Back to crack. "Regular" cocaine is generally expensive and usually appears on the street as a fine white powder. Supply, demand and other "market" factors play into the price, but it's relatively expensive. Crack, on the other hand, is available in cheaper chunks that deliver the same quick high as injection or freebasing (another method of smoking cocaine). Crack is often prepared by the dealer, offering him the ability to determine its purity. Crack's effects are immediate and intense, but short-lived. Of course, the cycle of behavioral effects only moves faster.

There are several tests used by cops, and dealers, to quickly identify cocaine. Obviously, for official purposes like a criminal trial, tests are conducted in a lab by trained professionals. However, there are a couple of testing options to use on the streets:

- **Cobalt-potassium thiocyanate test**—widely used by law enforcement, who carry a solution containing these chemicals, water and hydrochloric acid in small vials into the field. To use, the tester puts a small amount of suspected cocaine into a vial with the liquid. Cocaine produces a blue flaky precipitate in the solution.
- **Water test**—a small amount of suspected cocaine is dropped into a clear glass of water. Cocaine will dissolve very quickly, while the "cut" dissolves much slower or not at all.
- **Clorox test**—a small amount of alleged cocaine is dropped into a clear glass of Clorox. If it's cocaine, the substance will drop to the bottom in a milky form with a "trail" visible in the liquid. If the substance turns red, it's procaine.
- **Heat test**—a small amount of suspected cocaine is placed on a piece of tinfoil. The foil is heated by holding a match under it. If it's cocaine, it will smoke excessively and burn clearly to a gold color. If it burns black, the black residue is probably adulterants, which can be scraped off. If cocaine is present, it should be fused to the foil.
- **Whiskey test**—a small amount of purported cocaine is dropped into a clear glass of liquor. Cocaine will settle at the bottom, while other substances should float to the top.

Flunitrazepam (Rohypnol®)

Flunitrazepam, which is marketed under the brand name Rohypnol and also known as "roofies," is not legitimately available in the United States. It is prescribed legally in fifty other countries where it's used as a preanesthetic and to treat insomnia. It has a potent sedative effect for which it has become widely known in its use as a date-rape drug. Roofies cause partial amnesia—individuals don't remember certain events they experienced while under its influence. If used in a sexual assault, the victim may not be able to clearly recall the assault, the assailant or related events. This a Schedule IV controlled substance despite its U.S. status.

Ketamine

Also known as "Special K" or "K," Ketamine's legitimate use is for general anesthesia for humans and veterinary animals. Ketamine produces effects similar to PCP with the visual effects of LSD. Users tout its trip as better than PCP or LSD because hallucinations last only an hour or less. Its appearance is similar to pharmaceutical-grade cocaine. Users snort it, put it in drinks or smoke it with marijuana. Ketamine is a Schedule III controlled substance.

MDMA (Ecstasy)

Ecstasy gained popularity in the late 1980s and early 1990s for its stimulating and hallucinatory effects at "raves," nightclubs and high-energy music events. MDMA is taken orally, usually in tablet or capsule form, and its effects last approximately four to six hours. Users claim the drug produces profoundly positive feelings, empathy for others, elimination of anxiety and extreme relaxation. It's also said to suppress the need to eat, drink or sleep, enabling users to party for two or three days nonstop. Ecstasy users also report aftereffects of anxiety, paranoia and depression. MDMA is a Schedule I controlled substance.

Methamphetamine

Also known as "meth," "speed," "ice" and "crystal," this is the fastest-growing drug of abuse in the United States today. Meth can be smoked, snorted, injected or taken by mouth, and its appearance varies depending on how it's used. Typically, it's a white, odorless, bitter-tasting powder that is easily dissolvable in water. Crystal meth, or "ice" because of its similar appearance, can be smoked much like crack. Users refer to smoking ice as a "cool" smoke, whereas crack is a "hot" smoke. The euphoric effect of smoking ice lasts longer than crack.

Meth users frequently behave violently because of the drug's physiological effects. Other indications of meth use include hyperactivity, euphoria, increased energy and tremors. High doses or chronic use are associated with nervousness, irritability and paranoia. Withdrawal from high doses and chronic abuse produces severe depression, and a psychosis similar to schizophrenia characterized by paranoia, picking at the skin, self-absorption and auditory and visual hallucinations. Chronic, high-dose meth use frequently leads to violent and erratic behavior. Meth use can lead to a dangerous cycle, the peak of which is called "tweaking." During this stage, meth users can go from three to fifteen days without sleep. Irritable and paranoid, the tweaker craves one thing—more meth—but no dosage re-creates the euphoric high. This often leads to frustration, unpredictability and the potential for violence. Methamphetamine is produced in clandestine labs, largely in the southwest United States and Mexico.

Methylphenidate (Ritalin®)

Manufactured under the brand name Ritalin, Methylphenidate is a Schedule II stimulant that produces effects similar to cocaine or amphetamines. In the United States, doctors prescribe Ritalin to treat attention deficit hyperactivity disorder. Abuse occurs when the drug is used for its stimulant and euphoric effects.

Phencyclidine (PCP)

PCP, also known as "angel dust," "supergrass," "embalming fluid" and "rocket fuel," originated as a possible anesthetic for human use. Bad side effects caused discontinuance of its use on humans. Veterinarians used the drug until 1978 when abuse became so widespread that the drug earned a Schedule II rating and legitimate manufacturing was discontinued. Today, PCP that is available on the illicit market is produced in clandestine labs.

The chemicals needed to manufacture PCP are easy and inexpensive to obtain. PCP in liquid form is typically sprayed onto leafy material, such as marijuana, and smoked. The drug's effects vary. A moderate amount of PCP may cause the user to feel detached, distant and estranged from their surroundings. Numbness, slurred speech and loss of coordination may be accompanied by a sense of strength and invulnerability. A blank stare, rapid and involuntary eye movements and an exaggerated gait are among the observable effects. Auditory hallucinations, image distortion, severe mood swings and amnesia may also occur. In some users, PCP may cause acute anxiety and a feeling of impending doom; in others, it causes paranoia and violent hostility; and in some, it produces a psychoses indistinguishable from schizophrenia.

In chapter thirteen, "Crime Tools Guide," I described an encounter I had with a knife attack. In court, the guy who did it claimed to have smoked a marijuana cigarette laced with PCP prior to the assault. Considering his behavior and apparent obliviousness to injury or pain, I believed him.

Inhalants

Glues, hair spray, air fresheners, lighter fluid, paint products and thousands of other common household products contain a chemically diverse group of psychoactive drugs composed of organic solvents and volatile substances. While not regulated by the Controlled Substance Act, inhalant intoxication or huffing can cause effects resembling those of alcohol inebriation: stimulation, loss of inhibition and, ultimately, depression. Users report distortion in perceptions of time and space, headache, nausea or vomiting, slurred speech, loss of motor coordination and wheezing. "Glue sniffer's rash" around a user's mouth and nose might erupt. The odor of paint or solvents on clothes, skin and breath are also a sign of huffing.

Huffing's rapid absorption of chemicals into the bloodstream resembles the intensity of effects produced by the intravenous injection of other psychoactive drugs. I've met an avowed huffer, a prostitute from a low-income inner-city neighborhood. She claimed she "couldn't get off" any other way than whiffing paint thinner and, consequently, she used it all the time. I don't know if impaired judgment played a part in her demise, but several years ago she was found murdered in a cheap downtown hotel room.

Heroin

In my younger days, I worked the streets in a police capacity and had the opportunity to see all kinds of drugs and what they did in real-life situations. During that time, I didn't encounter heroin. In the 1980s, when "T's & B's" or "Blue Heaven" were supposed to be a heroin substitute, a heroin user I had arrested told me, with sentimental tears of joy, "T's ain't nothing. Nothing, nothing, nothing beats a heroin buzz!" I don't know if the guy was alone in his appraisal, but the amount of heroin we see coming off the streets these days is alarming. Could it be a resurgence of a killer drug for the new Millennium? If heroin is part of your story, consider these facts:

- The United States government considers heroin "a serious threat due to its expanded availability, cheap price and increasing abuse, as well as the devastating social and health consequences of heroin addiction."
- During the last decade, the purity of street heroin ranged from 1 to 10 percent. More recently, the purity of heroin, especially from South America, has skyrocketed to rates as high as 98 percent, with the national purity average at 41 percent.

- The *1998 National Household Survey on Drug Abuse* estimated there were 81,000 new heroin users in 1997 and that nearly 100 percent of them were under the age of twenty-six. The study also found the number of past-month heroin users had increased from 68,000 in 1993 to 130,000 in 1998.

Pure heroin is a white powder with a bitter taste. It's seen on the street in powder form, varying in color from white to dark brown due to impurities in the manufacturing process. Another form of heroin, "black tar," varies in color from dark brown to black and can be sticky like roofing tar or hard like coal. Black tar heroin is produced in Mexico and is generally available in the western United States.

Heroin's effects on the consumer include euphoria, drowsiness, respiratory depression, constricted pupils and nausea. Effects of heroin overdose include slow and shallow breathing, clammy skin, convulsions, coma and possibly death. Heroin is highly addictive. It's a Schedule I controlled substance.

Lysergic Acid Diethylamide (LSD)

LSD is the most potent hallucinogen known to man. Initially popular in the 1960s, its use declined until it made a comeback in the 1990s. LSD is produced in crystalline form and then mixed with excipients, or diluted as a liquid and sold in tablet form (microdots), on sugar cubes, in thin squares of gelatin (window panes) and, most commonly, on pieces of blotter paper (blotter acid).

An LSD user may experience physical reactions such as dilated pupils, lowered body temperature, nausea, goose bumps, heavy perspiration, increased blood sugar and a rapid heart rate. During the first hour after taking LSD, users may experience visual changes with extreme mood changes, and impaired depth and time perception with distorted perception of the size and shape of objects, movements, color, sound, touch and the user's own body image. Effects of higher doses last for ten to twelve hours. After an LSD trip, users may suffer acute anxiety or depression. They may also experience "flashbacks," or recurrences of LSD's effects, days or even months after the dose.

The U.S. Department of Justice believes most LSD is manufactured in clandestine labs in northern California by less than a dozen chemists and then distributed through the San Francisco Bay area.

LSD is a Schedule I controlled substance.

Marijuana

Marijuana is a Schedule I controlled substance but, specifications about penalties for mere possession vary across the country. In Ohio, for example, possession of less than one hundred grams of marijuana is considered a "minor misdemeanor," meaning a relatively small fine is the maximum penalty. There is considerable debate about the medicinal potential for marijuana. These issues vary so much from venue to venue that it's impractical to address them here.

Street-Level Drug Enforcement

Drug trafficking is a rather unique crime in that it involves a transaction, usually between two individuals, with no immediate victim involved. True, it can turn into a crime of violence with a rip-off robbery or retaliatory homicide, for example, but the bottom line is that it's an illegitimate business deal between two parties, therefore making it "victimless." In your writing, you can add or exaggerate whatever you want into a drug deal—nothing is too bizarre. But keep in mind, law enforcement's ultimate goal is a solid case and conviction in court. There isn't a victim per se; rather, the officer represents society at large by enforcing its laws. To do this, the officer, in a manner of speaking, participates in the crime when she engages in undercover work (buying drugs or being involved in drug transactions). This implies a degree of deceit. My opinion is that the best undercover work requires (in this order):

- Ethics
- Strict adherence to the law
- An excellent line of bullshit

Let's explore some undercover techniques. In your writing, the potential for variations on these themes is endless.

Undercover Techniques

The Buy

Most drug cases are made from some sort of "buy" or business transaction of illegitimate substances. Buys can take place one of three ways:

Undercover officer buy. This occurs when a police officer is involved in the transaction. Officers often meet dealers through confidential informants (CI). CIs are generally of questionable character themselves and are motivated by money or a lighter sentence for misdeeds they've been caught at. An officer-buy situation stands up best in court because juries get direct evidence of the crime from a credible source whose only motivation is doing her job.

One glitch appearing in some officer-buy drug cases is entrapment, or the argument that the officer somehow influenced the dealer to do something she wouldn't have ordinarily done. The defense goes something like this: "I would never have sold cocaine to that man, but he told me, begged me, to try to find some for him because he needed it for eye surgery he was going to perform on his aging grandmother who was about to go blind but doesn't have medical insurance, and if I could help, she wouldn't be in as much pain, so as a humanitarian effort and because he begged me. . . ."

There are a couple of issues that may make a dealer's lawyer think twice about using the entrapment defense:

- The dealer has a prior record of drug sales.
- Drugs and money were exchanged at the first meeting.
- The dealer had a large supply of drugs—much more than grandma could use.

To be as clear as possible about entrapment, here are some examples published by the IACP in *Legal Points No. 38 & 39*. The following were ruled in court as being lawful:

- Giving an informant marked money to make a purchase.
- Having an informant introduce a police officer as a relative.
- Having an officer pose as "being sick" from narcotics withdrawal.
- Having an officer introduce self as an "international smuggler" representing others.
- Having an officer tell a physician a drug prescription is needed for a nonexistent friend.
- Having an officer converse in the "jargon of the trade."
- Using decoy letters to consummate the sale.
- Having an officer present a valid search warrant, then ask the dealer to save everyone time and trouble and voluntarily give up the drugs.
- Having an officer tell minor lies, such as what his occupation is or criminal connections are.
- Having an officer wear old clothes, have grease on his hands and nails or act intoxicated.
- Having an officer dress the part, use an alias, be introduced to

the dealer by one of his friends or misrepresent the purpose for seeking drugs.

On the other hand, courts have held the following as examples of entrapment:

- Involving a first offender in a scheme where the illegal act is only incidental to the plan. Example: The CI, a "low character individual," enticed a physician into a scheme to bet on race horses injected with heroin. The physician referred him to the defendant, a first offender of high reputation. On mentioning the doctor's name, the defendant was persuaded to buy the heroin from a dealer, induced by the chances of making large winnings.
- Playing on the sympathies of a first offender to alleviate pain or other suffering. Example: An addict who was placed under arrest and promised release for results persuaded a first offender to procure morphine for him, at no personal profit, to enable the addict to keep his job.
- Giving drugs to a first offender and inducing him into selling it, over his objections. Example: An undercover officer gave twenty-five marijuana cigarettes to a seventeen-year-old high school student and told him to sell them. The student tried to return them, but the officer refused. The student was subsequently arrested for possession. No prior possession was shown by the prosecution.
- Using a woman CI of questionable virtue, who suggests sexual favors as added inducement for the sale. Example: The police sent a young girl to see two men to purchase an illegal drug. She bought the drugs, with part of the price being an offer of sex. The dealers posed a successful entrapment defense, testifying that they were influenced to commit the crime based on the promise of the CI's sexual favors.
- Selling a suspect drugs through one operative then buying it through another to perfect a charge of sale. Or, manipulating the whole process and inserting the defendant into the dealer's role.

When a defendant pleads entrapment as a defense, courts can rule the direction of the judgment for the defendant if the events indicate it as a matter of law. In other cases, a jury will decide the issue at trial. Four things always tend to ruin the entrapment plea for dealers who find themselves in court:

- When the defendant, on his own, sets the price of the drug
- When the dealer immediately delivers the drug

- When the dealer has a record of a recent conviction for drug sales
- When more than one sale occurs

Second Party Buy. This occurs when an officer or surveillance team observes the drug deal. This can be tricky because probable cause needs to be established before an officer can take action. Let's consider a case I was involved in as a uniform police officer in a marked police car.

- On patrol in a neighborhood where many arrests had occurred for street drug dealing (prior occurrence), I noticed a car stopped in traffic with a young man who was standing by the driver's side and conversing with the driver (transaction taking place).
- The young man held about ten packets of aluminum foil in his hand (from experience, I knew dealers used this method to package marijuana). He was showing the packets to the car's driver. The driver selected one of the packets and passed the young man some U.S. currency (transaction completed).
- The car drove off and the young man looked in my direction, apparently finally noticing me. He backed up to a window well and surreptitiously threw the foil packets in.

Did I have probable cause to investigate and make an arrest? Yes. Experience in the neighborhood, familiarity with common packaging styles, observation of a money-for-item transaction and the young man's actions in trying to ditch the goods as I approached all added up to probable cause to investigate. When I found the ten packets contained marijuana, the number of items, coupled with the large sum of money on the guy, established a trafficking charge.

But every story has a different ending. The defendant gave the following account in court, which the magistrate, in the most charitable manner, found "plausible":

"The officer's right. I was involved in a dope deal. He got me. Only one thing—I wasn't selling the weed, I was buying it. See, I bought eleven bags from the guy in the car. Then the guy drove off and I checked the weed. One of 'em wasn't any good. I saw the guy drive around the block again and I stopped him and told him I wanted my money back. He gave me my money back and I gave him the bad batch. So I was *buying,* not dealing."

Plausible? What was it P.T. Barnum said?

Third Party Buy. This occurs when officers send an informant or someone else in to make the buy. This is the least desirable method of making a case for several reasons: First, chances are the informant is a criminal as well, which automatically brings the credibility issue into question. Second, any decent defense attorney will want to know your informant's motive for making the buy. It's probably for money or another consideration, such as a lighter jail sentence in his own case. This presents the argument that the informant has "every reason to lie."

Still, because dealers are a suspicious lot, sometimes the informant or third party buy is the investigator's only option. If that's the case, it has to be a strictly *controlled* buy, with the entire process monitored and documented. Consider the following process if you choose to use a third party buy scenario in your work:

- The informant needs to understand, and acknowledge the understanding, of exactly what she is expected to do. She can't do any more or less than she's told.
- A good investigator will make some independent effort to authenticate the informant's information.
- Make no promises to the informant. Her participation has to be voluntary and free of any implied coercion.
- If possible, you should have the informant telephone the dealer while monitoring the call.
- The investigator should try to set up the deal in a location where it can be monitored by officers as much as possible (e.g., outdoors, in the daytime, etc.).
- Debrief any involved personnel.
- Strip search the informant so you can testify as to everything she took into the buy.
- Give the informant money in marked bills.
- Tell the informant again *exactly* what she is to do.
- Make sure surveillance officers know what the informant looks like and how she is dressed.
- Try to set surveillance to begin at least one hour before the buy to see who or what comes and goes from the location.
- After the buy, get the informant and the evidence out as quickly as possible.
- Strip search the informant again so you can testify to everything the informant left the scene with.
- Get a detailed written statement from the informant about the trans-

action. This can be used in court to refresh the informant's memory, especially if her memory has "suddenly failed."
- Return the informant's personal belongings and get a receipt.
- Try to get a taped phone call of the informant to the dealer. The informant can complain about or praise the quality of the purchase. Don't leave any doubt about the identity of the purchased substance.
- Be sure you can find the informant again when needed.

Modern technology brings lab-accurate results right to the street drug trade. This compact digital scale offers accurate readings on weight for dealers and buyers alike.

Types of Buys

Once you've decided who the buyer will be, there are two ways to conclude the transaction: the "buy/bust" and the "walkaway."
- A buy/bust occurs when the dealer gets arrested immediately after the sale. The benefit to this method is immediate recovery of the buy money. Or, if preferred, one could make several small buys and finally arrange for a larger one without having to risk the big buy money.

- The walkaway occurs when an officer makes a buy, or any number of buys depending on the case, and walks away to document enough details and evidence to eventually sign warrants or seek indictments.

Your creative ability is your biggest asset in devising drug deal or drug enforcement scenarios. A character's acting ability, coupled with their ability to deal with big money, violence and corruption, may be the true measure of his success in the world of illicit drugs.

PART VI

BIG BROTHER

Chapter Twenty-Six

Surveillance: Part I

by John Boertlein

There are a lot of things for writers to consider when using surveillance issues in their work. Most information-gathering procedures are tightly regulated by legislation, and we'll discuss some of those rules. And, considering the surreptitious nature of information or evidence-gathering processes, we'll examine a couple of law enforcement techniques. Finally, we'll look at some of the hardware used to keep an eye on one's "target."

Legal Issues

Federal and individual state laws restrict the use of information, or its collection, by surreptitious means. Obviously, federal laws apply nationwide. For our purposes, we'll consider the state of Ohio's laws concerning surveillance. Comparatively, Ohio is fairly strict, so if your story involves a specific locale, you may want to consider that venue's restrictions. The following statutes cover surveillance issues:

- 42 USC (United States Code) Section 2000aa—The Privacy Protection Act
  - No items, that are intended for publication, may be seized by law enforcement without a warrant.

If your suspect character's business is publishing, your law enforcement character needs to get a search warrant prior to looking at any written material, listening to dictation to be transcribed and so on. More simply, if I am writing the latest version of *The Great American Novel*, I *am* a publisher and the cops can't look at my stuff (on my computer, tape recorder, whatever) or use it against me without a warrant.

- 18 USC Sections 2510 and 2701—The Electronic Communications Privacy Act (ECPA)

- Law enforcement may not intercept the transmission of communications by means of any device without a warrant. (2510 paraphrased)
- Law enforcement may not seize the contents of electronic communications held in electronic storage without a warrant. (2701 paraphrased)

These sections require your law enforcement character to obtain a warrant prior to using a wiretap or looking into e-mails or any other information storage device.

(*Note:* The following examples apply only in the state of Ohio, although comparable legislation exists in every state.)

- Ohio Revised Code (ORC) 2933.52
  - No *person* (not only law enforcement) shall intercept, attempt to intercept or procure any other person to intercept or attempt to intercept any wire communication, oral communication or electronic communication.
  - No person shall use, attempt to use or procure any other person to use any communication interception device which is affixed to or otherwise transmits a signal through a wire, cable, satellite, microwave or other similar method of connection used in wire communications or transmits communications by radio, or interferes with communication by radio, to intercept any wire, oral or electronic communication.
  - No person shall use or attempt to use the contents of any wire, oral or electronic communication knowing or having reason to know the contents were obtained through the interception of wire, oral or electronic communication in violation of this section.
- ORC 2933.59 (C)—Presenting Altered Record of Intercepted Communication
  - No person shall edit, alter or tamper with any recording or resume of any intercepted wire or oral communication with the intention of presenting the altered recording or resume in any judicial proceeding or under oath or affirmation, without fully indicating the nature of the changes made.

Now that we know the rules, let's consider the investigative value of surveillance and look at a couple of techniques. When an investigator uses surveillance, here are some of the things she hopes to accomplish:

- Establish evidence of a crime in a legal manner that is of use in court
- Corroborate testimony and protect undercover officers
- Locate people by watching their associates or places they frequent
- Confirm an informant's reliability
- Locate hidden property or contraband
- Obtain information establishing probable cause and possibly leading to a search warrant
- Apprehend wanted subjects or prevent the commission of a crime
- Obtain information for later use in interrogation
- Develop leads

The following guidelines will help you write convincingly about your character's preparation for and effectiveness in surveillance work:

- When I was assigned an undercover job years ago, a narcotics investigation veteran gave me some good advice: "You're a white guy from the west side," he told me. "If you try to be anything else, they'll make you every time." Successful surveillance means going unnoticed or fitting in. What is considered to be an "ordinary appearance" changes from location to location and neighborhood to neighborhood. The point is not to try to be something you can't. Being aware of this can make or break your character's surveillance.
- Along the same lines, an investigator should strive to be as ordinary as possible. This means no orange hair, crazy clothes or anything else that sets him apart. The same goes for the investigator's car— no loud mufflers, mag wheels or "striped tomatoes" like Starsky and Hutch had.
- Your character needs to be patient. Most of the time, surveillance is incredibly boring. Sometimes it even ranges from uncomfortable to painful. I spent one Christmas season sitting in the back of a parked van waiting for a purse snatcher to strike. Another officer drove the van in and then left. There I sat with no bathroom facilities, heat or relief.
- Investigators should do everything possible to familiarize themselves with their target's appearance, dress, car, residence, neighborhood— *anything* they can find out about.
- Any surveillance is only as good as the records you keep. Detailed,

factual reports are crucial in making a case. A good investigator can't record or document enough!

- Your character may have "confidential informants" or CIs. The motivation, reliability and accuracy of CIs will be put to the test when it's time to get a search warrant or use their information in court. Cases can be made or lost by CIs. In your writing, a CI provides all kinds of character possibilities.

Your character is now ready to "do a surveillance." There are four methods he might use:

- Moving surveillance on foot
- Moving surveillance with a vehicle
- Fixed surveillance
- Electronic surveillance

Moving Surveillance on Foot

Foot surveillance is only effective over relatively short distances or to stay with a target after they've exited a vehicle. When I attended "undercover investigator" school, our instructors had us practice foot surveillance at a mall. It was difficult then, and never got easier. The following are foot surveillance methods:

- One-Man Surveillance. A lone officer attempts to follow the target. This is difficult to accomplish because the target must be kept in sight at all times. The surveyor must stay close enough to detect the target entering a building, turning a corner or making any other sudden moves. Uncontrollable factors like pedestrian traffic and the physical characteristics of the area challenge the effectiveness of one-man surveillance.
- Two-Man Surveillance. This affords greater security against detection and reduces the risk of losing the suspect. On a crowded street, both officers remain on the same side of the street that the target is on, with one officer in close proximity to the target and the other officer some distance behind. On a less crowded street, one officer walks on the opposite side of the street abreast with the target while the other follows some distance behind. Officers should alternate places to avoid detection.
- Surveillance Using Three or More Officers. This obviously presents opportunities for any combination of schemes to follow a target on foot without detection. Officers can "leap frog," play "pass and catch

up" or devise and customize their own plans to maintain surveillance of a target undetected.

It's impossible to predict every problem the surveyor might encounter during foot surveillance. The following tips come directly from an investigator's manual published by the U.S. Department of Justice and the IACP. There's nothing classified here. To put you in a "howdunit" frame of mind, try to write your own plans or solutions to these particular problems:

- When a suspect enters a building . . . at least one officer should follow the suspect inside, unless the building is a private home or small shop, or if entry would expose the officer. In the case of large public buildings with many exits, all officers should follow the suspect into the building. It is prudent for one officer to remain in the lobby or at a door to spot the suspect if he leaves the building.

- Situations where a suspect enters an elevator also present unique problems. If a suspect is the lone passenger and has reason to suspect surveillance, it may not be advisable to accompany him into the elevator. The surveillance officer should watch the indicator for the floor stop, and then proceed to that level to pick up the suspect's route. If the officer chooses to get on the elevator with the suspect, he should wait until the suspect departs, then go to the next higher floor before leaving the elevator. When two officers accompany the suspect into an elevator, they should wait for him to choose his floor, and then pick the next higher and lower floors for their own exit. Whatever method of surveillance is selected inside the building, one officer should remain in the lobby since the suspect may be using the elevator merely to elude the surveillance.

- In instances where a suspect enters a restaurant, at least one officer should enter behind the suspect and note any contacts made inside. If possible, the officer should pay his check before the suspect so that he can be prepared to leave with him. In some cases, it is desirable for the officer to leave shortly before the suspect and wait for him outside.

- In situations where a suspect hires a taxi, the officer should make a note of the time, the place, the name of the cab company and the license or cab number. The cab's destination can be obtained from the driver through the company office by using the cab's radio. When a suspect purchases a ticket on a train, boat, plane or long-distance bus, the decision to follow the suspect depends on the length of the trip, the circumstances regarding the surveillance and the officer's instructions from his superior. The suspect's destination can be determined by questioning the ticket agent. Examination of the exterior of the suspect's luggage should not be overlooked for indications of the suspect's destination.

- Suspects who enter a theater, racetrack or amusement park should be followed by all officers on the surveillance team. The regular admission charge should be paid. It is important that close surveillance be maintained in a crowd. In darkened theaters, the suspect must be closely watched. If possible, one officer should sit directly behind the suspect to observe if contact is made with another person. Exits must be covered to prevent the suspect from leaving undetected.
- Should the suspect register in a hotel, the room number and length of anticipated stay may be obtained from the manager or desk clerk.
- A clever suspect, discovering that he is under surveillance, may not reveal this knowledge, but may attempt to lose his followers by means of false contacts or decoys. For example, he may leave a package full of worthless papers or materials with a contact, thereby causing unwary officers to redirect or discontinue their surveillance, leaving him free to make his real contacts unobserved. Similarly, the suspect may attempt to lure an officer into a trap. A thorough knowledge of the locality, tempered with good judgment and alertness to realize when trailing becomes too easy, is a good defense against such traps.

If a suspect resorts to trickery, it is good policy to change surveillance officers. Some common methods that a suspect may use to detect a foot surveillance are:

- Stopping to tie a shoestring, meanwhile looking for followers
- Stopping abruptly and looking at people to the rear, or reversing course and retracing his steps
- Stopping abruptly after turning a corner, or alternately walking slowly or rapidly
- Arranging with a friend in a shop or other place to watch for surveillants behind him
- Riding short distances on buses and taxis, or circling the block in a taxi

- Entering a building and leaving immediately via another exit
- In hotel lobbies and restaurants, watching in wall mirrors to see who is coming and going
- Starting to leave a place quickly, then suddenly turning around to see if anyone also suddenly rises
- Opening and closing his hotel door to indicate that he has left his room, and then waiting inside his room with the door slightly ajar to see if anyone leaves an adjacent room

Moving Surveillance With a Vehicle

Conducting a surveillance from moving vehicles is very similar to foot surveillance only with the difficulties presented from being in a car. There should be at least three vehicles involved with one containing two people so that the passenger can follow on foot if needed.

With enough time and preplanning, officers can consider using parallel routes, "mixing it up" by changing tail cars from time to time or "leap frogging." But, for every one plan, there are a thousand ways to mess it up.

Again, from the Department of Justice's manual:

"As in the case of foot surveillance, a suspect who believes he may be followed can resort to various techniques to detect a surveillance automobile. Some of the most common techniques are:
- Alternating fast and slow driving or frequent parking
- Stopping suddenly around curves or corners or speeding up a hill, then coasting slowly downhill
- Driving into dead-end streets or pulling into driveways

"Once a suspect has confirmed his suspicion, he can use a variety of techniques to elude automobile surveillance. Some examples are:
- Committing flagrant traffic violations, such as making U-turns, driving against traffic on one-way streets and running through red lights
- Using double entrances to driveways—in one entrance and out the other
- Cutting through parking lots
- Driving through congested areas
- Deserting the vehicle beyond a blind curve or corner"

To apply what you've just learned, we'll examine "Operation Impala," an illegal gambling investigation based on an actual case. Visual surveillance, evidence collected from search warrants and numerous court-ordered wiretaps led to convictions in this case. You can use Impala in your writing as a model of successful surveillance. Although the documents you'll see are genuine, the names, dates and addresses have been changed. The following is an actual investigative report filed by Impala surveillance officers. As you're reading, imagine how you might expand on the text to write a story containing elements of surveillance.

INVESTIGATIVE REPORT
CASE TITLE: IMPALA
CASE NUMBER: EX-123
DATE: January 1, 1995
ACTIVITY: Surveillance at 123 Anywhere Street,
Cincinnati, Ohio 45238
DETAILS:

1. On January 1, 1995, Detective N. One, Sergeant N. Two and Detective N. Three set up surveillance on the residence of Jack SUSPECT at 123 Anywhere Street in the southside area of Cincinnati, Ohio. The surveillance began at 6:00 A.M.

2. At approximately 9:20 A.M., SUSPECT left his residence in his red Ford, two door, bearing Ohio license XXX555 and drove up East State Road to the entrance of the Self Serve storage lot at 1122 Anywhere Street, Cincinnati, Ohio, telephone number (555) 555-5555. He arrived at the location at approximately 9:28 A.M. and went to a storage area in the complex.

3. SUSPECT then pulled back out of the storage area at 9:33 A.M. using the Anywhere Street exit and pulled directly across Anywhere Street to the Rolling Hills Shopping Center lot where he parked and entered the URSick Pharmacy at 5222 Anywhere Street, telephone number (555) 555-5551. He remained in the store from 9:35 A.M. to 9:47 A.M.

4. During the time SUSPECT was in the pharmacy, Detective N. Four and Detective N. Five were notified of the movement. Detective N. Four responded to the area and Detective N. Five remained in the downtown area.

5. At 9:47 A.M., SUSPECT left the URSick Pharmacy parking lot and drove to eastbound 1099 to southbound I-75. The moving

surveillance followed him to the Second Street exit of southbound I-75, where he drove to a parking spot at Second and Pike Street, Cincinnati, Ohio.

6. SUSPECT then walked down Pike Street, where he was observed speaking to a male white subject in front of the SoLow Art store at 777 Pike Street, telephone number (555) 555-5552. He then proceeded on foot on Pike Street where Sergeant N. Two took up a foot surveillance at 10:10 A.M.

7. At this time, Detective N. Three radioed that he saw a male white subject, known to him as a gambler, on Pike Street in an older blue Buick with Indiana license plates.

8. The officer was able to locate the Buick and followed it to 122nd Avenue in Cincinnati, Ohio. The vehicle bore Indiana license 111YYY and is registered to B. Target of 111 Nowhere Street, Sunman, Indiana.

9. Upon obtaining the license plate of Target, Detective N. One was advised to return to the area to resume the surveillance on SUSPECT.

Get the idea? Document, document, document. Details, details, details.

Fixed Surveillance

Fixed surveillance, or the ever-popular "stakeout," is one of the easiest information-gathering techniques. It's also one of the easiest to blow. I remember setting up a surveillance of drug dealers at a small grocery store in an urban neighborhood. My partner and I managed to get an apartment across the street from the target. The building was under renovation, but there was heat, plumbing, electricity—all of the amenities that make for a successful surveillance involving sitting for hours while watching through binoculars and recording descriptions, license plates and activities of everyone who comes or goes.

The place had a back entrance and we had a key, so we came and went undetected. We had no problems and everything was great until one of the construction workers barged in about five hours into the job, apparently intending to use *our* facility. He must've told anybody who would listen about the two guys on the third floor who were looking out the window with binoculars and a camera. They had guns too! Afterward, you might've thought we had a big screen TV showing the Super-bowl out of our window for all the people who were watching it.

Where did we go wrong? Did we do anything right? Let's take a look:

- We were investigating a drug trafficking complaint in an African-American neighborhood. Being two thirty-something white guys, we knew we wouldn't blend in, so we did a reconnaissance of the area. Good job!

- During the recon, we noticed a building being rehabed right across the street from our intended target. What a break! Good observation.

- We checked the building, noting there was a rear entrance off an alley that we could reach from an adjacent street. We could come and go, and no one would be the wiser. Perfect spot.

- The building owner was more than happy to help. It turned out he was one of the people who had made a complaint. He gave us a key and we were in.

- Day one, fifth hour—We have our binoculars, a camera, a police radio and we're doing well. Our log is filling up with useful information. We also have a bathroom, heat, even tunes from a portable stereo. The vantage point is great. I brought my lunch and came in the back door. All is well.

- Day one, fifth hour-plus—A construction foreman answers nature's call by coming to use *our* facility. He looks surprised to find us inside the apartment. He looks scared as he stares at the guns in our shoulder holsters and makes a quick exit. Minutes later, other workers cross the street to the general target area, pointing and staring at our window. So we pack up and call it a day. The next time, we'll get the owner to restrict access or find a way to lock the door from the inside. You can't plan too much for a successful surveillance!

Electronic Surveillance

We began this chapter with some of the legislation restricting electronic surveillance. We'll conclude with some legislation as well because the government takes this issue very seriously. An illegal wiretap will not only blow a case for your character, it could even put him in the penitentiary. Even sterling intentions to get the bad guy at all costs won't save somebody on this one. *You've got to have a court order to do electronic surveillance.* To get one, you'll need:

- The identity of the individual whose communications are to be intercepted

- The nature and location of the communications facilities where authority to intercept is granted
- A particular description of the type of communications to be intercepted and a statement of the particular offense to which it relates
- The identity of the agency authorized to intercept the communications, and the person authorizing the application
- The period of time during which interception is authorized, including a statement as to whether or not the interception shall automatically terminate when the described communication has been obtained

As I mentioned before, state laws vary in electronic surveillance restrictions. Some, for example, permit "consensual eavesdropping" where one of the parties grants permission to listen in while the other party may be unaware of the eavesdropping; other jurisdictions prohibit it without a court order. Your best bet is to check the rules for the particular venue where your story takes place.

Hardware

The communications source, usually the phone company or carrier, is generally served with a court order for "trap and trace." They can identify the lines that are used and capture conversations or provide access to do so. But there are also gadgets available to do similar jobs. For example, the wristwatch video camera is a tiny camera hidden inside a wristwatch housing. It's battery operated and can be plugged into any video cam or a wireless transmitter. The hidden clock-radio transmitter looks like a normal clock radio, but there's a pinhole camera hidden in the lens and a microphone attached. The transmitter will broadcast anything in the room up to five-hundred feet. Even amateurs can purchase calculator transmitters (look like calculators but transmit audio), pager transmitters, neckties with hidden cameras and other hardware to suit legitimate, or not-so legitimate, surveillance needs.

Chapter Twenty-Seven

Surveillance: Part II

by Greg Fallis

from *Just the Facts, Ma'am: A Writer's Guide to Investigators and Investigation Techniques*

T his is one of the tasks most often associated with private detectives. The trench-coated private eye leaning against the lamppost and burning a butt is a stock image in American popular culture. Of course, it's a dreadful way to conduct a covert surveillance, but the image is more about style than substance.

When we speak of surveillance, we're generally talking about stationary surveillance. Mobile surveillance is commonly called tailing. It's a small distinction, but one worth noting. Small distinctions are important to writers and detectives alike.

Surveillance refers to the act of watching, preferably without being observed. While there are certain circumstances when a police detective or a private investigator will conduct an overt surveillance, most surveillance is done covertly.

Surveillance is a quiet craft, although you wouldn't know it from the way it's portrayed in the entertainment media. In the movies surveillance is often shown as a sort of pajama party. Somebody is always slipping out to get food. There is some giggling, some deep and meaningful personal discussion, the occasional spat. There are almost always two characters involved and always in the same room or car—there isn't much cinematic tension in a person sitting quietly and alone.

Unfortunately, many writers seem to take their cues on surveillance from the movies. Folks, it just ain't that way. At least not if it's done properly. In this chapter we'll take a look at how to do it properly. We'll also discuss some of the common errors and problems that take place in the field. It's important for the writer to remember that the field has no respect for the textbook.

There isn't much difference between the surveillance techniques used by police detectives and private investigators. Each group has some advantages over the other, which I'll point out as they arise.

Overt Surveillance

Overt surveillance is the least common form of surveillance. It's a violation of all the standard rules of surveillance (which is generally the act of seeing without being seen). In overt surveillance the investigator takes pains to make certain the subject is aware he is being watched. This is done simply by being obvious. By standing in the open, by smiling and nodding and waving at the subject. Maybe even by wearing a trenchcoat and leaning against the lamppost while burning a butt.

Overt surveillance is conducted for two reasons:

- To make an announcement
- To make the subject nervous

Although overt surveillance is rarely used, it is used more by police detectives than by private investigators.

When used as an announcement, overt surveillance is meant to intimidate the subject. The detective is gloating, informing the subject, "You're nailed. I own you. There is nothing you can do, no way you can avoid the inevitable. It's only a matter of time until I arrest your butt."

Overt surveillance is also used to make the subject nervous. Sometimes it is used as a bluff, a last-ditch attempt to force the subject's hand. If nothing else works, perhaps the police can rely on their coercive power to make the subject jittery and apprehensive enough to make a mistake.

The police, of course, have the corner on the legal coercion market, but there are occasions (most commonly in domestic matters) when private detectives use overt surveillance. When it is used, it is used for the same reasons: to either make the subject uncomfortable and nervous or to announce that the game is over.

The problem with overt surveillance is that it is harassment. Harassment is illegal, for both police and private detectives. Overt surveillance is stalking (though stalking laws often require some form of threat). The very fact that it is illegal is, sometimes, part of the intimidation. The detective is announcing that not even the law can keep him from getting to you.

Overt surveillance can be unnerving to the subject. That's the point.

Covert Surveillance

This is the most common form of surveillance. The reason is obvious: People don't behave normally (whatever that means) if they know they're being watched.

Why conduct a covert surveillance? Police detectives generally have only two reasons: They either want to catch somebody committing a crime (or prevent them from committing that crime), or they want to learn the contacts of a known criminal (knowing who visits a drug dealer, for example, is valuable information). Private detectives, on the other hand, may just want to see if somebody is doing something she shouldn't be doing (an "injured" worker chopping wood, for example, or a spouse engaging in illicit sex), or may simply be trying to learn who the subject meets (or who visits a certain building).

The focus of covert surveillance can be:

- A person
- A location

In essence the focus depends on the object of suspicion. Most commonly the object is a person—an errant spouse, a suspected criminal, a distrusted employee. However, sometimes the focus is a location. For example, the police may surveil a suspected crack house or a private investigator may try to locate a bail jumper by staking out his mother's house.

Obviously a person is far more difficult to surveil than a location. People are mobile, they're quirky and unpredictable. On the other hand, people are usually more interesting to watch. Surveillance of a location offers the detective a variety of advantages. The more familiar a detective is with the surroundings, the better. Of course, familiarity breeds contempt; surveillance of a location is generally duller, and it's easier to make a mental mistake.

There are basically three aspects to covert surveillance: preparation, the surveillance itself and breaking off the surveillance. Proper preparation will make it easier to conduct the surveillance and to break it off at the appropriate time (which, essentially, is before you get caught).

Surveillance Preparation

A successful surveillance is predicated on proper preparation (if you'll forgive the alliteration). Preparation should always be the detective's

GETTING GOTTI

Surveillance of a location can be a pure nightmare. Consider the difficulties faced by the FBI in maintaining a surveillance on the Ravenite Social Club on Mulberry Street in New York City's Little Italy. This small, unassuming little building was the headquarters of Mafia don John Gotti.

In theory it should not have been difficult to maintain a surveillance of the club. It was, after all, a small building with a clearly visible entrance on a fairly well-lighted street. However, the street is quite narrow and, although it's located in Little Italy, the club is located away from the more crowded restaurant section. The narrow street makes it difficult for the subject to slip away unnoticed; however, it also makes it difficult for surveillance to go unnoticed. The area has the feel of a small neighborhood, where people are wary of strangers. And, of course, the fact that the folks who frequented the club (Mafia soldati) were constantly on guard didn't help. Yet because they prepared properly, the FBI managed to maintain surveillance on the club for a long time.

first concern. As a writer, you have an active imagination. In preparing for a surveillance of any length, use that imagination to speculate on all the things that might possibly go wrong. You won't think of them all, but this exercise will help you think of many.

There are four main steps a good detective takes to prepare for a surveillance:
- Scout the area.
- Wear the appropriate clothes.
- Bring the proper equipment.
- Bring the necessary amenities.

It's certainly possible to conduct a successful surveillance operation without good preparation, just as it's possible to write a best-selling novel in one draft. It can be done; it's just not very likely.

Scout the Area. Scouting permits a good detective to become intimately familiar with the site of the surveillance. It allows the detective to locate several alternate spotting sites and to determine which will be best under what conditions. For example, one location might be best in the morning when the sun is low, and another might be best at night when the surveillance will be dependent on the street lighting and a clear line of sight.

Scouting also gives the detective the opportunity to consider the traffic patterns in the area, both foot and motor. It's possible that the success of the surveillance will depend on a detective's foreknowledge of the times of day when the streets and sidewalks are busiest or quietest.

Another advantage of scouting is that it allows the detective the chance to become familiar with the various entrances and exits to the area. There is no point in concentrating on the front door of an apartment building if you know the underground garage opens onto a side street.

Finally, scouting is important when a surveillance is expected to last any length of time. Smart detectives will become acquainted with the entire neighborhood—the stores, the gas stations, the markets, the places that have public toilet facilities. It may not be necessary to know about these places, but you never know.

Wear the Appropriate Clothes. It's important to wear the appropriate clothing for several reasons. First, it's necessary for the investigator to blend in with the surroundings. If the surveillance is being conducted by the docks and the detective is dressed in a sport coat and tie, he's going to get burned (caught, that is) rather quickly. Similarly, an investigator wearing an aloha shirt and Ray-Bans will attract attention if surveilling a tavern frequented by Wall Street bond traders. A surveillance is supposed to be inconspicuous.

A second reason the appropriate clothes are important is the investigator's personal comfort. It goes without saying that a detective should dress warm in the winter and cool in the summer, but consider the fact that detectives don't always have the luxury of moving around a lot when conducting a surveillance. You get both hotter in the summer and colder in the winter when you can't move around. And moving around too much on surveillance attracts attention.

Bring the Proper Equipment. Binoculars, monoculars, night vision (or starlight) scopes, still cameras (with the appropriate film and lenses), video cameras, voice-activated tape recorders, transmitters and receivers, audio amplification devices—these are all tools that might be used by police and private detectives during surveillance. A good detective generally carries more than he thinks will be needed. And batteries, batteries, batteries. Nothing will make you feel sillier than to be sitting in a car surrounded by tens of thousands of dollars of high-tech surveillance equipment, only to discover that you can't use the one device you need because you don't have fresh double-A batteries.

Bring the Necessary Amenities. What is "necessary"? Necessity is determined by the situation. Sunscreen might be necessary. Or bug spray. Or a cotton sweater. Some items, however, should always be in the detective's vehicle when on surveillance:

- A small medical kit (including aspirin, bandages, eyedrops, tweezers, ointment) for all those bites, scrapes, nicks, cramps and headaches that plague humankind.
- Paper towels. Stuff gets spilled, messes are made, things drip. It's not pleasant working in a messy environment. A few clean rags are also nice for those situations that are too tough for paper towels.
- Tape (both duct tape and Scotch tape). Tape is a remarkably versatile tool. I've used Scotch tape to affix seven photographs of the legitimate inhabitants of a four-apartment unit to my window visors (I needed to be able to distinguish between folks who belonged in that unit and those who didn't). And when breaking off surveillance for the night, I've often put a small bit of duct tape on the tread of a vehicle's rear tire; when my replacement arrived early in the morning, he could determine if the car had been used after I'd left. I've used duct tape for everything from temporarily patching a fiberglass canoe to taping plastic bags over my feet to keep them warm in the winter.
- Plastic bags. Large self-sealing ones are best. These are handy for holding greasy radio frequency vehicle-tracking transmitters after they've been removed from the target car, for holding everything from trail mix to Polaroid photographs and, of course, for keeping your feet warm when it gets really cold in the car.
- Survival tool. This is a terrific all-purpose folding device. It functions as pliers and wire cutters, has one or more knife blades, a screwdriver blade, a Phillips blade and a saw-edged blade. I used to carry a small tool kit; this one device allowed me to pitch the whole thing.
- String. It isn't used often, but when you need string, nothing else will do. I've used string to replace a broken shoelace, to tie an ink pen I kept losing to the door handle and, yes, to tie around my finger as a reminder to do something.

- Flashlights—a large four- or five-cell light and a pocket light. The big lights not only cast a high-powered beam, they can also double as effective clubs. Be sure to have extra batteries for both flashlights.

It's also wise to bring along extra pens or pencils, some breath mints and as many extra batteries as you can manage. Good detectives don't bring books or magazines; they're supposed to be paying attention to the subject, not catching up on their reading. I know some detectives who listen to audio books, but I've always found them distracting.

One category of amenity needs to be discussed: food and drink. A good detective gives this matter careful thought. It's important to find a balance between feeding the body and disposing of the waste (and I'm not talking about the wrapper on your Hi-Energy bar). From experience I recommend trail mix and a large thermos filled with ice chips. Trail mix can be a nice source of needed energy, it doesn't run through your intestinal system in a hurry, and a little of it can last a long time. Ice chips will quench your thirst without filling your bladder.

Food and drink are less of an issue for police detectives than for private investigators. Police detectives are rarely engaged in solo surveillance. They generally have the luxury of breaking away from the surveillance long enough to take care of those pesky bodily needs. Private investigators, on the other hand, may dislike solo surveillance but are more likely to find themselves conducting one. It's largely a matter of economics; a private client may not be willing to foot the cost of two, three or four agents conducting a surveillance. Police detectives also face budgetary constraints, but when a surveillance is approved, it is generally accepted that several officers will be involved.

Surveillance Techniques

When you consider it, the actual act of surveillance is absurdly simple. One simply watches and pays attention. Anybody with decent vision (or vision correctable by eyeglasses) who can manage to remain awake can theoretically engage in surveillance. The techniques are basically the same whether the surveillance is being conducted by one person or by a team (although it's almost always easier and more effective with a team).

Of course, surveillance isn't simple at all. There are a great many things that have to be taken into account when conducting a surveillance. Among them are:

- Mode of surveillance
- Surveillance location(s)
- Concealment

OH, WHAT A RELIEF . . .

Bladders and bowels. They have to be discussed. Nature can be stalled for a time but cannot be denied. At some point in a long surveillance the detective will almost certainly find it necessary to urinate and perhaps defecate. This may be one of the few areas of investigative work in which men have a true advantage over women. Men, after all, can urinate into a milk carton (I suppose a determined woman could also, but certainly not as easily).

If conducting a surveillance on foot, the detective can usually find some public or commercial building with a toilet—a gas station, a store, a hotel. If not, well, there are no rules covering this. Find a private spot and take care of business (again, easier for male detectives). I suppose it's possible to wear those adult diapers. I've never tried this, so I can't offer any advice.

The situation is somewhat improved when conducting a surveillance from a vehicle. Some surveillance vans have the luxury of built-in toilets, but a great deal of surveillance is conducted from a car. Although men have the advantage of being better equipped for this situation, don't imagine it's an easy process. I also highly recommend milk cartons for this procedure; most bottles have too small an opening—and this is not a project that is forgiving of mistakes.

In regard to how women investigators deal with this situation, I'm afraid I'm clueless.

Good detectives give some thought to each of these aspects of surveillance, both in preparation for and periodically during the surveillance.

Mode of Surveillance

There are three primary modes of surveillance:
- From a parked vehicle
- On foot
- From a building

Each mode has its advantages and disadvantages. Sometimes detectives, especially police detectives, will employ more than one mode during a surveillance. For example, one investigator may be surveilling the subject (or location) from a parked van while a second ghosts about the area on foot.

Of the three modes of surveillance I have a preference for surveillance on foot. It's more physically demanding, but I generally feel more involved in the case when I'm on foot. Being on foot also gives me a greater illusion of freedom (although, in fact, I'm still anchored to the target person or location).

ROUGHING IT

The different expectations of private detectives versus police detectives in regard to food and creature comforts during surveillance were made clear to me several years ago. I was one of two PIs hired on a subcontract by a small investigative firm to maintain a surveillance of a doctor's office. The other subcontractor was a former police officer turned PI. This man arrived with a small cooler in his car. In the cooler he had three or four Dagwood-size sandwiches, a bag of tortilla chips, a container of jalapeno cheese dip and a six-pack of Jolt cola (a highly caffeinated soda; he correctly thought the caffeine would help keep him alert, but he didn't realize caffeine increases the need to urinate). You'd have thought he was going to watch the Super Bowl, not conduct a surveillance.

Surveillance From a Parked Vehicle. Although I have no data on this, I suspect the majority of surveillances are conducted from parked vehicles. This has the distinct advantage of leaving the investigator instantly prepared to tail the subject should she leave. In addition, vehicles are large and can hold a great deal of equipment. Vehicles also provide the investigator with a certain level of concealment (especially if the vehicle is specifically designed for surveillance work). Finally, a vehicle offers some protection from the elements. Nothing is more miserable than conducting a surveillance on foot and being caught in a sudden downpour.

Vehicles, however, can't fully protect the investigator from the heat and cold because the heater or air conditioner can't be operated during the surveillance. A parked vehicle with either the air conditioner or heater running attracts far too much attention.

Perhaps the primary disadvantage of surveillance from a vehicle is that vehicles limit the locations from which investigators can conduct the surveillance. Vehicles are pretty much restricted to streets and parking lots.

Police detectives and a great many private investigators have access to vehicles (usually small vans) specially modified for surveillance. These are nondescript vehicles, usually having at least one one-way window with a reflective surface. Surveillance vehicles have several advantages, including storage room for a tremendous amount of surveillance equipment (some of which will be discussed in the chapter on investigative technology). In addition, surveillance vans often have small refrigerators or coolers for food and drink. Finally, surveillance vans possess that bit of technology most prized by experienced investigators—a toilet.

Surveillance on Foot. Foot surveillance is often used in conjunction with the other modes of surveillance. It has the distinct advantage of mobility. A detective on foot generally has a much larger selection of spotting locations—those places where investigators set up to conduct the surveillance. Also, moving around helps the detective to remain alert. An investigator on foot is much less likely to fall asleep on the job (although there have been times I've considered that a disadvantage).

There are two primary disadvantages to foot surveillance. First, the detective isn't immediately prepared to tail the subject if she should suddenly succumb to the urge to go for a drive. Second, it radically reduces the amount of equipment available to the detective. Certainly a detective engaged in foot surveillance can wear a small fanny pouch without attracting too much attention, but it's risky to tote around a small knapsack. Any carrying case large enough to haul around a useful variety of gear is going to be both too heavy and too conspicuous.

Surveillance From a Building. Under certain circumstances, surveillance will be conducted from a building. Obviously, this mode of surveillance is more likely to be used when the focus of attention is a location rather than a person. The location may be a public building, such as a bar or restaurant, or a private one, such as an office or apartment.

Buildings have two great advantages, the first being the ability to hold huge amounts of equipment. Tripods, for example, which allow the investigator to use long lenses, powerful telescopes and more sophisticated electronic equipment. The second advantage is personal convenience, such as running water, a refrigerator and a toilet.

Surveillance Location(s)

As I noted earlier when discussing preparation, it's important for the detective to select one or more surveillance sites. Obviously, when conducting a surveillance from a building this is only a factor once; you make whatever arrangements are necessary and you move in. However, surveillances on foot and, to a lesser extent, those conducted from a parked vehicle, require more than one surveillance location.

The advantages of multiple surveillance locations are twofold. First, a person or a vehicle that never moves from a location is likely to attract attention. People in the area (neighbors, shop owners, etc.) will begin to grow suspicious and may even notify the police. Second, moving around helps prevent the investigator from becoming bored and distracted.

If possible, good detectives scout primary and secondary sites in advance and become familiar with them. The primary site may change as the conditions of the surveillance change.

Concealment

Obviously, the point of covert surveillance is to see without being seen. That makes it necessary for the detective to blend into the environment. How this is done depends on the environment. While engaged in a foot surveillance I've dressed in dirty overalls and field jacket and sat on a stoop with drunks; a pint of vodka made me welcome, although I sipped from a bottle of water wrapped in a paper bag. I've dressed in poet's black and sat for hours with cafe writers in coffee shops. I've worn T-shirts and shorts and hung around a basketball court outside a gym (my ankle conspicuously taped up so nobody would ask me to play).

Surveillance from a parked vehicle, of course, offers a sort of built-in concealment. As noted earlier, most police departments and large private investigative firms maintain a surveillance van, but as long as the investigator doesn't drive a flashy car, a personal vehicle works just fine. When operating from my car, I liked to recline the seat until I could just see above the dashboard. I'd pull a baseball cap over my eyes and sink into a sort of meditative state. I was rarely noticed, but even on those few occasions when people did pay attention, they usually thought I was napping and left me alone.

Breaking Off

When does a detective break off a surveillance? Obviously, surveillance should be terminated if the detective gets burned (discovered). Other than that, there are no hard-and-fast rules. It's a situational decision, a judgment call. Still, there are some general guidelines. Surveillance should (or could) be terminated

- If the detective thinks he *might* have been burned. This is not the time to take a chance.
- If the detective attracts any sort of attention. I had a friend who was keeping an eye on a person attending one of those Renaissance fairs (where a lot of folks dress up in medieval costume). He was drifting along in the crowd, doing his job quietly and efficiently, when he was accosted by a group of women street buskers. He suddenly found himself part of their act, standing in the middle of a circle of onlookers while these women sang a bawdy song mocking his manhood.
- When the risk gets too high. Again, *any* sort of risk—the risk of falling asleep, the risk of getting burned, the risk of getting mugged.
- About an hour after a detective who's working alone is *absolutely* certain the subject is in for the night. Ninety minutes is better.

Remember the O'Hara Rule: Tomorrow is another day. It's frustrating to be forced by circumstances to break off a surveillance, especially when you think you might be getting good information. Still, it's almost always better to break off and try again later than to get burned and blow the whole surveillance.

Mental Preparation: The Zen of Surveillance

Surveillance can be the most dreary and tedious form of drudgery imaginable. It may sound sexy in theory, but in practice it can be like having your mind injected with novocaine. The detective may have to spend hours watching the outside of a building, waiting for the door to open or for the subject to walk by a window.

And yet, the detective has to remain alert. He can't be distracted by the weather, by passersby, by insects, by music, by aches or pains or by his bodily needs. After all, something could happen at any time.

This is without a doubt the single most difficult aspect of surveillance. It's the facet of surveillance that is the downfall of a great many detectives. All the other considerations may be bothersome, but they can be dealt with through foresight and preparation. But how does one manage to remain separate but involved? How does one stay detached but remain alert?

Not only is this difficult to do, it's difficult to explain. I suspect all good detectives have their own techniques, and I suspect each of them would find it hard to describe them. I'll try to explain how I did it, although it's much easier to do than to describe.

I sort of detached my brain from my body. It's easier to do when surveilling from a parked vehicle than when on foot. I'd get settled and comfortable, then sort of let my body drift away until it no longer seemed connected to me. Shut down all unnecessary systems. Become just a brain in a lump of meat. I was able to remain aware of what was going on around me, very alert—almost hyperalert—yet somehow unaffected by it all.

On foot the experience wasn't quite so pronounced, but it still kicked in. After all, a lot of our behavior is controlled at a subconscious level. We don't have to pay attention to walking. We don't have to think about adjusting our caps. We just do it. When conducting a surveillance on foot, I simply assign more functions to that lizard part of my brain and let my mind focus on the subject. Hours can fly by.

I realize this sounds absurd. But it worked for me, and I learned not to examine it too closely. And I never discussed it with any other detectives.

Conclusion

As a writer of detective and mystery fiction, you need to understand both the mechanics of surveillance and the odd Zen quality of waiting without anticipation, being aware without being involved. Surveillance is one of those package deals; a good detective needs to be good at both aspects. It's pointless to master the mechanics of surveillance unless you can also induce in yourself the proper mind-set to do the work. Conversely, the ability to sit quietly alert is worthless unless you know *where* to sit, *when* to sit there and *when* to get up and leave.

This is one of the few areas in which fiction and film occasionally get the detective game right. It's while on surveillance that detectives become the most philosophical. You start by thinking how much your knees hurt and suddenly find yourself pondering the intricate workings of the universe, and you've no idea how the one thought led to the other but you *know* they're inextricably linked together.

Surveillance is also an area that fiction and film get entirely wrong. Although there are times when conducting a surveillance with a partner that you'll find yourselves sitting together in a car having a clever or a heartfelt conversation, those times don't last long. The whole point of having two folks on surveillance, after all, is usually to cover more territory—and that means you spend most of the time apart.

I'd advise all of you to go out and conduct a surveillance. Pick out a bar or coffeehouse, one not in your own neighborhood. Spend eight to twelve hours hanging around outside. Create a scenario for yourself to explain why you need to keep an eye on this place (you're a writer, you can do this). Find out for yourself how to blend into the area, find your own spotting locations, figure out how to relieve those pesky bodily needs and try to remain alert without wearing out your brain.

You may not enjoy it, but it will help you understand the process, and that's got to add something to your writing.

Chapter Twenty-Eight

Tailing

by Greg Fallis

from *Just the Facts, Ma'am: A Writer's Guide to Investigators and Investigation Techniques*

Tailing is surveillance on the move. Take the difficulties of maintaining a stationary surveillance and multiply them by—pick any number you want. Tailing is infinitely more complex than stationary surveillance. Tailing is to stationary surveillance what combat is to target practice. The entire universe opens itself up to potential chaos.

The craft of tailing requires a remarkable synthesis of skills and knowledge. It calls on the detective's understanding of individual psychology, of social behavior, of traffic laws and herd instinct. It tests the detective's skills in driving, in concentration, in dealing with ambiguity and confusion. It demands the detective engage in a delicate balancing act—recklessness against prudence, confidence against cockiness, patience against the necessity of action. In my opinion tailing is the most frustrating, exciting, anxiety-producing and rewarding of the detective's many chores.

There is only one firm rule to tailing: Don't get caught. Beyond that, all we have are general guidelines. Although tailing is best done as a team, it can be done solo. Most of the guidelines we'll discuss apply to both team and solo tailing. It is far more common for private detectives to find themselves engaged in a solo tail. Again, it's a matter of resources.

Solo tailing is much more of a reactive skill. The subject acts; the detective reacts. While there are times when it becomes necessary for the detective to try to predict the subject's behavior—when you lose sight of the subject, for example—it's always a last resort. Teamwork allows the detective more discretion and reduces the risk involved in predicting the subject's behavior.

Tailing generally falls into two categories:
- On foot
- By motor vehicle

Of course, tailing can also involve other modes of transportation: boats, aircraft, horseback, snowmobile, bicycles, golf carts, snowboards. Anywhere people go, there is a detective willing to follow. We'll focus, however, on the most common methods of tailing—by foot and motor vehicle.

It's not uncommon for these two methods to be combined; for example, a detective may follow the subject from his home as he drives to the beach, then follow him on foot at the beach.

Tailing on Foot

In major cities, the majority of people travel on foot in conjunction with public transportation. As I write this I live in the borough of Manhattan in New York City; I only know one person here who owns a car, and she keeps it in New Jersey. But whether a detective lives in New York City, Columbus, Ohio, or Sioux City, Iowa, it's likely she'll have to conduct a tail on foot. People don't live in their cars, after all. They may drive to the mall, to the market and to work, but once there, they have to get out and walk.

Preparation

It's amazingly easy to lose track of somebody—even somebody you know well—in a crowd. It happens all the time. I can't count the number of times I've been shopping with a woman friend, got distracted for just a moment, and she would disappear. Right there in a store, an enclosed space with only a single public entrance, and she would just vanish. Imagine how easy it is to lose track of a stranger.

As with so many other things, preparation is the key to tailing on foot. A smart detective will study the subject as much as possible before initiating the tail.

What should be studied? There's not much point in studying features such as the subject's ear shape or eye color (although I've seen both described as essential features in some mystery novels). If you're close enough to the subject that you can distinguish his ear shape, you've probably already made a mistake.

For the most part, detectives concentrate on gross physical characteristics: the shape of the subject's head, the slope of the shoulders, the length of the arms and legs. These are things that can be recognized half a block away.

Just as important as the subject's physical features are the following:

WATCH THE WATCH

There are occasions when the subject is suspicious and considers that he might be tailed (a member of an organized crime gang, for example, or a husband who is cheating on his wife). If so, the subject may attempt to elude the tail by disguising himself. After all, it's as easy for the subject to change his appearance as it is for the detective.

In these cases, it's necessary for the investigator to study certain identifying features more closely. There are some items that a clever detective can key in on. For example, even when a male subject brings along a change of clothing to throw off a possible trail, he rarely brings a different belt or pair of shoes. And almost nobody, male or female, bothers to change watches.

- Clothing and accessories
- Walk, including his gait and stride
- Posture
- Idiosyncratic movements

Obviously, each of these characteristics can be changed or modified if the subject chooses, but if the surveillance and tail are done correctly, the subject shouldn't have any reason to change them.

Clothing and Accessories. These are the most obvious features of a subject's appearance, and usually it makes perfect sense to focus on them. Unfortunately, we live in an age of uniformity. In every city in the United States (and, for the most part, in the world), you'll find the same stores selling the same clothes. A black T-shirt sold at the Gap in Los Angeles is exactly the same as one sold in the Gap in Columbus, Ohio. There are certain neighborhoods where every third person is wearing a Tommy Hilfiger jacket or carrying a Lands' End knapsack. This means, of course, that the clothing your subject wears is likely similar or identical to that of hundreds of other people on the street.

The good news, however, is that this uniformity can work in the investigator's favor. It makes it easier for a detective to blend into the surroundings (more on this later).

Walking Patterns. A lot of people have distinctive walking patterns. Some bounce, some swagger, some waddle. Some walk quickly, some stroll leisurely, some walk with a precise military bearing. Some take long strides, others take quick little steps.

For example, when I was young I had a pronounced bounce when I walked. I paid no attention to it until I found myself in military basic training. An absurd amount of time in basic training is spent in learning how to march, and a drill instructor's dream is even columns and rows of soldiers moving in perfect unison at a uniform pace. The sight of my lone bald head bouncing up and down during drill training regularly sent my DI into an incoherent fury. I no longer walk with a bounce.

The older a person is, the more likely he is to have a distinct walk. Every small ache and minor injury adds a little something to that person's walk. People grow into their ways of walking.

A person's walk may also change according to her pace. A person may walk differently at a shopping mall (where the pace tends to be more leisurely) than in a downtown shopping area (where people tend to be much more brisk).

Posture. Posture can also be highly revealing and distinctive. Some folks carry themselves loosely, as if they have fewer bones than the rest of us. Others have rigid, inflexible, almost brittle postures. Many of the same factors that influence a person's walk affect his posture—all those small hurts and pains that accumulate over the years. I once had to tail a man who had been a photographer for years. He habitually carried his camera bag on one shoulder; even when he didn't have the bag, he still seemed to be leaning against its weight. He was an absolute delight to tail.

Idiosyncratic Movements. Most people have a series of odd gestures that are unique to them. A habit of brushing hair out of one's face, for example, or a nervous rolling of the neck muscles. Anybody who has seen the Akira Kurosawa movie *Yojimbo* is familiar with the distinctive shoulder twitch used by the actor Toshiro Mifune. Good detectives pay attention to these gestures and rely on them.

Concealment

Just as clothing, walk, posture and idiosyncratic movements allow the detective to maintain surveillance on the subject, the detective's own clothing, walk, posture and personal idiosyncrasies work against her. Good detectives are almost never flashy or obvious; they prefer to blend in with their surroundings. This is certainly one area in which Sergeant

Joe Friday would excel—nobody would look twice at the Bland Buddha of the LAPD.

It is also a good idea for the investigator to be able to quickly change her appearance. That way the subject, especially a suspicious subject, does not become familiar with the investigator's appearance. It is even acceptable to occasionally violate the rule of being as invisible as possible. Sometimes it can be effective to wear an article of clothing that draws attention to the article of clothing itself. The subject sees the article of clothing, not the person wearing it. Of course, immediately after the subject notices the article of clothing, it should be discarded or covered. Personally, I avoid this tactic, but I've known other investigators who swear by it.

As with so many aspects of detective work, there are no hard-and-fast rules in regard to concealment for foot surveillance. However, in regard to clothing and other accoutrements, generally good detectives

- Wear layers. This allows the detective to quickly change her appearance, which decreases the likelihood of being spotted.
- Avoid bright colors. Bright colors attract attention. The exception to this, as mentioned above, is when the brightly colored article is just one layer. In that case a brightly colored article can actually be useful. As noted, when a person first notices a person in a brightly colored T-shirt, for example, the attention is more on the T-shirt than on the person wearing it. If the subject glances at an investigator in a brightly colored article of clothing, and the investigator then removes (or covers) that article, it can create a radical change in appearance.
- Wear comfortable, breathable shoes. Detectives quickly learn to be kind to their feet.
- Wear clothing in which they feel at ease. Of course, good detectives are capable of being comfortable in a wide variety of clothing styles. The more at ease the detective is, the less likely she will attract attention. This is an area in which private detectives generally excel over police detectives; too often police detectives wear every item of clothing as if it were a uniform.
- Dress appropriately for the location. Don't wear high heels or dark socks and wing-tip shoes to the beach. Of course, this isn't always possible since the detective rarely knows in advance where the subject is heading.

- Avoid new clothing, clothing with slogans or anything that *might* attract attention.
- Wear glasses or sunglasses, which are a quick way to slightly alter one's appearance. Even if they don't wear corrective lenses, detectives can buy frames with clear glass at most good eyewear stores.
- Don caps and hats. Men often feel funny wearing hats, and hats are very visible and can attract attention. However, most men feel relatively comfortable in baseball caps (and, of course, they can be removed to change the detective's appearance). Other hats are trickier. A male detective might be able to wear a beret without causing comment in New York City or Seattle, but it might not be a wise choice in Boise or Kansas City.
- Tie back long hair, which can sometimes make radical changes in appearance.

Good detectives learn to subordinate their own personal sense of style and comfort. The only consideration should be the job.

Tactics

Tailing, whether on foot or in a vehicle, is best done by a team of investigators. Three is best; two is fine. A single detective, when necessary—and it's often necessary—will do. As with surveillance, police detectives are more likely to engage in team tailing; private detectives are more likely to engage in solo tails. The tactics discussed here apply whether the detective is conducting a solo tail or is part of a team.

Tactics in tailing on foot all revolve around maintaining visual contact with the subject. There are two factors that need to be addressed in regard to maintaining visual contact: interval and direction.

Direction is easy. With a solo tail, the subject will almost always be in front of the detective—off to one side, perhaps, but still in front. I've heard of detectives who claim to use small mirrors (attached to their glasses or to the bills of their caps), which allow them to tail a subject from in front. I've never tried this and I've never seen it actually done. Frankly, it sounds loopy to me. I'd think the mirrors would be too small to provide much in the way of visual contact or would attract attention from passersby.

Interval is a far more complicated matter. What is meant by "interval"? In the military we were always admonished to "watch your interval" when moving down a trail. That meant maintaining an appropriate distance from the man in front of you—close enough to keep an eye on him but far enough away to be safe if—when—something unexpected happened. The same is true for tailing.

Just how far away from the subject should the detective be? Far enough away to avoid attracting attention, but close enough not to lose the subject when he does something unexpected. And if there is a universal truth in tailing, it is that the subject will *always* do something unexpected. I have seen subjects suddenly dart across a street. I've seen them stop unexpectedly in the middle of a crosswalk. I've seen them stop in front of shop windows and reapply makeup. I had one subject who hesitated in front of a building, then suddenly reversed direction and walked directly toward me. I ignored him and continued several yards in the same direction before stopping in front of a store window. As I glanced back toward my subject, I was surprised to see him coming toward me again. I continued to study whatever was in the store window, waiting to see his reflection in the glass. After a moment I glanced back in his direction again. This time he was walking away from me. I stayed in front of the window for another moment, glanced at my watch (and took a quiet peek in his direction). Again, he was walking in my direction. I finally realized the subject was just pacing back and forth in front of the building, waiting for somebody.

Obviously, the appropriate tailing interval can vary radically from situation to situation. Forty feet in some circumstances is too far away; in other circumstances it is too close. Usually the investigator should be closer in a crowd, farther away in a less frequented area.

Maintaining visual contact doesn't mean the detective must always be looking directly at the subject. In fact, it's a good idea *not* to look directly at the subject—at least not very often. However, if the subject does something that attracts general public attention (spills a drink or knocks over a grocery store display of Cheez Whiz, for example), then a good detective will turn and watch. A determined refusal *not* to look directly at the subject when everybody else is can actually attract attention to the detective.

A lot of good detectives are more than a little superstitious; they tend to believe that looking too closely at the subject will somehow communicate itself to the subject.

Instead, good detectives tend to rely on:
- Reflective surfaces
- Peripheral vision
- Placement

WHEN YOU GOT TO GO . . .

Certainly the best people to tail on foot are those who are busy, hurrying from place to place, intent on their purposes. It may be tiring for the detectives to keep up, but at least the subjects are too focused to pay any attention to the world around them.

I think the worst experience I've had tailing on foot was a case involving a man who experienced diarrhea after a greasy lunch. You'd think that people who are worried about their bowels would have more immediate concerns than being tailed, and so they do. But my one experience of tailing a man with diarrhea taught me that people with diarrhea pay close attention to their surroundings. They're always looking around, trying to find the nearest rest room. It's probably true that unless I was wearing a sign that said "Men's Room," it's unlikely the subject would have noticed me. But the very fact that he kept stopping, turning and looking around anxiously was terribly disconcerting.

These techniques allow the detective to keep an eye on the subject without having to maintain continuous direct visual contact.

Reflective Surfaces. Every city, every mall, every public space is jammed with reflective surfaces. Markets and shops often have convex mirrors designed to allow clerks and loss prevention staff to be aware of shoplifters. Many buildings are now made of reflective glass. Windows cast reflections. Each of these allows the detective to keep track of the subject without having to look directly at him. However, the detective needs to keep in mind that the popular polarizing sunglasses designed to reduce glare can also deaden reflections.

Peripheral Vision. You often hear someone claim to see something "out of the corner of my eye." Obviously, our eyes don't have corners, but we all have the capacity to see something without looking directly at it. Good detectives learn to rely on their peripheral vision to gather and process information. It takes a bit of practice, but a person can actually learn to expand the use of her peripheral vision.

Placement. By "placement" I refer to the practice of estimating the subject's direction in relation to yours and the speed at which he is walking. If the subject is across the street walking north at a leisurely pace, with only one doorway between him and the end of the block, the detective can estimate approximately how long it will take the subject to reach the corner. That allows the detective to look elsewhere for a period of time. There is only so far and so many places the subject can go in that time.

The trick—one of the tricks—in tailing by foot is not to grow complacent, not to take too much for granted. Simply because the subject has taken the same route from his office to the parking garage four days in a row does not mean he will do the same on the fifth day.

Tailing by Motor Vehicle

I dearly love to watch television and movie detectives tailing folks by car. They drive the most inappropriate vehicles, they use the most absurd tactics, they never get caught by traffic signals and they always find good parking places. My favorite was the Hawaiian private detective who tailed folks in a bright red Ferrari. It looked like a UFO tooling around the island of Oahu. And this detective would usually follow almost directly behind his subject so that the subject's rearview mirror must have been filled with the sight of this brightly colored exotic car. Yet the PI never got burned. Bright red Ferraris must be as common as Toyotas in Honolulu.

Although many detectives use electronic vehicle-tracking devices, this chapter will concentrate on visual tailing.

Preparation

Again, preparation is vital in tailing by car. Obviously, the detective needs to become familiar with the subject vehicle, but the detective also needs to prepare the vehicle in which he'll be conducting the tail.

Preparation for the Subject Vehicle. A good detective always learns as much as possible about the vehicle he'll be tailing. In fact, a really good detective tries to learn more than is necessary and is never surprised to discover that it's not enough. In addition to the most obvious factors (make, model, color, year, license number), the detective should attempt to become familiar with individual aspects of the subject vehicle, including:

- Dents, nicks, scrapes and other blemishes
- Bumper stickers
- Taillight assembly (especially important when tailing at night)

If tailing in a rural area it's also appropriate for the detective to examine the vehicle's tire tread. Not only do different brands and models of tires have distinctive treads, the older the tires are, the more distinctive the tread becomes. A set of well-used tires can leave tracks as distinctive as a fingerprint.

Preparation of the Pursuit Car. Much of what is discussed here is just common sense, but it's amazing how often detectives—even experienced detectives—neglect to make sure their vehicles are properly prepared for tailing jobs. The smart detective plans the tail as if it's going to last all day and cover hundreds of miles—even if he's *certain* he's only going to follow the subject the usual 7.4 miles from her office to her home. Most detectives have been caught short once; good detectives try to make sure it's only once.

The following should always be checked prior to beginning the tail:
- Gasoline. Always have a nearly full tank.
- Maps, both highway and local street maps.
- Spare change for tolls, phone calls, unexpected road emergencies and snacks.
- Sunglasses. These should be polarized, unlike the sunglasses used for tailing on foot. Road glare can be a killer.
- Flashlights. And, of course, a trunk full of extra batteries.
- Obviously, the vehicle should be in good working order. You don't want backfires and clouds of blue smoke calling attention to your car.

A few minutes of preparation can spare the detective untold hours of regret and self-recriminations.

Concealment

This is primarily a matter of common sense. A pursuit vehicle should be as inconspicuous as possible. This means no bright red Ferrari. When choosing a pursuit vehicle, a detective might want to consider the following:
- It should be clean, but not obsessively so. People tend to pay more attention to meticulously maintained cars.
- It should be a common color. A neutral blue is good.
- It should be free of bumper stickers, decals, antenna art or anything else that might attract attention.

- No vanity license plates. I knew a man who obtained his private investigator's license, left his job as an insurance adjustor and opened a small detective agency. One of his first concerns was to get a vanity license plate for his car. It spelled "SNOOP." How could he expect to tail anybody? How could he expect to be taken seriously as an investigator? Nobody was surprised when his business folded in less than a year.

Tactics

There is one primary disadvantage to tailing by car: the inability of the detective to respond as quickly or readily as he could on foot. Even the most nimble of cars is still a ton of steel on rubber wheels. In addition, cars are bound by tens of dozens of purposely restrictive traffic laws. You can't just go anywhere you want, when you want. You're required to stay on a road and in an assigned lane. You're restricted from turning except at certain designated places. You're compelled to go in one specific direction. You're not even allowed to stop where and when you want.

Fortunately, those same restrictions apply to the subject being tailed. Although a lot of people routinely violate traffic laws, the scale of those violations is limited. The subject is unlikely to suddenly stop the car in the middle of the street and begin backing up. It's not impossible, but it's unlikely.

As with tailing on foot, tailing by car is best done with a team of at least three operatives. Again, this ideal is more likely to take place with police detectives than with private detectives. Private investigators often find themselves forced to engage in solo tails. Since solo tails are more common in fiction, I'll focus on them.

There are two factors to consider when engaged in a solo tail: interval and the number of shield cars. We've discussed the concept of interval already. The same vague rule applies to tailing by cars: The detective needs to be close enough but not too close, far enough but not too far.

Shield cars are vehicles the detective allows between himself and the subject vehicle. The number of shield cars depends on the detective's self-confidence and a variety of external conditions, including:

- Traffic density, speed and flow
- Lighting conditions
- Weather

Too many shield cars makes it difficult to maintain visual contact with the subject, increasing the odds of losing her. Too few shield cars increases the likelihood of getting burned. On an interstate highway—where exits are limited and fewer surprises can happen—the detective can allow more shield cars. City traffic, on the other hand, is much more treacherous; fewer shield cars are appropriate. In poor lighting and bad weather conditions, tighten the interval.

Some writers seem to think the most difficult people to tail are those who race madly down the highway. Not so. They may be a danger to other drivers, but speeders are usually fairly easy to follow. Speeders are paying attention to the road, looking for openings in the traffic. When they look in their rearview mirrors, they're usually watching for traffic cops.

Loafers, on the other hand, are exceedingly difficult to tail. They drive so slowly that it's difficult to remain behind them without attracting attention. They disrupt traffic patterns, and they spend a great deal of time glancing fearfully in their rearview mirrors. Slow drivers are also far more sensitive to cars behind them. They're expecting to get either rear-ended or honked at, so they spend more time studying the traffic behind them.

Getting Burned

Regardless of how well prepared the detective is, regardless of how skillful and methodical the detective is, something will inevitably go wrong. It's yet another universal truth of detective work: Every detective eventually gets burned—or at least singed around the edges.

It's important to remember that all detective work is, at its heart, intrusive. It consists of poking around in the personal affairs of other people. Most folks, if they discover they're being followed, tend to resent it, especially if they've been doing something they shouldn't be doing. This is much more of a problem when tailing on foot than when tailing by car. The subject is less likely to be able to physically confront the detective when both are in cars.

So how should a detective behave when he gets burned or is about to get burned? If burned, or almost burned, when tailing in a car, the detective can simply drive away. And never use that car again to tail that subject.

If burned, or almost burned, when tailing on foot, all the rules go by the board. The only thing the detective can do is to rely on his wits. Every situation is different, and every detective will respond to the situation differently.

Usually when I found myself face-to-face with the subject I was tailing—whether I'd been burned or not—I generally did something physically rude and repulsive. I scratched my crotch or picked my nose or let some slobber dribble down my chin. That sort of offensive behavior usually makes people look away, or at least it keeps them from looking you in the face. It costs a little dignity, but it usually kept me from being confronted—and sometimes allowed me to continue the tail on another day (although more cautiously).

Conclusion

Following people is like good jazz, a heady mix of improvisation grounded in a deep understanding of fundamental principles. When it all comes together it can be an exhilarating experience; when it doesn't, it's terribly frustrating and exasperating.

As a writer you should be aware of the perverse thrill that comes from successful tailing, but it's also important that you understand tailing is a difficult process that must be grounded in dull, routine preparation. In a way, it's this contrast that makes it difficult to find detectives who are adept at solo tailing. Those detectives who are good at routine tasks may lack the boldness and audacity required to work a tail; those who have the requisite brashness may not have the patience to do the necessary preparation.

Chapter Twenty-Nine

Information Sources

by Greg Fallis

from *Just the Facts, Ma'am: A Writer's Guide to Investigators and Investigation Techniques*

There are some facets of detective work that rarely appear in detective and mystery fiction. Perhaps the most important of these ignored facets is the amount of time detectives spend either gathering information or maintaining the networks necessary to gather information. I suspect the reason this aspect of investigative work is ignored by writers is because it's, well, sometimes it's pretty dull. Unfortunately, it's also pretty important.

We live in an information age. Information is a commodity, just like coal, coffee or ball bearings. You can buy and sell information. You can even buy and sell *access* to it. Although all detectives, police and private, deal in information, only private detectives treat information as their stock in trade. Police detectives use their information-gathering skills to serve the community at large; private detectives use their skills to serve their clients and make a buck. But both need to build and nourish information networks, both need to find their way through the bureaucratic maze of information available to the public, and both understand information as an object of value.

There are two basic sources of information available to detectives: people and archives. A good detective needs to be able to work with both.

Human Sources

Interviewing and interrogation are merely the final step in the information-collection process. Think of interviewing and interrogation as different ways of cooking. Before you can cook, you have to know where to get the ingredients. You can't make a file and andouille gumbo unless you can track down the file and andouille sausage. One of the sources for the fixings of detective work is people.

It's more difficult to get information from people than from documents. People have to be coaxed, flattered, threatened, charmed. People are complicated creatures. But they respond well to genuine interest. The best detectives have a deep and abiding interest in and concern for people. They may have ulterior motives in some of their working relationships, but they genuinely like people. And people recognize that and respond to it.

Good detectives cultivate a variety of contacts—people in information-rich environments. Clerks, bartenders, secretaries, social workers, probation and parole officers, nurses, receptionists. The world is full of people who have access to unique information, information that is difficult or impossible to obtain anywhere else.

Cultivating Contacts

How do investigators acquire and maintain networks of contacts? It's a long process, one that can't be rushed. Cultivating a contact is rather like growing bonsai, those tiny, twisted Japanese trees. Contacts don't need constant, lavish attention, but they do need careful, periodic, thoughtful attention. It's important for the detective to take the long view. A contact may not produce any worthwhile information for a long time and may not produce it often. What the detective is really cultivating is the *potential*.

THE HIDDEN POWER

It's not widely recognized, but clerks and secretaries run the entire world. They are the glue that binds organizations—private and public—together. They control access to the people who manage the organizations. They produce the documents necessary for organizations to operate. They schedule appointments. They know where everything is located. If every secretary and clerk in the world refused to go to work one day, the world would rapidly grind to a halt. Nothing would get done.

Good detectives recognize this fact and treat clerks and secretaries with the respect they deserve.

To develop a contact the detective needs to consider:
- The purpose of the contact
- The contact's daily routine and interactions
- A contact maintenance program

These are general guidelines, of course. (I know I keep repeating the phrase "general guidelines," but detective work isn't like engineering; general guidelines are all we have.)

Purpose of the Contact

The first thing the detective needs to consider is *why* she needs to develop a specific contact. The obvious answer would be that the person has access to information the detective needs. That's why detectives develop relationships with secretaries and phone company employees and petty criminals.

But the truth is detectives often develop contacts who produce no information at all. Some contacts simply produce *access* to other folks who have information. Some produce introductions. One of my best contacts was an old retired woman who volunteered her services at the information desk of a county courthouse. Every time I went to that courthouse I stopped to visit with her. She had friends in every department of the court. Whenever I needed to go to a particular department to get information, I'd stop at the information desk, chat for a bit and ask who I should talk to in that department. She'd give me a name and would sometimes even call that person and say she was sending me. It made my life a lot easier. Besides, she was a cheerful old woman who'd lived an interesting life.

Private detectives tend to have a wider, more varied network of contacts than police detectives do. That's because a PI has a more diverse caseload. Police detectives are restricted to criminal work; private investigators often work several types of cases simultaneously—a criminal case, an asset location case, an insurance fraud case. Each type of information requires different sources. On top of that, PIs have to cultivate sources in areas where police detectives get information as a matter of course (criminal records clerks, for example).

Police detectives, on the other hand, tend to have a more extensive network of contacts in the criminal world (snitches). This, of course, is a reflection of the purpose of their work.

Private investigators also generally put more effort into cultivating and maintaining sources. Police detectives tend to rely on the authority of their position to compel folks to give them information. It's not uncommon for police detectives who enter into private investigative work on retirement to discover that many of their sources dry up; the basis of their relationship ended when the detective turned in her badge.

Contact's Daily Routine and Interactions

When developing a contact, the detective needs to understand the nature of the contact's work life. Take, for example, a low-level clerk in a city hall office. The work is often dull and unrewarding. Clerks are often treated like serfs by members of the public and by their own superiors. All day long clerks face people who are impatient and inconsiderate. Members of the public view the clerks as the physical manifestation of a malevolent bureaucracy. Their own superiors tend to see them primarily as adjuncts to the computers and typewriters—mere extensions of the machines they work. Clerks often feel alienated from the people they work for, from the people who give them orders and from the product of their work. It's little wonder they are sometimes less than enthusiastic in their interactions with others.

Knowing that, consider the best way to approach a clerk in a city hall office. Try to consider the daily routines and interactions of, say, an emergency room nurse. Or a police dispatcher. Or a waitress in a bar frequented by lawyers, or one in a bar frequented by firefighters. Really think about who and what they face every working day. Each of these potential contacts faces radically different social situations.

A good detective makes the necessary effort to understand the reality of the contact's work life. This is necessary for the detective to both empathize with the contact and develop a pattern for maintaining the contact.

Contact-Maintenance Program

Once the detective determines the need for a contact in a certain situation, she needs to cultivate a relationship with that contact. It's a flagrant error for the detective to seek out the contact only when information is needed. The contact will feel used—and rightfully so. Good detectives develop *relationships*. It's critical for the detective to show herself routinely, to be friendly, courteous and genuinely interested.

I used to make rounds. Periodically I'd spend an afternoon and evening visiting bars, letting the bartenders and wait staff see my smiling face, engaging them in casual conversation, asking them nothing important, leaving them a healthy tip. Or I'd visit city hall or a courthouse or a hospital and do the same thing (without the overt tip, of course, although I might bring along a few boxes of chocolates or fresh-baked cookies).

Short-Term Contacts

For every long-term source of information a detective cultivates there are three or four short-term contacts. These are people who have information the detective wants, but who aren't in positions the detective will routinely find useful. For example, a detective based in Ohio may find himself needing information from a clerk in a social services office in Wisconsin.

A BRIBERY PRIMER

Bribery of public officials is a crime. Committing a crime is a bad thing. Nonetheless, detectives (mostly private detectives) occasionally find themselves in situations in which the offer of a little financial assistance is needed to obtain the information desired. There is an unspoken etiquette about those situations.

- Discretion is advisable. Don't make an overt offer. Simply put the money where only the target can see it.
- Avoid any suggestion that the money is a bribe. Offer it to defray copying costs, for example. Or don't mention it at all; simply let the target know you need the information. The target will know what the money is for.
- Don't scrimp. No singles. No fives. No tens. Never offer anything less than a twenty. This is a *bribe*, even if neither of you acknowledges it.
- Don't be smug. If the target accepts the offer, thank him sincerely. *Never* let the target think you look down on him for accepting a bribe.
- Accept a refusal gracefully. Apologize and leave.

When there is no need to cultivate the source as a long-term contact, the detective has more options. What matters is getting the information as efficiently as possible. These are Capone situations. Al Capone is credited with saying, "You can get farther with a kind word and a gun than with a kind word alone." I'm speaking of a metaphorical gun, of course (although I suspect Capone wasn't). A Capone situation is merely one in which the detective is free to use *any* technique to get the needed information. This includes intimidation, threats, bullying or bribery.

Capone situations may allow the detective a broader range of options, but just because you *can* do a thing doesn't mean you *should* do it.

A good detective uses rude behavior as a last resort even in Capone situations. Remember, even Capone stressed the importance of the kind word.

Archival Sources

As noted earlier, it's easier to get information from a document than from a person. A document is like physical evidence; it's just there. It can be held in the detective's hot little hands, it can be read, it can be photocopied, it can be faxed, it can be scanned onto a computer diskette. Archival information is available to anybody who knows where to find it.

I'm not going to spend a great deal of time on the traditional archival sources. It would take an entire book to accurately convey the breadth and depth of the amount of information available to the general public. Instead, I'll simply give a general overview of the types of information available through traditional sources, then turn our attention to a less traditional source of archival information—the trash can.

Traditional Sources of Archival Information

Certain types of information, such as arrest records, are theoretically available only to police officers (I say "theoretically" because most private investigators who need that sort of confidential information have usually developed contacts willing to provide it). Still, the vast majority of information of use to detectives is available to the public—if they know where to look.

Below I've listed places where certain types of information can be obtained. All the detective needs to do is go to those places and politely ask for the information. Again, most clerks will be helpful *if* they are treated decently. Far too many detectives, both police and private, expect clerks to drop whatever they're doing and offer assistance. If the clerk can't help, she (since most clerk positions pay relatively poorly and these employees are expected to take abuse, they are staffed almost exclusively by women) can usually suggest another option.

Financial Information
- Clerk of Court, Civil Files. It's a common practice in a divorce for the parties involved to be required to provide accounts of their financial statuses—income, debts, expenses and so forth. The Clerk of Court will also have a record of bankruptcy and possibly small claims suits.

- City Clerk. Maintains files on deeds, mortgages and liens against property.
- Tax Assessor. Records location, purchase price and current value of real property.

Legal Matters (Criminal and Civil)
- Clerk of Court, Criminal Files. Criminal convictions are a matter of public record, as are appeals.
- Department of Corrections/Bureau of Prisons. Sentences, inmate behavior infractions are available.
- Clerk of Court, Civil Files. Documents lawsuits (both plaintiff and defendants are named), personal injury matters, awards of damages and judgments (both for and against), certain contracts and names of representing attorneys.

Family Information
- City Clerk/County Recorder/Department of Vital Statistics. Files birth certificates (which include dates, times, places, names of parents, mothers' maiden names, parents' occupations, attending physicians), death certificates (which include causes of deaths, next of kin, burial locations), marriage licenses (which include names of witnesses, names of parents, maiden names of mothers, signatures of both parties) and marriage applications (not every marriage license applied for is used).
- Public Library. Newspapers on microfiche include information on births, deaths and marriages and generally include more detailed information on families than provided in public records. City directories list the number of dependents and sometimes their names.

Business Information
- Better Business Bureau/Chamber of Commerce. Maintains files of complaints against specified businesses.
- Clerk of Court, Civil Files. Records civil suits and criminal complaints against businesses.
- Alcoholic Beverage Control Board. Collects information on tavern owners (including names, addresses, DBAs—doing business as, names under which businesses operate—and fingerprints).
- Public Library. Keeps registers of corporations that list subsidiaries (Dun and Bradstreet, Standard and Poor's, Moody's). Newspapers

on microfiche often note staff promotions and other pertinent information.

- Secretary of State, Corporate Division. Maintains files of DBAs. Sometimes oversees professional licensing (physicians, nurses, private detectives, haircutters, lawyers, bondsmen, etc.).
- Securities and Exchange Commission. Holds records of public corporations, investment services and stockbrokers.

Property

- Department of Motor Vehicles. Operator licenses (including restrictions; also give weights, heights, eye colors of operators), vehicle registrations (include descriptions of registered vehicles, including boats), vehicle identification numbers (VINs), accidents and revocations of licenses.
- Tax Assessor. Records location, purchase price, current value and description of real property.
- City Clerk/Clerk of Court, Civil Files. Plat books give boundaries of property, restrictions on property use and improvements to property.

These are, of course, only a few of the traditional sources of archival information.

Dumpster Diving

Some of the best information isn't given away, isn't purchased, isn't delivered; it's tossed in the trash. The garbage cans and dumpsters of the nation are an overlooked and valuable source of information.

According to waste management professionals, there are two types of refuse: trash and garbage. Most people aren't aware of the distinction—nor do they need to be. In general garbage consists of organic remains, such as leftover food, cigarette butts, bones, rinds. Everything else—empty bottles, burned-out lightbulbs, cereal boxes, that old manuscript—is trash. Both contain useful information.

Garbage

Garbage is most commonly found in the trash cans of dwelling places rather than businesses. The information found in garbage may be interesting, but it is of limited use to most detectives. By and large, only private detectives engaged in child neglect cases find garbage of much benefit. The organic remains can give the detective some insight into the children's diet.

Trash

Trash is the more revealing aspect of refuse. Trash comes in two general categories: personal trash and business trash. Personal trash consists of the trash found in the home trash can; business trash is, obviously, trash that comes from businesses.

Personal Trash. Unless the detective is searching for a particular item (a telephone bill, for example, or credit card receipts), *everything* should be examined.

The following is a partial list of things that might be found in personal trash:

- Empty prescription medicine bottles. These are always labeled with the patient's name and are usually labeled with the name and dosage of the drug. The drug can be looked up in the *Physicians' Desk Reference (PDR)*, which can be found in the reference section of most public libraries. Prescription medications can provide insight into an individual's medical and/or emotional condition.

- Credit card receipts. These list the cardholder's name, credit card data and often the items recently purchased. An interesting sidenote: A new criminal market has sprung up, sparked by dumpster divers who search for all those preapproved credit card applications that get tossed as junk mail. The applications are filled out, the credit cards are sent to post office boxes and the thieves have the chance to max out brand-new credit cards.

- Personal letters. Gentlemen may not read other people's mail, but detectives do. Then again, nobody ever accused a good detective of being a gentleman.

- Empty alcohol containers. Obviously, it can be important to know how much a person drinks—and how much money is being spent on drink.

- Contraceptive materials, such as condom wrappers, birth control pill packages and empty tubes of spermicide. These give some indication of the subject's sexual habits.

- Telephone bills. These list all the long-distance numbers called, including the dates and durations of the calls.

- Magazines, newsletters and other materials that provide some indication of the reader's political, religious and social interests.

Even hard-boiled detectives often find it morally distasteful to nose around in other people's trash, but it remains a source of valuable information.

Business Trash. Nearly half of all the nation's trash is paper. Almost one million tons (that's two billion pounds) of office wastepaper find their way to the nation's landfills every year. Some of that wastepaper contains information of value to the detective.

Legally, a business has no right of privacy. The courts have concluded that the concept of privacy attaches only to individuals, not corporate entities. Businesses, however, do have certain rights that are analogous to the right of privacy. For example, corporate espionage might be prosecuted as an improper acquisition of a trade secret. A PI who finds a document containing a trade secret of an engineering firm may be within the law to remove the document from the trash, but he might be committing a crime if he sold that information to a competing firm.

Many businesses (and some individuals) attempt to protect themselves by shredding sensitive documents. This is not always as effective as people like to think. Cheap shredders simply don't slice the documents into small enough strips. Further, they tend to clump the strips together so that it's easy to know which strips go together. A determined and patient investigator can often reassemble these "shredded" documents. In fact, by shredding the document the business is in some ways making the detective's job easier; it points out which documents are the most important.

Legal Considerations
As it currently stands, federal law states that individuals have no reasonable expectation of privacy in regard to the contents of personal trash cans, even when the trash and/or garbage is placed in opaque bags (*California v. Greenwood*, 486 U.S. 35 1988). In effect, individuals relinquish their property interests in their own trash when they place the trash cans out for collection.

However, some individual states offer their citizens somewhat more protection against this sort of intrusion. California, Hawaii, New Jersey, Washington and Vermont all have laws limiting access to trash. Other states will likely follow suit. It would be wise for writers to research the laws of the states where their stories are located. This can be done at a local law library with the help of a reference librarian or, for those writers with access to the World Wide Web, by accessing a legal reference URL.

While the law generally says trash set out for collection is fair game, detectives cannot trespass on private property to take it. Trespassing is a crime.

Conclusion

OK, I admit gathering information is not the most exciting aspect of detective work. It doesn't offer the dramatic opportunities of tailing or undercover work. Maybe it's the groundwork that allows detectives to do the more interesting things, but it's not always easily translated onto the page.

And yet, it can add something to the depth of the character or the breadth of the narration. It can offer writers the opportunity to instill a sense of verisimilitude, an aura of authenticity, into their work. All too often we see fictional detectives spend hours running around trying to track down information real detectives can get in half an hour of talking to a contact or looking in a plat book. It can also allow the writer to develop the character a bit more.

One of my favorite scenes in the movie Chinatown (one of the best detective movies ever made, in my opinion) takes place in a dusty county clerk's office. Watching how Jake Gittes, the protagonist, interacts with the clerk tells us a lot about the sort of person Gittes is.

Gathering information *can* be made interesting.

About the Contributors

Russell Bintliff was an investigations professional for more than twenty years, working with the Arkansas State Police, the Criminal Investigation Division of the Army and the CIA. He wrote four books for the investigative profession and *Police Procedural: A Writer's Guide to Police and How They Work* and served as technical advisor for the Sylvester Stallone film *Nighthawks*.

Mauro V. Corvasce is a detective with the Monmouth County Prosecutor's Office in New Jersey. He is the co-author of *Modus Operandi: A Writer's Guide to How Criminals Work* and *Murder One: A Writer's Guide to Homicide*.

Greg Fallis is an experienced private investigator in both the public and private sectors. He holds a Ph.D. in Sociology of Justice and teaches college-level courses on Criminology and Policing. His published works include *Just the Facts, Ma'am: A Writer's Guide to Investigators and Investigation Techniques*, the novel *Lightning in the Blood*, the instructional guide *Be Your Own Detective* and the ongoing column "Fact and Fiction" for the mystery-writing magazine *Murderous Intent*.

Fay Faron runs her own detective agency, specializing in missing persons, crimes against the elderly and confidence schemes. Her column "Ask Rat Dog" appears in more than forty newspapers across the country, and she is also a popular guest on TV shows such as *The Oprah Winfrey Show*, *20/20*, *Larry King Live* and *Good Morning America*. She is the author of *Missing Persons: A Writer's Guide to Finding the Lost, the Abducted and the Escaped* and *Rip-Off: A Writer's Guide to Crimes of Deception*.

Sean Mactire has written many articles on violent crime and is the author of several nonfiction books, including *Victims of Domestic Violence* (1987) and *Victims of Trauma* (1986). He also designed and coordinated a project (later adopted by the U.S. Public Health Service) that focused on the prevention of child abuse, domestic violence and crimes against women and children. He served as associate director of a data collection project that focused on crimes and violence against children as well as serial crime patterns. He is the author of *Malicious Intent: A Writer's Guide to How Murderers, Robbers, Rapists and Other Criminals Think.*

Alan March Alan March has been a member of the Cincinnati Police Division for more than nineteen years. He is a lieutenant currently assigned to the Criminal Investigations Section. A graduate of the University of Cincinnati in Law Enforcement and Psychology, he is also an instructor for the Tri-State Regional Community Policing Institute. He has had several short fiction and nonfiction works published.

Joseph R. Paglino is a detective with the Monmouth County Prosecutor's Office in New Jersey. He is the co-author of *Modus Operandi: A Writer's Guide to How Criminals Work* and *Murder One: A Writer's Guide to Homicide.*

Katherine Ramsland, Ph.D., has written fourteen books, including biographies of Dean Koontz and Anne Rice. She has master's degrees, respectively, in clinical and forensic psychology, and a Ph.D. in philosophy. She has practiced as a therapist, taught at Rutgers University and did research for former FBI agent, John Douglas.

Keith D. Wilson, M.D., is a graduate of Ohio State University School of Medicine, where he earned several academic honors and graduated cum laude. Following medical school, he completed his residency in Denver, Colorado. He has served as the director of the Magnetic Resonance Imaging Section at the Toledo Hospital. His first novel, *Life Form*, a medical thriller, was published by the Putnam-Berkley Publishing Group. He is also the author of *Cause of Death: A Writer's Guide to Death, Murder and Forensic Medicine.*

Anne Wingate, Ph.D., has published seventeen mystery novels. A Writer's Digest School instructor, she has taught writing at the university level. She was in police work for seven years in Albany, Georgia, and Plano, Texas, where she headed the criminal identification section of the Plano Police Department. She has qualified in both state and federal court as a fingerprint expert. She is the author of *Scene of the Crime: A Writer's Guide to Crime-Scene Investigations.*

Index

Read More Howdunits!

Amateur Detectives—Here you'll find the information you need to keep your amateur-crime-solver novels and stories factually accurate and completely convincing. You'll learn about gun laws, the Freedom of Information Act, information-gathering methods and how real amateurs solve real crimes. *#10487/$16.99/240 pages/paperback*

Body Trauma—This incredible book explains what happens to body organs and bones maimed by accident or intent. You'll learn about agonizing injuries and the small window of opportunity for emergency treatment, while adding a new level of realism to your stories and novels. *#10488/$16.99/240 pages/paperback*

Deadly Doses—When it comes to poisoning your characters, this book will be your lifesaver. Written in understandable English, it provides you with easy access to all the important details, including symptoms, forms, lethality and methods of administration. *#10177/$16.99/304 pages/paperback*

Missing Persons—This book goes beyond the basics and details the professional's methods for finding lost lovers, missing relatives, old friends and vanishing villains. If you, or your PI, need to find someone, this is the only place you need to look to find out how it's done! *#10511/$16.99/272 pages/paperback*

Murder One—From accidental murder to a crime of passion, *Murder One* gives you the nuts and bolts necessary to build your fiction murder scenario. You'll investigate weapons, kidnapping, homicide, cover-up crimes and more. *#10498/$16.99/224 pages/paperback*

Private Eyes—Get the inside scoop on how private eyes really work, from their education and acquisition of clientele to in-depth investigations, tricks, tactics and more! All the procedures and details you need to know to write private investigators that come to life. *#10373/$15.99/208 pages/paperback*

Scene of the Crime—The evidence found at the scene of a crime—from latent fingerprints to bloodstains—is the lifeblood of your mystery novel or detective story. This book provides accurate, up-to-date details of criminal investigations—your window on the world of crime. *#10319/$16.99/240 pages/paperback*

Armed & Dangerous—In this fascinating reference, you'll find guidelines and advice for arming your characters with weapons perfectly suited for their crime. Hundreds of examples and easily understood language make complicated details completely accessible. *#10176/$15.99/192 pages/paperback*

Malicious Intent—Create unforgettable villains with the help of this guide to criminal psychology. You'll explore the facts and fictions of who these people are, why they commit their crimes, how they choose their victims and more! #10413/$16.99/240 pages/paperback

Police Procedural—In this in-depth reference you'll learn how police officers work, how they train, when they work, what they wear, who they report to, and how they go about controlling and investigating crime. #10374/$16.99/272 pages/paperback

Cause of Death—Discover how to accurately "kill-off" your characters as you are led step-by-step through the process of trauma, death and burial. Learn how police distinguish between an accident and foul play, details of an autopsy and what happens when a criminal is executed. #10318/$16.99/ 240 pages/paperback

Just the Facts, Ma'am—Former PI Greg Fallis uses real-life scenarios to show you how investigative professionals gather evidence, interview witnesses, determine motives and find the answers they're looking for. Also explored are the qualifications, powers and restrictions of investigators as well as fact-finding techniques such as surveillance and interrogation. #10569/$16.99/208 pages/paperback

Rip-Off—From street-level shell games to high-stakes real estate swindles, professional PI Fay Faron profiles the con artists, the cons and the victims. She provides you with the facts on classic scams like three-card monte, identity theft and insurance fraud, "white-collar" crimes and Internet rip-offs. #10570/$16.99/240 pages/paperback